A Comic Strip
History of England

Dedicated to Luiz Felipe Anchieta Guerra

A Comic Strip History of England

From Caesar's Invasion to Richard III

VOLUME THE FIRST

Written by Gilbert á Beckett between 1846 and 1847

Edited with an introduction in 2024 by Stephen Basdeo

PEN & SWORD HISTORY

First published in Great Britain in 2025 by
Pen & Sword History
An imprint of Pen & Sword Books Limited
Yorkshire – Philadelphia

ISBN 978 1 39901 568 4

Typeset by Mac Style
Printed in the UK by CPI Group (UK) Ltd, Croydon, CR0 4YY.

The Publisher's authorised representative in the EU for product
safety is Authorised Rep Compliance Ltd., Ground Floor,
71 Lower Baggot Street, Dublin D02 P593, Ireland.
www.arccompliance.com

For a complete list of Pen & Sword titles please contact

PEN & SWORD BOOKS LIMITED
47 Church Street, Barnsley, South Yorkshire, S70 2AS, England
E-mail: enquiries@pen-and-sword.co.uk
Website: www.pen-and-sword.co.uk
or
PEN AND SWORD BOOKS
1950 Lawrence Road, Havertown, PA 19083, USA
E-mail: uspen-and-sword@casematepublishers.com
Website: www.penandswordbooks.com

Contents

Acknowledgements

My former Ph.D. supervisor, Rosemary Mitchell, was responsible for introducing me to the text that is reproduced here. And to both Rosemary and Prof. Paul Hardwick, my other Ph.D. supervisor, I would like to, as always, extend my thanks for everything they have helped me with throughout my career. Rosemary passed away in 2021 and it was she who introduced me to Beckett's *Comic History* when she allowed me to read a manuscript of a conference paper she had written that (if I recall correctly) was titled something like "The Past Laugh" (a pun on the saying "The Last Laugh"). Alas! If I had been able to find and include that conference paper here so readers could see it, I would have—this was not to be! That being said, in Rosemary's absence, readers have the benefit of Mauricio Albuquerque's insights on Beckett's book, and Albuquerque's remarks form the introduction to the second volume of this work. Albuquerque, hailing all the way from Pelotas in Rio Grande do Sul, is an expert on British appropriations of the past and one of my very good friends. Thus, Mauricio, much thanks for all your work here!

Finally, to my ever-supportive colleagues at the brilliant Elizabeth School of London: You all know who you are, but I think especially two of you deserve a special mention. To Alex James Walker and Ravi Grewal, thanks for putting up with me during lunch hours while I go on about various historical things. This little shout-out is a token of my appreciation for having had the privilege of working with both of you until now.

Gilbert Abbot à Beckett.

Introduction

In George W.M. Reynolds's best-selling novel *The Mysteries of London* (1844–48), a butler, a lawyer, and a parson are congregated in a public house. The three of them strike up a conversation with a bookseller, for the parson reveals that he has written a new romance; a tale in which vice is punished and virtue is rewarded. The bookseller tells the parson not to bother taking his very serious and sober manuscript to a publisher because

> …said the bookseller, after a pause; "nothing now succeeds unless it's in the comic line. We have comic Latin grammars, and comic Greek grammars; indeed, I don't know but what English grammar, too, is a comedy altogether. All our tragedies are made into comedies by the way they are performed; and no work sells without comic illustrations to it. I have brought out several new comic works, which have been very successful. For instance, *The Comic Wealth of Nations*; *The Comic Parliamentary Speeches*; *The Comic Report of the Poor-Law Commissioners*, with an Appendix containing the *Comic Dietary Scale*; and the *Comic Distresses of the Industrious Population*. I even propose to bring out a *Comic Whole Duty of Man*. All these books sell well: they do admirably for the nurseries of the children of the aristocracy. In fact they are as good as manuals and text-books."

These remarks in Reynolds's book were a nod to Gilbert Abbot á Beckett's corpus of "comic" history books, which included the work offered to the public in this volume, *The Comic History of England*, as well as *The Comic History of Rome* and *The Comic Blackstone*, the last of which was a satirical law textbook lampooning William Blackstone's *Commentaries on the Laws of England* (originally published in four volumes in 1765).

People from the nineteenth century appear to us, in surviving portraits and photographs, often as stern and pompous people. Yet they liked to laugh. The novels they read made them laugh. Several magazines were printed with the intention of making their readers laugh—among these were *Fun*, *Judy*, *The Man in the Moon*, and last but certainly by no means least: the famous *Punch*. As Gilbert Abbot á Beckett's *Comic History of England* shows us, they also laughed at their history.

Born in 1811 to a middle-class family in Wiltshire, young Beckett was educated at Westminster School and was destined for the legal profession. Although he was called to the bar he decided to pursue the career of a writer. He became a regular contributor to the *The Times* and also wrote "adaptations" of Dickens's novels. From Beckett's pen flowed such classics as the *Posthumous Papers of the Wonderful Discovery Club* (1838), which was a thinly veiled copy of Dickens's *Posthumous Papers of the Pickwick Club* (1837). He also turned his attention to theatre writing and wrote several humorous plays before writing *The Comic History of England*.

Parts of Beckett's *Comic History of England* were originally published in serial instalments in *Punch* in the latter half of 1846, and ended early in 1847.[1] Founded in 1841 by social investigator Henry Mayhew and Ebenezer Landells, the magazine featured humorous short stories, jokes, and funny illustrations. Some of the Victorian era's best writers made their mark in *Punch*; among these were the poet Thomas Hood and the novelist William Makepeace Thackeray. In its early years the magazine could, at times,

---

1. Some historians have asserted that Beckett's Comic History was published in *Punch* in full as a serial first before it appeared in book form (see, for example, *The Cambridge History of Victorian Literature 2012*). Beckett's *Comic Blackstone* was fully serialised yet the *Comic History of England* was not. Some isolated sketches from the History appear in its columns, but unless I'm mistaken or even blind, I simply cannot find any record of the full run of the history.

be quite radical; some of its illustrations drew attention to social ills such as poverty, pollution, and the wrongs of the factory system. The magazine was therefore a suitable outlet for Beckett to contribute to for, in addition to his efforts as an author, Beckett was also a philanthropist and contributed to several government reports on social issues.

Politicians were also considered fair game for *Punch* writers and illustrators; a little later in the century William Ewart Gladstone and Benjamin Disraeli—or 'Dizzy', as the magazine affectionately called him—were routinely mocked. Not even the royal family was sacred—Queen Victoria was one "star" of the magazine who regularly appeared as a cartoon in its columns. Although *Punch* faced some financial difficulties when it first started the magazine soon became a household name. As the historian Richard Altick notes:

> To judge from the number of references to it in the private letters and memoirs of the 1840s ... *Punch* had become a household word within a year or two of its founding, beginning in the middle class and soon reaching the pinnacle of society, royalty itself.

Although she was regularly portrayed in *Punch*'s columns, Queen Victoria herself must have been amused indeed, and had no issue reading the magazine (perhaps she even secretly let out an unconstitutional chuckle when a politician she disliked was lampooned).

After Beckett had written the *Comic Blackstone* and a few historical sketches of kings and queens' follies, he must have set to work and decided to expand these comic history vignettes into a serialised publication that, though published by the *Punch* office, never appeared in the pages of the magazine itself (my late Ph.D. supervisor, Prof. Rosemary Mitchell, seems to so far be the only other historian who has gotten this point correct in her book titled *Picturing the Past*). The serials were then presented as a two-volume history book that was continually republished throughout the nineteenth century, and most editions retained John Leech's fantastic illustrations. Although at a basic level Beckett wanted to show that the writing of history could be funny while being factual—the footnotes throughout, unless otherwise stated, are Beckett's own—he also made a wider point. While a lot of early Victorian history writing was unashamedly patriotic and cast the actions of its historic rulers in a wonderful light, Beckett showed these historical statesmen up for what they really were: thugs and brutes who were often embroiled in scandals. Most of the 'great men' from English history were rarely worthy of admiration.

Beckett died in 1856 and his *Comic History* is presented to the reading public once more. I hope you enjoy it as much as the present editor has enjoyed it. A truly horrible history, it is in some respects the forerunner of *1066 and All That* and the *Horrible Histories* series of books—and in the latter case television shows—which are enjoyed by young and old alike to this day.

Stephen Basdeo

Further Reading

Altick, Richard, *Punch: The Lively Youth of a British Institution, 1841–1851* (Ohio State University Press, 1997)

Gray, Donald J., 'The Uses of Victorian Laughter', *Victorian Studies*, 10: 2 (1966), 145–76

Korte, Barbara and Doris Lechner, eds. *History and Humour: British and American Perspectives* (Verlag: Transcript, 2013)

Leary, Patrick, *The Punch Brotherhood: Table Talk and Print Culture in Mid-Victorian London* (London: British Library, 2010)

Mitchell, Rosemary, *Picturing the Past: English History in Text and Image, 1830–1870* (Oxford University Press, 2000)

Ross, A. *The Language of Humour* (London and New York: Routledge, 1998)

Note on the Text

The following text is taken from the first edition of the *Comic History of England* that was published in two volumes in 1848 that revised and expanded upon several comic history sketches which originally appeared in the magazine. The original text and images are reproduced in full.

Gilbert Abbot á Beckett's
Preface to the First Edition

In commencing this work, the object of the Author was, as he stated in the Prospectus, to blend amusement with instruction, by serving up, in as palatable a shape as he could, the facts of English History. He pledged himself not to sacrifice the substance to the seasoning; and though he has certainly been a little free in the use of his sauce, he hopes that he has not produced a mere hash on the present occasion. His object has been to furnish something which may be allowed to take its place as a standing dish at the library table, and which, though light, may not be found devoid of nutriment. That food is certainly not the most wholesome which is the heaviest and the least digestible.

Though the original design of this History was only to place facts in an amusing light, without a sacrifice of fidelity, it is humbly presumed that truth has rather gained than lost by the mode of treatment that has been adopted. Persons and tilings, events and characters, have been deprived of their false colouring, by the plain and matter-of-fact spirit in which they have been approached by the writer of the "Comic History of England." He has never scrupled to take the liberty of tearing off the masks and fancy dresses of all who have hitherto been presented in disguise to the notice of posterity. Motives are treated in these pages as unceremoniously as men; and as the human disposition was much the same in former times as it is in the present day, it has been judged by the rules of common sense, which are alike at every period.

Some, who have been accustomed to look at History as a pageant, may think it a desecration to present it in a homely shape, divested of its gorgeous accessories. Such persons as these will doubtless feel offended at finding the romance of history irreverently demolished, for the sake of mere reality. They will – perhaps honestly though erroneously – accuse the author of a contempt for what is great and good; but the truth is, he has so much real respect for the great and good that he is desirous of preventing the little and bad from continuing to claim admiration upon false pretences.

Volume 1

Landing of Julius Cæsar.

Book I

Henry VIII.th meeting Francis I.st

CHAPTER THE FIRST

THE BRITONS—THE ROMANS—
INVASION BY JULIUS CÆSAR

It has always been the good fortune of the antiquarian who has busied himself upon the subject of our ancestors that the total darkness by which they are overshadowed, renders it impossible to detect the blunderings of the antiquarian himself, who has thus been allowed to grope about the dim twilight of the past, and entangle himself among its cobwebs, without any light being thrown upon his errors.

But while the antiquarians have experienced no obstruction from others, they have managed to come into collision among themselves, and have knocked their heads together with considerable violence in the process of what they call exploring the dark ages of our early history. We are not unwilling to take a walk amid the monuments of antiquity, which we should be sorry to run against or tumble over for want of proper light; and we shall therefore only venture so far as we can have the assistance of the bull's-eye of truth, rejecting altogether the allurements of the Will o' the Wisp of mere probability. It is not because former historians have gone head over heels into the gulf of conjecture that we are to turn a desperate somersault after them.[2]

The best materials for getting at the early history of a country are its coins, its architecture, and its manners. The Britons, however, had not yet converted the Britannia metal— for which their valour always made them conspicuous—into coins, while their architecture, to judge from the Druidical remains, was of the wicket style, consisting of two or three stones stuck upright in the earth, with another stone laid at the top of them; after the fashion with which all lovers of the game of cricket are of course familiar. As this is the only architectural assistance we are likely to obtain, we decline entering upon the subject through such a gate; or, to use an expression analogous to the pastime to which we have referred, we refuse to take our innings at such a wicket. We need hardly add that in looking to the manners of our ancestors for enlightenment, we look utterly in vain, for there is no Druidical Chesterfield to afford us any information upon the etiquette of that distant period. There is every reason to believe that our forefathers lived in an exceedingly rude state; and it is therefore perhaps as well that their manners—or rather their want of manners—should be buried in oblivion.

It was formerly very generally believed that the first population of this country descended from Æneas, the performer of the most filial act of pick-a-back that ever was known; and that the earliest Britons were sprung from his grandson—one Brutus, who, preserving the family peculiarity, came into this island on the shoulders of the people. Hollinshed, that greatest of antiquarian gobemouches,

---

2. Some historians tell us that the most conclusive evidence of things that have happened is to be found in the reports of the *Times*. This source of information is, however, closed against us, for the *Times*, unfortunately, had no reporters when these isles were first inhabited.

has not only taken in the story we have just told, but has added a few of his own ingenious embellishments. He tells us that Brutus fell in with the posterity of the giant Albion, who was put to death by Hercules, whose buildings at Lambeth are the only existing proofs of his having ever resided in this country.[3]

Time Bowling out the Druids.

Considering it unprofitable to dwell any longer on those points, about which all writers are at loggerheads, we come at once to that upon which they are all agreed, which is that the first inhabitants were a tribe of Celtæ from the Continent: that, in fact, the earliest Englishmen were all Frenchmen; and that, however bitter and galling the fact may be, it is to Gaul that we owe our origin. We ought perhaps to mention that Cæsar thinks our sea-ports were peopled by Belgic invaders, from Brussels, thus causing a sprinkling of Brussels sprouts among the native productions of England.

The name of our country—Britannia—has also been the subject of ingenious speculation among the antiquarians. To sum up all their conjectures into one of our own, we think they have succeeded in dissolving the word Britannia into Brit, or Brick, and tan, which would seem to imply that the natives always behaved like bricks in tanning their enemies. The suggestion that the syllable tan, means tin, and that Britannia is synonymous with tin land, appears to be rather a modern notion, for it is only in later ages that Britannia has become emphatically the land of tin, or the country for making money.

The first inhabitants of the island lived by pasture, and not by trade. They as yet knew nothing of the till, but supported themselves by tillage. Their dress was picturesque rather than elegant. A book of truly British fashions would be a great curiosity in the present day, and we regret that we have no *Petit Courier* des Druides, or Celtic *Belle Assemblée*,[4] to furnish figurines of the costume of the period. Skins, however, were much worn, for morning as well as for evening dress; and it is probable that even at that early age ingenuity may have been exercised to suggest new patterns for cow cloaks and other varieties of the then prevailing articles of the wardrobe.

The Druids, who were the priests, exercised great ascendancy over the people, and often claimed the spoils of war, together with other property, under the plea of offering up the proceeds as a sacrifice to the divinities. These treasures, however, were never accounted for; and it is now too late for the historians to file, as it were, a bill in equity to inquire what has become of them.

Cæsar, who might have been so called from his readiness to seize upon everything, now turned his eyes and directed his arms upon Britain. According to some he was tempted by the expectation of finding pearls, which he hoped to get out of the oysters, and he therefore broke in upon the natives with considerable energy.

Whatever Caesar looking for the Pearls for which Britain was formerly celebrated, may have been Caesar's motives, the fact is pretty well ascertained that at about ten o'clock one fine morning in August—some say a quarter past—he reached the British coast with 12,000 infantry, packed in eighty vessels. He had left behind him the whole of his cavalry—the Roman horse-marines—who were detained by contrary winds on the other side of the sea, and though anxious to be in communication with their leader, they never could get into the right channel.

---

3. The story of Brutus and the Trojans has been told in such a variety of ways that it is difficult to make either head or tail of it. Geoffrey of Monmouth says that Brutus found Britain deserted, except by a few giants—from which it is to be presumed that Brutus landed at Greenwich about the time of the fair. Perhaps the introduction of troy-weight into our arithmetic may be traced to the immigration of the Trojans, who were very likely to adopt the measures—and why not the weights—with which they had been familiar.
4. *Famous "lifestyle" magazines around when Beckett was writing—Editor.*

Cæsar looking for the Pearls for which Britain was formerly celebrated.

At about three in the afternoon, Cæsar, having taken an early dinner, began to disembark his forces at a spot called to this day the Sandwich Flats, from the people having been such flats as to allow the enemy to effect a landing. While the Roman soldiers were standing shilly-shallying at the side of their vessels, a standard-bearer of the tenth legion, or, as we should call him, an ensign in the tenth, jumped into the water, which was nearly up to his knees, and addressing a claptrap to his comrades as he stood in the sea, completely turned the tide in Caesar's favour. After a severe shindy on the shingles, the Britons withdrew, leaving the Romans masters of the beach, where Cæsar erected a marquee for the accommodation of his cohorts. The natives sought and obtained peace, which had no sooner been concluded, than the Roman horse-marines were seen riding across the Channel. A tempest, however, arising, the horses were terrified, and the waves beginning to mount, added so much to the confusion that the Roman cavalry were compelled to go back to the point they started from. The same storm gave a severe blow to the camp of Cæsar, on the beach, dashing his galleys and transports against the rocks, which they were sure to split upon. Daunted by these disasters, the invaders, after a few breezes with the Britons, took advantage of a favourable gale to return to Gaul, and thus for a time the dispute appeared to have blown over.

Cæsar's thoughts, however, still continued to run in one, namely, the British, Channel. In the spring of the ensuing year, he rigged out 800 ships, into which he contrived to cram 32,000 men, and with this force he was permitted to land a second time by those horrid flats at Sandwich. The Britons for some time made an obstinate resistance in their chariots, but they ultimately took a fly across the country, and retreated with great rapidity. Cæsar had scarcely sat down to breakfast the next morning when he heard that a tempest had wrecked all his vessels. At this intelligence he burst into tears, and scampered off to the sea coast, with all his legions in full cry, hurrying after him.

Cæsar receiving Intelligence of the Destruction of his Fleet.

The news of the disaster turned out to be no exaggeration, for there were no penny-a-liners in those days; and, having carried his ships a good way inland, where they remained like fish out of water, he set out once more in pursuit of the enemy. The Britons had, however, made the most of their time, and had found a leader in the person of Gassivelaunus, alias Caswallon, a quarrelsome old Celt, who had so frequently thrashed his neighbours that he was thought the most likely person to succeed in thrashing the Romans. This gallant individual was successful in a few rough offhanded engagements; but when it came to the fancy work, where tactics were required, the disciplined Roman troops were more than a match for him. His soldiers having been driven back to their woods, he drove himself back in his chariot to the neighbourhood of Chertsey, where he had a few acres of ground, which he called a Kingdom. He then stuck some wooden posts in the middle of the Thames, as an impediment to Cæsar, who, in the plenitude of his vaulting ambition, laid his hands on the posts and vaulted over them.

The army of Cassivelaunus being now disbanded, his establishment was reduced to 4000 chariots, which he kept up for the purpose of harassing the Romans. As each chariot required at least a pair of horses, his 4000 vehicles, and the enormous stud they entailed, must have been rather more harassing to Cassivelaunus himself than to the enemy.

This extremely extravagant Celt, who had long been the object of the jealousy of his neighbours, was now threatened by their treachery. The chief of the Trinobantes, who lived in Middlesex, and were perhaps the earliest Middlesex magistrates, sent ambassadors to Cæsar, promising submission. They also showed him the way to the contemptible cluster of houses which Cassivelaunus dignified with the name of his capital. It was surrounded with a ditch, and a rampart made chiefly of mud, the article in which military engineering seemed to have stuck at that early period. Cassivelaunus was driven by Cæsar from his abode, constructed of clay and felled trees, and so precipitate was the flight of the Briton that he had only time to pack up a few necessary articles, leaving everything else to fall into the hands of the enemy.

The Roman General, being tired of his British campaign, was glad to listen to the overtures of Cassivelaunus; but these overtures consisted of promissory notes, which were never realised. The Celt undertook to transmit an annual tribute to Cæsar, who never got a penny of the money; and the hostages he had carried with him to Gaul became a positive burden to him, for they were never taken out of pawn by their countrymen. It is believed that they were ultimately got rid of at a sale of unredeemed pledges, where they were put up in lots of half a dozen, and knocked down as slaves to the highest bidder.

Ancient Armed Briton.

Before quitting the subject of Caesar's invasion, it may be interesting to the reader to know something of the weapons with which the early Britons attempted to defend themselves. Their swords were made of copper, and generally bent with the first blow, which must have greatly straitened their aggressive resources, for the swords thus followed their own bent, instead of carrying out the intentions of the persons using them. This provoking pliancy of the material must often have made the soldier as ill-tempered as his own weapon. The Britons carried also a dirk, and a spear, the latter of which they threw at the foe, as an effectual means of pitching into him. A sort of reaping-hook was attached to their chariot wheels, and was often very useful in reaping the laurels of victory.

For nearly one hundred years after Cæsar's invasion, Britain was undisturbed by the Romans, though Caligula, that neck-or-nothing tyrant, as his celebrated wish entitles him to be called, once or twice had his eye upon it. The island, however, if it attracted the Imperial eye, escaped the lash, during the period specified.

CHAPTER THE SECOND

INVASION BY THE ROMANS UNDER CLAUDIUS— CARACTACUS—BOADICEA—AGRICOLA—- GALGACUS—SEVERUS—VORTIGERN CALLS IN THE SAXONS

It was not until ninety-seven years after Cæsar had seized upon the island that it was unceremoniously clawed by the Emperor Claudius. Kent and Middlesex fell an easy prey to the Roman power; nor did the brawny sons of Canterbury—since so famous for its brawn—succeed in repelling the enemy. Aulus Plautius, the Roman general, pursued the Britons under that illustrious character, Caractus. He retreated towards Lambeth Marsh, and the swampy nature of the ground gave the invaders reason to feel that it was somewhat too

"Far into the bowels of the land
They had march'd on without impediment."

Vespasian, the second in command, made a tour in the Isle of Wight, then called Vectis, where he boldly took the Bull by the horns, and seized upon Cowes with considerable energy. Still, little was done till Ostorius Scapula—whose name implies that he was a sharp blade—put his shoulder to the wheel, and erected a line of defences—a line in which he was so successful that it may have been called his peculiar forte—to protect the territory that had been acquired.

After a series of successes, Ostorius having suffocated every breath of liberty in Suffolk, and hauled the inhabitants of Newcastle over the coals, drove the people of Wales before him like so many Welsh rabbits; and even the brave Caractacus was obliged to fly as well as he could, with the remains of one of the wings of the British army. He was taken to Rome with his wife and children, in fetters, but his dignified conduct procured his chains to be struck off, and from this moment we lose the chain of his history.

Portrait of Julius Agricola.

Ostorius, who remained in Britain, was so harassed by the natives that he was literally worried to death; but in the reign of Nero (a.d. 59), Suetonius fell upon Mona, now the Isle of Anglesey, where the howlings, cries, and execrations of the people were so awful that the name of Mona was singularly appropriate. Notwithstanding, however, the terrific oaths of the natives, they could not succeed in swearing away the lives of their aggressors. Suetonius, having made them pay the penalty of so much bad language, was called up to London, then a Roman colony; but he no sooner arrived in town, than he was obliged to include himself among the departures, in consequence of the fury of Boadicea, that greatest of viragoes and first of British heroines. She reduced London to ashes, which Suetonius did not stay to sift; but he waited the attack of Boadicea a little way out of town, and pitched his tent within a modern omnibus ride of the great metropolis. His fair antagonist drove after him in her chariot, with her two daughters, the Misses Boadicea, at her side, and addressed to her army some of those appeals on behalf of "a British female in distress," which have since been adopted by British dramatists. The valorous old vixen was, however, defeated; and rather than swallow the bitter pill which would have poisoned the remainder of her days, she took a single dose and terminated her own existence.

Suetonius soon returned with his suite to the Continent, without having finished the war; for it was always a characteristic of the Britons that they never would acknowledge they had had enough at the hands of an enemy. Some little time afterwards, we find Cerealis engaged in one of those attacks upon Britain which might be called serials, from their frequent repetition; and subsequently, about the year 75 or 78, Julius Frontinus succeeded to the business from which so many before him had retired with very little profit.

The general, however, who cemented the power of Rome—or, to speak figuratively, introduced the Roman cement among the Bricks or Britons—was Julius Agricola, the father-in-law of Tacitus, the historian, who has lost no opportunity of puffing most outrageously his undoubtedly meritorious relative.

Agricola certainly did considerable havoc in Britain. He sent the Scotch reeling over the Grampian Hills, and led the Caledonians a pretty dance.

He ran up a kind of rampart between the Friths of Clyde and Forth, from which he could come forth at his leisure and complete the conquest of Caledonia. In the sixth year of his campaign, a.d. 83, he crossed the Frith of Forth, and came opposite to Fife, which was played upon by the whole of his band with considerable energy. Having wintered in Fife, upon which he levied contributions to a pretty tune, he moved forward in the summer of the next year, a.d. 84, from Glen Devon to the foot of the Grampians. He here encountered Galgacus and his host, who made a gallant resistance; but the Scottish chief was soon left to reckon without his host, for all his followers fled like lightning, and it has been said that their bolting came upon him like a thunderbolt.

Agricola having thoroughly beaten the Britons—on the principle, perhaps, that there is nothing so impressible as wax—began to think of instructing them. He had given them a few lessons in war which they were not likely to forget, and he now thought of introducing among their chiefs a tincture of polite letters, commencing of course with the alphabet. The Britons, finding it as easy as A, B, C, began to cultivate the rudiments of learning, for there is a spell in letters of which few can resist the influence. They assumed the toga, which, on account of the comfortable warmth of the material, they very quickly cottoned; they plunged into baths, and threw themselves into the capacious lap of luxury.

For upwards of thirty years Britain remained tranquil, but in the reign of Hadrian, a.d. 120, the Caledonians, whose spirit had been "scotched, not killed," became exceedingly turbulent. Hadrian, who felt his weakness, went to the wall of Agricola,[5] which was rebuilt in order to protect the territory the Romans had acquired. Some years afterwards the power of the empire went into a decline, which caused a consumption at home of many of the troops that had been previously kept for the protection of foreign possessions. Britain took this opportunity of revolting, and in the year 207, the Emperor Severus, though far advanced in years and a martyr to the gout, determined to march in person against the barbarians. He had no sooner set his foot on English ground than his gout caused him to feel the greatest difficulties at every step, and having been no less than four years getting to York, he knocked up there, a.d. 211, and died in a dreadful hobble. Caracalla, son and successor to the late Emperor Severus, executed a surrender of land to the Caledonians for the sake of peace, and being desirous of administering to the effects of his lamented governor in Rome, left the island forever.

The history of Britain for the next seventy years may be easily written, for a blank page would tell all that is known respecting it. In the partnership reign of Dioclesian and Maximian, a.d. 288, "the land we live in" turns up again, under somewhat unfavourable circumstances, for we find its coasts being ravaged about this time by Scandinavian and Saxon pirates. Carausius, a sea captain, and either a Belgian or Briton by birth, was employed against the pirates, to whom, in the Baltic sound, he gave a sound thrashing. Instead, however, of sending the plunder home to his employers, he pocketed the proceeds of his own victories, and the Emperors, growing jealous of his power, sent instructions to have him slain

---

5. The remains of this wall are still in existence, to furnish food for the Archeologians who occasionally feast on the bricks, which have become venerable with the crust of ages. A morning roll among the mounds in the neighbourhood where this famous wall once existed, is considered a most delicate repast to the antiquarian.

The Emperor Severus leads his Army against the Northern Barbarians.

at the earliest convenience. The wily sailor, however, fled to Britain, where he planted his standard, and where the tar, claiming the natives as his "messmates," induced them to join him in the mess he had got into. The Roman eagles were put to flight, and both wings of the imperial army exhibited the white feather. Peace with Carausius was purchased by conceding to him the government of Britain and Boulogne, with the proud title of Emperor.

The assumption of the rank of Emperor of Boulogne seems to us about as absurd as usurping the throne of Broadstairs, or putting on the imperial purple at Herne Bay; but Carausius having been originally a mere pirate, was justly proud of his new dignity. Having swept the seas, he commenced scouring the country, and his victories were celebrated by a day's chairing, at which he assisted as the principal figure in a procession of unexampled pomp and pageantry. The throne, however, is not an easy fauteuil, and Carausius had scarcely had time to throw himself back in an attitude of repose, when he was murdered at Eboracum (York) (a.d. 297), by one Alectus, his confidential friend and minister. In accordance with the custom of the period that the murderer should succeed his victim, Alectus ruled in Britain until he, in his turn, was slain at the instigation of Constantius Chlorus, who became master of the island. That individual died at York (a.d. 306), where his son Constantine, afterwards called the Great, commenced his reign, which was a short and not a particularly merry one, for after experiencing several reverses in the North, he quitted the island, which, until his death in 337, once more enjoyed tranquillity.

Rome, which had so long been mighty, was like a cheese in the same condition, rapidly going to decay, and she found it necessary to practise what has been termed "the noble art of self-defence," which is admitted on all hands to be the first law of Nature. Britain they regarded as a province, which it was not their province to look after. It was consequently left as pickings for the Picts,[6] nor did it come off scot free from the Scots, who were a tribe of Celtæ from Ireland, and who consequently must be regarded as a mixed race of Gallo-Hibernian Caledonians. They had, in fact, been Irishmen before they had been Scotchmen, and Frenchmen previous to either. Such were the translations that occurred even at that early period in the greatest drama of all—the drama of history.

The Britons being shortly afterwards left once more to themselves, elected Marcus as their sovereign (a.d. 407); but monarchs in those days were set up like the king of skittles, only to be knocked down again. Marcus was accordingly bowled out of existence by those who had raised him; and one, Gratian, having succeeded to the post of royal ninepin, was in four months as dead as the article to which we have chosen to compare him. After a few more similar ups and downs, the Romans, about the year 420, nearly five centuries after Cæsar's first invasion, finally cried quits with the Britons by abandoning the island.

In pursuing his labours over the few ensuing years, the author would be obliged to grope in the dark; but history is not a game at blind-man's-buff, and we will never condescend to make it so. It is true that with the handkerchief of obscurity bandaging our eyes, we might turn round in a state of rigmarole,

---

6. The Picts," says Dr. Henry, "were so called from Pictich, a plunderer, and not from picti, painted." History, in assigning the latter origin to their name, has failed to exhibit them in their true colours. Britain continued for years suspended like a white hart—a simile justified by its constant trepidation and alarm—with which the Romans and others might enjoy an occasional game at bob-cherry. Maximus (a.d. 382) made a successful bite at it, but turning aside in search of the fruits of ambition elsewhere, the Scots and Picts again began nibbling at the Bigaroon that had been the subject of so much snappishness.

and catch what we can; but as it would be mere guesswork by which we could describe the object of which we should happen to lay hold, we will not attempt the experiment.

It is unquestionable that Britain was a prey to dissensions at home and ravages from abroad, while every kind of faction—except satisfaction—was rife within the island.

Such was the misery of the inhabitants that they published a pamphlet called "The Groans of the Britons" (a.d. 441), in which they invited Ætius, the Roman consul, to come over and turn out the barbarians, between whom and the sea, the islanders were tossed like a shuttlecock knocked about by a pair of battledores. Ætius, in consequence of previous engagements with Attila and others, was compelled to decline the invitation, and the Britons therefore had a series of routs, which were unattended by the Roman cohorts.

The southern part of the island was now torn between a Roman faction under Aurelius Ambrosius, and a British or "country party," at the head of which was Vortigern. The latter is said to have called in the Saxons; and it is certain that (a.d. 449) he hailed the two brothers Hengist and Horsa,[7] who were cruising as Saxon pirates in the British Channel. These individuals being ready for any desperate job, accepted the invitation of Vortigern, to pass some time with him in the Isle of Thanet. They were received as guests by the people of Sandwich, who would as soon have thought of quarrelling with their bread and butter as with the friends of the gallant Vortigern. From this date commences the Saxon period of the history of Britain.

---

7. *Horen*, means a horse; and the white horse, even now, appears as the ensign of Kent, as it once did on the shield of the Saxons. It is probable that when Horsa came to London, he may have put up somewhere near the present site of the White Horse Cellar. Vide "Palgrave's Rise and Progress of the English Commonwealth."

CHAPTER THE THIRD

THE SAXONS—THE HEPTARCHY

In obedience to custom, the etymologists have been busy with the word Saxon, which they have derived from *seax*, a sword, and we are left to draw the inference that the Saxons were very sharp blades; a presumption that is fully sustained by their fierce and warlike character. Their chief weapons were a battleaxe and a hammer, in the use of which they were so adroit that they could always hit the right nail upon the head, when occasion required. Their shipping had been formerly exceedingly crazy, and indeed the crews must have been crazy to have trusted themselves in such fragile vessels. The bottoms of the boats were of very light timber, and the sides consisted of wicker, so that the fleet must have combined the strength of the washing-tub with the elegant lightness of the clothes' basket. Like their neighbours the wise men of Gotham, or Gotha, who went to sea in a bowl, the Saxons had not scrupled to commit themselves to the mercy of the waves, in these unsubstantial cockle-shells. The boatbuilders, however, soon took rapid strides, and improved their craft by mechanical cunning.

Another fog now comes over the historian, but the gas of sagacity is very useful in dispelling the clouds of obscurity. It is said that Hengist gave an evening party to Vortigern, who fell in love with Rowena, the daughter of his host—a sad flirt, who, throwing herself on her knee, presented the wine-cup to the king, wishing him, in a neat speech, all health and happiness. Vortigern's head was completely turned by the beauty of Miss Rowena Hengist, and the strength of the beverage she had so bewitchingly offered him.

Rowena and Vortigern.

A story is also told of a Saxon *soirée* having been given by Hengist to the Britons, to which the host and his countrymen came, with short swords or knives concealed in their hose, and at a given signal drew their weapons upon their unsuspecting guests. Many historians have doubted this dreadful tale, and it certainly is scarcely credible that the Saxons should have been able to conceal in their stockings the short swords or carving-knives, which must have been very inconvenient to their calves. Stonehenge is the place at which this cruel act of the hard-hearted and stony Hengist is reported to have occurred; and as antiquarians are always more particular about dates when they are most likely to be wrong, the 1st of May has been fixed upon as the very day on which this horrible réunion was given. It has been alleged that Vortigern, in order to marry Rowena, settled Kent upon Hengist; but it is much more probable that Hengist settled himself upon Kent without the intervention of any formality.

It is certain that he became King of the County, to which he affixed Middlesex, Essex, and a part of Surrey; so that, as sovereigns went in those early days, he could scarcely be called a petty potentate. The success of Hengist induced several of his countrymen, after his death, to attempt to walk in his shoes; but it has been well and wisely said that in following the footsteps of a great man an equally capacious understanding is requisite.

The Saxons who tried this experiment were divided into Saxons proper, Angles, and Jutes, who all passed under the common appellation of Angles and Saxons. The word Angles was peculiarly appropriate to a people so naturally sharp, and the whole science of mathematics can give us no angles so acute as those who figured in the early pages of our history.

In the year 447, Ella the Saxon landed in Sussex with his three sons, and drove the Britons into a forest one hundred and twenty miles long and thirty broad, according to the old writers, but in our opinion just about as broad as it was long, for otherwise there could have been no room for it in the place where the old writers have planted it. Ella, however, succeeded in clutching a very respectable slice, which was called the kingdom of South Saxony, which included Surrey, Sussex, and the New Forest; while another invading firm, under the title of Cerdic and Son, started a small vanquishing business in the West, and by conquering Hampshire and the Isle of Wight, founded the kingdom of Wessex. Cerdic was considerably harassed by King Arthur of fabulous fame, whose valour is reported to have been such, that he fought twelve battles with the Saxons, and was three times married. His first and third wives were carried away from him, but on the principle that no news is good news, the historians tell us that as there are no records of his second consort, his alliance with her may perhaps have been a happy one. The third and last of his spouses ran off with his nephew Mordred, and the enraged monarch having met his ungrateful kinsman in battle, they engaged each other with such fury, that like the Kilkenny cats, they slew one another.

About the year 527, Greenwine landed on the Essex flats, which he had no trouble in reducing, for he found them already on a very low level. In 547, Ida, with a host of Angles, began fishing for dominion off Flamborough head, where he effected a landing. He, however, settled on a small wild space between the Tyne and the Tees, a tiny possession, in which he was much teased by the beasts of the forest, for the place having been abandoned, Nature had established a Zoological Society of her own in this locality. The kingdom thus formed was called Bernicia, and as the place was full of wild animals, it is not improbable that the British Lion may have originally come from the place alluded to.

Ella, another Saxon prince, defeated Lancashire and York, taking the name of King of the Deiri, and causing the inhabitants to lick the dust, which was the only way they could find of repaying the licking they had received from their conqueror. Ethelred, the grandson of Ida, having married the daughter of Ella, began to cement the union in the old-established way, by robbing his wife's relations of all their property. He seized on the kingdom of his brother-in-law, and added it to his own, uniting the petty monarchies of Deiri and Bemicia into the single sovereignty of Northumberland.

Such were the several kingdoms which formed the Heptarchy. Arithmeticians will probably tell us that seven into one will never go; but into one the seven did eventually go by a process that will be shown in the ensuing chapter.

Ida quitting his Kingdom.

CHAPTER THE FOURTH

THE UNION OF THE HEPTARCHY UNDER EGBERT

If it be a sound philosophical truth that two of a trade can never agree, we may take it for granted that, à fortiori, seven in the same business will be perpetually quarrelling. Such was speedily the case with the Saxon princes; and it is not improbable that the disturbed condition, familiarly known as a state of sixes and sevens, may have derived its title from the turmoils of the seven Saxon sovereigns, during the existence of the Heptarchy. Nothing can exceed the entanglement into which the thread of history was thrown by the battles and skirmishes of these princes. The endeavour to lay hold of the thread would be as troublesome as the process of looking for a needle,[8] not merely in a bottle of hay, but in the very bosom of a haystack. Let us, however, apply the magnet of industry, and test the alleged fidelity of the needle to the pole by attempting to implant in the head of the reader a few of the points that seem best adapted for striking him.

We will take a run through the whole country as it was then divided, and will borrow from the storehouse of tradition the celebrated pair of seven-leagued boots, for the purpose of a scamper through the seven kingdoms of the Heptarchy.

We will first drop in upon Kent, whose founder, Hengist, had no worthy successor till the time of Ethelbert. This individual acted on the principle of give and take, for he was always taking what he could, and giving battle. He seated himself by force on the throne of Mercia, into which he carried his arms, as if the throne of Kent had not afforded him sufficient elbow-room. This, however, he resigned to Webba, the rightful heir: but poor Webba was kept like a fly in a spider's web, as a tributary prince to the artful Ethelbert. This monarch's reign derived, however, its real glory from the introduction of Christianity and the destruction of many Saxon superstitions. He kept up a friendly correspondence with Gregory, the punster pope, and author of the celebrated jeu de mot on the word Angli, in the Roman market-place.[9]

"Non Angli sed Angeli forent si fuissent Christiani."

---

8. "A needle in a bottle of hay," is an old English phrase, of which we cannot trace the origin. Bottled hay must have been sad dry stuff, but it is possible the wisdom of our ancestors may have induced them to bottle their grass as we in the present day bottle our gooseberries.

9. The pun in question is almost too venerable for repetition, but we insert it in a note, as no History of England seems to be complete without it. The pope, on seeing the British children exposed for sale in the market-place at Rome, said they would not be Angles but Angels if they had been Christians. *Non Angli sed Angeli forent si fuissent Christiani.*

Ethelbert died in 616, having been not only king of Kent, but having filled the office of Bretwalda, a name given to the most influential—or, as we should call him, the president or chairman—of the sovereigns of the Heptarchy. His son, Eadbald, who succeeded, failed in supporting the fame of his father. It would be useless to pursue the catalogue of Saxons who continued mounting and dismounting the throne of Kent—one being no sooner down than another came on—in rapid succession. It was Egbert, king of Wessex, who, in the year 723, had the art to seat himself on all the seven thrones at once; an achievement which, considering the ordinary fate of one who attempts to preserve his balance upon two stools, has fairly earned the admiration of posterity.

Let us now take a skip into Northumberland—formed by Ethelred in the manner we have already alluded to, out of the two kingdoms of Deiri and Bernicia—which, though not enough for two, constituted for one a very respectable sovereignty. The crown of Northumberland seems to have been at the disposal of anyone who thought it worth his while to go and take it; provided he was prepared to meet any little objections of the owner by making away with him. In this manner, Osred received his quietus from Kenred, a kinsman, who was killed in his turn by another of the family: and, after a long series of assassinations, the people quietly submitted to the yoke of Egbert.

The kingdom of East Anglia presents the same rapid panorama of murders which settled the succession to all the Saxon thrones; and Mercia, comprising the midland counties, furnishes all the materials for a melodrama. Offa, one of its most celebrated kings, had a daughter, Elfrida, to whom Ethelbert, the sovereign of the East Angles, had made honourable proposals, and had been invited to celebrate his nuptials at Hereford. In the midst of the festivities Offa asked Ethelbert into a back room, in which the latter had scarcely taken a chair when his head was unceremoniously removed from his shoulders by the father of his intended.

Offa having extinguished the royal family of East Anglia, by snuffing out the chief, took possession of the kingdom. In order to expiate his crime he made friends with the pope, and exacted a penny from every house possessed of thirty pence, or half-a-crown a year, which he sent as a proof of penitence to the Roman pontiff. Though at first intended by Offa as an offering, it was afterwards claimed as a tribute, under the name of Peter's Pence, which were exacted from the people; and the custom may perhaps have originated the dishonourable practice of robbing Paul for the purpose of paying Peter.

After the usual amount of slaughter, one Wiglaff mounted the throne, which was in a fearfully rickety condition. So unstable was this undesirable piece of Saxon upholstery that Wiglaff had no sooner sat down upon it than it gave way with a tremendous crash, and fell into the hands of Egbert, who was always ready to seize the remaining stock of royalty that happened to be left to an unfortunate sovereign on the eve of an alarming sacrifice.

The kingdom of Essex can boast of little worthy of narration, and in looking through the Venerable Bede, we find a string of names that are wholly devoid of interest.

The history of Sussex is still more obscure, and we hasten to Wessex, where we find Brihtric, or Beortric, sitting in the regal armchair that Egbert had a better right to occupy. The latter fled to the court of Offa, king of Mercia, to whom the former sent a message, requesting that Egbert's head might be brought back by return, with one of Offa's daughters, whom Beortric proposed to marry. The young lady was sent as per invoice, for she was rather a burden on the Mercian court; but Egbert's head, being still in use, was not duly forwarded.

Battle between the Mercians and Egbert.—*Cotton MS.*

Feeling that his life was a toss up, and that he might lose by heads coming down, Egbert wisely repaired to the court of the Emperor Charlemagne. There he acquired many accomplishments, took lessons in fencing, and received that celebrated French polish of which it may be fairly said in the language of criticism that "it ought to be found on every gentleman's table."

Mrs. Beortric managed to poison her husband by a draft not intended for his acceptance, and presented by mistake, which caused a vacancy in the throne of Wessex. Egbert having embraced the opportunity, was embraced by the people, who received him with open arms, on his arrival from France, and hailed him as rightful heir to the Wessexian crown, which he had never been able to get out of his head, or on to his head, until the present favourable juncture. In a few years he got into hostilities with the Mercians, who being, as we are told by the chroniclers, "fat, corpulent, and short-winded," soon got the worst of it. The lean and active troops of Egbert prevailed over the opposing cohorts, who were at once podgy and powerless.

As they advanced to the charge, they were met by the blows of the enemy, and as "it is an ill wind that blows nobody good," so the very ill wind of the Mercians made good for the soldiers of Egbert, who were completely victorious.

Mercia was now subjugated; Kent and Essex were soon subdued; the East Angles claimed protection; Northumberland submitted; Sussex had for some time been swamped; and Wessex belonged to Egbert by right of succession. Thus, about four hundred years after the arrival of the Saxons, the Heptarchy was dissolved, in the year 827, after having been in hot water for centuries. It was only when the spirit of Egbert was thrown in that the hot water became a strong and wholesome compound.

CHAPTER THE FIFTH

THE DANES—ALFRED

An Illuminated Letter.

carcely had unanimity begun to prevail in England, when the country was invaded by the Danes, whose desperate valour there was no disdaining. Some of them, in the year 832, landed on the coast, committed a series of ravages, and escaped to their ships without being taken into custody. Egbert encountered them on one occasion at Char-mouth, in Dorsetshire, but having lost two bishops—who, by the bye, had no business in a fight—he was glad to make the best of his way home again.

The Danes, or Northmen, having visited Cornwall, entered into an alliance with some of the Briks, or Britons, of the neigh-bourhood, and marched into Devonshire; but Egbert, collecting the cream of the Devonshire youth, poured it down upon the heads of his enemies. According to some historians, Egbert met with considerable resistance, and it has even been said that the Devonshire cream experienced a severe clouting. It is certainly sufficient to make the milk of human kindness curdle in the veins when we read the various recitals of Danish ferocity. Egbert, however, was successful at the battle of Hengsdown Hill, where many were put to the sword, by the sword being put to them, in the most unscrupulous manner. This was the last grand military drama in which Egbert represented the hero. He died in 836, after a long reign, which had been one continued shower of prosperity.

Ethelwolf, the eldest son of Egbert, now came to the throne, but misunderstanding the maxim, *Divide et impera*, he began to divide his kingdom, as the best means of ruling it, and gave a slice consisting of Kent and its dependencies to his son Athelstane.

The Scandinavian pirates having no longer an opponent like Egbert, ravaged Wessex; sailed up the Thames, which, if they could, they would have set on fire; gave Canterbury, Rochester, and London a severe dose, in the shape of pillage; and got into the heart of Surrey, which lost all heart on the approach of the enemy. Ethelwolf, however, taking with him his second son Ethelbald, met them at Okely—probably in the neighbourhood of Oakley Street—and at a place still retaining the name of the New Cut, made a fearful incision into the ranks of the enemy. The Danes retired to settle in the isle of Thanet, to repose after the settling they had received in Surrey, at the hands of the Saxons. Notwithstanding the state of his kingdom, Ethelwolf found time for an Italian tour, and taking with him his fourth son, Alfred the Great—then Alfred the Little, for he was a child of six—started to Rome, on that very vague pretext, a pilgrimage. He spent a large sum of money abroad, gave the Pope an annuity for himself, and another to trim the lamps of St. Peter and St. Paul, which has given rise to the celebrated *jeu de mot* that, "instead of roaming about and getting rid of his cash in trimming foreign lamps, he ought to have remained at home for the purpose of trimming his enemies."

On his return through France, he fell in love with Judith, the daughter of Charles the Bald, the king of the Franks, who probably gave a good fortune to the bride, for Charles being known as the bald, must of course have been without any heir apparent. When Ethelwolf arrived at home with his new wife, he found his three sons, or as he had been in the habit of calling them, "the boys,"—indignant at the marriage of their governor. According to some historians and chroniclers, Osburgha, his first wife, was not dead, but had been simply "put away" to make room for Judith. It certainly was a practice of the kings in the middle age, and particularly if they happened to be middle-aged kings, to "put away" an old wife; but the real difficulty must have been where on earth to put her. If Osburgha consented quietly to be laid upon the shelf, she must have differed from her sex in general.

Athelstane being dead, Ethelbald was now the king's eldest son, and had made every arrangement for a fight with his own father for the throne, when the old gentleman thought it better to divide his crown

Guthrum pays an Evening Visit to Alfred.

than run the risk of getting it cracked in battle. "Let us not split each other's heads, my son," he affectingly exclaimed, "but rather let us split the difference." Ethelbald immediately cried halves when he found his father disposed to cry quarter, and after a short debate they came to a division. The undutiful son got for himself the richest portion of the kingdom of Wessex, leaving his unfortunate sire to sigh over the eastern part, which was the poorest moiety of the royal property. The ousted Ethelwolf did not survive more than two years the change which had made him little better than half-a-sove-reign, for he died in 867, and was succeeded by his son Ethelbald. This person was, to use an old simile, as full of mischief "as an egg is full of meat," and indeed somewhat fuller, for we never yet found a piece of beef, mutton, or veal, in the whole course of our oval experience. Ethelbald, however, reigned only two years, having first married and subsequently divorced his father's widow Judith, whose venerable parent, Charles the Bald, was happily indebted to his baldness for being spared the misery of having his grey hairs brought down in sorrow to the grave by the misfortunes of his daughter. This young lady, for she was still young in spite of her two marriages, her widowhood, and divorce, had retired to a convent near Paris, when a gentleman of the name of Baldwin, belonging to an old standard family, ran away with her. He was threatened with excommunication by the young lady's father, but treating the menaces of Charles the Bald as so much balderdash, Mr. Baldwin sent a herald to the Pope, who allowed the marriage to be legally solemnised.

We have given a few lines to Judith because, by her last marriage, she gave a most illustrious line to us; for her son having married the youngest daughter of Alfred the Great, was the ancestor of Maud, the wife of William the Conqueror.

Ethelbald was succeeded by Ethelbert, whose reign, though it lasted only five years, may be compared to a rain of cats and dogs, for he was constantly engaged in quarrelling. The Danes completely sacked and ransacked Winchester, causing Ethelbert to exclaim, with a melancholy smile, to one of his courtiers, "This is indeed the bitterest cup of sack I ever tasted." He died in 866 or 867, and was succeeded by his brother Ethelred, who found matters arrived at such a pitch that he fought nine pitched battles with the Danes in less than a twelvemonth. He died in the year 871, of severe wounds, and the crown fell from his head onto that of his younger brother Alfred. The regal diadem was sadly tarnished when it came to the young king, who resolved that it should not long continue to lack lacker; and by his glorious deeds he soon restored the polish that had been rubbed off by repeated leathering. He had scarcely time to sit down upon the throne when he was called into the field to fulfil a very particular engagement with the Danes at Wilton. They were compelled to stipulate for a safe retreat, and went up to London for the winter, where they so harassed Burrhed the king of Mercia, in whose dominions London was situated, that the poor fellow ran down the steps of his throne, left his sceptre in the regal hall, and, repairing to Rome, finished his days in a cloister.

The Danes still continued the awful business of dyeing and scouring, for they scoured the country round, and dyed it with the blood of the inhabitants. Alfred, finding himself in the most terrible straits, conceived the idea of getting out of the straits by means of ships, of which he collected a few, and for a time he went on swimmingly.

He taught Britannia her first lesson in ruling the waves, by destroying the fleet of Guthrum the Dane, who had promised to make his *exit* from the kingdom on a previous defeat, but by a disgraceful quibble he had, instead of making his *exit*, retired to Exeter. From this place he now retreated, and took up his quarters at Gloucester, while Alfred, it being now about Christmas time, had repaired to spend the holidays at Chippenham. It was on Twelfth-night, which the Saxons were celebrating no doubt with cake and wine, when a loud knocking was heard at the gate, and on someone going to answer the door, Guthrum and his Danes rushed in with overwhelming celerity. Alfred, who had been probably favouring the company with a song—for he was fond of minstrelsy—made an involuntary shake on hearing the news, and ran off, followed by a small band, in an allegro movement, which almost amounted to a galop.

The Saxon monarch finding himself deserted by his coward subjects, and without an army, broke up his establishment, dismissed every one of his servants, and, exchanging his regal trappings for a bag of old clothes, went about the country in various disguises. He had taken refuge as a peasant in the hut of a swineherd or pig-driver, whose wife had put some cakes on the fire to toast, and had requested Alfred to turn them while she was otherwise employed in trying to turn a penny.

His Majesty being bent upon his bow, never thought of the cakes, which were burnt up to a cinder, and the old woman, looking as black as the cakes themselves, taunted the king with the smallness of the care he took, and the largeness of his appetite. "You can eat them fast enough," she exclaimed, "and I think you might have given the cakes a turn."[10] "I acknowledge my fault," replied Alfred, "for you and your husband have done me a good turn, and one good turn, I am well aware, deserves another."

The monarch retired to a swamp, which he called Aethelingay—now Athelney—or the Isle of Nobles, and some of his retainers, who stuck to their sovereign through thick and thin, joined him in the morasses and marshes he had selected for his residence. Alfred did not despair, though in the middle of a swamp he had no good ground for hope, until he heard that Hubba, the Dane, after making a hubbub in Wales, had been killed by a sudden sally in an alley near the mouth of the Tau, in Devonshire. Alfred, on this intelligence, left his retreat, and having recourse to his old clothes bag, disguised himself as the "Wandering Minstrel," in which character he made a very successful appearance at the camp of Guthrum. The jokes of Alfred, though they would sound very old Joe Millerisms in the present day, were quite new at that remote period, and the Danes were constantly in fits; so that the Saxon king was preparing, by splitting their sides, to eventually break up the ranks of his enemy. He could also sing a capital song, which with his comic recitations, conundrums, and charades, rendered him a general favourite; and his vocal powers may be said to have been instrumental to the accomplishment of his object.

Having returned to his friends, he led them forth against Guthrum, who retreated to a fortified position with a handful of men, and Alfred, by a close blockade, took care not to let the handful of men slip through his fingers.

Guthrum, tired of the raps on the knuckles he had received, threw himself on the kind indulgence of a British public, and appeared before the Saxon king in the character of an apologist. Alfred's motto was, "Forget and Forgive;" but he wisely insisted on the Danes embracing Christianity, knowing that if their conversion should be sincere, they would never be guilty of any further atrocities. He stood godfather himself to Guthrum, who adopted the old family name of Athelstane, and all animosities were forgotten in the festivities of a general christening. A partition of the kingdom took place, and Alfred gave a good share, including all the east side of the island, to his new godson. The Danes settled tranquilly in their new possessions, though in the very next year (879), a small party sailed up the Thames and landed on the shores of Fulham; but finding the hardy sons of that suburban coast in a posture of defence, the Northmen took to their heels, or rather to their keels, by returning to their vessels. The would-be invaders repaired to Ghent to try their luck in the Low Countries, for which their ungentle-manly conduct in violating their treaties most peculiarly fitted them.

---

10. Though all the historians have given this anecdote, they vary in the words attributed to the old woman, and make no allusion to the reply of Alfred. So accomplished a monarch would hardly have found nothing at all to say for himself; and though he did not turn the cakes, he most probably turned the conversation in the manner we have described.

Alfred employed the period of peace in building and in law, both of which are generally ruinous, but which were exceedingly profitable in his judicious hands. He restored London, over which he placed his son-in-law, Ethelred, as Earl Eolderman or Alderman, and he established a regular militia all over the country, who, if they resembled the militia of modern times, must have kept away the invaders by placing them in the position familiarly known as "more frightened than hurt."

In the year 893, however, the Danes under Hasting, having ravaged all France, and eaten up every morsel of food they could find in that country, were compelled to come over to England in search of a meal. A portion of the invaders in two hundred and fifty ships, landed near Romney Marsh, at a river called Limine, and there being no one to oppose them in Limine, they proceeded to Appledore. Hasting, with eighty sail, took Milton; but he was soon routed out, and cutting across the Thames, he removed to Banfleet, which was only "over the way;" where he was broken in upon by Alderman Ethelred at the head of some London citizens. The cockney cohorts seized the wife and two sons of Hasting, who would have been killed but for the magnanimity of Alfred, though it has been hinted that in sending them back to his foe, the Saxon king calculated that as women and children are only in the way when business is going forward, their presence might add to the embarrassments of the Danish chieftain. That such was really the case, may be gleaned from the fact that on a subsequent occasion Hasting and his followers were compelled to leave their wives and families behind them in the river Lea, into which the Danish fleet had sailed when Alfred ingeniously drew all the water off, and left the enemy literally aground. This manoeuvre was accomplished partially by digging three channels from the Lea to the Thames, and partially by the removal of the water in buckets, though the bucket got very frequently kicked by those engaged in this perilous enterprise.

The river Lea would have been sufficiently deep for the purposes of Hasting had not Alfred been deeper still, and the fleet, which had been the floating capital of the Danes, became a deposit in the banks for the benefit of the Saxons. In the spring of 897 Hasting quitted England; but several pirates remained; and two ships being taken at the Isle of Wight, Alfred, on being asked what should be done with the crews, exclaimed, "Oh! they may go and be hanged at Winchester!" The king's orders having been taken literally, the marauders were carried to Winchester, and hanged accordingly.

Alfred, having tranquillised the country, died in the year 901, after a glorious reign of nearly thirty years, and is known to this day as Alfred the Great, an epithet which has never yet been earned by one of his successors.

The character of this prince seems to have been as near perfection as possible. His reputation as a sage has not been injured by time, nor has the mist of ages obscured the brightness of his military glory. He was a lover of literature, and a constant reader of every magazine of knowledge that he could lay his hands upon. An anecdote is told of his mother, Osburgha, having bought a book of Saxon poetry, illustrated according to the taste of our own times, with numerous drawings. Alfred and his brothers were all exclaiming, "Oh give it me!" with infantine eagerness, when his parent hit on the expedient of promising that he who could read it first should receive it as a present. Alfred, proceeding on the modern principle of acquiring "Spanish without a Master," and "French comparatively in no time," succeeded in picking up Anglo-Saxon in six self-taught lessons. He accordingly won the book, which was, no doubt, of a nature well calculated to "repay perusal."

Nor were war and literature the only pursuits in which Alfred indulged; but he added the mechanical arts to his other accomplishments. The sun-dial was probably known to Alfred; but that acute prince soon saw, or, rather, found from not seeing, that a sun-dial in the dark was worse than useless. Not content with being always alive to the time of day, he became desirous of knowing the time of night, and used to burn candles of a certain length with notches in them to mark the hours.[11] These were indeed melting moments, but the wind often blew the candles out, or caused them to burn irregularly. Sometimes they would get very long wicks, and, if every one had gone to bed, no one being up to snuff,

---

11. The practice of telling the time by burning candles was ingenious, but could not have been always convenient. It must have been very awkward when a thief got into one of the candles, thus exposing time to another thief besides procrastination. After Alfred's invention of the lanthorn, it might have been worn as a watch, in the same manner as the modern policeman wears the bull's-eye.

might render the long wicks rather dangerous. In this dilemma he asked himself what could be done, and his friend Asser, the monk, having said half sportively, "Ah! you are on the horns of a dilemma," Alfred enthusiastically replied, "I have it; yes; I will turn the horns to my own advantage, and make a horn lanthorn." Thus, to make use of a figure of a recent writer, Alfred never found himself in a difficulty without, somehow or other, making light of it.

He founded the navy, and, besides being the architect of his own fortunes, he studied architecture for the benefit of his subjects, for he caused so many houses to be erected that during his reign the country seemed to be let out on one long building lease. He revised the laws, and his system of police was so good that it has been said any one might have hung out jewels on the highway without any fear of their being stolen. Much, however, depends on the kind of jewellery then in use, for some future historian may say of the present generation that such was its honesty, precious stones,—that is to say, precious large stones,—might be left in the streets without anyone offering to take them up and walk away with them.

Alfred gave encouragement not only to native, but to foreign talent, and sent out Swithelm, bishop of Sherbum, to India, by what is now called the overland journey, and the good bishop was therefore the original Indian male—or Saxon Waghom. He brought from India several gems, and a quantity of pepper—the gems being generously given by Alfred to his friends, and the pepper freely bestowed on his enemies.

He died on the 26th of October, 901, in the fifty-third year of his age, and thirtieth of his reign, having fought in person fifty-six times; so that his life must have been one continued round of sparring with one or other of his enemies. All the chroniclers and historians have agreed in pronouncing unqualified praise upon Alfred; and unless puffing had reached a perfection, and acquired an effrontery which it has scarcely shown in the present day, he must be considered a paragon of perfection who never yet had a parallel. It is certain we have had but one Alfred, from the Saxon period to the present; but we have now a prospect of another, who, let us hope, may evince, at some future time, something more than a merely nominal resemblance to him who has been the subject of this somewhat lengthy chapter.

CHAPTER THE SIXTH

FROM KING EDWARD THE ELDER TO THE NORMAN CONQUEST

 n the death of Alfred, his second son, Edward, took possession of the throne, when he was served with a notice of ejectment by his cousin Ethelwald. Preparations were made for commencing and defending an action at Wimbum, when Ethelwald, intimidated by the strength of his opponent, declined to go on with the proceedings, and judgment, as in case of a nonsuit, was claimed on Edward's behalf. Subsequently, however, Ethelwald moved, apparently with a view to a new trial, towards Bury, where some of the Kentish men had ventured; and an action having come off, he incurred very heavy damage, which ended in his paying the costs of the day with his own existence. Edward derived much aid from Ethelfleda, a sister, who acted as a sister, by assisting him in his wars against his enemies. This energetic specimen of the British female inherited all the spirit of her father, as well as his mantle, which we find in looking into our own Mackintosh.[12] She is called "The Lady of Mercia" by the old chroniclers; but as she was always foremost in a fight, there seems something slyly satirical in giving the name of lady to a person of the most fearfully unladylike propensities. She beat the Welsh unmercifully, filling their country with wailings as well as covering their backs with wails, and she took prisoner the king's wife, with whom it may be presumed she came furiously to the scratch before the capture was accomplished. Ethelfleda died in the year 920, and her brother in 925, the latter being succeeded by his natural son, Athelstane, who had no sooner got the crown on his head, than he found several persons preparing to have a snatch at it. He, however, defeated all his enemies, and devoted his time to polishing his throne, adding lustre to his crown, and giving brightness to his sceptre. It was in this reign that England first became an asylum for foreign refugees, to whom Athelstane always extended his hospitality. Louis d'Outremer, the French king, and several Celtic princes of Armorica or Brittany, played at hide-and-seek in London lodgings, while keeping out of the way of their rebellious subjects.

It is probable that the part of the metropolis called Little Britain, may have derived its name from the princes having established a little Brittany of their own in that locality. Athelstane appears also to have taken a limited number of pupils into his own palace to board and educate, for Harold, the king of Norway, consigned his son Haco to the care and tuition of the Saxon monarch.

Athelstane died in the year 940, in his forty-seventh year, and was succeeded by Edmund the Atheling, a youth of eighteen, whose taste for elegance and splendour obtained for him the name of the Magnificent. He gave very large dinner parties to his nobles, and at one of these his eye fell upon one Leof, a notorious robber, returned from banishment, one of the Saxon swell mob who had been transported, but had escaped; and who, from some remissness on the part of the police, had obtained admission to the palace. Edmund commanded the proper officer to turn him out, but Leof—tempted no doubt by the sideboard of plate—insisted on remaining at the banquet. Edmund, who, as the chroniclers tell us, was heated by wine, jumped up from his seat, and forgetting the king in the constable, seized Leof by his collar and his hair, intending to turn him out neck and crop. Leof still refusing to "move on," the impetuous Edmund commenced wrestling with the intruder, who, irritated at a sudden and severe kick on his shins, drew a dagger from under his cloak, and stabbed the sovereign in a vital part. The nobles, who had formed a circle round the combatants, and had been encouraging their king with shouts of "Bravo,

12. Sir James Mackintosh's "History of England," Vol. I. chap, ii., p. 49.

Edmund!" "Give it him, your majesty!" were so infuriated at the foul play of the thief, and his un-English recourse to the knife, that they fell upon him at once, and cut him literally to pieces.

Edred, the brother and successor of Edmund, though not twenty-three years of age, was in a wretched state of health when he came to the throne. He had lost his teeth, and of course had none to show when threatened by his enemies; and he was so weak in the feet that he literally seemed to be without a leg to stand upon. Nevertheless he succeeded in vanquishing the Danes, who could not hurt a hair of his head; but, as the chroniclers tell us that every bit of his hair had fallen off, his security in this respect is easily accounted for. The vigour that marked his reign

Edmund and Leof.

has, however, been attributed to Dunstan, the abbot, who now began to figure as a political character.

Edred soon died, and left the kingdom to his little brother Edwy, a lad of fifteen, who soon married Elgiva, a young lady of good family, and took his wife's mother home to live with them. On the day of his coronation he had given a party, and the gentlemen, including Odo, Archbishop of Canterbury, and Dunstan, the monk, were still sitting over their wine, when Edwy slipped out to join the ladies. Odo and Dunstan, who were both six-bottle men, became angry at the absence of their royal host, and the latter, at the suggestion of the former, went staggering after the king to lug him back to the banquet-room. Edwy was quietly seated with his wife and her mother in the boudoir—for it being a gentlemen's party, no ladies seem to have been among the guests—and the monk, hiccuping out some gross abuse of the queen and her mamma, collared the young king, who was dragged back to the wine-table.

Though this outrage may have been half festive, interlarded with exclamations of "Come along, old boy," "Don't leave us, old chap," and other similar phrases of social familiarity, Edwy never forgave the monk, whom he called upon to account for money received in his late capacity of treasurer to the royal household. Dunstan being what is usually termed a "jolly dog," and a "social companion," was of course most irregular in money matters; and finding it quite impossible to make out his books, he ran away to avoid the inconvenience of a regular settlement.

Dunstan, nevertheless, resolved to pay his royal master off on the first opportunity; and a rising having been instigated by his friend and pot-companion, Archbishop Odo, Edgar, the brother of Edwy, was declared independent sovereign of the whole of the island north of the Thames. Dunstan returned from his brief exile; but, in the mean time, Edwy had been deprived of his wife, Elgiva, by forcible abduction, at the instigation of the odious Odo. The lovely unfortunate had her face branded with a hot iron, and the most cruel means were taken to deprive her of the beauty which was supposed to be the cause of her ascendancy over the heart of her royal husband. Some historians have attributed this outrage to the designs of Dunstan, and among the many irons that monk was known to have had in the fire, may have been the very irons with which this horrible barbarity was perpetrated. Her scars were, however, obliterated by some Kalydor known at the time, and probably the invention of some knightly Sir Rowland of that early era. She was on the point of rejoining Edwy at Gloucester, when she was savagely murdered by the enemies of her husband, who did not long survive her, for in the following year, 958, he perished either by assassination or a broken heart.

Edgar, a mere lad, of whom Dunstan had made a ladder for his own ambition, now succeeded to his brother's dignities, if a series of nothing but indignities can deserve to be so called. The wily monk had now become Archbishop of Canterbury, and encouraged the new king to make royal progresses among his subjects, in the course of which he is said to have gone up on the river Dee, in an eight-oared cutter, rowed by eight crowned sovereigns. In this illustrious water party Kenneth, king of Scotland, pulled the stroke oar, their majesties of Cumbria, Anglesey, Galloway, Westmere, and the three Welsh sovereigns, making up the remainder of the royal crew, over which Edgar himself presided as coxswain.

Though the young king gave great satisfaction in his public capacity, his private character was exceedingly reprehensible. His inconstancy towards the fair got him into sad disgrace, and his friend Dunstan on one occasion administered to him a severe reprimand. The monk, however, finished by fining him a crown, prohibiting him from putting on, during a period of seven years, that very uncomfortable article of the regalia. As the head is proverbially uneasy which wears a crown, the sentence passed upon the king must have been a boon rather than a punishment.

Among the events connected with the reign of Edgar, his marriage with Elfrida must always stand conspicuous. He had heard much of a provincial beauty, the daughter of Olgar, or Ordgar, Earl of Devonshire, and the king sent his favourite, the Earl of Athelwold, to see this rustic *belle*, with a view of ascertaining whether the flower would be worth transplanting to the palace of the sovereign. Athelwold, on seeing the young lady, fell in love with her himself, from her extreme beauty; but wrote up to Edgar, declaring that she might well be called "the mistress of the village plain," for her plainness was absolutely painful; and indeed he added in a P.S., "She is so disfigured by a squint, as to give me the idea of the very squintes-sence of ugliness." Athelwold attributed her reputation for beauty to her fortune, and declared that her money turned her red hair into golden locks, causing her to be well "worthy the attention of Persons about to Marry."

Edgar soon gave his consent to Athelwold's espousing the lady, on the ground of her being a good match for him; but she proved more than a match for him a short time afterwards. Edgar, at the expiration of the honeymoon, proposed to visit his friend, who made excuses as long as he could, inasmuch that he was seldom at home, and that he could not exactly say when his majesty would be sure of catching him. The king, however, good-naturedly promising to be satisfied with pot-luck, fixed a day for his visit; and Athelwold, confessing all to his wife, begged her to disguise her charms, by putting on her shabbiest gown, and to behave herself in such a manner as to make the king believe he had lost nothing in not having married her.

"I should like to see myself appearing as a dowdy before my sovereign," was the lady's feminine reply, and she paid more than usual attention to her *toilette* in order to attract the favourable notice of Edgar. The monarch finding himself deceived by Athelwold, asked him to come and hunt in a wood, when, without any preliminary beating about the bush, and exclaiming, "You made game of me, thus do I make game of you," he stabbed the unfortunate earl, and returned home to marry his widow. Edgar did not live many years after this ungentlemanly conduct, but died at the early age of two-and-thirty. Though he had been favourable to priestcraft, and patronised the cunning foxes of the Church, he was an enemy to wolves, and offered so much per head for all that were killed, until the race was exterminated, and the cry of "Wolf" became synonymous with a false alarm of danger.

Edgar was succeeded (a.d. 975) by Edward, his son by his first wife, who was not more than fourteen or fifteen years old; and thus, at that age before which an individual in the present day is not legally qualified to drive a cab, this royal hobbledehoy assumed the reins of government. His mother-in-law, Elfrida, endeavoured to grasp them for her own son Ethelred, an infant of six, but Dunstan having at that moment the whip hand, prevented her from reaching the point she was driving at.

Edward, who acquired the name of the Martyr, was accordingly crowned at Kingston, where coronations formerly came off; but he did not long survive, for hunting one day near Corfe Castle, he made a morning call on his mother-in-law, Elfrida, and requested that a drop of something to drink might be brought to him. As Elfrida was offering him the ale in front, her porter dropped upon him in the back, and inflicted a stab which caused him to set spurs to his horse; but falling off from loss of blood, he was drawn—a lifeless bier—for a considerable distance. Elfrida has been acquitted by some of having been the instigator of this cruel act, but as it is said she whipped her little son Ethelred for crying at the news of the death of his half-brother Edward, we can scarcely admit that there is any doubt of which we can give her the benefit. Both mother and son became so exceedingly unpopular that an attempt was made to set up a rival on the throne, to the exclusion of Ethelred, and the crown was offered to the late king's natural daughter, whose name was Edgitha.

Edgitha, however, having observed that the regal diadem was looked upon as a target, at which any one might take the liberty to aim, preferred the comfortable hood of the nun—for she was the inmate of a monastery—to the jewelled cap of royalty. The crown was accordingly placed by Dunstan, at Easter, a.d. 979, on the weak head of Ethelred; and it is said that the monk was in such a fit of ill-temper at the coronation that he muttered some frightful maledictions against the boy-king, while in the very act of crowning him. The youthful sovereign was also indebted to Dunstan for the nickname of the Unready, which was probably equivalent to the term "slow coach," that is sometimes used to denote a person of sluggish disposition and not very brilliant mental faculties.

Coronation of Ethelred the Unready.

Ethelred was wholly incompetent to wear the crown, which was so much too heavy for his weak head that he appeared to be completely bonneted under the burden. It sat upon him more like a porter's knot than a regal diadem; while the sceptre, instead of being gracefully wielded by a firm hand, was to him no better than a huge poker in the fragile fingers of a baby.

During the early part of his reign, his mother Elfrida exercised considerable influence, but she at length retired from government, and took to the building business, erecting and endowing monasteries in order to expiate her sins. She became a sort of infatuated female Gubitt, and at every fresh qualm of conscience ran up another floor, which was, familiarly speaking, the "old story" with persons in her unfortunate predicament. The money expended in the erection of religious houses was thought to be an eligible investment in those days for sinners, who having no solid foundation for their hopes, were glad to take any ground to build upon.

The Danes had for some time been tranquil, but their natural fearlessness made them ready for anything, and seeing Ethelred in a state of utter unreadiness on the throne, they indulged the hope of driving oft the "slow coach" in an early stage of his sovereignty.

It happened that young Sweyn, a scapegrace son of the king of Denmark, had been turned out of doors by his father, and having become by the injudicious step of his parent a gentleman at large, amused himself by occasional attacks upon the kingdom of Ethelred. This sovereign, who, instead of being born with a silver spoon in his mouth, appears to have been born one entire spoon of the real fiddleheaded pattern,[13] commenced the dangerous practice of paying the foe to leave him alone, which was of course holding out the prospect of a premium to all who took the trouble to bully him. He paid down £10,000 in silver to the sea-kings, on condition of their retiring from his country, which they did until they had spent all the money, when they returned, threatening to pay him off, or be paid off themselves, an arrangement that Ethelred three times mustered the means of carrying into operation.

Young Sweyn had now become king of Denmark, and had made friends with Olave, king of Norway, the son of old Olave, a deceased pirate, who had made his fortune by sweeping the very profitable crossing from his own country to England. These two scamps ravaged the southern coast in 994, and Ethelred, the unready king, was obliged to buy them off with ready money. In the year 1001, they made

13. Others think this royal spoon was not fiddle headed, but that he was the earliest specimen of the king's pattern, of his enemy. Emma, who was called the "Flower of Normandy," consented to transplant herself to England, and became the acknowledged daisy of the British Court.

another demand of £24,000, which left the sovereign not a single dump, except those into which he naturally fell at the draining of his treasury.

Ethelred, who, if he was unready for everything else, appears to have been always ready for a quarrel, had contrived to fall out with Richard the Second, Duke of Normandy, and he was on the point of taking up arms, when he laid his hand at the feet of Emma.

We would willingly take an enormous dip of ink, and letting it fall on our paper, blot out for ever from our annals the Danish massacre, which occurred at about the period to which our history has arrived. Unfortunately, however, were we to overturn an entire inkstand, we should only add to the blackness of the page, which tells us that the Danes were savagely murdered at a time when they were living as fellow-subjects among the people.

It was on the feast of St. Brice, soon after his marriage with Emma, that the order to commit this sanguinary act was given by Ethelred. It is true that the Danish mercenaries had given great provocation by their insolence. They had, according to the old chroniclers, sunk into such effeminacy that they washed themselves once a week and combed their heads still more frequently. We cannot perhaps accuse the chroniclers of being over nice in their objections to the Danish habits of cleanliness, but we really are at a loss to see the effeminacy of taking a bath every seven days, and preventing the hair from becoming in appearance little better than a quantity of hay in a state of unraked roughness. It was on the 15th of November, 1002, which happened to be one of their weekly washing days, that the Danes were surprised and treated in the barbarous manner we have alluded to. The Lady Gunhilda, the sister of Sweyn, and the wife of an English earl of Danish extraction, was one of the victims of the massacre, and died fighting to the last with that truly feminine weapon, the tongue, predicting that her death would be followed by the downfall of the English nation. This act of ferocity naturally exasperated Sweyn, who resolved on invading England, and he prepared a considerable fleet, the vessels belonging to which appear to have been got up much in the same style as the civic barges on the Thames, for they were gaily gilded, and had all sorts of emblematical devices painted over them. Sweyn himself arrived in the *Great Dragon*, a boat made in the inconvenient form of that disagreeable animal. Had the patron saint of England been at hand to do his duty at that early period, the great dragon would have been speedily overcome, but it is a familiar observation that people of this-sort are never to be found when they are really wanted.

The invaders landed at Exeter, which was governed by a Norman baron, a favourite of the queen; but, as frequently happens in the course of events as well as on the race-course, the favourite proved deceptive when the enemy took the field, and resigned the place to pillage. The Danish foe marched into Wiltshire, and in every town they passed through they ordered the best of everything for dinner, when, after eating to excess of all the delicacies of the season, they had the indelicacy to settle their hosts when the bill was brought to them for settlement. To prevent even the possibility of old scores being kept against them, which they might one day be called upon to pay off, they burned down the houses, thus making a bonfire of all the property, including account books, papers, and wooden tallies that the establishment might contain. The entertainers or landlords had no sooner presented a bill, than it was met by a savage endorsement on their own backs; and, though drawing and accepting may be regarded as a very

Settling the Bill.

customary, commercial transaction, still, when the drawer draws a huge sword the acceptor is likely to get by far the worst of it.

An Anglo-Saxon army was, however, organised at last, to oppose the Danes; but Alfric the Mercian— an old traitor, who had on a former occasion played the knave against the king—was put at the head of it. Ethelred had punished the first treachery of the father by putting out the eyes of the son; but this castigation of the "wrong boy," the young one instead of the old one, had not proved effectual. His majesty must have been as blind as he had rendered the innocent youth, to have again entrusted Alfric with command; and the consequences were soon felt, for the old impostor pretended to be taken suddenly ill, just as his men were going into battle. He called them off at the most important moment; and instead of stopping at home by himself, putting his feet in warm water, and laying up while the battle was being fought under directions which he could just as easily have given from his own room, he shouted for help from the whole army; and by sending some for salts, others for senna, a cohort here for a pill, and a legion there for a leech, he managed to keep the whole of the forces occupied in running about for him.

Sweyn in the meantime got clear off with all his booty, and by the time that Alfric announced himself to be a little better, and able to go out, the enemy had vanished altogether from the neighbourhood.

An appetite for conquest was not, however, the only appetite which the Danes indulged, for their voracity in eating was such that they created a panic wherever they showed themselves. They ravaged Norfolk, and having reduced it to its last dumpling, they fell upon Yarmouth, whose bloaters they speedily exhausted, when they tried Cambridge, having probably been attracted thither by the fame of its sausages. Subsequently they advanced upon Huntingdonshire and Lincolnshire, where they continued as long as they could find a bone to pick with the inhabitants. They then crossed the Baltic (a.d. 1004), having been obliged to quit England on account of there being literally nothing to eat; so that a joint occupation with the natives had become utterly impossible. Those only, who from its being the land of their birth, felt that they must always have a stake in the country, could possibly have mustered the resolution to remain in it. The vengeance of Sweyn being unsatisfied, he returned in the year 1006, when he carried fire and sword into every part, and it has been said with much felicity of expression that amidst so much sacking the inhabitants had scarcely a bed to lie down upon.

Unable to offer him any effectual check, the Great Council tried what could be done with ready money, and £36,000 was the price demanded to pay out this formidable "man in possession" from the harassed and exhausted country. The sum was collected by an income-tax of about twenty shillings in the pound, or even more, if it could be got out of the people by either threats or violence. Such as had paid the Danes directly to save their homes from destruction were obliged to pay over again, like a railway traveller who loses his ticket; and the natives seem to have got into a special train of evils, in which every engine of persecution was used against them.

A Dane securing his Booty.

In 1008 new burdens were thrown upon the people, who for every nine hides of land were bound to find a man armed with a helmet and breastplate. This would seem no very difficult matter, considering that two or three such men are found annually at the Lord Mayor's show; but in former times they had something more difficult to do than walk in a procession. Though two shillings and his beer will, it is believed, secure the services of an ancient knight, armed *cap-d-pie* at an hour's notice in our own day, such a person was not to be had so cheap in the time of Ethelred. In addition to this infliction, every three hundred and ten hides of land were bound to build and equip a ship for the defence of the country; but it seems, after all, nothing but fair that the hides should club together to save themselves from tanning. The fleet thus raised was, however, soon rendered valueless, in consequence of the various commanders having refused to row in the same boat, or rather insisting on pulling different ways, to the utter annihilation of their master's interest.

Ethelred had selected for his favourite a low fellow of the name of Edric, who was exceedingly eloquent, and had not only talked one of the king's daughters into accepting his hand, but had even talked the monarch himself into sanctioning the unequal marriage. Edric had obtained for his brother Brightric a high post in the navy, as commander of eight vessels; but the latter got into a quarrel with his nephew, Wulfnoth, who was known by the odd appellation of the "Child of the South Saxons," or the Sussex lad, as we should take the liberty of calling him. The "child" determined on flight; but with a truly infantine objection to run alone, he got twenty of the king's ships to run along with him. Brightric cruised after him with eighty sail, but the tempest

Soldier of the Period.

rising, and the rudders at the stem refusing to act, he was driven on shore by stem necessity. Wulfnoth, who had done a little ravaging on his own private account along the southern coast, returned to make firewood of the timbers of Brightric, which fortune had so cruelly shivered.

Ethelred was completely panic-stricken at the news of this reverse, and hurried home as fast as he could to summon a council, but every resolution that was passed no one had the resolution to execute. To add to the king's embarrassments, "Thurkill's host" came over, com-prising the flower of the Scandinavian youth, which planted itself in Kent, and caused a sad blow to the country. Various short peaces were purchased by the Saxons at so much a piece; but, as Pope Gregory would have had it, every arrangement was not a sale, but a sell on the part of Thurkill, who continued sending in a fresh account for every fresh transaction. Ethelred was now in the very midst of traitors, and it was impossible that he should ever be brought round in such a circle. He had not a single officer to whom a commission could be safely entrusted. Edric, his favourite, having taken offence, joined the enemy in an attack upon Canterbury, which had lasted for twenty days, when some one left the gate of the city ajar, either by design or accident.

Alphege, the good archbishop, who had defended the place, was instantly loaded with chains; and though he felt himself dreadfully fettered, he declined to purchase his ransom, for the very best of all reasons, namely that he had not the money to pay for it. The old man, wisely making a virtue of necessity, proclaimed his determination not to part with a shilling, "and indeed," said he, "I couldn't if I would; for to tell you the truth, I haven't got it."

The venerable prelate turning his pockets inside out, proved that he was penniless, when they offered to release him if he would persuade Ethelred to subscribe handsomely to the Danish rent, as we are fully justified in calling it. The archbishop, however, grew exceedingly saucy, when they pelted him with the remains of the feast, throwing bones, bottles, and bread, in rapid succession at the primate, who meekly bowed his head—or perhaps bobbed it up and down—to the treatment he experienced. The good old man remained for some time unshaken, till a shower of marrow-

Thurkill's little Account.

bones threw him on his knees, and one of the ruffians with a coarse pun exclaiming, "Let us make no more bones about it, but despatch him at once," brutally realised his own ferocious suggestion.

Thurkill now sent in another account of £48,000 as the price of his promised allegiance, which was certainly not worth a week's purchase, but Ethelred somehow or other found and paid the money. Sweyn, on hearing of this proceeding, pretended to be very angry with Thurkill, and fitted out a formidable fleet, with the avowed intention of killing with one stone two birds—namely, the Danish crow, and the Saxon pigeon. The ships of Sweyn were elaborately carved for show, and consequently not very well cut out for service. Nevertheless they were quite strong enough to vanquish the dispirited Saxons, who would have been overawed at the sight of a Danish oar, and might have been knocked down with a feather.

Sweyn landed at York, and leaving his fleet in the care of his son Canute, carried fire and sword into the north; but as the inhabitants were all favourable to his cause, he had no more occasion to take fire into the north, than to carry coals to Newcastle. The king had sought refuge in London, which refused to give in until Ethelred sneaked out, when the citizens having been threatened, according to Sir Francis Palgrave, with damage to their "eyes and limbs," threw open their gates to the conqueror. The unready monarch made for the Isle of Wight, but finding apartments dear and living expensive, he packed off his wife and children to his brother-in-law, Richard of Normandy, who lived in a court at Rouen. The duke made them as comfortable as he could, and the lady Emma having fished for an invitation for her husband, at length succeeded in getting him asked, to the infinite delight of old "Slowcoach," who for once got ready at a very short notice to avail himself of the asylum that was offered him. Sweyn was now king of England, a.d. 1013, but after a reign of six weeks, entitling him to only half a quarter's salary, he died at Gainsborough, very much lamented by all who did not know him. The Saxon nobles who had so recently sent Ethelred away, now wanted him back again. They despatched a message, however, to the effect that, if he would promise to be a good king, and never be naughty any more, they would be glad to accept him once more as their sovereign. Ethelred turning his son Edmund into a postman, forwarded a letter by hand, promising reform, but stipulating that there should be no "fraud or treachery," or in other words, no humbug on either side. This arrangement, though growing out of mutual distrust, and being little better than a provision which each party thought necessary in consequence of the dishonesty of both, must be regarded as highly important in a constitutional point of view, for it is evidently the germ of those great compacts, which have since been occasionally concluded between the sovereign and the people.

Ethelred, on his arrival at home, found that Canute, the son of Sweyn, having been declared king by the Danes, had coolly set himself up as landlord of the Crown and Sceptre at Greenwich. Ethelred and Canute continued for three years like "the Lion and the Unicorn, fighting for the Crown," with about equal success, when death overtook "Slowcoach," after a long and inglorious reign. He died on St. George's Day, 1016, having been for five-and-thirty years man and boy, on and off the throne of England.

Ethelred despatching a Letter by his Son.

CHAPTER THE SEVENTH

EDMUND IRONSIDES—CANUTE— HAROLD HAREFOOT—HARDICANUTE— EDWARD THE CONFESSOR—HAROLD— THE BATTLE OF HASTINGS

On the decease of Ethelred the citizens of London offered the throne to his son Edmund, who had got the strange nickname of Ironsides. He obtained this appellation from his extreme toughness; for it has been said by a contemporary that if you gave him a poke in the ribs they rattled like the bars of a gridiron, or the railings round an area. There can be no doubt that Edmund had strength on his side, as far as he was personally concerned, but Canute, or as some called him, C'nute and 'Cute, often overreached young Ironsides in cunning.

In one of their battles—the fifth of a series—the Danes were on the point of defeat, when Edric, whom Edmund, however hard in the ribs, was soft enough in the head to trust after former treachery, raised the cry that the young leader had fallen. By some ingenious contrivance, Edric had cut off somebody's head which resembled Edmund in features, and, perhaps, improving the likeness with burnt cork or other preparations, raised it on a spear in the field, exclaiming "Flee, English! flee, English! dead is Edmund."[14] The whole army became paralysed at the sight, and even Ironsides himself was completely put out of countenance, for he was unable to tell at the moment whether his head was really upon his own shoulders. How Edric could have had the face to practise such an imposition may puzzle the reader of the present day; but

"Flee, English! dead is Edmund!"

it was exceedingly likely that the trick would be aided by Edmund undergoing, as he no doubt would at the moment, a sudden change of countenance.

Ironsides, though for the moment put to flight, having been as it were frightened at his own shadow, found on reflection, in the first piece of water he came to, that his head was in its right place, though

---

14. These are the very words, exactly as they have been preserved—Vide Sir F. Palgrave, chapter xliii. page 308.

his heart had slightly failed him, and he consequently paused in his retreat, and met Canute face to face, on the road to Gloucestershire. Ironsides, stepping forward in front of his army, made the cool proposition to Canute that instead of risking the lives of so many brave men, they should settle the quarrel by single combat. Considering that Edmund had not only the advantage of patent-safety sides, which rendered him nearly battle-axe proof, but was also about twice the height of his antagonist, it is not surprising that Canute declined coming in immediate contact with the metallic plates, which would have acted as a powerful battery upon the diminutive Dane. Had he accepted the crafty challenge, every blow inflicted on Ironsides would have been a severe rap on the knuckles to Canute, who might as well have run his head against a brick wall as engage in a single combat with a person of such undoubted metal. It was, however, agreed that they should divide the realm, and though as a general rule it is not advisable to do anything by halves, this arrangement was decidedly beneficial to all parties. The armies were both delighted at the proposal, and their joy affords proof that their discretion formed a great deal more than the better part of their valour.

Canute took the north, and Edmund the south, with a nominal superiority over the former, so that the crown is said by the chroniclers to have belonged to Ironsides. It was certainly better that the ascendency should have been given to one of the two, for if their territory had been equal the crown must have been divided, and he that had the thickest head might have claimed the larger share of the regal diadem. Edmund lived only two months after the agreement had been signed, and as Canute took the benefit of survivorship, it has been good-naturedly suggested that he must have been either the actual or virtual murderer of Ironsides. There are only one or two facts which spoil this ingenious and amiable theory; the first of which is that there is no proof of his having been killed at all—an uncertainty that is quite sufficient to allow the benefit of the doubt to those who have been named as his murderers. Hume has, without hesitation, appointed Oxford as the scene of the assassination, and has been kind enough to select two chamberlains as the perpetrators of the deed, but we have been unable to collect sufficient evidence to go to a jury against the anonymous chamberlains, whom we beg leave to dismiss with the comfortable assurance that they quit these pages without any stain on their characters.

Canute, as the succeeding partner in the late firm of Edmund and Canute, found himself, in 1017, all alone in his glory on the British throne. His first care was to call a public meeting of "bishops," "duces," and "optimates," at which he voted himself into the chair; and he caused it to be proposed and seconded that he should be king to the exclusion of all the descendants of Ethelred. There can be no doubt that the meeting was packed, for every proposition of Canute was received with loud cries of "hear," and repeated cheers. Strong resolutions were passed against Edwy, the grown-up brother of Edmund Ironsides. Proceedings were instantly commenced; he was declared an outlaw, and was soon taken in execution in the then usual form.

Edmund and Edwy, the two infant sons of Ironsides, were protected by the plea of infancy; but Canute sent them out to dry-nurse to the king of the Swedes, with an intimation that if their mouths could be stopped by Swedish turnips, or anything else, the arrangement would be satisfactory to the English monarch. His Swedish majesty, whether moved by pity or actuated by the feeling of "None of my child," sent the babies on to Hungary, where they were taken in, but not done for, as Canute had desired. The little Edmund died early, but his brother Edward settled respectably in life, married a relation of the Emperor of Germany, became a family man, and one of his daughters was subsequently a Mrs. Malcolm, the lady of Malcolm, king of Scotland.

Edmund and Alfred, the other sons of Ethelred by Emma of Normandy, who were still living with their uncle Robert, had a sort of lawyer's letter written in their name to Canute, threatening an action of trover for the sceptre, unless it were immediately restored.

After offering a moiety—being equal to a composition of ten shillings in the pound—he proposed to settle the matter by marrying their mamma, who consented to this arrangement; and the claims of the infants were never heard of again. Neglected by their mother, they forgot their mother tongue—they grew up Normans instead of Saxons, say the old chroniclers, which seems to be going a little too far, for a Saxon cannot become a Norman by living in Normandy, any more than a man becomes a horse by residence in a stable.

After triumphing over his enemies, Canute somewhat altered for the better, and became a quiet, gentlemanly, but rather jovial man. He was fond of music, patronised vocalists, and occasionally wrote ballads, one of which is still preserved. As it was said of a certain performer that he would have been a good actor if he had been possessed of figure, voice, action, expression, and intelligence; so we may say of Canute that if he had known anything of sense or syntax, if he had been happy at description, or possessed the slightest share of imagination, he would have been a very fair poet.

A portion of one of Canute's once popular ballads has been preserved, and if the other verses resembled the one that has come down to us, there is no reason to regret that the rest is out of print and that nobody has kept the manuscript.

The following is the queer quatrain which remains as the sole specimen of his majesty's poetical abilities:—

> "Merrily sing the monks within Ely,
> When C'nute King rowed there by;
> Row, my knights, row near the land,
> And hear we these monks sing."

This dismal distich is said to have been suggested by his hearing the solemn monastic music of the choir as he rowed near the Minster of Ely; but we suspect the song must have been rather of a secular kind, or the term merrily would have been exceedingly inappropriate.[15]

About the year 1017, Edric, the royal favourite, evinced some disposition to strike for an advance of salary, when Canute resisting the demand, the king and the courtier came to high words. Eric of Northumbria, who happened to be sitting in the room with his battle-axe—which was in those days as common a companion as an umbrella or a walking-stick in the present age—got up, on a hint from the king, and axed the miserable Edric to death.

Canute, who was also king of the Danes, the Swedes—whose sovereign was his vassal—and of the Northmen, had many turbulent subjects abroad as well as at home, but he was in the habit of employing one against the other, so that it was utterly immaterial to him which of them were slain, so that he got rid of some of them. He kept a strong hand over his Danish earls, and even his nephew, "the doughty Haco"—though why he should have been called "doughty," is a matter of much doubt—was exiled for disregard of the royal authority.

Canute performing on his favourite Instrument.

The Swedes, who were always boiling over, got at last completely mashed by Earl Godwin; and the kings of Fife, who, although mere *piccoli*,[16] were monarchs of some note, having exerted themselves in a melancholy strain for independence, at length fell, for the sake of harmony, into the general submission

15. Some writers have endeavoured to justify the royal author or vindicate the characters of the monks of Ely, by saying that in those days "merry" meant "sad." These gentlemen might just as well argue that black meant white—a proposition some people would not hesitate to put forth as a plea for the errors of royalty.
16. *A group of small animals—Editor.*

to Canute. Six nations were now reduced into one general subordination to the English king, who of course became the object of the grossest flattery, and upon one memorable occasion was nearly sacrificed to the puffing system of his injudicious friends. One day, when in the plenitude of his power, he caused the throne to be removed from the throne-room and erected, during low tide, on the sea-shore. Having taken his seat, surrounded by his courtiers, he issued a proclamation to the ocean, forbidding it to rise, and commanding it not, on any account, to leave its bed until his permission for it to get up was graciously awarded. The courtiers backed the royal edict, and encouraged with the grossest adulation this first great practical attempt to prove that Britannia rules the waves. Such a rule, however, was soon proved to be nothing better than a rule *nisi*, which it is impossible to make absolute when opposed by Neptune's irresistible motion of course. Every wave of Canute's sceptre was answered by a wave from the sea, and the courtiers, who were already up to their ankles in salt water, began to fear that they should soon be pickled in the foaming brine.

At length the monarch himself found his footstool disposed to go on swimmingly of its own accord, and there was every prospect that the whole party would undergo the ceremony of an immediate investiture of the bath. The sovereign, who was very lightly shod, soon found that his pumps were not capable of getting rid of the water, which was now rising very rapidly. Having sat with his feet in the sea for a few minutes, and not relishing the slight specimen of hydropathic treatment he had endured, he jumped suddenly up, and began to abuse his courtiers for the mess into which he had been betrayed by their outrageous flattery.

One of the attendants who had remained at the back of the others during this ridiculous scene, observed drily that the whole party would have been inevitably washed and done for, if Canute had not made a timely retreat. The sovereign was so humbled by this incident that he took off his crown upon the spot, made a parcel of it at once, forwarded it to Winchester Cathedral, and never wore it again.

Water, as we all know, can subdue the strongest spirit, and though the spirit of Canute could bear a great deal of mixing, it is evident that the sea had shown him his own weakness. In the year 1030 he went on a pilgrimage to Rome, with no other staff than a wooden one in his hand; and instead of a valet to follow him, he had a simple wallet at his back. From a letter he

Canute reproving his Courtiers.

wrote to his bishops while abroad, it would seem that he received presents of "vases of gold and vessels of silver, and stuffs, and garments of great price;" so that by the time he got home again, his wallet must have been a tolerable burden for the royal back. He died at Shaftesbury, in 1035, about three years after his return from Rome, and was buried at Winchester; so that he finally laid his head where his crown had been already deposited.

On the death of Canute there was the usual difficulty as to what was to be done with the British crown; for there were two or three who thought the cap fitted themselves, and who consequently claimed the right to wear it. There is no doubt that Hardicanute, the only legitimate son of the late king, would have tried it on had it not been left by will to Harold, while his brother Sweyn was the legatee of Norway. A compromise was, however, effected, by which Harold took everything north of the Thames, including, of course, the Baker Street and Finsbury districts, while Hardicanute, to whom Denmark had been bequeathed, took the territories on the south shore, commencing in the Belvidere Road, Lambeth, and terminating at the southern extremity of the kingdom. He, however, left his English dominions to the management of his mother and Earl Godwin, while he himself lingered in Denmark; on account of the convivial habits of the Scandinavian chiefs; for Hardicanute drank, as the phrase goes, "like a fish," though the liquid he imbibed was very different from that which the finny tribe are addicted to.

Edward and Alfred, the two sons of Ethelred, had come over to be in the way in case of anything turning up on the death of Canute, but Edward finding himself rather too much in the way, and fearing an unpleasant removal, took a return ticket for himself and party for Normandy. Alfred, after vainly attempting to land at Sandwich, happily thought of Herne Bay, and though it was in the height of the season, he of course found no one there to resist his progress. Having ventured up to Guildford on the invitation of Godwin, Alfred and his soldiers found a sumptuous repast and comfortable lodgings prepared for them. But Godwin had been more downy even than the beds, and the soldiers having been seized and imprisoned found wet blankets thrown on their hopes of hospitable treatment. Edward himself was cruelly murdered, and Harold, who was called Harefoot, from the speed with which he could run, was now able to walk over the course, for there was no opposition to him in the race for the stakes of Royalty.

He was fond of nothing but hunting, and as he could catch a hare by his own velocity he generally had the game in his own hands. He died a.d. 1040, after a short reign of four years; and though, if he had lived to old age, he might have proved a good sovereign in the long-run, he was certainly not happy in the walk of life where fortune had placed him.

Hardicanute, a name signifying Canute the Hardy, or the tough, came over on the death of Harold; but with all his toughness he evinced or assumed some tenderness at the cruel fate of his brother Alfred. He showed his sympathy for one by brutality towards another, and subjected Harold's memory to the most barbarous indignities.

Godwin, fearing that he might share the obloquy of his former master, propitiated Hardicanute by giving him a magnificent toy, consisting of a gilt ship, with a crew of eighty men, each having a bracelet of pure gold weighing sixteen ounces, and dressed in the most valuable habiliments. The new king no doubt melted the gold very speedily in drink, to which he was so much addicted that he actually died intoxicated at a party given at Clapham, by one Clapa, from whose name, or home, that suburb was called. His majesty was, according to the chroniclers, "on his legs," and the waiters had of course left the room, when Hardicanute unable to get further than "Gentlemen," staggered into his seat, and was carried out—mortally inebriated.[17]

The throne being now vacant, Edward, the half-brother of the late king, who happened to be on the spot, was induced to step up and take a seat, though he was the senior of the late sovereign. In those days, however, the rules of hereditary descent were not very rigidly followed, for it was success that chiefly regulated succession. Edward's cause had, however, derived much support from Earl Godwin, the most extraordinary teetotum of former times. He had practised the political *chassez croisser* to an extent that even in our own days has seldom been surpassed. He had turned his

A frightful Example.   Death of Hardicanute.

---

17. Other historians say in so many words that "he died drunk." We prefer using the milder expression of "mortally inebriated."

coat so frequently that he had lost all consciousness of which was the right side and which the wrong; but he always treated that side as the right which happened to be uppermost.

Godwin had, it is said, commenced life as a cowboy, but he soon raised himself above the low herd, and eventually succeeded in making his daughter Editha the queen of Edward. The king, who had lived much in Normandy, and had derived some assistance from Duke William, afterwards the Conqueror, had formed many Norman predilections, which created jealousy among his Saxon subjects. In 1061, he had received as a visitor his brother-in-law, one Eustace, Count of Boulogne, who, on returning home with his followers through Dover, insolently demanded gratuitous lodgings of one of the inhabitants. The Dover people, who are still remarkable for their high charges, and who seldom think of providing a cup of tea under two shillings, or a bed for less than half-a-crown, resisted the demands of Eustace and his friends, when a fight ensued, and the Normans were compelled to make the best of their way out of the neighbourhood.

Eustace, still smarting under the blows he had received, ran howling to Edward, like a boy who, upon receiving a thrashing, flies to his big brother for redress. The king desired Godwin, who was governor of Dover, to chastise the place; but the earl positively refused, and insisted that the Count of Boulogne could not complain if, when he required to be served gratuitously, he had got regularly served out. Edward, irritated at this message, prepared for war, and Godwin, who was joined by his sons, Sweyn and Harold, had collected a powerful army; but when it came to the point, the soldiers on both sides gave evident symptoms of a desire to see the matter amicably arranged. As the king's forces consisted chiefly of the fryd or militia, there can be little doubt where the panic commenced; and Godwin's men, recognising among the foe some of their fellow-countrymen trembling from head to foot, immediately commenced shaking hands, so that there was an end to all firmness on both sides. A truce was consequently concluded, and the disputes of the parties referred to the arbitration of the Witenagemote; who doomed Sweyn to outlawry, and Godwin and Harold to banishment. Thus the "king's darlings," as they had been called, were disposed of, and the pets became the object of petty vengeance. Editha, the daughter of Godwin, shared in the general disgrace of her family; for the king, her husband, "reduced her," say the chroniclers, "to her last groat;" and with this miserable fourpence she was consigned to a monastery, where she was waited on by one servant of all-work, and controlled by the abbess, who was the sister of her royal tyrant.

Edward being now released from the presence of Godwin, began to think of seeing his friends, and invited William of Normandy to spend a few months at the English court. He came with a numerous retinue, and finding most of the high offices in the possession of Normans, he was able to feel himself perfectly at home. On the conclusion of his stay he departed, with a gift of horses, hounds, and hawks; in fact, a miniature menagerie, which had been presented to him by his host, without considering the inconvenience occasioned by adding "a happy family" to the luggage of the Norman visitor.

Edward was not allowed much leisure, for his guest had no sooner departed, than he found himself threatened by Earls Godwin and Harold, who sailed up to London, and landed a large army in the Strand. This important thoroughfare, which has been in modern times so frequently blockaded, was stopped up at that early period by men who were paving their way to power; so that paviours of some kind have for ages been a nuisance to the neighbourhood.

Edward agreed to a truce, by which Godwin and his sons were restored to their

Unpleasant Position of King Harold.

William inspecting the Volunteers previous to the Invasion of England.

rank; but the earl, while dining soon afterwards with Edward at Windsor, was, according to some, choked in the voracious endeavour to swallow a tremendous mouthful. Thus perished, from an appetite larger than his windpipe, one of the most illustrious characters of his age. Harold, his son, succeeded him in his titles and estates; but as the latter are said to have consisted chiefly of the Goodwin Sands, the legatee could not hope to keep his head above water on such an inheritance.

Harold commenced his career by worrying Algar, a rival earl, who got worried to death (a.d. 1059), and he then turned his attention to the father-in-law of his victim, one Griffith, a Welsh sovereign, whose army not liking the bother of war, cut off his head and sent it as a peace-offering to the opposite leader. This unceremonious manner of breaking the neck of a difficulty by decapitating their king, says more for the decision than the loyalty of the Welsh people.

It was not long after this circumstance that Harold, going out in a fishing-boat on the coast of Sussex with one or two bungling mariners, got carried out to sea, and was ultimately washed ashore like an old blacking-bottle in the territory of Guy, Count of Ponthieu. Having been picked up by the count, poor Harold was treated as a waif, and impounded until a heavy sum was paid for his ransom. William of Normandy, upon hearing that an earl and retinue were pawned in the distinguished name of Harold, good-naturedly redeemed them, at a great expense, but made the English earl solemnly pledge himself to assist his deliverer in obtaining the English crown at the death of Edward. The king expired on the 5th of January, 1066, leaving the crown to William, according to some, and to Harold, according to others; but as no will was ever found, it is probable enough that he agreed to leave the kingdom first to one and then to the other, according to which happened to have at the moment the ear of the sovereign.[18]

---

18. This Edward was generally called the Confessor, but how he got the name we are unable to say with certainty. It has been ingeniously suggested that it was on the *lucus a non lucendo* principle, and that he was called the Confessor, from his never confessing anything.

Harold, forgetting the circumstance of his awkward predicament in the fishing-boat, and ungrateful of William's services, immediately assumed the title of king, and got his coronation over the very same evening. It is even believed by some that the ceremony was so hastily performed as to have been a mere *tête-à-tête* affair between Stigand, the Archbishop of Canterbury, and the new sovereign.

When William received the news of Harold's accession he was having a game with a bow and arrows in his hunting-ground near Rouen. His trembling knees suddenly took the form of his bow, and his lip began to quiver. He threw himself hastily into a skiff, and crossing the Seine, never stopped till he reached his palace, where he walked up and down the hall several times, occasionally sitting down for a moment in the porter's chair, then starting up and resuming his promenade up and down the passage. On recovering from his reverie he sent ambassadors to demand of Harold the fulfilment of his promise; but that dishonest person replied that he being under duress when he gave his word, it could not be considered binding.

William accordingly called a public meeting of Normans, at which it was resolved unanimously that England should be invaded as speedily as possible. A subscription was immediately entered into to defray the cost, and volunteers were admitted to join the expedition without the formality of a reference. Tag from Maine and Anjou, Rag from Poitou and Bretagne, with Bob-tail from Flanders, came rapidly pouring in; while the riff of the Rhine, and the raff of the Alps, formed altogether a mob of the most miscellaneous character. Those families who are in the habit of boasting that their ancestors came in with the Conqueror, would scarcely feel so proud of the fact if they were aware that the companions of William comprised nearly all the roguery and vagabondism of Europe.

A large fleet having been for some time in readiness at St. Valery, near Dieppe, crossed in the autumn of 1066, and on the 28th of September the Normans landed without opposition at Pevensey, near Hastings. William, who was the last to step on shore, fell flat upon his hands and face, which was at first considered by the soldiers as an evil omen; but opening his palm, which was covered with mud, he gaily exclaimed, "Thus do I lay my hands upon this ground—and be assured that it is a pie you shall all have a finger in." This speech, or words to the same effect, restored the confidence of the soldiers, and they marched to Hastings, where they waited the coming of the enemy.

Harold, who had come to London, left town by night for the Sussex coast, and halted at Battle, where the English forces kept it up for two or three days and nights with Bongs and revelry. At length, on Saturday, the 14th of October, William gave the word to advance, when a gigantic Norman, called Taillefer, who was a minstrel and a juggler, went forward to execute a variety of tricks, such as throwing up his sword with one hand and catching it with the other; balancing his battle-axe on the tip of his chin; standing on his head upon the point of his spear, and performing other feats of pantomimic dexterity. He next proceeded to sing a popular ballad, and having asked permission to strike the first blow, he succeeded in making a tremendous hit; but some one happening to return the compliment, he was very soon quieted. The men of London, who formed the bodyguard of Harold, made a snug and impenetrable barrier with their shields, under which they nestled very cosily.[19]

From nine in the morning till nine in the afternoon the Normans continued watching

The Landing of William the Conqueror.

---

19. Some of them, who were buried under their bucklers, may have been inhabitants of Bucklersbury, which may have derived its name from the practice we have described.

for the English to emerge from under their shields, as a cat waits for a mouse to quit its hiding-place. As the mouse refuses to come to the scratch, so the Londoners declined to quit their snuggery, until William had the happy idea of ordering his bowmen to shoot into the air; and they were thus down upon the foe, with considerable effect, by the falling of the arrows. Still the English stood firm until William, by a pretended retreat, induced the soldiers of Harold to quit their position of safety. Three times were the Saxon snails tempted to come out of their shells by this crafty manouvre, but their courage was still unshaken, until an arrow, shot at random, hit Harold in the left eye, when his dispirited followers fled like winking.

The English king was carried to the foot of the standard, where a few of his soldiers formed round him a little party of Protectionists. William fought with desperate valour, and was advancing towards the banner, when an English billman drew a bill which he made payable at sight on the head of the Duke of Normandy. Fortunately the precious metal of William's helmet was sufficient to meet the bill, which must otherwise have crushed the Norman leader. Harold, whose spirit never deserted him, observed with reference to the wound in his eye that it was a bad look-out, but he must make the best of it. At length he fell exhausted, when the English having lost their banner, found their energies beginning to flag, and William became the Conqueror.

Book II

THE PERIOD FROM THE NORMAN CONQUEST TO THE DEATH OF KING JOHN

CHAPTER THE FIRST

WILLIAM THE CONQUEROR

Before entering on our account of the reign of William the Conqueror, a bird's-eye view of the early biography of that illustrious person may be acceptable. He was born in 1024, of miscellaneous parents, and was a descendant of the illustrious Rollo, who wrested Normandy from Charles the Simple, whose simplicity consisted no doubt in his submitting to be done out of his possessions. William had been in his early days one of those intolerable nuisances, an infant prodigy, and at eight years old exhibited that ripeness of judgment and energy of action for which the birch is in our opinion the best remedy. He had quelled a disturbance in his own court, when very young; but a beadle in our own day can do as much as this, for a disturbance in a court is often quelled by that very humble officer. His marriage with Matilda, daughter of the Earl of Flanders, gave him the benefit of respectable connection, so useful to a young man starting in life; and after trying with all his might to acquire Maine, his success in obtaining it added to his influence.

Such was the man whom we left in our last chapter on the field of Battle, and on our return to him we find him building Battle Abbey in memory of his victory. He caused a list or roll to be made of all the nobles and gentlemen who came over with him from Normandy, and many of them were men of mark, if we are to judge by their signatures. This earliest specimen in England of a genuine French roll was preserved for some time under the name of the roll of Battle Abbey, but the monks were in the habit of making it a medium for advertisement, by allowing the insertion of fresh names, to gratify that numerous class who are desirous of being thought to have come in with the Conqueror. The roll of Battle Abbey was no longer confined to the thorough-bred, but degenerated into a paltry puff, made up in the usual way, with paste—and scissors.

William, instead of going at once to London, put up for a few days at Hastings, expecting the people to come and ask for peace; but though he remained at home the greater part of the day, the callers were by no means numerous. He accordingly took his departure for Romney, which he savagely rummaged. He then went on to Dover, which Holinshed describes as the lock and key of all England, but the inhabitants, finding the lock and key in hostile hands, sagaciously made a bolt of it.

William's soldiers had no sooner taken possession of Dover than they were all seized with severe illness, but whether they availed themselves of the celebrated Dover Powders is exceedingly dubious. The Conqueror at length went towards London, where the Witan had proclaimed as king a poor little boy of the name of Edgar Atheling, the son of Edmund Ironsides. William, however, nearly frightened the Witan out of its wits by burning Southwark, and a deputation started from town to Berkhampstead, to make submission to the Conqueror. Young Edgar made a formal renunciation of the throne, which was not his to renounce, and indeed, when he sat upon it the child fell so very far short that for him to feel the ground under his feet was utterly impossible.

After these concessions, the day was fixed for William's coronation in Westminster Abbey, on the 26th of December, 1066, when the ceremony was performed amid enthusiastic cheering which lasted for several minutes.

The Normans outside not being accustomed to Saxon habits, mistook the applause for disapprobation, and thinking that their duke was being hooted, or perhaps pelted, with "apples, oranges, nuts, and pears," they began to avenge the fancied insult by taking it out in violence towards the populace. Houses were burnt down in every direction, when the noise made without became audible to those within, who rushed forth to join in the row, and William, it is said, was left almost alone in the abbey, to finish his own coronation. He, however, went through the whole ceremony, and even added a few extemporaneous paragraphs to the usual coronation affidavit, by the introduction of an oath or two of his own, after the interruption of the ceremony.

The Conqueror having taken some extensive premises at Barking, went to reside there for a short time, and was visited by several English families, among whom that of the warrior Coxo—since abbreviated into Cox—was one of the most illustrious. William found considerable difficulty in satisfying the rapacity of his followers, who thought nothing of asking for a castle, a church, an abbey, or a trifle of that kind by way of remuneration for their services. He scattered those articles right and left, according to the chroniclers; but it would be difficult to say where he got them from, were it not that the chroniclers are so skilled in castle-building that they have always a stock on hand to devote to the purposes of history.

After six months' residence in England, William, having got his half-year's salary as king, was in funds to enable him to take a trip to Normandy. He took with him a complete sideboard of English—not British—plate, and with the treasures of this country dazzled the eyes of his continental friends and subjects. A party of Young England gents who accompanied him attracted also, by their long flowing hair, the admiration of foreigners.

Odo, William's half-brother, who had been left at home to rule in the absence of the king, soon—as the reader may anticipate from the obvious pun that must ensue—rendered himself utterly odious. His treatment of the conquered people was cruel in the extreme; he filled the cup of misery not only to the brim, but degradation was kept continually on draft, every new blow being a fresh tap for the victims of tyranny. The very smallest beer will, however, ferment at last if kept continually bottled up; and though the Entire of England had been for a time rendered flat, there was a good deal of genuine British stout at bottom. A general effervescence broke out on the departure of William, who had acted hitherto as a cork; but Odo evinced a disposition to play the screw, by drawing out whatever he could in the absence of his superior.

A general conspiracy seemed to be on the point of breaking out, when William, who had allowed letter after letter to remain unanswered which had been sent to entreat him to come home, started late one night for Dieppe, on his return to England. His first care was to assuage the discontent, and he had already learned the acknowledged trick that the shortest way of stopping a British mouth is by liberally feeding it. He accordingly gave a series of Christmas dinners, and he invited several Saxon earls to meet a succession of bovine barons. If the banquets were intended as a bait, there is no doubt that the English very readily swallowed them. By way of further propitiating the people, he published a law in the Saxon tongue, decreeing "that every son should inherit from his father," or in other words, should take after him. If, however, he was liberal in his invitations to dinner, he took care that the people should pay the bill, for he had scarcely finished entertaining them, when he began taxing them most oppressively.

William did not acquire the title of Conqueror quite so speedily as has been generally imagined, for he was occupied at least seven years in running about the country from one place to the other, wiping out, by many severe wipes, the remaining traces of insubordination to his government. In the year 1068 he besieged Exeter, where Githa, the aged mother of Harold, was leading a quiet life, surrounded by a bevy of venerable gossips. The Conqueror routed them out, and they repaired to Bath, where their taste for tittle-tattle might have been indulged, but meeting with rudeness from the celebrated Bath chaps, they hastened to Flanders. William now sent for his wife Matilda, whom he had not brought over until he could form some idea how long he was likely to remain in his new quarters. A cheap coronation was got up for her at Winchester, the contract having been taken by Aldred, Archbishop of York, who it is believed found all the materials for the ceremony, without extra charge; and as the queen was rather short, we may presume that everything was cut down to a low figure. A little after this event, Harold's two sons, Godwin and Edmund, with a little brother, facetiously called Magnus, came over from Ireland, and hovered about the coast of Cornwall, where young Magnus, being a minor, perhaps hoped for sympathy. They planted their standard, expecting that the inhabitants would fly to it, but they only flew at it, to tear it in pieces. Poor Magnus, with infantine tenderness, cried like a baby over the insulted bunting. Tired with their ill success, the three brothers eventually went over as suppliants to Denmark, where the unhappy beggars were received by Sweyn with amiable hospitality.

In the ensuing year, William turned Somerset so completely upside down that it could not have known whether it stood on its head or its heels; and in every shire he took, he built a castle, by way of insuring the lives of himself and his followers in the county. According to Hollinshed, the greatest indignities were passed upon the conquered people. They were compelled even to regulate their beards in a particular fashion, from which the youngest shaver was not exempt. They were obliged to "round their hair," which probably means that they were obliged to keep it curled, and thus even in their *coiffure* they were ruled by a rod of iron. In addition to this, they were forced to "frame themselves in the Norman fashion," which must have made them the pictures of misery.

William had, in one of his amiable moods, probably over a bottle of wine, promised Edwin, the brother-in-law of Harold, his daughter in marriage. When, however, the earl came to claim his fair prize, the Conqueror not only withdrew his consent, but insulted the suitor, and a scene ensued very similar to the common incident in a farce, when a testy old father or guardian flies into a passion with the walking gentleman, exclaiming "Hoity-toity!" and calling him a young jackanapes. Edwin, irritated at this treatment, collected an army in the north, and waited near the river Ouse; but the courage of his soldiers soon oozed out when the Conqueror made his appearance. William was victorious; but he had much to contend against during the

William refusing his Daughter to Edwin.

first few years of his reign, and an invasion of the Danes, under Osborne, was a very troublesome business.

The Normans, having shut themselves up in York, set fire to some of the houses outside the city, to check the approach of the foe; but the flames catching the minster, a "night wi' Burns" seemed to be inevitable. Not wishing to remain to be roasted, they risked the minor inconvenience of being basted, and made a very lively sally out of the city. They were nearly all killed, and the Danes took possession of York; but the place being reduced to ashes, was little better than an extensive dust-hole. Osborne and his followers not wishing to winter among the cinders, retired to their ships, and William thus had time to make further arrangements.

The Conqueror was hunting in the Forest of Dean when he heard of the catastrophe, and having his lance in his hand, he swore he would never put it down until he had exterminated the enemy. This must have been a somewhat inconsiderate vow, for though it may have been chivalrous to declare he would never put down his lance until a certain remote event, the weapon must have been at times a very inconvenient companion, as he did not commence his campaign until the spring; but as his vow came into operation immediately, the lance must have been a dead weight in his hand during the whole of the winter season. At length he mounted his horse, and rode rough-shod over the people of York, after which he took Durham, and ultimately repaired to Hexham, to which he administered a regular Hexham tanning.

Robbery, under the less obnoxious name of confiscation, now became very general, and William commenced the wholesale subtraction of lands, with a view to their division among his Norman followers. The conquered English had nearly all their property seized, and those who had but little shared the lot of the wealthiest in the spoliation to which all were subjected. William de Percy profited largely in purse; and if in those days manners made the man, he must have been a made man indeed, for he got no less than eighty manors. Several other names will be found in the Domesday Book, drawn up about fifteen years after the conquest, from which some of our oldest ancestors may learn full particulars of their early ancestors.

The title of Richmond had its origin from a Breton ruffian of the name of Allan, who having got a mount near York as his share of the plunder, gave it the name of Riche-Mont, or Rich-Mount; and the first Earl of Cumberland was a low fellow named Reuouf Meschines, the latter title being no doubt derived from *mesquin*, to express something mean and pitiful in this individual's character. The boast of having come in with the Normans is equivalent to a confession of belonging to a family whose founder was a thief, or at least a receiver of stolen articles.

The resistance to the Conqueror was, in many parts of England, exceedingly obstinate, and Hereward of Lincoln, commonly called "England's Darling," or the Lincoln pet, was one of the most resolute of William's enemies. Such was the impetuosity of the pet that the Normans imagined he must be a necromancer: and William, in order to turn the superstitions of the people to his own account, engaged a rival conjuror, or sorceress, who was placed with much solemnity on the top of a wooden tower, among the works that were proceeding for the defence of the invader's army. Hereward, however, seizing his opportunity, set fire to the wizard's temple, and the unfortunate conjuror being puzzled, terminated his career amidst a grand pyrotechnic display, which proved for Hereward and his party a blaze of triumph.

The English had established a camp of refuge at Ely, but the hungry monks, whose profession it was to fast, were the first, when provisions ran short, to grumble at the scarcity. Their vows were evidently as empty as themselves, and though they had pledged themselves to abstinence, they began eating their own words with horrible voracity. They betrayed the isle to the Conqueror; but Hereward refusing to submit, plunged, like a true son of the soil, into the swamps and marshes, where the Normans would not venture to follow him. Protected to a certain extent in the bosom of his mother earth, he carried on a vexatious warfare, until William offered terms which took the hero out of the mud, and settled him in the estates of his ancestors.

It has been customary with historians to cut the conquest exceedingly short, as if *Veni, vidi, vici*, had been the motto of William; and that, in fact, the Anglo-Saxons had surrendered at his nod—overcome by the waving of his plume—if he ever wore one; or in other words, knocked down with a feather. Such, however, was not the case; for it took seven years' apprenticeship to accustom the hardy natives of our isle to the subjection of a conqueror.

While William was in Normandy, whither he had been called to protect his possessions in Maine—for, as we are told by that mad wag, Matthew Paris, he never lost sight of the Main chance—Philip of France offered some assistance to Edgar Atheling. This individual accordingly set sail, but the unlucky dog had scarcely got his bark upon the sea, when the winds set up a dismal howl, and he was driven ashore near Northumberland. Edgar and a few friends escaped to Scotland, and at the advice of his brother-in-law, Malcolm sought a reconciliation with the Conqueror, who allowed the Atheling his lodging in the palace of Rouen, with a pound's worth of silver a day for his maintenance.

The king was soon recalled to England by an insurrection, got up by Roger Fitz Osborn, who, together with a large number of persons who were all subject to Fitz, determined on resisting the insolent oppression of the Conqueror. Young Roger, whose father, William Fitz Osborn, had been of great service to the Norman invader, was engaged to Emma de Gael, a daughter of the Duke of Norfolk, when the banns were most unreasonably forbidden by the sovereign. The young couple, however, determined not to be foiled, had made a match of it; and at the wedding feast, which was given at Norwich, some violent speeches were made, in the course of which William was denounced as a tyrant and a humbug, amid repeated shouts of "hear, hear," from the whole of the company.

The grand object of the Norman rebels was to bring round Earl Waltheof, and having taken care to heat him with wine, they did succeed in bringing him round in a most wonderful manner. He assented to every proposition, and his health was drunk with enthusiasm, followed, no doubt, by the usual complimentary chorus, attributing to him the festive virtues of jollity and good fellowship. The next morning, however, after "a consultation with his pillow," according to the Saxon chroniclers—from which we are to infer that he and his pillow laid their heads together, on the principle of goose to goose—he began to think he had acted very foolishly at the party of the previous night, and, jumping out of bed, packed off a communication to those with whom he had promised to co-operate. After presenting his compliments, he "begged to say, that the evening's amusement not having stood the test of the morning's reflection, he was under the painful necessity of withdrawing any consent he might have given to any enterprise that might have been proposed at the meeting of the day preceding."

The conspiracy, which had commenced in drinking, ended, very appropriately, in smoke; nearly all who took a part in the Norwich wedding were killed, and it has been well said by a modern writer that a share in the Norwich Union was not in those days a very profitable matter. It was about the year 1077 that William began to be wounded by that very sharp incisor—the tooth of filial disobedience. When preparing for the conquest of England he had promised, in the event of success, to resign Normandy to his son Robert, and had even taken an oath—clenched, probably, with the exclamation, "So help me, Bob!"—that if Robert assisted in his father's absence the boy should have the Duchy.

Having conquered England, the Governor returned, and wanted Normandy back again, observing, with coarse quaintness, that he was "not going to throw off his clothes till he went to bed," or, in other words, insisting that Robert, who had got into his father's shoes, should instantly evacuate the paternal high-lows. Robert was brave, but by no means foppish in his dress, and had acquired the nickname of Robert Curt-hose or Short-stockings. He probably derived this appellation from a habit of wearing socks, and it is not likely that he was familiarly known as Bob Socks among his friends and acquaintances. Young Socks, who had always been irritable, was on one occasion roused to a pitch of passion by having the contents of a pitcher pitched upon his head by his two brothers, from the balcony of his own lodging. He became mad with rage, and, irritated by the water on the brain, he ran upstairs with a drawn sword in his hand, when the king, hearing the row among the three boys, rushed to the spot, and succeeded in quelling it in a manner not very favourable to Young Socks, who ran away from home towards Rouen. Through the intercession of his mother, he was persuaded to return home, and it is probable that "B. S."—the initials of Bob Socks—was "entreated to return home to his disconsolate mother, when all would be arranged to his satisfaction." Nevertheless, his pocket-money continued to be as short as his hose, and his companions declared it to be a shame that he never had a shilling to spend in anything. He accordingly went to his father, and demanded Normandy, but the monarch refused him, reprimanded him for his irregular habits, and recommended him to adopt "the society of serious old men"—the "heavy fathers" of that early period. Robert declared irreverently that the old pumps were exceedingly dry companions, and reiterated his demand for Normandy. The king wrathfully refused, when Young Socks announced his determination to take his valour to the foreign market, and place it at the service of any one who chose to pay him his price for it.

He visited various localities abroad, where he recounted his grievances, and borrowed money, making himself a sort of begging-letter impostor, and going about as if with a board round his neck, inscribed "Turned out of doors," or "Totally destitute." Though he collected a good round sum, he spent the whole of it in minstrels, jugglers, and parasites, so that he divided his time between the enjoyment of popular songs, conjuring tricks, and paid paragraphs, embodying the most outrageous puffs of his own character. After leading a vagabond life for some time, he was set up by Philip of France, in a castle on the confines of Normandy; but as he was only allowed lodging, he had to find his board as he could, by plundering his neighbours. One day he had sallied forth in search of a victim, when he found himself engaged in single combat with a tall gentlemanly man in a mail coat and a vizor, forming a sort of iron veil, which covered his countenance. The combatants had been for some time banging at each other with savage vehemence, when Robert delivered "one, two, three," with such rapid succession on the head of his antagonist, that the latter, unable to resist so many plumpers coming at once to the pole, retired from the contest.

The stalwart knight being regularly knocked up, was glad to knock under, and fell to the earth with a piteous howl, in which Robert recognised the *falsetto* of his own father. Young Socks, who had a good heart, burst into tears, and instead of falling on his antagonist to finish him as he had designed, he fell upon his own knee to ask forgiveness of his parent. William, who would have been settled in one more crack, took advantage of his son's assistance, but went away muttering maledictions against Young Socks, who subsequently finding the vindictiveness of his father's character, declined any further communication with the "old gentleman," and never saw him again.

In the reign of William the Church was always disposed to be militant, and among the most pugnacious priests was Walcher de Lorraine, the Bishop of Durham, who, it is said, often turned his crozier into a lance, by having, we presume, a long movable hook at the end of it. He divided his time between preaching and plunder, correcting the morals of the people one day, and on the next picking their pockets. He was, in fact, alternately teaching and thrashing them, as if the only way to impress them with religious truth, was to beat it regularly into them.

At length, however, the right reverend robber having become very unpopular in his neighbourhood, agreed to attend a public meeting of the inhabitants at Gateshead, to offer explanations on the subject of the murder of one Liulf, a noble Englishman, and on other miscellaneous business. The attendance was far more numerous than select, and the old bishop becoming exceedingly nervous, ran away into the church with all his retinue. The people declared that if he did not come out they would smoke him out, by setting fire to the building; and they had proceeded to carry their threats into execution, when, half suffocated with the heat, the bishop came to the door with his face muffled up in the skirts of his coat, and addressed a few words to the mob in so low a tone that our reporters being at a considerable distance—almost eight centuries off—have not succeeded in catching them. The bishop, however, caught it at once, for he was slain after a short and rather irregular discussion. The words "Slay ye the bishop," were distinctly heard to issue from a voice in the crowd, and the speaker—whoever he was—having put the question, the ayes and the bishop had it.

William selected one bishop to avenge another, and chose the furious Odo, who in spite of cries for mercy, and piteous exclamations of "O! don't, Odo!" killed every one that came across his path, without judicial forms, or, familiarly speaking, without judge or jury. This ambitious butcher looked with a pope's eye at the triple crown of Rome, and set out for Italy, with plenty of gold, to carry his election to the papal chair by corruption and bribery. The virtues of the cardinals might not have proved so strong as the cardinal virtues; but Odo, the bishop of Bayeux, had no chance of trying the experiment, for he was stopped in his expedition to Rome, at the Isle of Wight, by his brother-in-law, the Conqueror. William ordered his arrest; but no one volunteering to act as bailiff, the king seized the prelate by the robe, and took him into custody. "I am a clerk—a priest," cried Odo, endeavouring to get away. "I don't care what you are," exclaimed William, retaining his hold upon his prisoner. "The pope alone has the right to try me," shrieked the bishop, getting away, and leaving a fragment of his robe in the king's hand. "But I've got you, and don't mean to part with you again in a hurry," muttered William, after darting forward and effecting the recapture of Odo, who was immediately committed to a dungeon in Normandy.

The king soon after this incident lost his wife Matilda, and he became, after her decease, more cruel, avaricious, and jealous of his old companions-in-arms, than ever. One of the worst acts of his reign was the making of the New Forest in Hampshire, which he effected by driving away the inhabitants without the smallest compensation, from a space of nearly ninety miles in circumference. He appointed a bow-bearer, whose office still exists as a sinecure, with a salary of forty shillings a year, for which the gentleman who holds the appointment swears "to be of good behaviour towards the sovereign's wild beasts," and of course, in compliance with his oath, would feel bound to touch his hat to the British Lion.

The Bishop of Durham.

After founding the New Forest, the king enacted the most oppressive laws; placing on the killing of a hare such penalties as are enough to cause "each particular hair to stand on end," by their extreme barbarity.

Towards the end of the year 1086 William, who had grown exceedingly fat, started for France, to negotiate with Philip about some possessions, when the latter indulged in some small puns at the expense of the corpulency of the Conqueror. By comparing him to a fillet of veal on castors, and suggesting

William departing for France.

his being exhibited at a prize monarch show, Philip so irritated William that the latter swore, with fearful oaths, to make his weight felt in France; and he kept his word, for falling upon Mantes, he succeeded in completely crushing it. Having, however, gone out on horseback to see the ruins, the gigantic animal he was riding stepped on some hot ashes, which set the brute dancing so vigorously that the pummel of the saddle gave the Conqueror a fearful pummelling. He was so much shaken by this incident that he resolved never to ride the high horse, or indeed any other horse again; and he was soon after removed, at his own request, to the monastery of St. Gervas, just outside the walls of Rouen. Becoming rapidly worse, his heart softened to his enemies, most of whom he pardoned, and he then proceeded to make his will, by which he left Normandy to his son Robert, and bequeathed the crown of England to be fought for by William and Henry, with a significant wish, however, that the former might get it. Henry exclaimed emphatically, "What are you going to give me?" and on receiving for his answer, "Five thousand pounds weight of silver out of my treasury," ungraciously demanded what he should do with such a paltry pittance. "Be patient," replied the king; "suffer thy elder brothers to precede thee—thy time will come after theirs;" but Henry, muttering "It's all very well to say 'be patient,'" hurried out of the room, drew the cash, weighed it carefully, and brought a strong box to put it in.[20]

To think of an iron chest at such a moment proved the possession of a heart of steel; and William, the elder son, was nearly as bad, for he hastened to England to look after the crown before his father had expired.

It was on the 9th of September, 1087, that the Conqueror died, and his last faint sigh was the signal for a rush to the door, in which priests, doctors, and knights joined with furious eagerness. In vain did a diminutive bishop ask a stalwart warrior "where he was shoving to?" and the expostulations of a prim doctor to the crowd, entreating them to keep back, as there was "plenty of time," were utterly disregarded. The scene resembled that which may be witnessed occasionally at the pit door of the Opera, for the whole of William's attendants were eager to get home for the purpose of being early in securing either some place or plunder. The inferior servants of the royal robber—like master, like man—commenced rifling the king's trunks and drawers of all the cash, jewels, and linen. There seemed scarcely more than it deserves, for there is no doubt that he was cruel, selfish, and unprincipled. It is, however, a curious fact that what receives blacking from one age gets polished by the next: and this may account for the brilliance that has been shed in this country over the name of one who introduced the feudal system, the Game Laws, and other evils, the escape from which has been the work of many centuries. Though a natural son, he was an unnatural father, and the result was that being an indifferent parent, his children became also indifferent. He had a violent temper, and was such a brutal glutton that he aimed a blow

---

20. For further particulars of Henry's conduct, vide Orderic, every prospect of the Conqueror being left in the city of Rouen to be buried by the parish, when a few of the clergy began to think of the funeral. The Archbishop ordered that it should take place at St. Stephen's, in Caen, and none of the family being present, the undertaker actually came down upon a poor good-natured old knight, who had put himself rather prominently forward as a sort of provisional committee-man. How the affair was settled we are unable to state, but we have it on the authority of Oderic that when the Bishop of Evreux had pronounced the panegyric, a man in the crowd jumped up, declaring the Conqueror was an old thief, and that he—the man in the crowd—claimed the ground on which they were then standing. Many of the persons round cheered him in his address, and the bishops, for the sake of decency, paid out the execution from the Conqueror's grave for sixty shillings.

at Fitz-Osborne, his steward, for sending to table an under-done crane, when Odo interfered to check his master's violence. Of his personal appearance we have an authentic record in a statue placed against one of the pillars of the church of St. Stephen, at Caen; but as the figure is without a head, we have tried in vain to form from it some idea of the Conqueror's countenance. From the absence of the face in the statue we can only infer that William wore an expression of vacancy.

CHAPTER THE SECOND

WILLIAM RUFUS

illiam, the son of the Conqueror, had obtained the nick-name of Rufus, from his red hair, and these jokes on personal peculiarities afford a lamentable proof of the rudeness of our ancestors. Having left his father at the point of death, he hastened to England, where he pretended to be acting for the king; resorting to what, in puffing phraseology, is termed the untradesmanlike artifice of "It's the same concern," and doing business for himself in the name of the late sovereign. One of his first steps was, of course, towards the treasury, from which he drew sixty thousand pounds in gold and silver. Having received from his father a letter of introduction to Archbishop Lanfranc, he rushed, with the avidity of a man who has got a reference to a new tailor, and presenting it to the primate, requested that measures might be taken for putting the crown on his head as soon as possible. Lanfranc, having secured the place of Prime Minister for himself, issued cards to a few prelates and barons, inviting them to a coronation on Sunday, the 26th of September, 1087, when the event came off rather quietly.

When Curt-hose—whom the reader will recognise as our old friend Socks—first heard of his father's death, he was living on that limited but rather elastic income, his wits, at Abbeville, or in some part of Germany. He, however, repaired to Rouen, where he was very well received; while Henry, the youngest brother, stood like a donkey between two bundles of hay, not knowing whether he should have a bite at Britain or a nibble at Normandy.

Rufus had, at the commencement of his reign, to contend with a conspiracy got up by his uncle Odo, to place Robert on the throne of England as well as on that of Normandy; for the great experiment of sitting on two stools at once had not then been sufficiently carried out to prove the folly of attempting it.

Odo took rapid strides, but as Robert, if he took any stride at all, must have attempted one from Rouen to Rochester, he remained in his Duchy, leaving his followers to follow their own inclination at their own convenience. They had fortified Rochester Castle, but being besieged, and a famine threatening, they were glad to find a loop-hole for escape, which they effected by capitulating on certain conditions, one of which, proposed by Odo, was a stipulation that the band should not play as the vanquished party left the Castle. Rufus, feeling that a procession without music would go off flatly, refused his assent to this proposal, and the band accordingly struck up an appropriate air at each incident.

As Odo left the Castle the "Rogue's March" resounded from tower to tower and

Odo dismissed from Rochester Castle.

battlement to battlement, while the people sang snatches of popular airs, among which "Go, Naughty Man," and "Down among the Dead Men," were perhaps the greatest favourites. Odo was eventually banished, and the insurrection was at an end, for Curt-hose had neither the money nor the inclination to carry on the war; and, like a defunct railway scheme, the plan took its place amongst the list of abandoned projects.

In the year 1088 Lanfranc, the king's adviser, died, and was succeeded by a Norman clergyman, named Ralph, who was called also Le Flambard, or the Torch, from his being a political incendiary, who had been ever ready to light up the flame of discontent at a moment's notice. His nominal offices were treasurer and chaplain, but his real duty was to raise money for the king, extort for his majesty a large income, and help him to live up to it. As a taxgatherer and a *bon vivant* he was unexceptionable; but we regret that we cannot say so much for him as a bishop and a gentleman.

This person, however, succeeded only to the political, not to the ecclesiastical dignities of Odo; for the king, finding the revenues of Canterbury very acceptable, determined on acting as his own archbishop. He professed a desire to improve the see by using his own eyes, but his real view was to get all he could for the indulgence of his pleasures. Ralph le Flambard seems to have possessed the talent of extortion to a wonderful degree, and he even set at nought the proverb as to the impossibility of making "a silk purse out of a sow's ear;" for he certainly extracted immense sums by getting hold of the ear of the swinish multitude.

William Rufus, having been successful against the friends of Robert in England, determined (a.d. 1089) on attacking the unfortunate and improvident Curt-hose on his own ground in Normandy. Socks had no money to carry on the war, for he had not only cleared out his coffers to the last farthing, but was up to his neck in promises which he never could hope to realise. His bills were flying like waste-paper about every Exchange in Europe, and the boldest discounters shook their heads when a document with the familiar words "Accepted, R. Curt-hose," was shown to them. He applied, therefore, for aid to the king of the French, his feudal superior, who sent an army to the confines of Normandy, but sent a messenger at the same time to the English king, stating the terms on which the army might be bought off and induced to march back again.

Rufus willingly paid the money, and Socks, in a fit of desperation, applied to his brother Henry, who had already lent him three thousand pounds, taking care, however, to get a third of the duchy by way of security for his money. He accordingly came to Rouen, where he put down a large sum of money: and what was better still, he put down a conspiracy to deliver up the city to the enemy. One Conan, a burgess, who was to have handed over the keys, was condemned to imprisonment for life; but Henry taking him up to the top of a tower under the pretence of showing him the scenery, brutally threw him over. The unhappy captive was beginning to expatiate on the softness of the landscape below, when Henry, seizing him by the waist, savagely recommended him to test the reality of so much apparent softness,

Robert Curt-hose trying to get a Bill discounted.

by throwing himself on the kind indulgence which the verdant landscape appeared to offer him. The burgess had no time to reply, before he found himself half-way on his down journey.

It is difficult in these days to fancy the brother of the sovereign visiting a condemned culprit in his prison, and taking a walk with him up to the top of the building, to point out to him the beauties of the surrounding prospect. That the royal visitor should suddenly turn executioner in the most barbarous manner, is still more unaccountable. Henry must surely have received a large quantity of the burgess's sauce before he could have been provoked to an act which redounds so much to his discredit in the pages of history.

In the year 1091, William and Robert settled their differences, after which they began to take advantage of their little brother Henry, whom they robbed of everything he possessed, until his suite was reduced to one knight, three esquires, and one chaplain. His flight was a series of rapid movements, to which this miserable quintette formed a kind of running accompaniment; but Henry, in spite of every *contretemps*, behaved himself with dignity as the leader and conductor of his little band.

Rufus, on his return to England, found it overrun by Malcolm, the Scotch king, who, however, made a regular Scotch mull of his enterprise. After a peace as hollow as the "hollow beech tree" which the woodpecker keeps continually on tap, poor Malcolm was invited to Gloucester, where he fell into an ambush—a bush in which he was torn to pieces by the sharp thorns of treachery.

Duke Robert having made repeated applications to his brother, William Rufus, for the settlement of his claims upon England, at length put the matter into the hands of his solicitor, Philip of France; who, after soliciting justice for Curt-hose, marched an army into Normandy. Rufus, knowing costs to be the only motive of Philip, who, on being handsomely paid, would certainly throw his client overboard, determined on raising a large sum; which he accomplished by levying twenty thousand men as soldiers, and allowing them to buy their discharge at ten shillings a head, an arrangement which nearly all of them gladly fell into. The proceeds of this transaction being handed over to Philip, that monarch shifted his forces from Normandy, leaving Robert to shift for himself; so that poor Socks was again driven to the most wretched extremities.

Rufus was now troubled by the Welsh, who had overrun Cheshire, probably on account of its cheeses, for the Welsh were attached to their rabbits even so early as the eleventh century. The Red King pursued them over hill and dale, but they daily obtained advantages over him, and on reaching Snowdon he saw that it would be the height of folly to proceed further. After a few ups and downs over the mountains, he retreated with shame, and found occupation at home, a.d. 1094—5, in quelling a conspiracy headed by Robert de Mowbray, Earl of Northumberland, aided by Richard de Tunbridge, with a variety of Johns, Williams, and Thomases de What-d'ye-call-'em and So-and-So. Some of the conspirators were imprisoned, and some hanged; but a few, in anticipation of the fatal bolt, ran away for the purpose of avoiding it.

Immediately after these events, Robert, roused by the preaching of Peter the Hermit, familiarly known as *Pietro L'Eremita*, determined on giving up business as Duke of Normandy and starting as a crusader for Palestine. In order to raise money for his travelling expenses, and after having vainly entreated discount for his bills, he proposed to sell his dukedom to his brother for ten thousand pounds, including the good-will of the house of Normandy, the crown, which was not a fixture, the throne with its appropriate hangings, the sceptre the sign of royalty, and all the palace furniture. The unscrupulous Rufus agreed to purchase, but being without a penny of his own, he made a demand on the empty pockets of his subjects.

Several bishops and abbots having already sold all the treasures of their churches, told the king in plain terms they had nothing more to give him, when the sovereign replied, "Have you not, I beseech you, coffins of gold and silver full of dead men's bones?" thus insinuating, according to Holinshed, "that he would have the money out of their bones if they did not pay him otherwise." The bishops and abbots were induced to take the hint of the king; and the term "boning" may have had its origin from this species of robbery.

Having paid the ten thousand pounds, Rufus went to take possession of his new purchase, and met with no resistance except from one Helie, Lord of La Flèche, who professed to have a previous mortgage on part of the property. Rufus treated him as a mortgagee so far as to pay him off in the current coin of the age, though a year or two after (a.d. 1100) as the Bed King was hunting in the New Forest, he heard that Helie had surprised the town of Mans, and of course astonished the men of Mans very unpleasantly.

William turned his horse's head towards the nearest seaport, which happened to be Dartmouth, plunged into the first vessel he found there, and ordered the sailors to start at once for Normandy. The crew suggested that it was a very odd start to think of setting off in a gale of wind; but his majesty began to storm with as much violence as the elements. He asked—if they ever knew of a king being drowned?—and if the adage applies to those who deserve hanging as well as to those who are born for that ceremony, Rufus might have relied on exemption from a watery terminus. He arrived safely at Harfleur, after one of the most boisterous passages in his life, which was one of considerable turbulence. The bare news of his arrival sufficed to frighten Helie, who first ordered his troops to fall in, and immediately ordered them to fall out, for he had no further use for them. Helie took to his heels, and William became sole master of Normandy.

We now come to one of the most remarkable incidents in English history, and in our desire for accuracy we have grubbed about the records of the past with untiring energy. We have blown away the dust of ages with the bellows of research, and have, we think, succeeded in investing this portion of our annals with a plainness of which the very pike-staff itself might be fairly envious.

It was on the 1st of August, in the year 1100, that William was passing the night at Malwood Keep, a hunting-lodge in the New Forest. Had there been a Court Circular in existence in those days, it would have recorded the names of Henry, the king's brother, and a host of sporting fashionables who were present, to share the pleasures of their sovereign. His majesty was heard at midnight to be talking loudly in his sleep, and his light having gone out, he was crying lustily for candles. His attendants rushed to his room, and found him kicking and plunging under a nightmare, from which he was soon released, when he requested them to sit and talk to him. When their jokes were on the point of sending him to sleep, their songs kept him awake: and in the morning an artisan sent him six arrows as a specimen, with an intimation that there would be a large reduction on his taking a whole quiver. The king took the half-dozen on trial, keeping four for himself, and giving two to Sir Walter Tyrrel, with a complimentary remark that "good weapons are due to the sportsman that knows how to make a good use of them."

During a boisterous *déjeûner d la fourchette*, at which the Red King greatly increased his rubicundity by the quantity of wine he consumed, a postman arrived with a dream, from the Abbot of St. Peter's, at Gloucester, done up in an envelope. "Read it out," exclaimed Rufus, after having glanced at its contents; and on its being found to forbode a violent death to the king, he ordered a hundred pence to be given to the dreamer, which, supposing him to have been taking "forty winks," would have been at the liberal rate of twopence-halfpenny a wink for his rather disagreeable doze over the destiny of his sovereign. Rufus laughed at the prediction, and repaired to the chase, accompanied by Sir Walter Tyrrel, when a

Reading the Dream.

hart, in all its heart's simplicity, came and stood between the illustrious sportsmen. The extraordinary hilarity of the bounding hart attracted the attention of Rufus, who drew his bow, but the string broke, and Rufus not having two strings to his bow, called out to Tyrrel to shoot at the bald-faced brute for his bare-faced impudence. Sir Walter instantly obeyed; but the animal, bobbing down his head, allowed the arrow to go through his own branches towards those of a huge tree, when the dart, taking a somewhat circuitous route, avoided the body of the hart and went home to the heart of the sovereign. Tyrrel ran towards his master, and attempted to revive him; but though there was plenty of harts-horn in the forest, none could be made available. The unfortunate regicide, merely muttering to himself some incoherent expressions as to his having "done it now," galloped to the sea coast, and tied to France—taking French leave of his country, according to the usual custom of malefactors.

The royal remains were picked up soon after by one Mr. Purkess, a respectable charcoal-burner, whose descendants still reside upon the spot, and who carted Henry off on his own responsibility to Winchester, where the king was honoured by a decent funeral. Though there were plenty of lookers-on, there were

Flight of Sir Walter Tyrrel. Horse of the Period.

very few mourners; and in a portrait of the tomb which has been preserved,[21] we recognise economy as the most prominent feature. Henry, the king's brother, made the usual rush to the treasury, where he filled his pockets with all the available assets; and the members of the hunting party, finding that the game was up, started off as fast as they could in pursuit of their own interests.

The character of Rufus is not one which the loyal historian will love to dwell upon. The philologist may endeavour to prove the brutal licentiousness of the king by deriving from Rufus the word ruffian; but the philologist will, however, be as much in error as the antiquarian who declared that Rufus, or Roofus, was so called from his being the builder of Westminster Hall, of which the roof was the most conspicuous ornament. The Red King died a bachelor, at the age of forty-three, after a very extravagant life, in the course of which he exhibited strong symptoms of the royal complaint—which shows itself in a mania for constructing and altering palaces. He would erect new staircases, and indulge in the most extravagant flights; but if this had been accompanied by a few steps taken in the right direction, Posterity would not have judged very harshly what are, after all, the mere whims of royalty.

---

21. The tomb still stands in the middle of the choir of Winchester Cathedral.

CHAPTER THE THIRD

HENRY THE FIRST, SURNAMED BEAUCLERC

n returning to Henry, we find him at the porter's lodge, imperiously demanding the keys of the treasury. While he had just succeeded, by alternate bribery and bluster, in obtaining the desired bunch from the hesitating janitor, William de Breteuil, the treasurer came running out of breath, and protested, as energetically as the state of his wind would allow, against the money being carried away, when Robert, the elder brother, had a prior right to it. Henry, having tried a little argument, of which he got decidedly the worst, suddenly drew his sword, and threatened to perforate the treasurer, or any one else who should oppose his progress. A mob of barons having collected round the disputants, took part with the new king, in expectation, no doubt, of getting a share of the plunder.

William de Breteuil was compelled therefore to look on at the pocketing of the cash and jewels by Henry and his supporters, the treasurer occasionally entering a protest by mildly observing "Mind, *I've* nothing to do with it." Having made use of the cash in buying the adherence of some of those mercenary weathercocks—from whom it is considered an honour, in these days, to be descended—Henry got himself crowned on the 5th of August, in the year 1100, at Westminster.

Finding his throne rather rickety, he tried a little of the "soft sawder" which has always been found serviceable as a cement between the sovereign and the people. He mixed up a tolerably useful compound in the shape of a charter of liberties, and by laying it on rather thick to the Church, he obtained the support of that influential body. He restored ancient rights, and promised that when he had to draw money from his people he would always draw it as mild as possible.

Henry's next "dodge" was to try the effect of an English marriage, and he therefore sent in a sealed tender for the hand of Miss Matilda Malcolm, or Maud, the daughter of the king of Scots, as she is commonly called in history. She had already refused as many offers as would have filled a moderate-sized bonnet-boxy and sent word back that she was "o'er young to marry yet," in answer to the application of the English sovereign. She was, however, advised that it would be a capital thing for the two countries, if she would consent to the match; and as it is one of the penalties of royalty to wed for patriotism instead of from choice, she was soon persuaded to agree to the union.

Such instances of devotion are, however, only found among royal families; for we doubt whether a fair Jemima Jenkins, or a bewitching Beatina Brown, would consent to become the wife of young Johnson in an adjacent street, for the sake of healing a parochial feud, or curing the heartburn of an entire neighbourhood.

The marriage between Maud and Henry was very nearly being prevented by a report that the young lady had formerly been a nun; but it was proved that her aunt had been in the habit of throwing over her head something in the shape of a veil or a pinafore, to prevent the Normans from staring at her when she went out walking. Miss Matilda had the candour to acknowledge that she always took off the unbecoming covering directly she got a little way from home, and it is evident she was not unwilling to have a sly peep at the Normans, when her aunt was not watching her. Her marriage was celebrated on the 11th of November; but Anselm, the Archbishop of Canterbury, who officiated, came out of the Abbey before the ceremony, and in order to answer all false reports, stuck an enormous poster on the door, intimating that Maud was "No Nun," in tremendous capitals.

Henry also obtained some popularity by expelling all the improper characters that his brother had patronised; but it does not seem that they were replaced by persons of a much more reputable order.

Henry, however, affecting the estimable qualities of a new broom, began by sweeping clean, and scavenged the court of all his brother's minions. Ralph le Flambard, the late king's tax-gatherer, was sent to the Tower, where he became one of the lions of the place, and by his wit captivated the keepers who were charged with his captivity. Henry on being urged to get rid of him, happened to say accidentally, "No, no, give the fellow sufficient rope and he will hang himself," upon which one of the courtiers taking his majesty at his word, sent an enormous quantity of stout cord to the prisoner. Flambard having reduced the guards to the state in which tipplers wish to be who love their bottles, took the rope, and hanging himself by the waist, lowered himself into the moat beneath, from which he escaped to Normandy.

Robert Curt-hose, who had turned crusader a year or two before, came back (a.d. 1101) with a perfect shrubbery of laurels from Palestine. The Normans, delighted at seeing their chief smothered in the evergreens of glory, were easily persuaded to join him in an attack upon England. The followers of Curt-hose, however, soon began to waver, and after having received several terrific stripes, their leader agreed to take 3000 marks, by way of annuity, as a compromise for all his claims upon England. Robert was true to his part of the engagement, but Henry, under various pretexts, soon discontinued his payments to Socks, who nevertheless lived in a style of great extravagance. He filled his court with bad characters, who not only emptied his pockets, but sold or pawned his clothes; and he is represented as often lying in bed for want of the necessary articles of attire to enable him to get up to breakfast. With the crown on his toilet table, and the regal robe hanging across the back of a chair—for these insignia of royalty were always left to him—he was still without the minor but indispensable articles of dress; and he often observed to his minister, "I can't very well go about with nothing on but that scanty robe and that hollow bauble." We can imagine him being reduced to the necessity of offering to pledge his crown, and being met by the depreciatory observation, "that the article was second-hand, had been a good deal worn, and seemed very much tarnished."

At length, in the year 1105, Henry, taking advantage of Robert's reduced circumstances, made an attack upon Normandy. The troops of Curt-hose were ill-paid, ill-clad, ill-conditioned, and ill-tempered. In vain did Curt-hose attempt to rally them; for they only rallied him on his poverty, and many of them deserted, leaving him to fight his own battles. His personal valour served him for a short time; he struck out right and left with enormous vigour, but his almost solitary efforts became at length absolutely absurd, and he was ultimately "removed in custody." He was subsequently committed to Cardiff Castle, where he died, in the year 1134, at the advanced age of nearly eighty; and it was said by a wag of the day that Curt-hose had such a facility

The Effects of Extravagance.

of running into debt that he ran up four scores with Time before the debt of Nature was satisfied.

Henry was now master of Normandy, whither he on one occasion took his son and heir, William, a lad of eighteen, to receive the homage of the barons. This was an idle ceremony, for the barons seldom kept their words; and homage, or hummage, was frequently a mere hum on the part of those who promised it. The English king was about returning from the port of Barfleur, when Thomas Fitz-Stephen, a sailor, originated the disgraceful touting system, by thrusting his card into Henry's hands, and offering to take the royal party over cheap, in a well-appointed vessel. His majesty replied, "I have already taken my own passage in another ship, but the prince and his suite have to be conveyed, and I shall be happy to hear what you will undertake it for, per head, provisions, of course, included." The terms were soon arranged, and the dangerous practice of overcrowding having, even at that time, prevailed among mercenary speculators, three hundred people were packed into a craft which might have comfortably accommodated about twenty. The prince and his gay companions insisted on having a party on board the night previous to starting, and the crew, as well as the captain, were more than half-seas-over before they started from the shore of Normandy. Fitz-Stephen was in such a state at the wheel that it seemed to him continually turning round, and the men employed in looking-out thought the *Bas de Catte*—a well-known rock—had been doubled, when in fact the vessel was driving rapidly on to it. This recklessness soon led to a wreck, and the sole survivor was one Berold, a butcher of Rouen, who has reported the catastrophe with so much accurate minuteness as to have deserved, though he never got it until now, the proud title of the father of the penny-a-liners.[22] When Henry heard the news he fainted away, and never "smiled as he was wont to smile" from that day to the present. Being deprived of his only legitimate son, he became anxious to secure the throne to his daughter, the widow Maud, or Matilda, relict of the Emperor Henry the Fifth; and on Christmas-day, 1126, the bishops, abbots and barons were assembled at Windsor Castle to swear to maintain her succession. These parties—the respectable families that "came in with the Conqueror"—were all guilty of the grossest perjury; which, a few years ago, would have rendered them all liable to the pillory, and would in the present day expose them to serious punishment. A quarrel arose between Stephen, Earl of Boulogne, the king's legitimate nephew, and Robert, Earl of Gloucester, his illegitimate son, as to which was entitled to swear first; the real object being to decide which, upon breaking their oaths as they both fully intended to do—would take precedence as the successor of Henry. After a good deal of desultory discussion, a division settled the point in the nephew's favour. Anxious to see his daughter settled in life, Henry got her married, rather against her will, to Geoffrey, Earl of Anjou; who, from an odd custom he had of wearing a piece of broom in his cap, instead of a feather, acquired the nickname of Plantagenet. The marriage was celebrated at Rouen, and Henry issued a proclamation ordering everybody to be merry. Long faces were thus entirely prohibited, there was a penalty on black looks, and persons unable to laugh on the right side of their mouths were made to laugh upon the other.

Some anxiety was, however, occasioned to Henry by the existence of his nephew, William Fitz-Robert, the son of Curt-hose, who had pretensions to the throne through Matilda, his grandmother, which of course gave him a claim on the friendship of the house of Baldwin, between whom and the grandmother there was a close relationship. The apprehensions of Henry were aroused by William Fitz-Henry being made Earl of Flanders, but the young man was unfortunately killed by receiving a poke from a pike; and though the wound was only in the finger, it grew worse from being placed in the hands of ignorant practitioners. Finding it did not get better, he observed that it was "really very mortifying," and so it was, for mortification ensued almost immediately. He died at St. Omer, on the 27th of July, 1128, in the twenty-sixth year of his age; and if his epitaph had been written, it would have run thus:

> "Here lies a young prince, whose life was cut short
> By medical quacks overturning the sand of it;
> His finger was wounded, but who could have thought
> The doctors would make such a very bad hand of it?"

Henry's latter days were employed in listening to the quarrels of his his daughter, Matilda, and her husband, who were never out of pickles, by reason of their family jars, which were very numerous. The king had resided four years abroad, and had been hunting, on the 25th of November, for the purpose of chasing sorrow as well as the game, when, on his return home, he insisted on eating a lamprey, against the orders of his physicians. The king did not agree with the doctors, and the lamprey did not agree with the king, who died on the 1st of December, 1135, at the age of sixty-seven.

Henry's chief merit was his love of learning, which had got him the name of Beau-clerc, or the pretty scholar. He loved the society of men of letters, and of wild beasts; but the literary lions were, perhaps, his greatest favourites. He nevertheless desired that these lions should only roar in his praise; for he punished Luke de Barré, a poet, very severely for having written some satirical verses, in which the king was made a laughing-stock. The poet, according to Orderic, burst from the executioners and dashed out his brains, which had been the cause of giving offence to his sovereign.

---

22. *An allusion to Victorian journalists, many of whom were paid one penny for every line they wrote—Editor.*

CHAPTER THE FOURTH

STEPHEN

If the oaths of the bishops and barons had been worth even the ink expended in alluding to them, there might have been some chance of Matilda coming quietly to the throne on the death of Henry. The Anglo-Normans, however, had as little respect for truth as for property, and were even destitute of the humbler virtue of gallantry towards the fair, for they began to clamour loudly against the notion of a woman reigning over them.

Stephen, the late king's nephew, and Robert, Earl of Gloucester, the illegitimate son of Henry, were the two favourites in the race for the throne; but the betting was at least ten to one upon the former, in consequence of his having married Maud, the daughter and heir of Eustace, Count of Boulogne.

On the arrival of Stephen in England, he made at once for the treasury, which he cleared completely out, and he devoted the proceeds to purchasing the fidelity, or rather the mercenary adherence, of the barons, prelates, and people. Having bribed a sufficiently numerous party, he procured a decent attendance at his coronation, which took place on St. Stephen's day, December 22, 1135, at Westminster. He sent a good round sum to the pope, Innocent the Second, whose innocence seems to have been chiefly nominal, for he was guilty of accepting a bribe to give a testimonial in favour of Stephen's title. As long as the money lasted the barons were tolerably faithful; but "no plunder no allegiance" was the ordinary motto of the founders of those families whose present representatives trace themselves up, or rather bring themselves down, to the days of the Conquest.

The Norman nobles complained that their perjury had not had its price, and began seizing various castles belonging to Stephen, who, by purchasing the services of other mercenaries, got his property back again. At length, however, a coalition was effected between Robert, Earl of Gloucester, and Matilda, his half-sister, who landed in England on the 1st of September, 1139, with a retinue of one hundred and forty knights, an empty purse, and very little credit. Several Normans ran to meet Matilda on her arrival; but these high-minded founders of our very first families, hearing that there was no cash, returned to the side of Stephen.

Matilda went on a visit to the Queen Dowager, Adelais, or Alice, at Arundel Castle, which was besieged by the king, who, however, respected the property on account of its owner, and sent Matilda in safety to join her half-brother Robert, at Bristol, whither he had gone with twelve followers in search of Bristol board—and lodging. Stephen, having exhausted the materials for making the golden links which had hitherto bound the Normans to his side, found them rapidly adhering to Matilda, whose expectations were not bad, though her present means were limited.

On the 2nd of February, 1141, the king was besieging Lincoln when the whole of his cavalry wheeled round to the side of the enemy. Relying on his infantry, he put himself at their head, but treachery was on foot as well as on horseback. He nevertheless fought desperately, breaking his sword and battle-axe over the backs of his foes, till he was left fighting with the hilt of one weapon and the handle of the other. Having lost the use of his arms, he was surrounded by the enemy, but he continued alive and kicking till the last, when he was taken prisoner. He was cruelly thrown into a dungeon at Bristol, and in order that his muscular activity might be checked, he was loaded with irons. He still retained his cheerfulness, and may probably have been the original composer of the celebrated "hornpipe in fetters," which is occasionally danced by dramatic prisoners.

Matilda now scraped together all the money she could, to purchase that very marketable commodity, the allegiance of the Norman nobles and prelates. Among the latter was Stephen's own brother, the Bishop of Winchester, who renounced his unfortunate relative, swore fidelity to Matilda, cursed all her enemies, and, as the price of all this swearing and cursing, received a large amount of church patronage.

Not only did he crown his new mistress at Winchester, but he crowned his own baseness by a slashing speech against his own brother, winding up with a fulsome puff for the new queen, whom he hailed as "the sovereign lady of England and Normandy." Matilda was by no means successful in handling the sceptre, which required a stronger arm and more dexterity than she was mistress of. The Londoners, in particular, showed symptoms of revolt, and the Bishop of Winchester having got all he could from the queen, turned round once more in favour of his brother. This episcopal roundabout was the first to set the example, so frequently followed in the present day, of blocking up the city; and it is an odd fact that paving was his pretext, for he stopped up the London thoroughfares in order to pave the way for the return of his brother to power.

King Stephen in Prison.

Matilda, who was in town—probably for the season—contrived to make her escape by the western suburb, with a small retinue. Some of her knights quitted her at the bridge which still retains their name; an earl or two followed her as far as Earl's Court; some turned off at Turnham Green; but by the time she had reached the little Wick of Chis, her party had dwindled down into absolute insignificance. Her brother Robert was taken prisoner, and Stephen being also in captivity, the two parties were brought to a deadlock for want of leaders. By negotiating a sort of Bill of Exchange, Robert was released, and Stephen was paid over, in the shape of "value received," to his own party.

The Bishop of Winchester, who appears to have been an exceedingly plausible mob orator, now made another speech, in which he showed a wonderful amount of face by regularly turning his back upon himself, and unsaying all that he had said in favour of Maud, and against his brother on a former occasion. He swore and cursed as before, merely altering the name of the objects of his oaths and execrations, for he now swore allegiance to his brother instead of to Maud, and cursed the former's, instead of the latter's enemies.

Stephen was accordingly raised, by the crane of circumstances, from the depth of his dungeon, and lifted on to his throne; but he found a new rival in the person of Matilda's son, Prince Henry, so that he had now a woman and a boy, instead of a mere woman to fight against. Henry, in a spirit of calculation far beyond his years, married Eleanor, the divorced wife of Louis the Seventh; but it was only for the sake of her money, which he expended in getting together an army for an attack upon England. The opposing forces met, but having already received their pay, they evinced a disposition to shirk their duty, and—like gentlemen of the bar, who having got their fees, propose that the matter should be referred to arbitration—the soldiers of Stephen and Henry recommended a quiet compromise.

Theobald, Archbishop of Canterbury, and Stephen, Bishop of Winchester, were appointed referees, and it was agreed that Stephen should wear the crown with remainder over to Henry.

A good deal of homage was interchanged, for Henry swore fealty to Stephen, and the son of the latter swore ditto to Henry. The king in fact cut off his own tail for the benefit of his former enemy, and Henry took a kind of *post obit* as a consideration for his not pressing

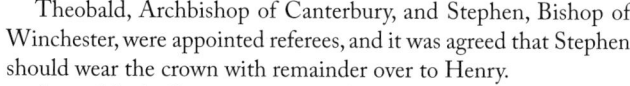

A Clerical Weathercock.

his claims to abbots, also exchanged affidavits, and swore in direct opposition to what they had sworn before, making altogether a mass of perjury that would have kept the Central Criminal Court occupied for half-a-dozen entire sessions. Stephen, however, died at Dover, on the 25th of October, 1154, so that he did not live long under the new arrangement.

The historian often finds himself awkwardly situated when called upon to give a character to a king, and there being a natural objection to written characters, the difficulty is greater on that account. It may be said for Stephen that he was sober and industrious, tolerably honest, not addicted to gluttony, or given to drink like many of his predecessors, and of course, therefore not so much accustomed to wait at table. He had a pleasing manner, and a good address, except while confined in prison, when his address was none of the pleasantest. On the whole, when we look at him as the paid servant of the public, we think him ill adapted for a steward, since England was always in confusion while under his care; and as a coachman he was even worse, for he was quite unfitted to hold the reins of power.

CHAPTER THE FIFTH

HENRY THE SECOND, SURNAMED PLANTAGENET

enry, who was amusing himself with besieging a castle in Normandy when he heard of Stephen's death, soon repaired to England with his middle-aged wife, Eleanor. They were crowned on the 19th of December, 1154; but he had no sooner got the crown on his head, than he went to business, and commenced a series of sweeping reforms. Finding the coinage reduced to a state of almost unutterable baseness, he issued a good supply of new money, and thus gave a fearful smash to the smashers. He drove out a quantity of foreign scamps, who had been made earls and barons in the reign of Stephen. After having enjoyed the fee-simple of castles and estates, they were sent back to take possession of the plough in tail, and to till as serfs the earth's surface. Finding the royal income very much reduced, Henry restored it by taking back what his predecessors had given away; an operation he performed with so much impartiality that he deprived his friends and his foes indiscriminately of all their possessions.

The policy of Henry the Second, on coming to the throne, seems to have differed from that of most of his predecessors; for while they had usually bought the allegiance of all the knaves and rogues about the court, he preferred the less costly process of rendering them perfectly powerless. He demolished many of the castles which had been erected by the barons, as fences rather than defences, for they were little better than receptacles for stolen property. Nor was he less vigorous in his measures against the clergy, for, like a skilful chess-player, he felt that it is better for the king that the bishops and the castles should be got out of the way when they are likely to prove troublesome. So far, therefore, from encouraging the exactions of the priesthood, he seems to have kept a supply of industrious fleas, for the purpose of putting one now and then into the ear of such of the clergy as came to make unreasonable requests to him. It is said that, on one occasion, the prior and monks of St. Swithin's threw themselves prostrate before the king imploring his protection against the Bishop of Winchester, who had cut off three meals a day from the ravenous fraternity. Henry perceiving that the monks were in tolerable condition, inquired how many meals were still left to them. "Only ten!" roared the prior, in recitative, while the rest of the party took up the words in dismal chorus.

How they could have contrived to demolish thirteen meals a day is an enigma to us; but the fact is a wondrous proof of monkish ingenuity. In the days of ignorance all classes were prepared, no doubt, to swallow a great deal, but thirteen meals must have required a power of digestion and a force of appetite that throw into the shade even the aldermanic attainments of a more civilised period. Henry, who took nothing but his breakfast, dinner, and tea, was shocked and startled by the awful avowal of gluttony on the part of the monks of St. Swithin, whom he placed at once on a diet similar to his own, by reducing them to three meals *per diem*. It is probable that the monks crammed into three repasts the quantity they had consumed in thirteen, and thus eluded the force of the royal order.

By a rigorous determination to "stand no nonsense," either with the clergy or the nobles, and by ordering the Flemish mercenaries of the army to the "right about," Henry seemed to commence his reign under very encouraging auspices.

Not content with his successes at home, he sought to increase his influence abroad by taking Nantes, and he sent Thomas à Becket to Paris to bamboozle the French court, lest his encroachments should excite jealousy in that quarter, Thomas à Becket was the son of Mr. Gilbert à Becket, a respectable tradesman of the city of London; and as his appears to be the first mercantile name on record, we are justified in calling him the Father of British Commerce. The chronicles of the Times—and we are justified in relying on the united evidence of the *Times* and *Chronicle*—relate that Gilbert à Becket,

Henry the Second dismissing the Foreign Barons.

in the way of business, followed the army to Palestine. What his business could have been we are unable to guess, but as it took him to the camp, he may perhaps have been a dealer in camp stools, or tent bedsteads. Mr. Gilbert à Becket unfortunately became a prisoner, and being sold to a rich Mussulman, fell in love with a young Mussul girl, his master's daughter. The affection was mutual, and the child of the Mussulman strained every muscle, or, at all events, every nerve to effect the escape of Gilbert à Becket, who, in the hurry of his departure, forgot to take the lady away with him. It is not unlikely that he had got half-way to London before he missed the faithful girl, and it would then have been the height of imprudence to return for the purpose of repairing the oversight. His *inamorata* made the best of her way after him, and arriving in London, ran about the streets, exclaiming, "Gilbert! Gilbert!" thus acting as her own crier, instead of putting the matter into the hands of the regular bellman.

The fact of a young woman continually traversing the great metropolis with Gilbert in her mouth, soon reached the ears of Mr. à Becket, who found the female in distress and his own Saracen maid to be the same individual. One of those frantic recognitions occurred, in which a rapid dialogue of "No!" "Yes!" "It can't be!" "It is!" "My long-lost Sara—!" "My Gil—!" was spasmodically went through, and the couple having rushed into each other's arms, got soon bound together by that firmest of locks familiarly known as wedlock. The fruit of their union was the celebrated Thomas, of whose career we are enabled from peculiar sources to furnish some interesting particulars.

Gilbert was determined to give his boy Tom a good education, and sent him to school at Merton Abbey, where a limited number of young gentlemen from three to eight were lodged, boarded, and birched—when necessary—at a moderate stipend. Young Tom was removed from Merton to a classical and commercial academy in London, which he quitted for Oxford, and he was ultimately sent to Paris to undergo the process of French polishing. While yet a young man, he got a situation in the office of the sheriff, and became, of course, a sheriff's officer; in which capacity he arrested, among other things, the attention of Theobald, Archbishop of Canterbury. His patron took young à Becket from the *ad captandum* pursuits in which he had been engaged, put him into the Church, gave him rapid preferment, and introduced him to the parties at the palace, which had, in those days, sufficient accommodation for the family and friends of royalty. Mr. à Becket became chancellor of the kingdom, though he never held a brief, or had even been called to the bar; and he was appointed tutor to the Royal Family, in which office he no doubt had the assistance of the Usher of the Black Rod. Of course, with his multiplicity of offices and occupations, it may be presumed that Mr. à Becket made a very excellent thing of it. His house was a palace, he drank nothing but the best wine, employed none but the best tailors, and when he went to Paris he took four-and-twenty changes of apparel—which may, perhaps, have been after all nothing more than two dozen shirts—so that he had a different costume for every hour of the day. In his progress through France he was preceded by two hundred and fifty boys, or charity children, singing national songs. These were followed by his dogs, in couples, who no doubt gave tongue, and made a sort of barking accompaniment to the music that went before.

Eight waggons came next, carrying his clothes and his crockery, his cooking apparatus, his bed and bedding, and his suite; when after a few led horses, some knights with their esquires, and some monkeys *à cheval* with a groom behind, on his knees, came à Becket himself and his familiar friends.[23] His entry into a town was more like that of an equestrian troop about to establish a circus than that of

---

23. Vide Fitz-Stephen, Secretary and Biographer of Thomas à Becket.

the Chancellor of England travelling in his master's behalf. He lived on terms of the closest intimacy with the king, who made him Archbishop of Canterbury, but not until thirteen months after the death of Theobald the First, for Henry always kept a good appointment open as long as he could that he might put the revenues into his own pocket.

From the time of his promotion to the see of Canterbury, à Becket became an altered man. He cut his gay companions, discharged his *chef de cuisine*, discontinued his dealings with his West-End tailor, and took to a kind of cheap blouse made of the coarsest sackcloth. He abandoned his sumptuous mode of living and drank water made unsavoury by herbs, victimising himself probably with cups of camomile tea, and copious doses of senna. But the most serious change in à Becket's conduct, was his altered behaviour to the king, whom he had previously backed in all his attacks on the Church revenues. The new archbishop stood up for all the privileges of the clergy, and a difference of opinion between à Becket and the king, as to the right to try a delinquent clergyman in the civil courts, led to the summoning of a council of nobles and prelates (a.d. 1164) at Clarendon. Some rules were drawn up, called the "Constitutions of Clarendon," which à Becket reluctantly agreed to sign; but Pope Alexander having rejected them, the archbishop withdrew his name from the list of subscribers.

Finding the vengeance of the king likely to prove too much for him, à Becket quitted the kingdom, and was very hospitably entertained during his stay on the Continent.

After an absence of about seven years, he returned in consequence of the king of France and others having persuaded Henry to make it up, though the reconciliation was never very cordial. Though à Becket was received with shouts of approbation by the mob, he was greeted, on his arrival, with menacing signs and abusive language from the aristocracy.

Gilbert à Becket.   Thomas à Becket.

There was a strong party against him at court, and one evening, at about tea-time, Henry and a few nobles were sitting round the palace fire, gossiping over the subject of à Becket's awful insolence. The king burst into a furious diatribe, stigmatising the archbishop as a beggar, and winding up with the suggestive observation that, "Not one of the cowards I nourish at my table—not one will deliver me from this turbulent priest." Four knights who were present took the royal hint, and gave the archbishop a call at his house in Canterbury, where having seated themselves unceremoniously on the floor, they got to high words very speedily. The archbishop refused to yield to low abuse, and went in the evening to vespers as usual. The feelings of the historian will not allow him to dwell much upon the *dénouement* of the drama in which à Becket had played the principal character. Suffice it to say, he was murdered in Canterbury Cathedral by four assassins, of whom Fitzurse—the son of a bear—was one, and Mireville, a name suggestive of mire and villainy, was another. The two remaining butchers were Britto, of Saxon descent, a low fellow, familiarly termed the Brick, and Tracey, who is not worth the trouble of tracing.

When Henry heard of this dreadful deed, he went without his dinner for three days, during which period he shut himself up in his own room, and refused to be "at home" to anyone.

By way of diverting his melancholy, he determined on joining in an Irish row, and finding the chiefs of the five principalities into which Ireland was divided at cross purposes, he espoused the cause of Dermot McMurrough, who seems to have been what the Milesians would term the "biggest blackguard" amongst them. Henry gave him a letter authorising him to employ any of the subjects of England that happened to be disengaged; and three ruined barons, with damaged reputations, chancing to be out of work in the neighbourhood of Bristol, were offered terms by Dermot. This precious trio consisted of two brothers, named Robert Fitz-Stephen and Maurice Fitz-Gerald, and Richard de Clare, Earl of Pembroke, surnamed Strongbow, though, as he was greatly addicted to falsehood, Longbow would have been a more appropriate name for him.

After talking the matter over for some time without any arrangement being come to, Strongbow cut the matter short by exclaiming, "I'll tell you what it is. If I'm to fight for your kingdom, I must have it myself when you have done with it. You must make me your heir, and, as a security that you will perform your part of the agreement, I must marry your daughter." Dermot, though rather taken aback by this proposal, invited Strongbow to a quiet chop, over which the latter's terms were acceded to; and the ruined baron, feeling that it was "neck or nothing" with him, succeeded in making it "neck" by the ardour with which he entered into the contest. Though he set to work in the spring of the year, his vengeance was truly summary, and in a few months he had restored everything to Dermot, who happened conveniently to die, and Strongbow came in for all that he had been fighting for.

Henry having become jealous, Strongbow thought it good policy not to overshoot the mark, and came to England to offer allegiance. The king at first refused to see him, and on calling at Newnham, in Gloucestershire, where Henry was staying, he was kept for some time eating humble-pie in the passage with the hall-porter. Strongbow having been sufficiently bent by this treatment, was at length asked to step up, and it was arranged that he should accompany the king to Ireland, surrender his possessions, and consent to hold them as the vassal of the English sovereign.

On his return to England, Henry, who had four sons, began to find "the boys" exceedingly troublesome. Their mother, once the middle-aged, but now the ancient Eleanor, had grown cross as well as venerable; and being exceedingly jealous of her husband, encouraged his own sons to worry him. Her jealousy had become a perfect nuisance; and jealousy is unfortunately one of those nuisances which never get abated.

A story is told of a certain Fair Rosamond; and, though there is no doubt of its being a story from beginning to end, it is impossible to pass it over in an English History. Henry, it is alleged, was enamoured of a certain Miss Clifford—if she can be called a certain Miss Clifford, who was really a very doubtful character. She had been the daughter of a baron on the banks of the Wye, when, without a why or a wherefore, the king took her away, and transplanted the Flower of Hereford, as she well deserved to be called, to the Bower of Woodstock. In this Bower he constructed a labyrinth, something like the maze at Rosherville; and as there was no man stationed on an elevation in the centre to direct the sovereign with a pole which way to go, nor exclaim,

"Right, if you please!"

"Straight on!"

"You're right now, sir!"

"Left!"

"Right again!" etc. etc., his majesty had adopted the plan of dragging one of Rosamond's reels of silk along with him when he left the spot, so that it formed a guide to him on his way back again.

This tale of the silk is indeed a most precious piece of entanglement; but it was perhaps necessary for the winding up of the story. While we cannot receive it as part of the thread of history, we accept it as a means of accounting for Eleanor having got a clue to the retreat of Rosamond.

The queen, hearing of the silk, resolved naturally enough to unravel it. She accordingly started for Woodstock one afternoon, and, suspecting something wrong, took a large bowl of poison in one hand, and a stout dagger in the other. Having found Fair Rosamond, she held the poignard to the heart, and the bowl to the lips of that unfortunate young person, who, it is said, preferred the black draught to the steel medicine.

Queen Eleanor and Fair Rosamond.

That such a person as Fair Rosamond existed is perfectly true, for she was buried at Godstow, near Oxford. The sensitive heart, which is ever anxious to inundate the page of sorrow with a regular Niagara of tears, is, however, earnestly requested to turn off the rising supply from the main of pity, for it is agreed on all hands that the death of Rosamond was perfectly natural. It has been convenient for the romancists to cut short her existence by drowning it in the bowl; but truth compels us to add that there is no ground for such a conclusion.

Henry devoted the remainder of his life to quarrelling, first with one of his children, then the other, and every now and then with all of them. He fully intended to divide his possessions among them; but they most unreasonably required to be let into possession before the death of the governor. The eldest ran away to France, and Eleanor had actually put on male attire, with the intention of abandoning Henry, when, unfortunately for him, he was silly enough to have her imprisoned for the purpose of stopping her. "Why didn't you let her go?" was the frequent exclamation of his intimate friends to the king, and a melancholy "Ha! I wish I had," was the only reply he was able to make them.

Finding himself threatened on all sides, and when he had exhausted every other expedient, he resolved on trying what penitence could do for him. His conscience no doubt often reminded him of the murder of poor à Becket, to whose shrine the king determined on making a pilgrimage. Purchasing some split peas, he put about a pint in each of his stockings, and started for Canterbury, where he threw himself madly upon à Becket's tomb, sobbing, yelling and shrieking in the most pitiable manner. Nor was this enough, for he threw off his robe, and insisted on receiving the lash from about eighty ecclesiastics. Though they administered the punishment so lightly that the cat caused only a few scratches, the peculiar circumstances attending it cause it to stand out in history as *par excellence* "the great flogging case."

The ecclesiastical authorities at Canterbury taking advantage of Henry's softened heart, which seems to have been accompanied by a sad softness of head, succeeded in extracting from him a promissory note to pay forty pounds a year for keeping lights constantly burning on the tomb of à Becket. There can be no doubt that the contract for lighting was taken cheaply enough by some tradesman of the town, and that the surplus went into the clerical coffers. Posterity regards with disgust the effrontery of the monks in making—for the sake of a few dips—such an enormous dip into the purse of the sovereign.

From this time affairs began to mend; and it would seem that the whipping his majesty had suffered had whipped his misfortunes completely out of him. If the king had been an old carpet the beating he received could not have proved more beneficial than it did, for it seemed to revive the brighter colours of his existence. He employed the peace he now enjoyed in carrying out some political reforms, divided England into six circuits, so that Justice might be brought home to every man's door; though, like everything else that is brought home to one's door, it must be paid for—sometimes after a little credit, but sometimes on delivery. He abolished the criminal tariff, by which it had been allowable for the rich to commute their offences, according to a certain scale of charges. Family quarrels unfortunately called him away from these wholesome pursuits, and his eldest son died of a fever brought on in consequence of a disagreement with his younger brother, Richard. Prince Henry expired on the 11th of June, 1183, in the twenty-seventh year of his age. Such was his remorse that, according to Roger Hoveden, he insisted on his attendants tying a rope to his foot and taking him in tow, until they dragged him out of his bed, in order to deposit him on a bed of ashes. This particular desire to die in a dusthole was accompanied by a request for a reconciliation with his father, who sent a ring as a token of forgiveness, with a message that he hoped the invalid might come, like the ring, completely round.

On the death of their elder brother, Richard and Geoffrey still continued to show fight against their father; who at length got so much the worst of it, that he was obliged to make the best of it by coming to a compromise. By one of the conditions he was to pardon all the insurgent barons, and having called for a list of them, found at the bottom of it the name of his favourite son John. This was too much for the persecuted parent, who flew into a furious passion, which he vented in the customary manner of royalty at that period, by pouring out a volley of execrations with frightful fluency. He jumped on to his bed, and, falling back upon it, turned round to the wall, exclaiming "Now then, let everything go—— as it will." Several ministers, priests, bishops, prelates, and barons were in attendance, under pretence of receiving his last sigh, but really with the intention of robbing him of his last shilling, for they rifled his pockets directly life was extinct.

The reign of Henry, though not very comfortable to himself, was undoubtedly beneficial to his country. He introduced many improvements into the law, and was the first to levy a tax on the goods of nobles as well as commoners, for the service of the state. He died at the Castle of Chinon, near Saumur, on the 6th of July, 1189, in the fifty-sixth year of his age. He left behind him a good name, which those who stole his purse were fortunately not able to filch from him. His wife caused all the quarrels in his family, showing that a firebrand may grow out of a very bad match. Eleanor was indeed a female Lucifer, lighting up the flame of discord between parent and children, until death gave her husband the benefit of a divorce.

CHAPTER THE SIXTH

RICHARD THE FIRST, SURNAMED COUR DE LION

ichard having secured the crown began to look after the cash, and pounced upon an unhappy old man named Stephen, of Tours, who had acted as treasurer to Henry the Second. The new king, not satisfied with cashiering the cashier, arrested him and threw him into prison, until he had given up not only all the late king's money, but had parted with every penny of his own, which was extracted in the shape of costs from the unfortunate victim.

Richard, on arriving in England, made for Winchester, where the sovereigns were in the habit of keeping their plate and jewels, all of which were turned at once into ready money in order to enable him to carry on the war, which he was very anxious to do, as a crusader in Palestine. It would seem that the treasury was regularly emptied at the commencement of every new reign, and filled again as speedily as possible by exactions on the people.

The coronation of Richard, which took place on the 3rd of September, 1189, was disgraced by an attack upon the Jews, who came to offer presents, which were eagerly received; but the donors were kicked out of Westminster Hall with the most ruthless violence. Nearly all the Jews in London were savagely murdered, all their houses were burnt and all their property stolen; when Richard issued a proclamation, in which he stated that he took them under his gracious protection: an act which would have been more gracious if it had come before instead of after the extermination of the ill-used Israelites.

How to go to Palestine was, however, the king's sole care; and to raise the funds for this trip he sold everything he possessed, as well as a great deal that rightfully belonged to others. He put up towns, castles, and fortresses to public auction, knocking down not only the property itself but those also who offered any remonstrance, or put in any claim to the goods he was disposing of. Such was his determination to clear off everything without reserve that he swore he would put up London itself if he could find a bidder—an assertion that was very likely to put up the citizens.

Some of the castles he sold two or three times over, leaving the purchasers to settle among themselves which should be the possessor of the property that had been paid for by every one of them. It is not unlikely that he caused glowing advertisements to be prepared, of "Little Paradises," standing "in their own fortifications;" and that he would have described a dead wall with a moat before it as "Elysium on a small scale," entrenched behind its own battlements. There can be little doubt that he would also have dilated in glowing terms upon the wealth of the neighbourhood offering unlimited pillage to an enterprising purchaser.

Richard's presence-chamber was, according to Sir Francis Palgrave, a regular market-overt, in which prerogatives and bounties were to be purchased by anyone coming with the money to pay for them. We can fancy a table laid out with a number of patents of nobility, labelled with a large ticket, announcing, "All these titles at an enormous sacrifice." We can imagine a row of velvet robes and coronets hanging up under a placard inscribed "Dukedoms at a considerable reduction;" while we can contemplate a quantity of knights' helmets lying in the window, marked at a very low figure, after the manner of the five thousand straw bonnets offered to the public by some dashing haberdasher at the commencement of the spring season.

Richard even went so far as to announce the stock of vacant bishoprics as "selling off," and it is not improbable that he may have caused tasteful arrangements of mitres and lawn sleeves to be arranged in different parts of the presence-chamber, to tempt the ambition of ecclesiastical purchasers. He likewise sold his own good-will for three thousand marks to his half-brother Geoffrey, who had been elected Archbishop of York; and wherever there was a penny to be turned, Richard had the knack of turning it.

Having left the regency in the hands of one Hugh Pudsey, the king repaired to France to meet Philip, who was to be his companion to Palestine. Their united forces amounted to a hundred thousand men; but Richard and Philip did not travel together farther than Lyons, and indeed it was as well they did not, for they were almost continually quarrelling. Numerous adventures befell Richard on his way; but the most awkward was his being dunned by the cardinal bishop of Ostia—where he had put in to repair—for a debt due to the see of Rome, on account of bulls and other papal articles.

Cour de Lion, instead of discharging the bill, abused and ill-treated the applicant, and made the best of his way to Naples, before there was time for ulterior proceedings. He went thence to Sicily, where his quarrel with Philip was renewed, and the latter demanded an explanation of Richard's refusal to marry the princess Aliz, the French king's sister. Cour de Lion, who had really formed another attachment, excused himself by blackening the character of the lady to whom he had been engaged, and her chivalrous brother agreed to take two thousand marks a year, as a compromise for the breach of promise of marriage which Richard had committed. "Such," exclaims Hume—and well he may—"were the heroes of this pious enterprise."

The Princess Aliz or Alice, having been regularly thrown overboard by the bargain between her own brother and her late lover, the latter was at liberty to follow his inclination by marrying Berengaria, daughter of the king of Navarre, with whom he had had a flirtation as early as during his residence at Guienne. Taking with him his latest affianced, he set sail for Palestine; but his ship being cast ashore at Cyprus, and plundered by the natives, he waited to chastise the people, and imprison an elderly person named Isaac, who called himself the emperor. He then ran off with the old man's only daughter, in addition to the princess of Navarre, whom he had the coolness to marry on the very spot from which he had seized this new addition to the female part of his establishment. The only reparation offered to the father was a set of silver fetters to wear instead of the common iron he had at first been thrown into.

Richard at length arrived in Palestine, and was not long in getting to work against the forces of Saladin, who, leading forth his battalions, mounted on their real Jerusalem ponies, proved exceedingly harassing.

Terrific Combat between Richard Cœur de Lion and Saladin.

Among the events of the crusade undertaken for the promotion of Christianity, on the side of the Lion Heart, his beheading of five thousand Turkish prisoners stands conspicuous. This act of barbarity arose out of some misunderstanding on the subject of a truce, and Saladin, by way of making matters square, slaughtered about an equal number of captive Christians. Such were the heroic defenders of the Cross on one side and the Crescent on the other. It is generally a libel to compare a human being to a brute, but in giving the title of Lion Heart to Richard, the noble beast is the party scandalised.

It is surprising that the British lion has never cited this as one of his numerous grievances, for he would certainly have a capital action for defamation if he were to sue by his next friend or *in forma pauperis* for this malicious imputation on his noble character.

On the 7th of September, 1191, the two chiefs came to a general engagement, near Azotus, about nine miles from Ascalon. Richard's prowess was tremendous; but, after himself, the most striking object was his battle-axe. This wondrous weapon had been forged in England by the very best Smiths, and there were twenty pounds of steel in the head, formed into a tremendous nob, which fell with fearful force on the nobs of his enemies. His battle-axe divided with him the attention of all beholders, and he divided the turbans of the foe with his battle-axe. The weapons of the Crusaders were certainly better adapted for havoc than those of the Saracens, who seem to have fought with an instrument less calculated for milling men than for milling chocolate. The armour of the knights was also more effective than that of their adversaries; for while the former had their heads comfortably secured in articles made on the principle of rushlight shades, with holes for seeing and breathing through, the partisans of the Crescent wore little more upon their heads than might have been supplied by the folding of a sheet or tablecloth into the form of a turban. The result was that Baladin was compelled to fly, with a loss of seven thousand men and thirty-two emirs, which so diminished his stock of officers that he was almost reduced, according to an old chronicler, to his very last emir-gency.

Richard went on to Jaffa, where he was delayed by an artful proposition to negotiate until the rainy weather set in; and he had to start off during November, in the midst of incessant showers. The Crusaders got regularly soaked; and being caught in the middle of the plain of Sharon with no place, not even a doorway, they could stand up under, they tried to pitch a tent, which was instantly pitched down by the fury of the elements. Their arms became perfectly rusty, and their horses, not liking the wet, got rusty also. Their provisions were all turned into water *souchet*, and indeed the spirit of the Crusaders became weakened by excessive dilution in the pelting showers.

The energies of Richard and his companions were of course considerably damped; but a positive inundation would scarcely have quenched the fire of chivalry. Cour de Lion retreated to Ascalon, the fortifications of which he found had been dismantled; but he worked to restore them like a common mason, mixing mortar on his shield for want of a hod, and using his axe as a substitute for a trowel. All the men of rank followed his example, except the Duke of Austria, who declared that he had not been brought up to it; upon which Cour de Lion kicked him literally through the breach in the fortification he had refused to repair, and turned him out of the town with all his vassals.

After a most uncomfortable sojourn in Palestine, Richard opened a negotiation with Saladin; and the ardour of both having been rather cooled, a truce was concluded. It was to last three years, three months, three weeks, and three days, the discussion on the subject occupying about three hours, the writing out the agreement three minutes, and the signing three seconds.

Taking advantage of the truce, Richard quitted Palestine for England; but sending the ladies home in a ship, he started to walk in the disguise of a pilgrim by way of Germany. Though his costume was humble his expenditure was lavish; and having sent a boy into the market-place of Vienna to buy some provisions, the splendid livery of the page, and his abundance of cash, excited suspicion as to the rank of his master. The secret of the Lion Heart was kept for some time by the faithful tiger, but he was at length forced into a confession, and Richard was arrested on the 20th of December, 1193, by the very Duke of Austria whom he had some time before kicked unceremoniously out of Ascalon.

The Emperor Henry the Sixth claimed the royal captive as a prize, and Richard was locked up in a German dungeon with German shutters, and fed alternately on German rolls and German sausages, while his enemies were doing their worst at home and abroad to deprive him of his sovereignty.

There is a legend attached to the incident of Richard's captivity: which has the slight disadvantage of being altogether fabulous, and we therefore insert it—under protest—in the pages of our faithful history. The story runs that the Lion Heart, who was fond of music, and had a tolerable voice, used to amuse himself and his gaolers by singing some of the most popular ballads of the period. It happened that Blondel, one of his favourite minstrels, of whom he had probably taken lessons in happier hours, was on an ambulatory tour, for professional purposes, when he chanced to tune his clarionet and clear his throat, with the intention of "striking up" under the walls of Richard's prison. At that moment the Lion Heart had just been called upon for a song, and his voice issued in a large octavo volume from the window of his dungeon. The tones seemed familiar to the minstrel, but when there came a tremendous trill on the low G, followed by a succession of roulades on A flat, with an abrupt modulation from the minor to the major key, Professor Blondel instantly

Blondel, the Minstrel, under the Walls of Richard's Prison.

recognised the voice of his royal pupil. The wandering minstrel, without waiting for the song to terminate, broke out into a magnificent *sol fa*, and the king at once remembering the style of his old master, responded by going through some exercises for the voice which he had been in the habit of practising. Blondel having ascertained the place of his sovereign's confinement, had the prudence to "copy the address," and went away, determining to do his utmost for the release of Richard. "I wish," thought the professor, as he retired from the spot, "that those iron bars were bars of music, for then I could show him how they are to be got through; or would that any of the keys of which I am master would unlock the door of his prison!" With these two melancholy puns, induced by the sadness of his reflections, Blondel hastened from the spot, and repaired to England with tidings of the missing monarch.

Such is the romantic little story that is told by those greatest of story-tellers, the writers of history.

Richard was at length brought up for examination before the Diet of Worms; and though several charges were alleged against him, he pleaded his own cause with so much address that he was discharged on payment of a fine of one hundred and fifty thousand marks, being about three hundred thousand pounds of our money. He at once put down thirteen and fourpence in the pound, giving good bills and hostages for the remainder; but the amount was soon raised by taxes and voluntary contributions from the English people. Churches melted down their plate, people born with silver spoons in their mouths came forward with zeal, whether the article happened to be a gravy, a table, a dessert, or a tea; and the requisite sum was raised to release him from captivity. He arrived in England on the 20th of March, 1194, and was enthusiastically welcomed home, where he got up another coronation of himself, by way of furnishing an outlet for the overflowing loyalty of the people. As if desirous of taming it down a little, he made some heavy demands upon their pockets; but nothing seemed capable of damping the ardour of the nation, which appeared ready to give all it possessed in change for this single sovereign.

About the middle of May, 1194, Richard revisited Barfleur, with the intention of chastising his brother John—who had shown symptoms of usurpation in his absence—and the French king, Philip. John, like a coward, flew to his mamma—the venerable Eleanor—requesting her to intercede for him. The old lady wrote a curt epistle, consisting of the words, "Dear Dick—Forgive Jack. Yours ever, Nell;" and John having fallen at the feet of Richard, was contemptuously kicked aside with a free pardon. Against the French king, however, several battles were fought, with fluctuating success, though Richard's fortunes now and then received a fillip which caused Philip to get the worst of it. A truce was concluded on the

23rd of July, 1194, but London beginning to rebel, cut out fresh work for Lion Heart. The discontented cockneys had for their leader one William Fitz-Osbert, commonly called Longbeard, who complained of the citizens having been so closely shaved by taxation; and Longbeard even dared to beard the sovereign himself, by going to the Continent to remonstrate with Richard. The patriot made one of those clap-trap speeches (of which mob-orators have in all ages been famous), and demanded for the poor that general consideration which really amounts to nothing particular. Richard promised that the matter should be looked into, but nothing was done—except the people and their advocate. In the year 1196 Longbeard originated the practice of forming political associations, and got together no less than fifty-two thousand members, who swore to stand by him as the advocate and saviour of the poor; an oath which ended in their literally standing by him and seeing him savagely butchered by his enemies. He was taking a quiet walk with only nine adherents, when he was dodged by a couple of citizens, who had been watching him for several days, and who pretended to be enjoying a stroll, until they got near enough to enable them to seize the throat of Longbeard. This movement instantly raised his choler, and drawing his knife, he succeeded in cutting completely away. He sought refuge in the church of St. Mary of Arches, which he barricaded for four days, but he was at last taken, stabbed, dragged at a horse's tail to the Tower, and forwarded by the same conveyance to Smithfield, where he was hanged on a gibbet, with the nine unfortunates who had been the companions of his promenade. The mob, who had stood by him while he was thus cruelly treated, pretended to look upon him as a martyr directly he was dead. This, however, seems to have been the result of interested motives, for they stole the gibbet, and cut it up into relics, which were sold at most exorbitant prices; so that, by making a saint of him, they gave a value to the gallows which they purloined. It is possible that they were not particular as to the genuineness of the article, so long as there was any demand for little bits of Longbeard's gibbet.

Richard was now engaged in almost continual quarrels with Philip, which were only suspended by occasional want of money to pay the respective barons, who always struck, or rather, refused to strike at all, when they could not get their wages. In the year 1198, hostilities were renewed with great vigour, and a battle was fought near Gisors, where Philip was nearly drowned by the breaking of a bridge, in consequence of the enormous weight of the fugitives. In his bulletin, Richard insultingly alluded to the quantity of the river the French king had been compelled to drink, and hinted, that as he was full of water it was quite fair to make a butt of him.

This was Cour de Lion's "positively last appearance" in any combat. A truce was concluded, and Richard quitted Normandy for the Limousin, where it was said in one of the popular ballads of the day that the point of the arrow was being forged for the death of the tyrant. Many dispute the point, and believe the story to be forged; but certain it is that Henry, the father of Richard, had frequently been shot at by an arrow, and had had, according to a lame pun of the period, many a-n-arrow escape from the hands of his secret enemies. According to the usual version of Cour de Lion's death, it seems that he went with an armed force to demand of Vidomar, Viscount of Limoges, a treasure, said to have been found in the domains of the latter. The viscount claimed halves, which Richard refused, and with a loud cry of "All or none," threatened to hang every man of the garrison. The king was surveying the walls to ascertain an eligible place for the assault, and had just raised his eyes, exclaiming—"Here's a weak point," when the point of an arrow came whizzing along and stuck in his left shoulder. Richard making some passing allusion to this novel mode of shouldering arms, took little notice of the wound, but went on with the assault, and soon seized the Castle.

Bertrand de Gourdon before Richard.

The business of the day being concluded, he sent for a surgeon, who took out the point of the arrow somewhat clumsily, causing Richard to remark, in allusion to the bungling manner in which the operation had been performed, that it could not be called a very elegant "extract." The wound, though slight, became worse from ill-treatment; and the king, feeling that there were no hopes of his recovery, would only reply to the encouraging remarks of his attendants by pointing mournfully yet significantly over his left shoulder.

It is said that he sent for Bertrand de Gourdon, the youth that inflicted the wound, and let him off for letting off the bow; but it is impossible to say what truth there is in this anecdote. The MS. chronicle of Winchester says that Richard's sister Joan expressed a truly female wish to have the prisoner given to her that she might "tear his eyes out," and that she literally put in force this threat which so many women are heard to make, but which not one of the sex was ever known to execute.

Richard died on Tuesday, the 6th of April, 1199, after a reign of ten years, not one of which had been passed in England, for he had led the life of a royal vagabond. He died at forty-two, and it is a remarkable fact, says one of the chroniclers—whom for the sake of his reputation we will not name—that, though Richard lived to be forty-two, fortitude was the only virtue he had ever exhibited. He loved the name of Lion Heart, and he certainly deserved a title that indicated his possession of brutish qualities. The British lion might, in justice to his own character, repudiate all connection with this contemptible Cour de Lion, who had at least as much cruelty as courage, and who had murdered many more in cold blood when prisoners than he had ever killed on the field of battle. His slaughter of the three thousand Saracen captives must be regarded as a proof that, whatever of the lion he might have had in his disposition, he had not much of the heart. This, however, such as it was, he never gave to England in his lifetime, and he left it to Rouen at his death, being certainly the very smallest and most valueless legacy he could possibly have bequeathed.

Arrival of Richard's Legacy at Rouen.

CHAPTER THE SEVENTH

JOHN, SURNAMED SANSTERRE, OR LACKLAND

ohn, who was in Normandy when Richard died, made every effort to secure that gang of humbugs, the mercenaries, by sending over to offer them an increase of salary, with the view of preventing them from taking engagements in the cause of his nephew, Arthur, the child of his elder brother, Geoffrey. Hubert Walter, the Archbishop of Canterbury, was despatched to England, to obtain the services of the barons by the usual means; and John himself repaired to Chinon, to ransack the castle where Richard had kept his treasures. Having chastised a few citizens for supporting Arthur, he repaired to Rouen, where on Sunday, the 25th of April, 1199, he was bedizened with the sword and coronal of the duchy. The English were not much disposed to favour the claims of John, but Archbishop Hubert purchased a few oaths of allegiance from the barons and prelates, who for the usual consideration were always ready to swear fealty to anyone.

John landed at Shoreham on the 25th of May, and on the 27th he knocked at the church door of St. Peter's, Westminster, to claim the crown. He seems to have encountered a tolerably numerous congregation, whom he endeavoured to convince by pulling out of his pocket an alleged will made in his favour by his brother Richard, and some other documents, which, backed by a speech from Archbishop Hubert, set everybody shouting "Long live the king!"

Poor little Arthur was completely overlooked in this arrangement, for he had scarcely anyone to take his part but a noisy scolding mother, who bore the name of Constance, probably on account of her shameful inconstancy. She had married a third husband while her second was still living; and it is even said that she contemplated adding trigamy to bigamy, for which purpose she sent her son to be out of the way at Paris, with Philip, the French king. The poor child had his interests fearfully sacrificed on all sides, for a treaty was agreed upon between John and Philip, according to which there would be nothing at all left for the unfortunate boy when the two sovereigns had helped themselves to their respective shares of the booty.

In the summer of the year 1200, John made a royal progress into France where he evinced a familiar and festive humour, which made him a favourite with a few of the "jolly dogs," but did not win the respect of the more sober classes of the community. He did not at all improve upon acquaintance; and he completed his unpopularity by running away with Isabella, the wife of the Count of La Marche, whom he married and brought to England, in spite of his having already a wife at home, and the lady's having also a husband abroad. A second coronation was performed in honour of his second marriage; but he seems to have soon got tired of his new match, for he marched into Aquitaine without his wife, under the pretence that he had business to attend to, but he really did no business at all. Little did he anticipate when he started *en garçon* on his tour that the historian nearly

Prince Arthur requires his Grandmother to surrender.

seven centuries afterwards would be recording the manner in which he passed his time, and proving the hollowness of the excuse for leaving his wife behind him when he took his trip to Aquitaine.

Young Arthur, who was but fifteen years of age, was advised by Philip (a.d. 1202) to try his hand in a military expedition. "You know your rights," said Philip to the youth, "and would you not be a king?"

"Oh! wouldn't I, just?" was the boy-like reply, and the French king counting off two hundred knights, as if they were so many bundles of wood, handed them over to the prince, telling him to go and make an attack upon some of the provinces. Arthur was recommended to march against Mirabeau, the residence of his grandmother, Eleanor, a violent old lady who had always been unfavourable to his claims. Arthur took the town, but not his grandmother, who, on hearing of the lad's intentions, exclaimed, "Hoity toity! would the urchin teach his grandmother to suck eggs, I wonder?"

"No, but I would teach my grandmother to succumb," was the dignified reply of the prince, when the message of his venerable relative was brought to him. The sturdy old female, who was rather corpulent, made, literally, a stout resistance, having thrown herself into a strong tower, which set rather tight upon her, like a corsage, and in this position she for some time defied the assaults of the enemy. Encased in this substantial breastwork, she awaited the threatened lacing at the hands of her grandson, when John came to her rescue. In the night between the 31st of July and the 1st of August, he took the town, dragged Arthur out of his bed, as well as some two hundred nobles who were "hanging out" at the different lodgings in the city. After cruelly beating them, he literally loaded them with irons, giving them cuffs first, and hand-cuffs immediately afterwards. Twenty-two noblemen were thrown into the damp dungeons of Corfe Castle, where they caught severe colds, of which they soon died, and they were buried under the walls of Corfe without coffins.[24] Young Arthur's tragical end has been the subject of various conjectures. Several historians have tried their hands at an interesting version of the young prince's death, but Shakspeare has given the most effective, and not the least probable, account of the fate of Arthur. The monks of Margan believe that John, in a fit of intoxication, slew his nephew; but we have no proof that Lackland was often in that disgraceful state, which in these days would have rendered him liable to the loss of a crown—in the shape of the five-shilling fine for drunkenness.

Ralph, the abbot of Coggeshall, who agrees with Shakspeare in many particulars, says that Arthur had been removed to Rouen, where his uncle called for him on the night of the 3rd of April, 1203, in a boat, to take a row on the river. It being time for all good little children to be in bed and asleep, Arthur was both at the moment of the avuncular visit. Boy-like, he made no objection to the absurd and ill-timed excursion, for it is a curious fact that infants are always ready to get up at the most unseasonable hours, if anything in the shape of pleasure is proposed to them. Arthur was soon in the boat for a row up the Seine with his uncle John and Peter de Maulac, Esquire, one of the unprincipled "men about town" at that disreputable period.

They had not proceeded far when either John or Mr. de Maulao seized the boy, as if he were so much superfluous ballast, and cruelly pitched him overboard. Some say that the squire was the sole executioner, while others hint that he turned squeamish at the last moment, and left the disgraceful business to John; but they doubtless shared the guilt, as they were both rowing in the same boat, and were in point of private character "much of a muchness." Shakespeare, as everybody knows, makes the young prince meet his death more than half-way by leaping on to the stones below his prison window, with a hope that they might prove softer than the heart of his uncle. It is not improbable that a child so young may have been foolish enough to jump to such a conclusion.

The rumour of the murder naturally occasioned the greatest excitement; and if we are to believe the immortal bard, five moons came mooning out upon the occasion, which may account for the moonstruck condition of the populace.

The Britons, amongst whom Arthur had been educated, were furious at the murder of their youthful prince, whose eldest sister, Eleanor, was in the hands of her uncle John. This lady was called by some, the Pearl of Brittany; but if she was really a gem, she must have been an antique, for she spent forty years of her life in captivity. The Britons, therefore, rallied round a younger heroine, her half-sister, Alice, and appointed her father, Guy de Thouars, the regent and general of their confederacy. De Thouars

---

24. Matthew Paris: It is to be regretted that the statement of a fact sometimes involves the necessity for a pun, as in the present instance. The faithful historian has, however, on such an occasion, no alternative. Fidelity must not be sacrificed even to a desire for solemnity.

was a Guy only in name, for he was extremely handsome, and had attracted the attention of the lady Constance, whose third and last husband he had become. Guy went as the head of a deputation to the French king, who summoned John to a trial; but that individual instead of attending the summons, allowed judgment to go by default, and was sentenced to a forfeiture of his dominions.

John for some time treated the steps taken against him with contempt, and remained at Rouen, until he thought it advisable to go over to England, to prepare for his defence by collecting money, for it was always by sucking dry the public purse that tyrants in those days were accustomed to look for succour.

It was by his efforts to extract cash from his people that he excited among his nobles the discontent which has rendered the discontented barons of his reign, *par excellence, the* discontented barons of English history. He continued to mulct them every day, and his reign was a long game of forfeits, in which the barons were always the sufferers. Still they refused to quit the country for the defence of their tyrant's foreign possessions.

By dint of threats and bribery he at last contrived (a.d. 1206) to land an army at Rochelle, and a contest was about to commence, when John proposed a parley. Without waiting for the answer, he ran away, leaving a notice on the door of his tent, stating that he had gone to England, and would return immediately, which, in accordance with the modern "chamber-practice," was equivalent to an announcement that he had no intention of coming back again.

John, who could agree with nobody, now began to quarrel with the pope by starting a candidate for the see of Canterbury, in opposition to Stephen Langton, the nominee of old Innocent. His holiness desired three English bishops to go and remonstrate with the king, who flew into a violent passion, and used the coarsest language, winding up with a threat to "cut off their noses," which caused the venerable deputation to "cut off" themselves with prompt King John threatens to cut off the Noses of the Bishops.

The bishops, however, soon recovered from the effects of their ill-treatment, and determined by the aid of the people to punish with papal bulls the royal bully.

On Monday, the 23rd of March, 1208, they pronounced an interdict against all John's dominions; but, like children setting fire to a train of gunpowder and running away, the bishops quitted the kingdom, as if afraid of the result of their own boldness. This was soon followed by a bull of excommunication against John, but the wary tyrant, by watching the ports, prevented the entrance of this bull, which would have made it a mere toss up whether he could keep possession of his throne.

John employed the year 1210 in raising money, by stealing it wherever he could lay his hands upon it; for, says the chronicler, "as long as there was a sum he could bone, he thought it the *summum bonum* to get hold of it." With the cash he had collected he repaired to Ireland, and at Dublin was joined by twenty robust chieftains, who might have been called the Dublin stout of the thirteenth century. Returning to England in three months with an empty pocket, he became alarmed at hearing of a conspiracy among his barons. He shut himself up for fifteen days in the castle of Nottingham, seeing no one but the servants, and not permitting the door to be opened even to take in the milk, lest the cream of the British nobility should flow in with it.

At length, in the year 1213, Innocent hurled his last thunderbolt at John's head, with the intention of knocking off his crown. The pope pronounced the deposition of the English king, and declared the throne open to competition, with a hint to Philip of France that he might find it an eligible investment. He prepared a fleet of seventeen hundred vessels at Boulogne, but some of the vessels must have been little bigger than butter-boats if seventeen hundred of them were crammed into this insignificant harbour. John, by a desperate effort, got together sixty thousand men, but they were by no means staunch, and he was as much afraid of his own troops as of those belonging to the enemy. Pandulph, the pope's legate, knowing his character, came to Dover, and frightened him by

King John threatens to cut off the Noses of the Bishops.

fearful pictures of the enemy's strength, while Peter the Hermit,[25] who was rather more plague than prophet, bored the tyrant with predictions of his death. John, who was exceedingly superstitious, was so worked upon by his fears that he agreed to Pandulph's terms, and on the 15th of May, 1213, he signed a sort of cognovit, acknowledging himself the vassal of the pope, and agreeing to pay a thousand marks a year, in token of which he set his own mark at the end of the document.

He next offered Pandulph something for his trouble, but the legate raising his leg, trampled the money under his foot. The next day was that on which Peter the Hermit had prophesied that John would die, and the tyrant remained from morning till night watching the clock with intense anxiety. Finding himself alive at bedtime, he grew furious against Peter for having caused him so much needless alarm, and the Hermit was hanged for the want of foresight he had exhibited. He died, exclaiming that the king should have been grateful that the prediction had not been fulfilled; "but," added he, as he placed his head through the fatal noose, "some folks are never satisfied." The French king was exceedingly disgusted at the shabby treatment he had received; but Philip expended his rage in a few philippics against Pandulph, who merely expressed his regret, and added peremptorily that England being now under the dominion of the pope, must henceforth be let alone. Philip alluded to the money he was out of pocket, but the nuncio politely observing that he was not happy at questions of account, withdrew while repeating his prohibition.

John, who had so lately eaten humble pie, soon began to regard his promises as the pie-crust, which he commenced breaking very rapidly. Wishing, however, to carry the war into France, he required the services of his barons, who were very reluctant to aid him, and he had got as far as Jersey, when happening to look behind him, he perceived that he had scarcely any followers. He had started with a tolerable number, but they turned back sulkily by degrees, without his being aware of it until he arrived at Jersey, when he was preparing to turn himself round, and perceived that his *suite* had dwindled down to a few mercenaries, who hung on to his skirts merely for the sake of what he had got in his pockets. Becoming exceedingly angry, he wheeled suddenly back, and vented his spite in burning and ravaging everything that crossed his path. He was in a flaming passion, for he set fire to all the buildings on the road till he reached Northampton, where Langton overtook him, and taxed him with the violation of his oath. "Mind your own business," roared the king, "and leave me to manage mine;" but Langton would not take an answer of that kind, and stuck to him all the way to Nottingham, where the prelate, according to his own quaint phraseology, "went at him again" with more success than formerly. John issued summonses to the barons, and Langton hastened to see them in London, where he drew up a strong affidavit by which they all swore to be true to each other, and to their liberties.

John was still apprehensive of the hostility of the pope, which might have been fatal at this juncture, had not Cardinal Nicholas arrived in the nick of time, namely, on the 12th of September, 1213, to take off the interdict. The court of Rome thus executed a sort of *chassez-croisez*, by going over to the side of John, but Langton did not desert his old partner, liberty. In the following year the English king was defeated at the battle of Bouvines, one of the most tremendous affrays recorded in history. Salisbury, surnamed Longsword, was captured by that early specimen of the church militant, the Bishop of Beauvais, who, because it was contrary to the canons of the Church for him to shed blood, fought with a ponderous club, by which he knocked the enemy on the head, and acquired the name of the stunning bishop. He banged about him in such style that he might have been eligible for the see of Bangor, had his ambition pointed in that direction. John obtained a truce; but the discontented barons had already placed a rod in pickle for him, and on the 20th day of November, they held a crowded meeting at St. Edmund's Bury, which was adjourned until Christmas. At that festive season, John found himself eating his roast beef entirely alone, for nobody called to wish him joy, or partake his pudding.

After dining by himself, at Worcester, he started for London, making sure of a little-gaiety at boxing-time, in the great metropolis.

Nobody, however, took the slightest notice of him until one day the whole of the barons came to him in a body, to pay him a morning visit. Surprised at the largeness of the party, he was somewhat cool, but on hearing that they had come for liberty, he declared that he would not allow any liberty to be taken while he continued king of England. The party remained firm with one or two exceptions,

---

25. Some writers have called Peter the Hermit a hare-brained recluse. As his head was closely shaved the epithet "hairbrained" seems to have been sadly misapplied.

when John began to shiver as if attacked with ague, and he went on blowing hot and cold as long as he could, until pressed by the barons for an answer to their petition. He then replied evasively, "Why—yes—no; let me see—ha! exactly—stop! Well, I don't know, perhaps so—'pon honour;" and ultimately obtained time until Easter, to consider the proposals that were made to him. The confederated barons had no sooner got outside the street-door than John began to think over the means of circumventing them. As they separated on the threshold, to go to their respective homes, it was evident from the gestures and countenances of the group that there had been a difference of opinion as to the policy of granting John the time he had requested. A bishop and two barons, who had turned recreants at the interview, and receded

The Bishop of Beauvais capturing Salisbury.

from their claims, were of course severely bullied by the rest of the confederates, on quitting the royal presence. At length the day arrived, in Easter week, when the barons were to go for an answer to the little Bill—of Rights—which they had left with John at the preceding Christmas. They met at Stamford, where they got up a grand military spectacle, including two thousand knights and an enormous troop of auxiliaries. The king, who was at Oxford, sent off Cardinal Langton, with the Earls of Pembroke and Warrenne, as a deputation, who soon returned with a schedule of terrific length, containing a catalogue of grievances, which the barons declared they would have remedied.

John flew into one of his usual passions, tearing his long hair, and rapidly pacing his chamber with the skirt of his robe thrown over his left arm, while, with his right hand, he shook his fist at vacancy. The deputation could merely observe calmly, "We have done our part of the business: that is what the barons want;" and a roll of parchment was instantly allowed to run out to its full length at the foot of the enraged sovereign. John took up the document and pretended to inspect it with much minuteness, muttering to himself, "No, I don't see it down," upon which Langton asked the sovereign what he was looking for. "I was searching," sarcastically roared the tyrant, "for the crown, which I fully expected to find scheduled as one of the items I am called upon to surrender." This led to some desultory conversation, in the course of which the king made some evasive offers, which the barons would not accept, and the latter, appointing Robert Fitz-Walter as their general, at once commenced hostilities.

They first marched upon the castle of Northampton, but when they got under the walls they discovered that they had got no battering-rams, and after sitting looking at the castle for fifteen days, they marched off again. At Bedford, where they went next, the same farce might have been enacted, had not the inhabitants opened the gates for them. Here they received an invitation from London, and stopping to rest for the night at Ware—on account, perhaps, of the accommodation afforded by the Great Bed—they arrived on Sunday, the 24th of May, 1215, in the City. Here they were joined by the whole nobility of England, while John was abandoned by all but seven knights, who remained near his person, the seven knights forming a weak protection, to the sovereign. His heart at first failed him, but he was a capital actor, and soon assumed a sort of easy cheerfulness. He presented his compliments to the barons, and assured them he should be most happy to meet them, if they would appoint a time and place for an interview. The barons instantly fixed the 19th of June at Runny-Mead, when John intimated that he should have much pleasure in accepting the polite invitation.

At length the eventful morning arrived, when John cantered quietly down from Windsor Castle, attended by eight bishops and a party of about twenty gentlemen. These, however, were not his friends, but had been lent by the other side, "for the look of the thing," lest the king should seem to be wholly without attendants. The barons, who had been stopping at Staines, were of course punctual, and had got the pen and ink all laid out upon the table, with a Windsor chair brought expressly from the town of Windsor for John to sit down upon. It had been expected that he would have raised some futile objections to sign; but the crafty sovereign, knowing it was a *sine qua non*, made but one plunge into the inkstand, and affixed his autograph. It is said that he dropped a dip of ink accidentally on the parchment, and that he mentally ejaculated "Ha! this affair will be a blot upon my name for ever." The facility with which the king attached his signature to Magna Charta—the great charter of England's liberties—naturally excited suspicion; for it is a remark founded on a long acquaintance with human nature that the man who never means to take up a bill is always foremost in accepting one. Had John contemplated adhering to the provisions of the document he would have probably discussed the various clauses, but a swindler seldom disputes the items of an account, when he has not the remotest intention of paying it.

John in a Passion.

Though Magna Charta has been practically superseded by subsequent statutes, it must always be venerated as one of the great foundations of our liberties. It established the "beautiful principle" that taxation shall only take place by the consent of those taxed—a principle the beauty of which has been its chief advantage, for it has proved less an article for use than for ornament. The agreeable figure that everyone who pays a tax does so with his own full concurrence, and simply because he likes it, is a pleasing delusion, which all have not the happiness to labour under. It was also provided that "the king should sell, delay, or deny justice to none," a condition that can scarcely be considered fulfilled when we look at some of the bills of costs that generally follow a long suit in that game of chance which has obtained the singularly appropriate title of Chancery. It may be perhaps argued that the article delayed and sold is law, whereas Magna Charta alludes only to Justice. This, we must admit, establishes a distinction—*not* without a difference.

Though John had kept his temper tolerably well at the meeting with the barons, he had no sooner got back to Windsor Castle, than he called a few foreign adventurers around him, and indulged in a good hearty swearing fit against the charter. He grew so frantic, according to the chroniclers, that he "gnashed his teeth, rolled his eyes, and gnawed sticks and straws," though he could scarcely have done all this without sending for the umbrella-stand, and having a good bite at its contents, or ordering in a few wisps from the stable.

That John was exceedingly mad with the barons for what they had made him do, is perfectly true, but we do not go the length of those who look upon a truss of straw as essential to a person labouring under mental aberration.

John now went to reside in the Isle of Wight, and tried to captivate the fishermen by adopting their manners. There is nothing very captivating in the manners of the fishermen of the Isle of Wight at the present day, whatever may have been the case formerly; but it is probable that the king became popular by a sort of hail-fellow-well-met-ishness, to which his dreadful habit of swearing no doubt greatly contributed. Having imported a lot of mercenaries from the Continent, he posted off to Dover to land the disgraceful cargo, and with them he marched against Rochester Castle, which had been seized by William D'Albiney. The larder was wretchedly low when D'Albiney first took possession, and the garrison was soon reduced to its last mouthful of provisions. This consisted of a piece of rind of cheese, which everybody had refused in daintier days, when provisions were plentiful. D'Albiney bolted the morsel and unbolted the gate nearly at the same moment, when John, rushing in, butchered all the supernumeraries and sent the principal characters to Corfe Castle.

John, who always grew bold when there was no opposition, committed all sorts of atrocities upon places without defence, and the barons shut up in Lincoln, held numerous meetings, which terminated in a resolution to offer the crown to Louis, the son of Philip of France, provided the young gentleman and his papa would come over and fight for it. Louis left Calais with six hundred and eighty vessels, but he had a terribly bad passage across to Sandwich, where the "flats," as usual, permitted the landing of an enemy. John, who had run round to Dover with a numerous army, fled before the French landed, and committed arson on an extensive scale all over the country. Every night was a "night wi' Burns," and the royal incendiary seems to have put himself under the especial protection of Blaise, as the only saint with whom the tyrant felt the smallest sympathy. John ultimately put up at Bristol, and the neighbourhood of Bath seems to have quenched for a time his flaming impetuosity.

Louis having besieged Rochester Castle, which seems in those days to have been very like a copy of the *Times* newspaper, which some one was always anxious to take directly it was out of hand, marched on to London. He arrived there on the 2nd of June, 1216, where he was received with that enthusiasm which the hospitable cockneys have ever been ready to bestow on foreigners of distinction. Nearly all the few followers that had hitherto adhered to John now abandoned him, and he was left almost alone with Gualo, the pope's legate, who did all he could to revive the drooping spirits of the tyrant. Vainly, however, did Gualo slap the sovereign on the back, inviting him to "cheer up," and ply him with cider, his favourite beverage. "Come! drown it in the bowl," was the constant cry of Gualo. "Talk not of bowls," was the reply of John; "what is life but a game at bowls, in which the king is too frequently knocked over?"

Louis, in the meantime, growing arrogant with success, commenced insulting the English and granting their property to his foreign followers. The barons began to think they had made a false step with reference to their own country by allowing the French prince to put his foot in it. This for a moment brightened the prospects of John, who started off and went blazing away as far as Lynn, where he had got a *dépôt* of provisions, and of course a change of linen. Hence he made for Wisbeach, and put up at a place called the "Cross Keys," intending to cross the Wash, which is a very passable place at low water.

John was nearly across when he heard the tide beginning to roar with fearful fury. Knowing that tide and time wait for no man, he felt he was tied to time, and hurried to the opposite shore with tremendous rapidity. He succeeded in reaching land; but his horses, with his plate, linen, and money were not so fortunate, for he had the mortification of seeing all his clothes lost in the Wash, and the utter sinking of the whole of his capital.

Venting his sorrow in cursory remarks and discursive curses, he went on to Swineshead Abbey, where he passed the night in eating peaches and pears, and drinking new cider.[26] The cider of course added to the fermentation that was going on in his fevered frame; and even without the peaches and pears, the efforts of his physicians might have proved fruitless. He went to bed, but could not sleep, for his conscience continued to impeach him in a series of frightful dreams, to which the peaches no doubt contributed. He nevertheless made an effort to get up the next morning, and mounted his horse on the 15th of October; but he was too ill to keep his seat, and his attendants, putting him into a horse-box, got him as far as Sleaford. Here he passed another shocking night, but the next day they again moved him into the horse-box, and dragged him to Newark, where he requested that a confessor might be sent for. The abbot of Crocton, who was a doctor as well as a divine, immediately attended, and this leech was employed in drawing a confession from the lips of the tyrant. He named his eldest son, Henry, his successor, and dictated a begging-letter to the new pope, imploring protection for his small and helpless children. He died on the 18th of October, 1216, in the forty-ninth year of his age, and the seventeenth of one of the most uncomfortable reigns recorded in English history. From first to last he seems to have been cut by his subjects, for we find him eating his Christmas dinner alone in the very middle of his sovereignty, and dragged about the country in a horse-box within a day of his death, when such active treatment could not have been beneficial to the royal patient in an advanced stage of fever.

The character of John has been so fully developed in the account of his reign that it is quite unnecessary to sum him up on the present occasion. If he harassed the barons, they certainly succeeded in returning the compliment; for he seems to have had a most unpleasant time of it. He had the title of king, but was often worse off.

---

26. Matthew Paris, point of accommodation than the humblest gentleman. His case reminds us of an individual, who, finding himself in a sedan with neither top nor bottom to it, came to the conclusion that he might as well have walked but for "the look of the thing." So it may be said of John that deprived of all the substantial advantages of a throne, he might but "for the name of the thing" have just as well been a private individual.

Book III

THE PERIOD FROM THE ACCESSION OF HENRY THE THIRD, TO THE END OF THE REIGN OF RICHARD THE SECOND. A.D. 1216—1399

CHAPTER THE FIRST

HENRY THE THIRD, SURNAMED OF WINCHESTER

enry, the eldest son of John, was a child under ten years of age at the time of his father's death, but his brother-in-law, the Earl of Pembroke, brought him to Gloucester and got him crowned by Gualo, who had always acted as a friend of the family. The coronation, which took place on the 28th of October, 1216, was very indifferently got up, for the crown had not come from the Wash, where it had been lying in soak ever since John's unfortunate expedition across the water from Wisbeach. Gualo therefore took a ring from his finger, and put it on the young king's head, as a substitute for the missing diadem. The coronation party consisted of three earls, three bishops, and four barons, with a sprinkling of abbots and priors, comprising altogether a retinue of about thirty individuals.

The clergy of Westminster and Canterbury complained bitterly of the ceremony having been "scamped," by which their rights had been invaded, or, in other words, by which they had been done out of their perquisites. The first coronation was therefore treated as a mere rehearsal, and a more regular performance afterwards took place, with new machinery, dresses, decorations, and all the usual properties.

On the 11th of the following November, Pembroke was appointed *rector Regis et Regni*—ruler of the king and kingdom—so that Henry the Third was sovereign *de jure* with a *de facto* viceroy over him. This arrangement was made at a great council held at Bristol, where Magna Charta was revised with a view to the publication of a new and improved edition.

Louis, on hearing of John's death, puffed himself up with a certainty of success, but he only realised the old fable of the French frog and the British bull; for, becoming inflated with pride, he was not long in bursting like an empty bubble.

As Christmas, 1216, was close at hand, a truce was arranged, to enable each party to enjoy the holidays. Louis took advantage of the vacation to go to Paris to consult his father Philip, who, like a modern French king of the same name, was remarkable for his tact in doing the best for his own family. On his return to England, Louis encountered some hostility from the hardy mariners of the Cinque Ports—the Deal and Dover boatmen of that day—but reaching Sandwich, he got over the flats with the usual facility. He, however, spitefully burned the town to the ground, merely because it was one of the Cinque Ports, which had turned crusty at his approach, though it was hardly fair of him to mull the only port that did not prove too strong for him. Hostilities were continued on both sides with varying success, until the Count de la Perche, a French general, flushed with a recent triumph at Mount Sorel, in Leicester, determined to attack the Castle of Lincoln. He would probably have succeeded, but for the resistance of a woman, the widow of the late keeper of the castle, who, with the obstinacy of her sex, refused to surrender. The Count de la Perche, ashamed of being beaten by one of the gentler sex, continued the attack, and refusing to quit the town, found himself involved in a series of street rows of the most alarming character.

Pembroke having collected a large force, sent part of it into the castle by the back garden gate, and the other part into the town, so that poor de la Perche found it impossible to move either one way or the other. The English literally gave it him right and left till he died; and after falling upon the almost defenceless French, they gave the name of "the fair of Lincoln" to a battle about as unfair as any recorded in the pages of history.

This event, which came off on the 20th of May, 1217, was followed in June by a conference which, like Panton Square, led to nothing. Louis made one more attempt upon Dover, but he had no means to carry on the war, and he was obliged to raise the siege, as he could not raise the money. He hastened to London, which he had no sooner entered than the English shut the gates and locked him in; while the pope sent a tremendous bull down upon him, to add to his annoyances. Louis began to feel that he had had quite enough of it, and being anxious for a little peace, he proposed one to Pembroke. The terms were soon agreed upon, but Louis was detained in town some little time for want of the money to pay his debts and his journey home again. The citizens of London forming themselves into a loan society, advanced a few pounds to the French prince, who deserves some credit for not having taken French leave of his creditors. By the terms of the treaty he surrendered all his claims upon the English crown, which seems to have been rather a superfluous sacrifice, as he had been trying it on for some time, and found that the cap never fitted.

As Louis went out of London at the East End, to embark for France, Henry, who had been at Kingston, came in at Hyde Park Corner. Pembroke, the regent, made him exceedingly popular by advising him to confirm Magna Charta, and to add a clause or two for the purpose of freshening it up, so that the new edition might repay perusal. Unfortunately for the prospects of the kingdom, Pembroke died, in May, 1219, and was buried in the Temple Church, where his tomb is still to be seen by anyone who can obtain a bencher's order. The regent's authority was now divided between Hubert de Burgh and Peter—or, as Rapin christens him—William des Roches, the Bishop of Winchester. These two individuals, though jealous of each other, agreed in the propriety of another coronation, probably on account of the patronage it gave to those who happened to be in power; and as the couple in question had just taken office, they were anxious to realise some of the profits at the earliest opportunity. In the quarrels between these two worthies, des Roches was getting rather the upper hand, when Hubert de Burgh, in 1223, got the pope to declare that the king, who was only sixteen years of age, had attained his majority. Thus, like the dog in the manger, Hubert determined that no one else should enjoy a position which he himself was unable to profit by. This was an "artful dodge" of the cunning Hubert, to get the game into his own hands, for Henry on being pronounced "of age," having received a surrender of various castles and fortified places from the barons, gave back those which he had no occasion for to the wily minister. The barons, finding themselves bamboozled, became exceedingly angry with the king and Hubert, but the latter went on, alternately hanging and excommunicating, until he had settled the obstreperous and quelled the turbulent.

The year 1225 must ever be remarkable for the refusal of Parliament—a name that was then coming into use—to grant supplies without asking any questions. This had formerly been the usual practice, but when Hubert coolly proposed a grant of a fifteenth of all the movable property in the kingdom for the use of the king, the Parliament said it was all very well, but if the money was given there ought to be something to show for it. Henry accordingly gave another ratification of Magna Charta, which was a good deal like the old superfluous process of putting butter upon bacon, for he had already twice ratified that important document. In those days, however, there was no objection to giving the lily an extra coat of paint, or treating the refined gold to an additional layer of gilding.

In the year 1228, Henry had collected an army at Portsmouth to sail for France, but Hubert de Burgh, who seems to have held the place of First Lord of the Admiralty as well as his other offices, had not provided a sufficient number of vessels. When the troops were about to embark it was found impossible to stow them away even with the closest packing. Henry flew into a violent passion with Hubert, accusing him of pocketing the money he ought to have laid Goode out in ships, and the king had

The Earl of Chester interposing between Henry the Third and Hubert de Burgh

drawn his sword, intending to run the minister through, when the Earl of Chester ran between them, exclaiming "Hold!" with intense significance.

This fine dramatic situation told exceedingly well; for Hubert de Burgh got off, though the king did not, and the expedition was postponed until the year following. He passed over into Normandy, a.d. 1229, but he preferred feasting to fighting, and the only advance he made was by continually running away, which kept him constantly ahead of the enemy. He, however, threw all the blame of the failure on Hubert, whose shoulders must have been tolerably broad to have borne all that his master chose to cast onto them.

The king returned to England very much out of pocket and completely out of spirits. He applied to his old paymaster, the Parliament, but his conduct had excited so much disgust that instead of money, or as it was then called, blunt, he got a blunt refusal. His majesty, whose tone had hitherto been that of command, now assumed the humble air of the mendicant, and he adopted the degraded clap-trap of his being "a real case of distress," in order to obtain a subsidy. He declared his inability to pay his way, but as his way was never to pay at all, this argument availed him very little. He was, however, getting rapidly shorter and shorter every day, when fearing that he would perhaps compromise the dignity of the crown by pawning it, or sell the regalia for the purpose of regaling himself, the Parliament agreed to let him have a trifle for current expenses. This consisted of three marks for every fief held immediately of the crown,[27] which was little enough to give him an excuse for not paying his debts, and yet sufficient to allow him to rush into fresh extravagances. In the year 1232, Henry, having of course spent every shilling of his small supply, renewed his application to Parliament, alleging that he was desirous of discharging the liabilities incurred in his expedition to France, but the barons firmly, and not very respectfully, refused any further pecuniary assistance. They urged in effect that they had already been doubly robbed of their services and their cash, for they had never been paid for the one, and had been almost drained of the other. The nobles, who had derived nearly all they possessed from plunder, could not see the justice of the principle that as they had done to others they deserved to be done, and they peremptorily refused to comply with the attempted exactions of the sovereign.

Having failed in his attack on the pockets of his Parliament, Henry looked with an envious eye on the comfortably lined coffers of his minister. Hubert de Burgh, though he enjoyed the reputation of a trusty servant, had taken care to feather his nest, nor did the feathers lie very heavily on his conscience, for in those days the greatest weight that could be placed upon the mind was always portable. The tonnage of Hubert's conscience appears to have been considerable, for though he carried a good cargo of peculation, he seems never to have evinced any disposition to sink under his burden. Henry became jealous of the good fortune of his minister, and resolved, for the purpose of getting his savings, to effect his ruin. Presuming Hubert to have been a dishonest man, and granting that there is policy in the recommendation to "set a thief to catch a thief," the king could not have done better than to send for des Boches, the Bishop of Winchester, to assist in cleaning out the favourite. Poor de Burgh was in the first instance charged with magic and enchantment; which may be considered equivalent to an impeachment of the minister of the present day for phantasmagoria and thimble-rig.

In these enlightened times we cannot conceive the Premier being sent to the Tower on a suspicion of jack-a-lantern and blind hookey, though it was for offences of this class that Hubert was at first arraigned on the prosecution of his sovereign. These frivolous charges having fallen to the ground, the king called upon him for an account of all the money that had passed through his hands; when the minister having kept no books and being wholly without vouchers, cut a very pretty figure. As he had been in the habit of cutting figures all through his career, this result was not to be wondered at. He, however, rummaged among his papers and found an old patent, given him by John, absolving him from the necessity of rendering any account, but his enemies replied that this was only a receipt in full

27. Rapin's *Histoire d'Angleterre*, tome ii., p. 386 of the second edition where he turned in to the priory. The king at first determined to have him out, dead or alive, and a mob of upwards of twenty thousand people, says Rapin, were about to start with the Mayor of London to take the ex-minister into custody. How such a crowd was got together in those days out of the mere superfluous idlers of the city, is not known, and we are equally in the dark how it happened that this mob continued doing nothing, while the king listened to remonstrances from various quarters against the violence of his measures.

up to the time of Henry's accession. Hubert finding he could not get out of the scrape, determined, if possible, to get out of the country; but he proceeded no further on the road than Merton. London mobs must have been rather more tractable in the thirteenth than in the nineteenth century, for the twenty thousand people dispersed when it was understood, after considerable negotiation, that their services would not be required. Indeed, according to a more recent historian, they had actually started when a king's messenger was despatched to call them back again.

Hubert, who had found the priory at Merton exceedingly slow, started off to St. Edmund's Bury to see his wife, who resided there. He had got as far as Brentwood, and had gone to bed, when he was roused by a loud knocking at the door, which caused him to put his head out of the window and inquire who or what was wanted. "Is there a person of the name of Hubert de Burgh stopping here?" exclaimed the captain of the troop; but the wily minister, for the sake of gaining time, pretended to misunderstand the question. "Hubert de What?" he exclaimed, as he slipped on a portion of his dress; but the soldier repeated the name with a tremendous emphasis on the syllable Burgh, which caused a shudder in the frame of Hubert. He, however, had the presence of mind to direct them to the second door round the corner. Having got them away from the front of the cottage by this manouvre, he ran downstairs into the street, and made his way to the chapel. Here he was seized by his pursuers, who placed him on a horse, and tied his feet together under the animal's stomach. Hubert must have had legs of a most extraordinary length, or the horse must have been a very genteel figure to have permitted this arrangement, which we find recorded in all the histories.

It is possible that the brute upon which de Burgh was secured may have been a donkey, in which case the legs of the ex-favourite might have been long enough to admit of their being tied in a double knot—and perhaps even in a bow—under the animal's stomach. In this uncomfortable position he was trotted off to the Tower; but the clergy being incensed at the violation of sanctuary, Hubert was remounted in the same style, and trotted back again. He was placed in the church as before, but all communication with it was cut off, a trench dug round it, and Hubert was left without any food but that which is always so plentiful under similar circumstances—namely, food for reflection.

After "chewing the bitter cud" until there was nothing left to masticate, he intimated from the steeple his desire to surrender. He had remained forty days shut up without food, fire, or any other clothing but the wrapper in which he had made his escape from his lodgings at Brentwood. The once burly de Burgh had, of course, become dreadfully thin, and the thread of existence seemed to be inclosed in a mere thread-paper. In this state he was taken to the Tower; but he was soon released to take his trial before his peers, who would have condemned him to death, but the king, looking on the minister as a golden goose, merely seized the accumulated eggs, and sent him to prison at the Castle of Devizes, until some other means were devised of getting hold of the remainder of his property.

Hubert had scarcely been in prison a year, when he took advantage of a dark night to drop himself over one of the battlements. He, however, found that one good drop deserved another, for he had fallen into a ditch containing a good drop of water, in which he remained absorbed for several seconds. Having crawled out, he commenced wringing his hands and his clothes, but feeling there was no time to be lost, he made his way to a country church, whither he was traced by the drippings of his garments, which had left a mark something like that of a water-cart, along the path he had taken. Though captured by one party, he was set at liberty by another, with whom the king had become very unpopular, and Hubert was carried off to Wales, where a sect of discontents, who, had they lived in these days, would have been called the Welsh Whigs, had long been gathering. Hubert in about a year and a half, obtained a return of part of his estates, and was even restored to his honours; but the king still kept him as a sort of nest-egg to plunder as occasion required. Hubert finally compromised the claims of the sovereign by surrendering four castles, in which Hollinshed is disposed to believe that Jack Straw's and the Elephant could not have been included.

The Bishop of Winchester, or as he is termed in history, the Poictevin bishop, succeeded to power on the downfall of Hubert, and des Boches soon filled the court with foreign adventurers. Two of a trade never agree; and the nobility, who had originally been foreign adventurers themselves, objected to the importation of any more scamps from abroad, on the principle, perhaps, that England had got plenty of that sort already. The Poictevin bishop was particularly hostile to the son of the late regent, the young

Earl of Pembroke, who inherited some of his father's virtues, and what was far more interesting to old des Boches, the whole of his father's property. Young P. was in Ireland, where he had large estates, which the Poictevin bishop desired the governors of that country to confiscate. He promised them a slice, and the governors being—as Rapin has it—*avides d'un si bon morceau*—(ravenous for such a tit-bit) determined on getting hold of it. Treachery was accordingly resorted to, and Pembroke was basely stabbed in the back whilst sitting unsuspectingly at his own Pembroke table. This was more than the barons could bear; and they told Henry very plainly, through Edmund, the new Archbishop of Canterbury, that if des Boches was not dismissed, the sovereign himself would be sent forthwith about his business. The Poictevin was ordered off to Winchester, with directions to limit his views to his own see; and the patriotic Canterbury, who had of course only been anxious for the good of his country, obtained the power from which his predecessor had been cleverly ousted.

The Bishop of Winchester was soon afterwards called to Rome by the pope, who pretended to require his advice, but really had an eye to his money. des Boches imagined that he was invited for protection, but he was in fact wanted for pillage. The Poictevin was glad to escape from English *surveillance*, and was quite content to eat his mutton under the pope's eye, though he was hardly prepared for the process of picking to which he was subjected. The predecessor of Urban was,[28] however, all urbanity, and thus made some amends to des Boches, who, like the majority of mankind, found victimisation a comparatively painless operation when performed by the gentle or light-fingered hands of an accomplished swindler.

In the year 1236, Henry married Eleanor of Provence, with immense pomp and another coronation—a ceremony the frequent repetition of which in former times was a proof of the uncertainty of regal power, for the crown could not be very firm that so often required re-soldering. The king's marriage formed, perhaps, a reasonable excuse for placing an extra hod of cement between the monarch's poll and the hollow diadem. The marriage festivities were followed by the summoning of a Parliament at Merton, where Henry passed a series of statutes that became famous under the name of the Statutes of Merton; and where he also pocketed, in the shape of subsidies, a considerable sum of money.

Eleanor, the new queen, brought with her to England a quantity of needy and seedy foreigners, most of whom were immediately promoted. One of her uncles, "named Boniface," says Matthew Paris, "from his extraordinary quantity of cheek," was raised to the see of Canterbury. She invited over from Provence a quantity of *demoiselles a marier*, whom she got off by palming them upon rich young nobles, of whom her husband held the wardship. The court was turned into a kind of matrimonial bazaar, where the wealthy scions of English aristocracy were hooked by the portionless but sometimes pretty spinsters of Provence. Nor was this all, for Isabella, the queen mother, sent over her four boys, Guy, William, Geoffrey, and Aymer, her sons, by the Count de la Marche, to be provided for. England was in fact regarded as an enormous common, upon which any foreign goose or jackass

Marriage of his most Gracious Majesty Henry the Third and Eleanor of Provence.

might be turned out to grass, provided he was patronised by a member of the reigning family. Henry, who was the victim of his poor relations, soon found himself short of cash, and he was obliged to get money in driblets from the Parliament, who never allowed him much at a time, and always exacted conditions which were invariably broken as soon as the cash was granted.

---

28. According to some authorities Celestine was pope at this period, and Urban did not reach the papal dignity till some time afterwards.

Henry had been married about a year, when he had the coolness to ask the nation for the expenses of his wedding. The barons declared that they had never been consulted about the match, and that the king up to the last hour of his remaining a single man had acted with great duplicity. Finding it useless to command, he resorted to the old plan of humbug, and fell back upon his old friend Magna Charta, which he confirmed once more, for about the fifth or sixth time, and of course got the money he required. This great Bill of Rights was to him a sort of stereotyped bill of exchange, upon which he could always raise a sum of money by going through the formality of a fresh acceptance.

The history of this reign for the next few years would furnish fitter materials for the accountant than the historian, and Henry's career would be better told in a balance-sheet than in the form of narrative. Had his schedule been regularly filed it would have disclosed a series of insolvencies, from which he was only relieved by taking the benefit of some act of generosity and credulity on the part of his Parliament. At one moment he was so fearfully hard up that he was advised to sell all his plate and jewels.[29] "Who will buy them?" he exclaimed—"though," he added, glancing at his four awkward half-brothers, "if anyone would give me anything for that set of spoons, I should be glad to take the offer." He was told that the citizens of London would purchase plate to any amount, at which he burst into violent invectives against "the clowns," as he termed them, probably on account of the presumed capacity of their breeches pockets. He made every effort to annoy the citizens, and showed his appreciation of their superfluous cash by helping himself to ten thousand pounds of it by open violence.

In the year 1253, Henry was once more in a fix, and again the Parliament had the folly to promise him a supply if he would go through another confirmation of Magna Charta. On the 3rd of May he attended a general meeting of the nobility at Westminster Hall where he found the ecclesiastical dignitaries holding each a burning taper in his hand, intending probably that the melting wax should make a deep impression on the sovereign. Some are of the opinion that this process was illustrative of the necessity sometimes said to exist for holding a candle to a certain individual. Henry took the usual quantity of oaths, and the priests dashed to the ground their tapers, which went out in smoke, and were so far typical of the king's promises. On receiving the money he went to Guienne, from which he soon came back—as a popular vocalist used to say by way of cue to his song—"without sixpence in his pocket, just like—Love among the roses."

The pope now brought in a heavy bill of £100,000 for money lent, of which Henry declared he had never enjoyed the benefit. The pope merely observed that he was clearing his books and must have the matter settled. The king turned upon the clergy, upon whom he drew bills, one of which was addressed to the Bishop of Worcester, who declared they might take his mitre in execution for the amount, and the Bishop of Gloucester said they might serve his the same; but if they did he would wear a helmet. Richard, the king's brother, who was very wealthy, hearing that the German empire was in the market for sale, made a bold bid for it. There was another competitor for the lot in the person of Alphonso, king of Castile, but Richard put down £700,000 and was declared the purchaser. This liberality was of course at the expense of poor England, which was so completely drained of cash that when Henry met his Parliament on the 2nd of May, 1258, he found the barons in full armour, rattling their swords, as much as to say that these must furnish a substitute for the precious metals.

Henry was alarmed at the menacing aspect of the assembly, but one of his foreign half-brothers began vapouring, in a mixed *patois* of bad French, to the bent down, but not yet broken, English. The king himself resorted to his old trick of promising, and pledged his word once more with his usual success, though it was already pawned over and over again for a hundred times its value. The barons, however, were still ready to take it in; though they had got by them already an enormous stock of similar articles, all unredeemed, and daily losing their interest. The leader of the country party was at this time Simon de Montfort, Earl of Leicester, a Frenchman, who had married Eleanor, the king's sister. He had quarrelled and made it up with Henry once or twice, and the following conversation is recorded to have taken place, in 1252, between the earl and his sovereign:—

"You are a traitor," said the king.

"You are a liar!" replied the courtier.

---

29. Matthew Paris, Mat. West. Chron. Duncl.

After this brief and decisive dialogue Leicester went to France, but his royal brother-in-law soon invited him back again.

On the 11th of June, 1258, there met, at Oxford, an assembly to which the Royalists gave the name of the Mad Parliament. There was a good deal of method in the madness of the members, for they appointed twenty-four barons and bishops as a committee of government. There was some insanity in the proposition to hold three sessions in a year, but it is doubtful whether Dr. Winslow, or any other eminent physician would have found, in the statutes passed at the time sufficient to form the foundation of a statute of lunacy. Henry seems to have been most in want of Dr. Winslow's care, for his majesty was exceedingly mad at the decisive measures of the barons, and would have been glad of an asylum where he would have been safe from their influence.

The Oxford Parliament, which was certainly an odd compound of good and bad, or light and dark—the regular Oxford mixture—passed some measures of a very miscellaneous character. The annual election of a new sheriff, and the sending to Parliament of four knights, chosen by the freeholders in each county, were judicious steps; but in some other respects the barons abused their power, and got a good deal of abuse themselves in consequence. The queen's relations and the king's half-brothers were literally scared out of the kingdom; but only to make way for the advancement of the friends and relatives of the Mad Parliament.

Soon after it met, Richard, who had emptied his pockets in Germany, wanted to come to England to replenish them. He was met at St. Omer by a messenger, stating that there would be no admittance unless he complied with the new regulations made by the barons. To this he reluctantly consented, and he joined his brother the king, with the full intention of organising an opposition, which he found already commenced by the Earl of Gloucester, who had grown jealous of Leicester's influence. Even at that early period the struggles between the "Ins and the Outs," which form the chief business of political life, had already commenced, and there was the same sort of shuffling from side to side, and principle to principle, which the observer of statesmanship at the present day cannot fail to recognise.

There was among all parties a vast protestation of regard for Magna Charta, which served the same purpose then as has since been answered by the British Constitution and the British lion. Henry, seeing with delight the divisions of the barons, got a bull from the pope to serve as a piece of india-rubber for his conscience, by rubbing out all the oaths he had taken at Oxford.

On the 2nd of February, 1261, he announced his intention of governing without the aid of the committee, and immediately went to the Tower, of which he took possession. He then dropped in at the Mint, where he emptied every till, and even waited, according to some, while a shilling, which was in the course of manufacture, got cool in the crucible. The Mint authorities were of course exceedingly obsequious, and may probably have offered to send him home a batch of new pennies that were not quite done, if his majesty desired it. "No, thank you," would have been Henry's reply, "I'll take what you've got;" and so he did, for off he marched with the whole of it.

The arbitrary conduct of the barons had somewhat disgusted the people, many of whom had discovered that one tyrant was not quite so bad as four-and-twenty. London declared for Henry, and Leicester ran away; but the vacillating cockneys soon declared for Leicester, which brought him back again. The king, who had been at such pains to secure the Tower, had the mortification to find it secured him, for he was safely locked up in it. Prince Edward, his son, flew to Windsor Castle, and the queen, his mother, was going down to the stairs at London Bridge to take a boat to follow him. She had shouted "Hi!" to the jack-in-the-water, and was stepping into a wherry, when she was recognised by the mob, who called after her as a witch, and pelted her with mud and missiles. The Lord Mayor, who happened to be passing, gallantly offered her his arm, walked with her to St. Paul's, and left her in the care of the doorkeeper. This anecdote is circumstantially given by all the chroniclers, among whom we need only mention Wykes, West, and Trivet—the correctness of the last being so remarkable that "right as a Trivet" is to this day a proverb. After a prodigious quantity of quarrelling between Henry and Son on one part, and Leicester and Co. on the other, the matters in dispute were referred to the arbitration of the French king, Louis the Ninth, who made an award in favour of Henry, which the barons of course refused to abide by. A civil war broke out with great fury, in which the Jews were victimised by both parties, though opposed to neither. They were slaughtered by the barons for being attached to the king, and were also slaughtered by the king's party for being attached to the barons. If they were attached to either it certainly was one of the most unfortunate attachments we ever heard of, and the strength of the attachment must have been great which could have survived such horrible treatment.

On the 14th of May, 1264, the king's party and that of Leicester met in battle. His majesty was at Lewes, in a hollow, where he thought himself deep enough to have got into a position of safety. The earl was upon the Downs, which Wykes calls a "downy move," for the spot was raised and commanded a view of the movements of the sovereign.

Leicester commenced the attack, which soon became general. Prince Edward charged the London militia, who could have charged pretty well in return if they had been behind their counters; but they had no idea of selling their lives at any price. They accordingly fled in all directions and the prince paid them off all he owed them for the manner in which they had served his mother. Leicester concentrated his force upon the king to whom he gave personally a sound thrashing.

Having cudgelled the king to his heart's content, he took him into custody. Prince Edward was seized, but the latter escaped on the Thursday in Whitsun week, 1265, and raised a powerful force, with which he marched to Evesham against his father's enemies.

Leicester had formed a camp near Kenilworth, and having got the king still in his possession, he encased the poor old man in armour, put him on a horse, and turned him into the field on the morning of the battle. The veteran was soon dismounted, and was on the point of being killed, when he roared out "Hollo! stop! I am Henry of Winchester!" His son recognising his voice, seized him and literally bundled him into a place of safety. "What do you do here?" muttered Edward, somewhat annoyed, but the aged Henry could not explain a circumstance which might have played old Harry with the cause of the Royalists. Leicester's horse fell under him, but the earl bounding to his feet, continued to fight, until finding the matter getting serious, he paused to inquire whether the Royalists gave quarter. "There is no quarter for traitors," was the only reply he received, followed by a poke in the shape of a home-thrust from the sword of one of the enemy. Deprived of their leader, Leicester's followers had nothing to follow, and the Royalists obtained a victory. The king was now restored to power, but there were still a few rebels in the forest of Hampshire, one of whom, named Adam Gourdon, came to a personal contest with Prince Edward, who got him down, placed his foot on his chest, and generously restored him to liberty. Gourdon was introduced to the queen the same night as a sort of prize rebel, and became a faithful adherent to the royal family.

Henry was now left at home all by himself, his son Edward having gone to Palestine. The old man often wrote to request the prince to return, for his majesty found himself unequal to the bother of ruling a people still disposed to be occasionally turbulent. A sedition had broken out at Norwich, which Henry had gone to quell, and he was on his way back to London, when he was laid up at St. Edmund's Bury by indisposition. Being considered a slight illness, it was at first slighted, but the royal patient became worse, and he died on the 16th of November, 1272, at the respectable age of sixty-eight, according to one historian,[30] sixty-four according to a second,[31] and sixty-six according to a third.[32] The last seems to be the nearest to the truth, for Henry had been a king about fifty-six years, and he was about ten when he came to the throne. He was buried at Westminster Abbey, where for nothing on Sundays and for twopence on week days, posterity may see his tomb.

The character of Henry the Third was an odd compound, a species of physiological grog, a mixture of generous spirit and weak water, the latter predominating over the former in a very considerable degree. He was exceedingly fond of money, of which he extracted such enormous quantities from his subjects that if the heart and the pocket were synonymous, as they have sometimes been called, Henry would have had the fullest possession of the hearts of his people. His manner must have been rather persuasive; for if the Parliament refused a subsidy at first they were always talked over by his majesty, and made to relax their purse-strings before the sitting closed. Some gratitude may perhaps be due to him on account of his patronage of literature, for he started the practice of keeping a poet, in an age

---

30. Macfarlane.
31. Hume.
32. Rapin.

when poets found considerable difficulty in keeping themselves. The bard alluded to was one Master Henry, who received on one occasion a hundred shillings,[33] and was subsequently "ordered ten pounds;" but, considering the unpunctuality of the king in money matters, it was doubtful whether the order for ten pounds was ever honoured. The persecution of the Jews was among the most remarkable features of the career of the king, who used to demand enormous sums of them, and threatened to hang them if they refused compliance. In this he only followed the example of his father, John, who, it is said, demanded ten thousand marks of an unfortunate Jew, one of whose teeth was pulled out every day, until he paid the money. It is said by Matthew Paris,[34] that seven were extracted before the cash was forthcoming. This was undoubtedly the fact, but it is not generally known that, with the cunning of his race, the Jew contrived to get some advantage out of the treatment to which he was subjected. It is said that he exclaimed, after the last operation had been performed, "They don't know it, but them teeth was all decayed. There's not a shound von among the lot, so I've done 'em nicely;" and with this piece of consolation, he paid the money.

To his reign has also been attributed the origin of the custom of sending deputies to Parliament to represent the commons, a practice that we find from looking over the list of the lower house, is liable to be in some cases greatly abused. "Take him for all in all," as the poet says, "we shall never"—that is to say, we hope we shall never—"look up on his like again."

33. Madox page 208.
34. Page 160.

CHAPTER THE SECOND

EDWARD THE FIRST, SURNAMED LONGSHANKS

dward was the first king who came to the throne like a gentleman, without any of that indecent clutching of the crown and sacking of the treasury which had been practised by almost every one of his predecessors. Perhaps his absence from England was the chief cause of this forbearance; but it is at all events refreshing to meet with a sovereign whose accession was not marked by a burglary upon the premises where the public treasure happened to be deposited.

On the 20th of November, 1272, four days after his father's death, Edward was proclaimed king by the barons at the New Temple. It was probably under the shade of the old fig-tree in Fig-Tree Court that they read his titles of King of England, Lord of Ireland, and Duke of Aquitaine. Edward had been engaged in the crusades, as one of those fighting missionaries who conveyed "sermons in stones" through the medium of slings, and knocked unbelief literally upon the head with the Christian battle-axe. One day he nearly lost his life, by the hands of an assassin, disguised as a postman from the Emir of Jaffa, who, feigning a wish to be converted, had opened a correspondence with Edward.

Edward's Arm in the hands of his Medical Advisers.

The English prince was lying in his *robe-de-chambre* on a couch, when the usual salaam—the emir's postman's knock—was made at the door of his apartment. The messenger had brought a letter, of which Edward had scarcely broken the wax, when his doom was nearly sealed by a blow from a dagger, hidden in the postman's sleeve. The prince parried the attack with his arms, which were his only weapons, until, wresting the dirk from his assailant's hands, he used it to put a period to the existence of the would-be murderer, by a process of punctuation which no grammarian has attempted to describe.

Edward's wound was not deep, but his enemies had been deep enough to introduce some venom into it. When he heard the fact he gave himself up to despair, for he considered that his existence was irretrievably poisoned. A romantic story is told of Queen Eleanor having sucked the poison from her husband's arm, but it is quite certain that such succour was never afforded him, and the anecdote is therefore not worth the straw that the operation would have required.

The prince owed his recovery to the prompt attendance of an English surgeon, who happened to be settled at Acre, and to some drugs supplied by the Grand Master of the Templars, who opened his heart and his chest—of medicine—for the relief of the suffering Edward. There is no doubt that Eleanor had sufficient affection for her husband, to have prompted her to draw the poison into her mouth had it ever entered her head; but the fact appears to be that the remedy was never thought of until a century after the infliction of the wound, which was a little too late to be of service to the patient, though nothing is ever too late to be made use of by the chroniclers. The notion was too good to be rejected by these very credulous gentlemen, who are easily induced to convert might have been, into has been, when the latter course is better adapted for exciting an agreeable interest.

Feeling tolerably secure of the throne, he was in no hurry to take possession, but enjoyed an agreeable tour before returning to England. He paid a visit to the new pope, his old friend Theobald, though there was some difficulty in getting into Theobald's road, for his holiness had left Rome for Civita Vecchia. Edward spent some time in Italy, for among the many irons he had in the fire were two or three Italian irons, which he desired to look after before arriving in his own country. He next visited Paris, and instead of coming straight home with the diligence that might have been expected, he turned back to Guienne, where he was invited by the Count of Chalons to a tournament.

"'Twas in the merry month of May," in the year 1274, "When bees from flower to flower did hum," exactly as they do in the present day, that the parties met lance to lance, each attended by a host of champions. Edward brought one thousand with him, but the Count of Chalons came with two thousand, an incident which at once raised a suspicion that the chivalrous knight intended foul play towards his royal antagonist. A tournament in sport soon became a battle in earnest, and the count rushed upon Edward, grasping him by the neck to embrace the opportunity of unhorsing him. Nothing, however, could make him resign his seat, and the Count of Chalons was soon licking the dust, or rather, the saw-dust spread over the arena in which the tournament was given. Edward was so angry at the trick which had been played that he hit his antagonist several times while down, and kept hammering at the armour of the count like a smith at an anvil. The Count of Chalons roared out lustily for mercy, but Edward refusing to grant it, continued to "give it him" in another sense for several minutes. At length the count offered to surrender his sword, which was ignominiously rejected by the English king, who called up a common foot soldier to take away the dishonoured weapon.

It was not till the year 1274 that Edward thought of returning to England, and he sent over to order his coronation dinner on a scale that would have done honour to a mayoral banquet. The bill of fare included so many heads of cattle that the shortest way to get through the cooking would have

Edward and the Count of Chalons.

been to light a fire under Leadenhall Market, and roast the whole of the contents by a single operation. If such a feast had really taken place, it was enough to put the times out of joint for a twelvemonth afterwards. On the 2nd of August, 1274, Edward arrived at Dover, and on the 19th of the same month he was crowned at Westminster Abbey, with his wife, Eleanor. This was the wonderful woman who was erroneously alleged to have sucked the poison from her husband's arm, a feat that has had no parallel in modern times, if we except the individual who undertook to swallow liquid lead and arsenic before a generous British public, and who, by surviving the operation, gave great offence to a portion of the enlightened audience. Edward, on coming to England, found plenty of loyalty, but very little cash; and though he had no objection to reign in the hearts of his people, he felt the necessity of making himself also master of their pockets. A crown without money would have been a mere tin kettle, tied to the head, instead of the tail, of the unlucky dog who might be compelled to wear it.

The king turned his attention to the unfortunate Jews, who seemed to be tolerated in England as human bees, employed in collecting the sweets of wealth only for the purpose of having it taken away from them. Edward literally emptied them out of the kingdom, for the purpose of plundering their hives more effectually. He allowed some of them their travelling expenses out of England, but even this was more than they required in many cases, for the inhabitants of the ports saved the Jews the cost of their journey by most inhumanly drowning them.

Edward, however unjust himself, disliked injustice in others; and indeed, with the common jealousy of dealers on a very large scale, he seemed to desire a monopoly of all the robbery and oppression practised within his own dominions. In the year 1289, the judicial bench was disgraced by a set of extortioners whose existence we can scarcely comprehend in the present age, when a corrupt judge would be as difficult to find as the philosopher's stone, or as that desirable but impossible boon to the briefless barrister, perpetual motion. The Chief Justice of the King's Bench had actually encouraged his own servants to commit murder, for the sake of the fees that would accrue upon the trial, and, of course, the acquittal of the culprits. The Chief Baron of the Exchequer had kept all the money paid into court upon every action that had been tried, and was even discovered going disgraceful snacks with the usher in illegal charges upon suitors. As to the puisnes, they had been detected in selling their judgments *in banco* at so much a folio, and even hiring pickpockets to rob the leading counsel as they went out of court with their fees in their pockets. The Chancellor had spent the money of nearly all his wards, and would never fix a day for a decree until he was positively forced, when he would pronounce a decision unintelligible to all parties. These disgraceful proceedings were made a pretext by the king for taking eighty thousand marks from the judges, his majesty observing that if he took from them all the marks they possessed, he could not remove the stains from their characters. This shallow sophism, though it might have satisfied the king himself, was not consolatory to the judges, nor was it calculated to reimburse the people for the losses sustained by judicial delinquency.

It is said that the first clock placed opposite the gate of Westminster Hall was purchased with a fine of eight hundred marks upon the Chief Justice of the King's Bench, and the popular saying "that's your time of day" is supposed to have arisen from a sarcasm that used to be addressed by the crowd outside to the judicial delinquent.

As a measure of further extortion, Edward became suddenly very particular as to the titles by which the nobles held their estates, and sent round commissioners to demand the production of the deeds by which the barons acquired their property. Earl de Warenne was called upon among the rest, and desired that the commissioners

Earl de Warenne producing his title to the Commissioners

might be politely shown in to him. "So, gentlemen," he mildly observed, "you wish to see the title by which I hold my property."

"Exactly so," was the reply, which was followed by a commonplace expression of sorrow at being obliged to trouble him. "It is no trouble in the least," rejoined Earl de Warenne, drawing a tremendous sword, which he brandished before the eyes of the commissioners, and begged their close inspection of the title by which his ancestors had acquired his possessions.

"You see, gentlemen," he continued, "there is no flaw to be detected, and if after looking at my title you want a specimen of my deeds, I can very speedily give you the satisfaction you require." The historian need scarcely add that the commissioners backed out, with an observation, "that a mere abstract of the title—a drawing of the sword out of its scabbard—was all that could possibly be required." Edward having other fish to fry, had hitherto neglected Wales, but that land of mountains was a scene of frequent risings, which he now determined to "put down" with promptitude and vigour. Llewellyn, the Prince of North Wales, was summoned to London to do homage as a tributary to the English crown, but his ambition having been fired by some prophecies of the famous Merlin, the fiery Welshman sent word that he would not come so far to see Edward, which was equivalent to a declaration that he would see him further. The English king having resolved to punish so much insolence, about Easter, 1277, crossed the Dee—not the sea, as some historians have alleged—with a large army and blocked poor Llewellyn up in his own principality. His brother David having been made an English baron, and married to the daughter of an English earl, was at first devoted to the English, but his native breezes fanned the still dormant flame of patriotism, and he joined his brother in resisting the foreign enemy. Edward occupied Anglesey, but in crossing over to the mainland he found himself in the most dreadful straits at the Menai. He lost several hundred men, and was obliged to fly for protection to one of his castles, but a king in those days could make every Englishman's house his castle, by unceremoniously walking into it. Llewellyn was somewhat emboldened by partial success, and foolishly advanced to the valley of the Wye, without anyone knowing wherefore. Roger, the savage Earl of Mortimer, was immediately down upon him, and sacrificed him before he had time even to put on his armour, in which he was only half encased when he was cruelly set upon by the enemy. He had buckled on his greaves, and was in the act of putting on his breast-plate over his head when he was decapitated with the usual disregard which was at that time continually shown to the heads of families. His brother David kept cutting about the country with his sword in his hand for at least six months, until he was basely betrayed into the hands of the English. He was condemned to die the death of traitors, which included a series of barbarities too revolting to mention. This sentence, which formed a precedent in the punishment of high treason for many ages, is one of the most disgraceful facts of our history. It casts a stigma upon every Parliament and every generation of the people in whose time this fearful penalty either was or might have been inflicted.

The leek of Wales was now entwined with the rose of England, and Edward endeavoured to propitiate his newly acquired subjects by becoming a resident in the conquered country. His wife Eleanor gave birth to a son in the castle of Caernarvon, and he availed himself of the circumstance to introduce the infant as a native production, giving him the title of Prince of Wales, which has ever since been held by the eldest son of the English sovereign.

After remaining about a year in Wales, Edward was enabled by the tranquillity of the kingdom to take a Continental tour, in the course of which he was often appealed to

King Edward introducing his Son as Prince of Wales, to his newly acquired Subjects.

as a mutual friend by sovereigns between whom there was any difference. He acted as arbitrator in the celebrated cause of Anjou against Aragon; but while settling the affairs of others, his own were getting rather embarrassed, and he was compelled in the year 1289 to return to England.

Upon reaching home he found that Scotland was in that state of weakness which offered an eligible opportunity to a royal plunderer. The king, Alexander the Third, had died, leaving a little grandchild of the name of Margaret, as his successor. This young lady was the daughter of Eric, king of Norway, who wrote over to Edward, requesting he would do what he could for her in case of her title being disputed. The English sovereign, with a cunning worthy of a certain French old gentleman whom we need not name, recommended a marriage with his son as the best mode of protecting the royal damsel. The preliminaries were all arranged, and Eric had agreed to forward the little Margaret, who was only eight years of age, by the first boat from Norway to Britain. The child had been shipped and regularly invoiced, when she fell ill, and being put ashore at one of the Orkney Islands, she unfortunately died.

On the death of the queen being made known, claimants to the Scottish crown started up in all directions, and it was necessary to find the heir by hunting among the descendants of David of Huntingdon. John Baliol was the grandson of David's eldest daughter, and John's grandmother therefore gave Baliol a right to the crown, which was disputed by Bruce and Hastings, the sons of the youngest daughters of Huntingdon senior, whose only son, Huntingdon junior, died without issue. An opening was thus left to the female tranches, and the introduction of those charming elements of discord—the ladies—into the question of succession, created, of course, all the confusion that arose.

Edward, having advanced to Norham, a small town on the English side of the Tweed, which, as everyone knows, forms a kind of Tweedish wrapper for Scotland, appointed a conference, which took place on the 10th of May, 1291, at which he distinctly stated that he intended regulating the succession to the Scotch throne. At this meeting Edward himself proposed the first resolution, which pledged the assembly to a recognition of the right of the English king not only to do what he liked with his own, but to do what he liked with Scotland also, which did not belong to him. One gentleman, in the body of the assembly, who remains anonymous to this day, ventured to suggest by way of amendment that no answer could be made while the throne was vacant, and an adjournment until the next morning was agreed upon. No business was, however, done on the morrow, but a further postponement till the 2nd of June was eventually carried. When that day arrived the attendance was numerous and highly respectable, for on the platform we might have observed no less than eight competitors for the crown. Robert Bruce, who was there in excellent health and spirits, publicly declared his readiness to refer his claims to Edward's arbitration, and all the other claimants did the same. On the next day, Baliol made his appearance and followed the example of the others, and it was agreed that one hundred and four commissioners should be appointed to inquire and report to Edward previous to his giving his final award. There is little doubt that this enormous number of commissioners could only have been intended to mystify the case, and to leave Edward at liberty to settle it his own way; a suspicion that is still further justified by his having reserved the right to add, without any limit or restriction, to the number of commissioners, and thus make "confusion worse confounded" should occasion require.

The wily Edward, pretending that it was necessary to the performance of his duty as arbitrator, got the kingdom, the castles, and other property surrendered into his hands on the 11th of June; though the Earl of Angus refused to give up Dundee and Forfar without an indemnity, which he stoutly stuck up for, and eventually obtained. None of the clergy joined in this disgraceful concession but the Bishop of Sodor, who ought to have been the very first to effervesce. The king himself went to the principal towns in Scotland with the rolls of homage, which were allowed to lie for signature, and he sent attorneys, empowered to take affidavits, into the various villages.

At length, on the 3rd of August, the commissioners met for the despatch of business, and, of course, came to no decision. In the year following they tackled the subject again, but it was found that the more they talked about it, the more they differed. Edward, by way of complicating the affair still further, summoned a Parliament to meet at Berwick on the 15th of October, 1292, at which Bruce and Baliol were fully heard, when the assembly laid down a general proposition that the lineal descendant of the eldest sister, however remote in degree, was preferable to the nearer in degree, if descended from a younger sister. This decision left everything undecided, and accordingly Edward gave judgment that

Baliol should be king of Scotland, with the simple proviso that Edward should be king of Baliol. The whole affair having been "a sell" got up between the English sovereign and the Scottish claimant, there was no demur on the part of the latter, who swore fealty, as he would have sworn that black was white, had such been the purport of the oath that his master required.

Edward took every opportunity of bullying Baliol, and even ordered him to come all the way to Westminster to defend an action brought against him for money due from Alexander the Third, his greatgrandfather. He was also served with process in the paltry suit of self *ats* Macduff; and other writs, to which he was forced to appear in person, were continually served upon him. For the smallest pecuniary claim the Scotch king was compelled to come to England to plead, until his patience at last gave way, and he turned refractory.

Edward was now at war with Philip of France, whom Baliol agreed to serve by harassing their mutual enemy. The Scotch king, who was at heart a humbug and a coward to the core, became exceedingly insolent, from the belief that Edward was somewhat down, and the proper time had arrived for hitting him. The English sovereign, who had been harassed at first by the Scotch cur, soon brought him howling for mercy, which was accorded on condition of his resigning the kingly office, a proposition which Baliol basely submitted to. Edward made a triumphal progress through Scotland, and taking a fancy to an old stone, upon which the kings had sat to be crowned at Scone, caused the very uncomfortable coronation chair to be removed to Westminster.[35] The people of Scotland had always considered this block to be the corner-stone of their liberties, and its removal seemed to take away the only foundation that their hopes of regaining their independence were built upon. As long as it was in their country, they believed it would bring them good fortune; but they dreaded the reverse if the stone should be removed even so far as a stone's throw from the borders of Scotland. Edward having appointed the Earl de Warenne governor of the vanquished kingdom, and given away all the appointments that were vacant to creatures of his own, returned in triumph to England.

In the year 1297 William Wallace, commonly known as the hero of Scotland, made his first appearance on the stage of history as a supernumerary, carrying a banner, for we find him engaged in unfurling the standard of liberty. He was at first merely the captain of a small band of outlaws—a sort of first robber—in the great drama in which he was soon to sustain a principal character. He was the second son of Sir William Wallace, of Ellerslie, and had all the qualities of a melodramatic hero, so far at least as we are enabled to judge by a description of him written a hundred years after his death with that minuteness which the old chroniclers were so fond of adopting when they knew that no one had the power of contradicting them. The celebrated Bower, who continued the Scotichronicon of Fordun, tells us that Wallace was "broad-shouldered, big-boned, and proportionately corpulent," so that his shoulders were broad enough to bear the burden he undertook; and his being corpulent gave him this advantage over his enemies, that if they had fifty thousand lives, he had undoubtedly "stomach for them all."

Mr. Tytler, who will perhaps excuse us for venturing on Tytler's ground, informs us in his History of Scotland that "Wallace had an iron frame," so that we have the picture of the man at once before us. For a quarrel with an English officer he had been banished from his home, and by living in fastnesses he acquired some of those loosenesses which are inseparable from a roving character. His followers comprised a few men of desperate fortunes and bad reputation, who had turned patriots, as gentlemen in difficulties generally do; for it is a remarkable fact that the men who endeavour to discharge a debt to their

Portrait of William Wallace, from an old Wood Block.

35. Hemingford.

country are those who never think of discharging the debts which they owe to their creditors. Success, however, covers a multitude of sins, and Wallace with his little band of outlaws, having achieved one or two small triumphs, soon found out the fact that the world which sneers at the very noblest cause in its early struggles, will always be ready to join it in the moment of victory. Wallace having been fortunate in his efforts, soon had the co-operation of Sir William Douglas and all his vassals; just as Mr. Cobden and the Anti-Corn-Law League, after having been denounced as turbulent demagogues, and threatened with prosecution, were assisted on the eve of the fulfilment of their object by the leaders of the Opposition and the principal members of the Government.

Edward, who had been in Flanders during the commencement of the Scotch rebellion, now returned to England, and by way of propitiating his subjects, he summoned a Parliament, at which Magna Charta was again voluntarily confirmed. It is true he made a cunning effort to insert at the end of it the words "saving always the rights of our crown,"[36] which would have been almost equivalent to striking out all the other clauses of the document. The Parliament hotly opposed the crafty suggestion, which was accordingly withdrawn, and supplies for carrying on the war against the Scotch insurgents were readily granted. In the summer of 1298, Edward came in person to Scotland at the head of a large army. Wallace, instead of waiting for a battle, retired slowly before the forces of the English king, clearing off all the provisions on the way, and thus aiming a blow at the stomach of the enemy. The invaders advanced, but there was nothing to eat; or as Mr. Tyler well expresses it, "they found an inhospitable desert" where—he might have added—they had occasion for a hospitable dinner. Wallace was now at Falkirk, from which he meditated an attack upon the king, but Edward, having been apprised of his intention, reflected that it was a game at which two could play, and he thought it as well to secure the first innings. The English king accordingly, finding the ball at his foot, took it up immediately, and at once bowled out the Scottish hero. The battle of Falkirk was fought on the 22nd of July, 1298, and the Scotch loss is variously stated at ten, fifteen, and sixty thousand men. In ordinary matters it is sometimes safe to believe half that we hear, but it would be more judicious to limit one's trust to ten per cent, in the records of history.

The Scotch war had of course been a very expensive business, and Edward had been sponging upon his subjects to an alarming extent during its continuance. In 1294 he had taken from the clergy half their incomes and nearly all their eatables. His purveyors first emptied their granaries, then robbed their farm-yards and ultimately pillaged their pantries; so that the king having already ransacked their pockets, the "reverend fathers," as he insultingly termed them, were in a very pretty predicament. Their larders were laid waste, their safes were no longer safe, they could not preserve their jam, their corn was instantly sacked, and even their joints of meat, from the leg to the loin, were walked off or pur-loined by the order of the sovereign. The pope, who had been applied to for protection when they were being deprived of their cattle, sent over a bull, which proved of very little use, for he soon despatched a second, by which the first was recalled in all its most important provisions.

The trading classes were not so easily robbed, for when the king began to deal with them in his own peculiar fashion, he found them rather awkward customers. Some wool had been prepared for shipping by the London merchants, when the king's agents came woolgathering to the wharfs, and carried it off with a high hand for the use of the sovereign. It is true they promised to pay, and ordered the owners to put it down to the bill; but the traders determined that they could not do business in that manner. They were joined by some of the nobles, and among others by Hereford, the constable, and Norfolk, the marshal of England, who had a joint audience of his majesty, who threatened to hang them if they did not do his bidding. "I will neither do so, nor hang, sir king," was Norfolk's reply, in which Hereford acquiesced; so that it was evident Edward could neither trample on the marshal, nor any longer overrun the constable. Thirty bannerets and fifteen hundred gentlemen whom the king had dubbed knights joined the two nobles in their refusal to dub up,[37] and Edward was left almost alone. In this dilemma he appealed to the people by the old trick of an effective speech, interlarded with those clap-traps which he knew so well how to employ. He caused a platform to be erected at the door of Westminster Hall,

36. Rapin, vol. iii., p. 72, second edition, quarto, 1727.
37. Heming.

and appeared upon it, supported by his son Edward, the Archbishop of Canterbury, and the Earl of Warwick. Like the schoolmaster who never administered a flogging without saying it hurt him a great deal more than the boy, the king told the people that it was more grievous to him to exact taxes from his dear people than it could be to them to bear the burden. "I am going," he exclaimed, "to expose myself to all the dangers of war for your sakes," and here he pulled out his pocket-handkerchief, behind which he winked at the Archbishop of Canterbury, who thrust his tongue into his cheek to show the prelate's relish for his master's hypocrisy.

"If I return alive," continued the royal humbug, "I will make you amends for the past; but if I fall, here is my dear son (step this way, Ned), place him on the throne (hold your head up, stupid), and his gratitude (bow, you blockhead) will be the reward of your fidelity." Here he fairly swamped his face in tears, while the archbishop turned on a couple of fountains, which came gushing through his eyes, and the meeting was literally dissolved by the practice of this piece of crying injustice towards the people. Not only had he melted the hearts of the traders by this manouvre, but he drew streams of coin for the liquidation of his debts from their pockets. With the cash thus collected he started to join Guy, Earl of Flanders, against Philip le Bel, a very pretty sort of fellow, between whom and Edward there was a contest for the possession of the daughter of the Guy, the fair Philippa. The English king had, as early as 1294, contracted a marriage for the Prince of Wales with this young lady, who was only nine when the match was agreed upon. The happiness of the Flemish infant of course went for nothing in the game of craft and ambition which was being played by the intriguing French king, who had no other object but the extension of his personal influence. Though he may have been the first, he was certainly not the last Philip on the throne of France to force the inclinations of royal children on the subject of marriage for his own purposes.

Edward the Fourth had expended a large amount of English money in purchasing the support of foreign mercenaries, who had no sooner spent their wages than they discontinued their services. The English king, finding he was likely to get the worst of it, concluded a truce in the spring of 1298, and left the unfortunate Guy to fight his own battles.

Before Edward's return home, the London citizens refused to pay the taxes, on the ground of their not having been imposed by the consent of Parliament. Many a tax-gatherer lost his time and his temper in going from door to door, and was told, tauntingly, to collect himself, when he sought to collect money for the royal treasury. The king, who was at Ghent, tried the never-failing experiment of another confirmation of Magna Charta, with the addition of what he called—in a private letter to his son—"a little one in," namely, a confirmation of the Statute *de Tallagio non concedendo*, which was an act declaring that no talliage or aid should be levied without the consent of the Parliament. This was the first occasion upon which the nation was formally invested with the sole right of raising the supplies, but the investment, after all, was not particularly eligible, as the sole right of raising the supplies carries with it the sole duty of finding the money. Not content with his confirmation of the charter, Edward, in May, 1298, was called upon to ratify, at York, the confirmation itself, and thus spread with additional butter the constitutional bacon. This he for some time evaded by a series of paltry excuses, in which "head-ache," "previous engagement," and "out of town," were pleaded from time to time, until the barons, by following him up, got him into a *cul*

Tax Collecting in the Reign of Edward the First.

de sac from which there was no escaping. He consented at last to ratify, but, in the most dishonourable manner, he contrived while signing to smuggle in a clause at the end, which, by saving the right of the Crown, rendered the whole document a wretched nullity. This was a trick he was much addicted to, for he had tried the paltry subterfuge on a previous occasion. The barons, when they saw the addition, merely shook their heads, murmured something about "a do," and returned to their homes; but Edward thought he should find no difficulty in coming over the citizens. He accordingly called a meeting in St. Paul's Churchyard, when the confirmation was read over, amid cheers, and cries of "Hear" at the end of every clause, until the last, when the shouts of "Shame!" "No, no!" "It's a dead swindle!" and "Don't you wish you may get it?" became truly terrible. Edward retained his usual self-possession during the meeting, but expressed, in side speeches to his attendants, his fears that the citizens were not such fools as he had taken them for. Making a virtue of necessity—though, by the way, virtues made out of that material very seldom appear to fit, but sit very awkwardly on the wearer—he withdrew the offensive clause at a Parliament that was held soon after Easter.

Edward and Philip, finding it convenient to make up their differences, threw overboard their respective allies, the French king giving up the Scots, and the English sovereign completely sacrificing the poor old Guy of Flanders. This earl has got the name of the Unfortunate, but he better deserves the title of the soft Guy, the silly Guy, or the Guy that, if there happened to be a difficulty within his reach, was sure to blunder into it. He had twice been fool enough to accept an invitation from Philip, and had twice been detained as a prisoner. We therefore have little sympathy with him when we hear of his being deserted by Edward; for "the man who" will continually run his head into a noose, must expect to find the stringency of the string at some time or another.

Peace was made between the French and English kings by means of two marriages; but it seems rash to calculate upon matrimony as a source of quietude. Edward, who was a widower, married Philip's sister, Margaret, and the Prince of Wales was affianced to little Isabella, aged only six years, the daughter of the French sovereign. A treaty was concluded between the two countries on the 20th of May, 1303, by which Edward took Guienne, and gave up Flanders. The unhappy Guy was sent thither to negotiate a peace with his own subjects, but, like everything else he undertook, the poor old man made a sad mess of it. Returning to Philip with the news of his failure, he was committed to prison, which really, considering all things, seems to have been the best place for him. He was, at all events, out of harm's way, and prevented from doing mischief to himself and others by his provoking stupidity. He remained in custody till he died, but it was said of him by a contemporary that he was never known to "look alive" during the whole of his existence.

Edward, having settled his dispute with France, had time to turn his attention to Scotland, which had always been his "great difficulty," as Ireland became the "great difficulty" to England at a later period. The English king advanced against the Scotch in a sort of hop-scotch style, first making for the North, then returning to the South, or going to the East, in a zig-zag direction. The Scots soon surrendered, and were allowed to go scot-free, with a very few exceptions. Stirling Castle proved itself possessed of sterling qualities. It held out against the besiegers with determined obstinacy, and Edward himself came to assist by throwing stones, which caused the remark to be made that the king had been brought to a very pretty pitch through the audacity of the Scotch rebels. When the provisions were exhausted, the garrison made an unprovisional surrender, and the governor gave out that he gave in, with all his companions. Wallace, having been betrayed into Edward's power, was cruelly murdered; but within six months of his death, Liberty, like a new-born infant, was in arms once more in Scotland. Robert Bruce, the grandson of old Bruce, was the new champion of his native land, and intrusted his scheme to Comyn. The latter proved treacherous, and Bruce, seeing what was Comyn, or rather, what Comyn was, killed him right off out of the way, in a convent at Dumfries. Young Bruce having mustered a party of about a dozen friends, took an excursion with them to Scone, where, in the course of a kind of picnic party, he was crowned on the 27th of March, 1306, with some solemnity. Edward was at Winchester when he heard the news, and, though very far from well, he determined on being carried to Scotland. Like John, who had been dragged about the country in a horse-box till within a few hours of his death, Edward was packed on a litter and conveyed with care to Carlisle, whence he wished to be forwarded to Scotland. Making a desperate effort, he mounted his horse, and went six miles in four days, a pace which could only have been performed by an equestrian prodigy; for the slowest animal, unless he were a determined jibber, could scarcely have accomplished a task so difficult.[38] This anything but "rapid act of horsemanship" was the last act of Edward's reign, for having got to Burgh upon the Sands, he found the sand of his existence had run out, on the 7th of July, 1307. He had lived sixty-eight years, and had reigned during half that time; so that for him the stream of life had been a sort of half and half—an equal mixture—crowned by a frothy, foamy diadem.

His remains were, some short time afterwards, sent to Westminster, *via* Waltham, and were buried on the 8th of October, with those of his father Henry.

The character of Edward has been generally praised, but we are compelled to tender a bill of exceptions to the report of previous historians. He certainly added to his dominions, but if this is a merit, it may be claimed for any man who, by fraud or violence, increases his own property at the expense of his neighbours. The improvements effected in his reign were rather in spite of him than owing to his sense of justice or his liberality. He had the talent of talking people out of their money, but this quality he has only shared with many equally accomplished, but less exalted, swindlers. His attempt to smuggle a clause into Magna Charta, before the face of the citizens, was an act calculated to ruin him in the City, where putting one's hand to paper is a proceeding that must not be trifled with. His treatment of Wallace proves him to have been a cruel and vindictive enemy; his abandonment of the poor Earl of Flanders shows that he was an insincere and treacherous friend: he was constant to his hatreds, and fickle in his likings: his animosity had the strength of fire, but in him the milk of human kindness was greatly diluted with water. He made some good laws, such as the statute of mortmain, which was first passed in his reign, but so far from there being any truth in the proverb, *necessitas non habet legem*, it is certain that necessity produced nearly every good law that Edward gave to his people.

In person, he was a head taller than the ordinary size, with black hair that curled naturally, and eyes that matched the hair in colour.[39] His legs were too long in proportion to his body, which gained him the nickname of Longshanks, though it would have been more respectful to have called him Daddy Long-legs, in allusion to his being the father of his people.

He observed the outward decencies of life, but in this he evinced the strength of his hypocrisy rather than the extent of his morality. It may be worthy of remark that the title of baron, which had hitherto been common to all gentlemen who held lands of the crown, was in this reign restricted to those whom the king called to Parliament.[40] During the monarchy of Edward, Roger Bacon lived and died; but as we have already expressed our antipathy to putting butter upon Bacon, we refrain from any eulogy upon that illustrious character.

---

38. It is possible that the horse hired by the king on this occasion may have been accustomed to draw a fly, the owner of which may have been in the habit of charging by the hour.
39. Rapin, vol. iii., p. 88.
40. The last of the Non-Parliamentary barons is the well-known Baron Nathan of Kennington. He still claims a seat among the Piers of Gravesend and Rosherrille.

CHAPTER THE THIRD

EDWARD THE SECOND, SURNAMED OF CAERNARVON

dward the Second was, in common phraseology, a very nice young man when he came to the throne, being twenty-three years of age, and tolerably good-looking, though he turned out eventually, according to one of the chroniclers of the times, "a very ugly customer." His first step on coming to the throne was to send for a scamp named Piers Gaveston, a Gascon youth who was full of gasconade, and had been sent out of England by the late king as an improper character. Young Edward, who had been much attached to this early specimen of the gent., recalled Piers Gaveston, and made him a nobleman by creating him Duke of Cornwall, but never succeeded in making him a gentleman. This step was in direct violation of a solemn promise to Edward the First, who had warned his son against Gaveston, as a bad young man and by no means a desirable acquaintance for an English sovereign. Directly Piers arrived, he and his young master began to play all sorts of tricks and, by way of change, dismissed the Chancellor, the Treasurer, the Barons of the Exchequer, and all the Judges. The whole of the judicial staff of the kingdom being thrown out of employ, a panic was created in all the courts, and some of their lordships, being unable to meet the demands upon them, were compelled to go to prison. Many were stripped of all their property by the king, at the instigation of Gaveston, and the Chancellor not only lost the seals, but his watch, and a number of other articles of value. Edward and his friend were determined to pay off those who had been instrumental to the latter's disgrace, and among others, Langton, the Bishop of Lichfield, was put into solitary confinement, no one being allowed to speak to him, so that the unfortunate Lichfield found himself literally sent to Coventry. Gaveston, who was a dashing young spark, nearly sent England in a blaze by his return, for he was very far from popular. He could dance and sing, was passionately fond of bagatelle, and as to wine, when he took it into his head he could always drink his bottle.

Edward went over to Boulogne, in January, 1308, to get married to Isabella, the daughter of the king of France, and left Gaveston regent of the kingdom. His majesty soon got tired of a French watering-place, and returned to England for his coronation, which took place on the 24th of February, at Westminster. All the honours were showered upon Gaveston, and instead of giving the perquisites to the proper officers, the king handed them over, one by one, to the favourite. "Put that in your pocket, Piers, my boy," exclaimed Edward, as he transferred to his disreputable friend each article that some officer of state was entitled to. The English nobility, as they saw everything passing into the hands of the Gascon, could only murmur to each other, "What a shame!"

"That's mine, by rights!" and "Well, I never! Did you ever?" But the Bishop of Winchester gave his majesty a dose, by mixing up a pretty strong oath and making him swallow every word of it. He undertook of course to confirm the Charter, which really becomes quite a bore to the historian, who cannot help feeling something of the satiety induced by *toujours perdrix*, and he draws the humiliating conclusion that his countrymen, having got hold of a good thing, never knew when they had had enough of it. Gaveston's conduct became so overbearing that a regular British cry of "Turn him out!" resounded from one end of the kingdom to the other. Englishmen seldom do things by halves, and having once raised a shout, they did not desist from it, but to the howl of "Turn him out," they added a demand for the sovereign to "Throw him over!" With this requisition Edward reluctantly complied, and Gaveston was expelled from England; but only to be made Governor of Ireland, until the king could get the permission of the barons to allow the favourite to come back again. This, with their usual imbecility, they speedily agreed to, and Piers soon returned to the court, which he filled with buffoons and parasites. Any mountebank who could make a fool of himself was sure of an engagement at the palace. The king's horse-collars were worn out with being grinned through, and the family circle of royalty was never without a clown to the ring, under the management of Piers Gaveston. The favourite himself became so arrogant that he would dress himself up in the royal jewels,[41] wearing the crown instead of his own hat, and turning the sceptre into a walking-stick.

Edward, being in want of supplies, called a Parliament in 1309, but the Parliament would not come, which caused him to call again; and the more he kept on calling the more they kept on not coming, until the month of March, 1310, when they came in arms, for they were determined no longer to submit to Gaveston's insolence. He had offended their order by giving them all sorts of nicknames, which are less remarkable for their wit than their coarseness. He called the Earl of Lancaster an old hog, or, perhaps, a dreadful bore; to Warwick he gave the name of the Black Dog, in reply, perhaps, to an insinuation that he, Gaveston, was a puppy; and the Earl of Pembroke was alliteratively alluded to as "Joe the Jew," by the abusive but not very facetious favourite.

Edward the Second and his Favourite, Piers Gaveston.

In August, 1311, Edward met the barons at Westminster. Their lordships would seem to have all got out of bed on the wrong side on the morning of the assembly, for their surliness and ill-temper were utterly unparalleled. They prepared forty-one articles, to which they insisted on having the consent of his majesty. Of course, in the catalogue of claims our old friend Magna Charta was not forgotten. This glorious instrument of our early liberties, was once more touched up, and a new clause introduced, which imparted freshness to the document. It provided "that the king should hold a Parliament once a year, or twice if need be," as if the barons had been impressed with the idea that "the more the merrier" was a sound maxim of politics. The banishment of Gaveston was, however, the grand desideratum, and this was at length consented to by Edward, who on the 1st of November, 1311, took leave of the favourite. His majesty retired to York, but soon began to ask himself—"What's this dull town to me?" in the absence of Piers, who, in less than two months, was again sharing the dissipations of his sovereign. The royal party had gone for a change to Newcastle, when the cry of "somebody coming" disturbed the revels of the king and his courtiers. This unwelcome "somebody" was no less a personage than Edward's cousin, the Earl of Lancaster, who had arrived with a few barons for the purpose of, as they said, "giving it" to Gaveston. The king and the favourite escaped from Newcastle in a ship—probably a collier—but the sovereign was heartless enough to leave his wife behind him with the utmost indifference. It was *sauve qui peut* with the whole court, and the queen was lost in the general scamper. The favourite, after running as hard as he could, threw himself, quite out of breath, into Scarborough Castle, which was strong in everything but eatables, for the supply of provisions was perfectly contemptible. Piers Gaveston, who had never been accustomed to short commons, went to the window of the castle, and calling out to the Earl of Pembroke, who was waiting outside, proposed to capitulate. "Can we come to any terms?" cried Piers; but the earl would at first hear of nothing short of an unconditional surrender.

---

41. Il joignoit à cela une vanité ridicule, en effectant de porter sur sa personne les joyaux du Roi et delà couronne meme.—Rapin, vol. iii., p. 94.

After some parleying, Pembroke exclaimed, "I'll tell you what I'll do for you. If you choose to place yourself in my hands, I'll promise to take you to your own castle at Wallingford."

"You're not joking?" cried Gaveston, as he looked through the rusty bars of the fortress.

"Honour bright," was the substance of the earl's reply, and Piers put himself at once into the hands of Pembroke. It was arranged that the king should meet the favourite at Wallingford; but one morning, on the road, he was ordered out of bed at an unusually early hour, when whom should he see, upon going downstairs, but the grim Earl of Warwick! Gaveston began to feel that it was all up with him. Putting him on a mule, they conveyed him to Warwick Castle, where a hurried council was got up—the Duke of Lancaster in the chair—for his trial. He was, of course, condemned, when he threw himself for pardon at the feet of Lancaster, who kicked him aside, and all the rest gave him a lesson on the Lancastrian system by a similar indignity.

Parley between Piers Gaveston and the Earl of Pembroke.

A proposition was made in the body of the hall to spare his life, but somebody exclaimed that "Gaveston had been the cause of all their difficulties, and that, when a difficulty came in the way, the best plan was to break the neck of it." The stem justice of this remark was instantly acknowledged, and amid savage cries of "Bring him along!" they dragged the favourite off to Blacklow Hill, where, by removing his head from his shoulders, they made what may be called short work of him. Upon hearing the news, the king cried for grief and then cried for vengeance. After reconciling himself to his loss, he reconciled himself to the barons, and the double reconciliation was greatly assisted by the barons having given up to him the plate and jewels of the deceased favourite.

Edward, on looking round him, found that the "Scots whom Bruce had often led" were making considerable progress. The English king at once ordered an army to meet him at Berwick, and by a given day one hundred thousand men had assembled. Bruce had got scarcely forty thousand, so that the chances were more than two to one against him. He took them into a field near Bannockburn, and spread them out so as to make the very most of them. On Sunday, the 23rd of June, 1314, Edward and his army came in sight. After some desultory fighting, the monotony of the day's proceedings was relieved by a somewhat curious incident. Bruce, who seems to have been rather eccentric in his turn-out, was riding on a little bit of a pony, quite under the duty imposed upon it, in front of his troops. He wore upon his head a skullcap, over that a steel helmet, and over that a crown of gold, while in his hand he carried an enormous battle-axe. He and his Shetland were frisking about, when an English knight, one Henry de Bohun, or Boone, came galloping down, armed at all points, upon a magnificent British dray-horse. Bruce, instead of getting out of the way, entered into the unequal combat amid cries of "Go it, Bob!" from his own followers. He instantly fell upon and felled to the earth the English knight, amid the acclamations of the surrounding soldiers. The battle was very vigorously fought on both sides, and victory seemed doubtful, when suddenly there appeared on a hill, at the back of the Scotch, an immense crowd that looked like a new army. The group, in reality, consisted of nothing but a mob of suttlers and camp-followers, who had been kept back by Bruce to look like a tremendous reserve, and who might be called the heavy scarecrows of the Scotch army. The plan succeeded admirably, for although the English did not receive a single blow, they were completely panic-struck, which had the same effect as the severest beating. They fled in all directions, with the Scotch in hot pursuit; and it is said that Edward himself had to run for it as far as Dunbar, a distance of sixty miles, with the enemy after him.

According to the Scotch historians, the results of this victory were truly marvellous, for the number of prisoners alleged to have been taken is actually greater than the number of the combatants. The chariots and waggons, it is also said, would have extended for many leagues, if drawn up into a line; but this is merely one of those lengths which are too frequently gone to by the old chroniclers. Though it is impossible that the Scotch could have killed fifty thousand, and made double the number of prisoners out of one hundred thousand men (unless they manufactured fifty thousand additional foes as readily as Vauxhall can put forth its fifty thousand additional lamps), it is, nevertheless, certain that on this occasion England experienced the severest defeat it had encountered since the establishment of the monarchy. Such was the effect created by the battle of Bannockburn that for some time after three Scotchmen were considered equivalent to a hundred Englishmen. There is every reason to believe that the Scotch were exceedingly vigorous in coming to the scratch at that early period.

Encouraged by the success of his brother Robert in Scotland, Edward Bruce thought that the crown of Ireland was a little matter that would just suit him, and he accordingly passed over to the Green Isle, in the hope of finding it green enough to accept him as its sovereign. He was, for a time, successful in his project, and was actually crowned at Carrickfergus on the 2nd of May, 1316. But after knocking about the country, and being knocked about in the country, for a year and a half, he got a decisive blow from the English on the 5th of October, 1318, at Fagher, near Dundalk. Though he had landed in Ireland with only five hundred Scotchmen, he was left dead in the field with two thousand of his fellow-countrymen. He had been joined, no doubt, by several after his first arrival, but if he had not, it would have been all the same to the chroniclers, who would not have scrupled to kill the same individuals four times over to make a total sufficiently imposing for historical purposes. The historians would have been invaluable to a minister of finance, for they could always create an enormous surplus out of a vast deficiency.

The Scotch continued their successes until a truce was agreed upon for two years, and thus Edward had leisure to look after domestic affairs, which had been fearfully neglected. Since the death of Gaveston, the royal favourite, there had been just room for one in the not very capacious heart of the English sovereign. A certain Hugh Spencer had been introduced to the court by the barons, as a sort of page, to act as a spy upon the king, and it is a curious fact that the spencer, or jacket, has been the characteristic of the page from that time to the present. Hugh Spencer had a shrewd father, who advised his son to care no more for the barons, who had got him his place, but to work it to his own advantage, and make the most of the perquisites.

Young Hugh, taking the parental hint, determined on booking himself for the inside place in Edward's heart, which has been already alluded to as vacant. Not only did he succeed in his design, but contrived to take up his old father, and carry him along as a sort of outside passenger. Riches and promotion were showered on the Spencers, who adopted a coat of arms, and made themselves Despencers, by prefixing the syllable de, which can impart a particle of aristocracy to the most plebeian of patronymics. The Despencers had obtained such influence over the king that he allowed them to do as they pleased; and as they took all the good things to themselves, the nobles—who were getting nothing—began to evince considerable anxiety for the public interest.

The Earl of Lancaster, a prince of the blood, felt his order insulted by the promotion of the two plebeians, and he one day energetically exclaimed, "that Spencers could not have anything in tail, though the king might try to fasten it on to them." Lancaster marched upon London, and pitched his tent in Holborn, among the hills that abound in that locality. He gave out jocularly that "he had come to baste a couple of Spencers, by trimming their jackets," but he was saved the trouble by a Parliament, which met armed at Westminster, and passed on the two Despencers a sentence of banishment.

They were accordingly exiled in August, but came back in October, presenting an instance of a quick return without the smallest profit. Lancaster retired to the north, and was met at Boroughbridge by Sir Simon Ward and Sir Andrew Barclay, a couple of stout English knights, who stopped up the passage. Lancaster endeavoured to swim across the river, but the tide had turned against him, and he was taken prisoner. The unfortunate earl having been tried, was condemned to an ignominious death, and the mob were allowed to pelt him with mud on his way to execution—a privilege of which a generous public took the fullest advantage.

Edward had now to encounter opposition from a new quarter, or rather from two quarters, for his better half, Isabella, the sister of Charles le Bel, was now plotting against him. She left him under the pretence of going to settle some business for him in France, and then refused to return to him. Some ambassadors volunteered to bring her back, but the ambassadors never came back themselves, for they had been in league with the queen, and only wanted an opportunity of joining her.

Their conduct brings to mind the anecdote of a scene that once passed in the shop of a shoemaker. A stranger had tried on a pair of shoes, and another stranger had been trying on a pair of boots at the same moment. Suddenly the shoes decamped without payment, when the boots standing upon their professed swiftness, offered to go in pursuit of the unprincipled shoes; and as neither shoes nor boots were ever seen again by the tradesman, it is probable that the "false fleeting perjured Clarences" are still being pursued by the immortal Wellingtons. Thus the Earl of Kent, the king's own brother, the Earl of Richmond, his cousin, and others, who had undertaken to go after the queen to bring her back, remained with her, until she returned as an enemy to her own husband. Edward was now compelled to run away in his turn from his angry wife; and rather than encounter the fury of a domestic storm, he got into a ship with young Despencer, to brave the elements. Old Despencer was taken and hanged, without the ceremony of a trial.

The Prince of Wales was appointed guardian of the kingdom on account of the absence of his father, who had been regularly advertised, but had declined to come forward lest he should hear of something to his disadvantage. Having been tossed about upon the waves for several days, he came ashore on the coast of Wales, and hid himself for some weeks, with young Despencer and another, in the mountains of Glamorganshire. His two companions were one day startled by a cry of "We've got you!" and were instantly seized, upon which, Edward exclaiming, "It's no use: you've got the two birds in the hand, and may as well have the one in the bush," rolled out of a hedge and gave himself up to his pursuers.

Young Despencer was taken to Hereford, and hanged at once, upon a gallows fifty feet high; but why severity was carried to such a height is a question we have no means of answering. It has been brutally said by an annotator that the culprit had been accustomed to the high ropes during his life, and it was therefore determined that they should accompany him even to the gibbet.

The king was sent in custody to Kenilworth Castle, and Parliament met on the 7th of January, 1327, to consider what should be done with him. His deposition was a preliminary step; for it was the custom in those days to punish first and try the culprit afterwards. It was determined to place his son upon the throne in his stead, and on the 20th of January, 1327, a deputation went to Kenilworth to receive his abdication, if he liked to give it, or take it by force if he should prove refractory. The king, seeing Sir William Trussel, the Speaker, at the head of his enemies, observed calmly, but sadly, "Alas! the Trussel I depended upon for support has joined in dropping me." He renounced the regal dignity, and on the 24th of January, Edward the Third was proclaimed king, and crowned on the 29th at Westminster.

This proceeding is on many accounts remarkable, and of the utmost value, as settling a point of constitutional practice, which had never before been recognised. It established a precedent for dissolving under extraordinary circumstances the compact between the king and the people. It negatived the alleged "right divine of kings to govern wrong," and proved that it was not always necessary to take violent means for ridding a country of a tyrant. It showed that the crown might be removed from the head without taking off the head and all, which had been hitherto the recognised mode of effecting a transfer of the royal diadem.

The unhappy Edward was kept for a time at Kenilworth; but ultimately by command of Lord

Fancy Portrait of Inspector Baliol.

Mortimer, who had entire influence over the queen, the deposed king was removed to Berkeley Castle. Here it is believed he was most cruelly murdered, though it was given out by his keepers that his death was perfectly natural. He died on the 21st of September, 1327, in the forty-third year of his age, and the nineteenth of his reign. No inquiry took place, and although no coroner's inquest was held, "Wilful Murder against some person or persons unknown" is the almost unanimous verdict of posterity.

The character of this king has been said to have been chiefly disfigured by feebleness of judgment, which prevented him from knowing what was good for him. He managed, nevertheless, to find out what was bad for his subjects, and he was never at a loss to secure the means of enjoyment for himself and his favourites, at the expense of his people.

In the reign of Edward the Second the order of Knights Templars was abolished, a circumstance which arose from the king of France being short of cash, and casting a longing eye upon the rich possessions of the order. In France they were put to the torture to force them into confessions of crimes they had never committed; but in England the same effect was produced by imprisonment; for instruments of cruelty were never recognised by English laws, or encouraged as articles of British manufacture. The Archbishop of York finding nothing of the kind in the country, wished to send abroad for a pattern,[42] but it must be spoken to the credit of our ancestors that though, in a pecuniary sense, they were famous for applying the screw, the thumb-screw was never popular.

Rapin mentions among the great events of this reign, a tremendous earthquake, but it can have been no great shakes, for we do not find any details of its destructive effects in the old chronicles. It occurred on the 14th of November, 1320, to the unspeakable terror of all classes; but it did not swallow up half as much as is swallowed up annually on the 9th of November at the Mansion House in London.

---

42. Vide Rapin, vol. iii., p. 95, and also a Note in Lingard.

CHAPTER THE FOURTH

EDWARD THE THIRD

The young king did not upon his father's death come to the throne, for he had taken his seat upon the imperial cushion eight months before the decease of his by no means lamented parent. Mortimer had caused a medal to be struck in celebration of the accession of Edward the Third, in which he was represented receiving the crown, with the motto, "*Non rapit sed recipit*," which we need scarcely translate into "He did not snatch it, but got it honestly."[43] A council of regency was appointed, to which Mortimer, with affected modesty, declined to belong, but he and the queen did as they pleased with the affairs of government. Her majesty got an enormous grant to pay her debts, but knowing the extravagant and dishonest character of the woman, we have reason to believe that she pocketed the money and never satisfied the demands of her creditors. She obtained, also, an allowance of twenty thousand a year, which was better than two-thirds of the revenues of the crown; so that a paltry six-and-eightpence in the pound was the utmost that young Edward could have to live upon. The Earl of Lancaster was appointed guardian, and began doing the best for himself, after the approved fashion of the period. The attainders against the great Earl of Lancaster were of course reversed, and the confiscation of the estates of the Despencer afforded some very pretty pickings to the party that was now dominant.

Though the king was too young to govern, his admirers persuaded him that he was quite old enough to fight, and he was recommended to try his hand against Bruce, who was getting old; so that, in the language of the ring, the British pet was not very ill matched against the Scottish veteran. The Caledonian Slasher, as Bruce might justly have been called, had broken the truce agreed upon with Edward the Second, and had sent an army into Yorkshire, which plundered as it went every town and village. The stealing of sheep and oxen was carried on to such an extent by the Scotch troops that their camp resembled Smithfield market, or a prize cattle show. Sixty thousand men gathered round the standard of Edward, but the foreign and native troops quarrelled with such fury among themselves that they had little energy left to be expended on the enemy. Fortunately for the English king the vastness of his army made up for its want of discipline. Bruce, directly he saw the foe, waited only to take their number, and retired with the utmost rapidity, amusing himself with the Scotch favourite Burns, by setting fire to all the villages.

The English, instead of following the enemy, waited a night upon the road for some provisions expected by the Parcels Delivery, which had been delayed by some accident. The Scotch were thus allowed to get ahead, and Edward sent a crier through his camp, offering a hundred a year with the honour of knighthood to anyone who would apprise him of the place where he should find the opposing army. Thomas of Rokeby, so called from his habit of rokeing about, was successful in the search, and came galloping into the English camp with a loud cry of Eureka, and a demand of "money down," with knighthood on the spot, before he divulged his secret. "You're very particular, sir," said Edward, flinging him a purse, containing his annuity for the first year, and dubbing him a knight by a blow on the head from the flat of the sword, administered with unusual vehemence.

Thomas of Rokeby having pocketed the money, and secured the dignity, pointed to a hill three leagues off, observing, "There they are!", an observation which caused a general exclamation of "Well, it's very funny! To think that they should have been so near us all the while and we not aware of it!" The English having made for the spot, sent a challenge, inviting the Scotch to meet them in a fair open field,

---

43. It is a curious fact that Mortimer should have been in the medal line, a business in which his namesake of the house of Store and Mortimer has since become so illustrious.

Thomas of Rokeby receiving the honour of Knighthood.

but the proposition was declined, with thanks and compliments. The English, on the return of the herald, went to sleep, for the presence of the herald always had a soporiferous influence. Edward was exceedingly severe upon the occasion, and commented upon the herald's news, which the king declared was always most unsatisfactory. For three days and three nights, the English lay by the side of the river, having been thrown by the herald into a state of dreamy inactivity. At length, on the fourth day, they woke from their transient trance, when they found that the Scotch had once more changed their position. Edward moved higher up, keeping opposite to the foe, and the two armies lay facing each other for eighteen days and nights, like two great cowardly boys, both afraid of "coming on," but each assuming a menacing attitude. There is every reason to believe that the herald had mesmerised the whole of the English troops, for they allowed the Scotch to go away in the dead of the night for want of proper vigilance. The probability, however, is that both armies were illustrating the proverb that "none are so blind an those who won't see," and that their aversion to "come on," was mutual.

A truce was concluded, and Edward, according to Froissart, returned "right pensive" to London; but his "right pensiveness" may have been accounted for by the fact that he was on the eve of marriage. His mother had, during her visit to the Continent, arranged to wed him to Philippa of Hainault, a lady who, to judge from her portrait on her tomb in Westminster Abbey, was one of those monsters commonly called a "fine woman." This fineness in the female form consists of excessive coarseness, which is better adapted to the laundry than the domestic circle. She, however, made Edward an excellent better half—or perhaps a better two-thirds is a more suitable term to indicate the relative proportions of the royal couple. She was brought to London by her uncle John, surnamed of Hainault, and, it being Christmas-time, she was taken out to enjoy all the amusements of the festive season. Jousts and tournaments, balls and dinnerparties, were given in her honour during her stay in town; and on the 24th of January, 1328, the nuptial ceremony was performed with great solemnity.

Edward being now married, was desirous of avoiding that roving life which the constant pursuit of Bruce had rendered necessary. The English king thought it better to settle down into the domestic habits of a family man, which was impossible as long as he was compelled to be out all night, watching the foe and bivouacking with his soldiers. Bruce, who had grown old and gouty, was also eager for peace, which was concluded on the condition of his little boy, David, aged five, being married to Edward's little sister Joanna, aged seven. The English king gave up all claim to the sovereignty of Scotland, causing even the insignia of Scotch royalty to be carefully packed and forwarded to Bruce, who, on opening the parcel, was delighted to find himself in possession of the crown and sceptre of his predecessors. He did not, however, get quite the best of the bargain, for he undertook to pay thirty thousand marks into Edward's court as compensation, in the form of liquidated damages, for the mischief that the Scotch invaders had committed. Bruce had obtained a sort of letter of licence, allowing him to take three years for the payment of the sum agreed upon. A more formidable creditor, however, took him in execution, for he was called upon to pay the debt of nature within the ensuing twelvemonth. Mortimer, who had advised the peace with Scotland, which was by no means popular, got himself created Earl of March, for it is the policy of crafty politicians to obtain rewards for their most objectionable measures.

It will be remembered that the Earl of Lancaster had been appointed guardian of the young king, but no scapegrace in a comedy ever made such an undutiful ward as the youthful Edward. He remained with his mother and Mortimer, the latter of whom was particularly distasteful to Lancaster, who endeavoured to get up a party to oppose the favourite. This association was joined by the Earls of Kent and Norfolk, two of the king's uncles, as well as by some other gentlemen, who set forth in an advertisement the reason of their having combined. The statement of grievances was drawn up with the usual tact of red-hot patriots, who always put down a few impossibilities in the list of things to be achieved, for the impracticability of their objects prevents their trade from being suddenly brought to a dead stand-still. There were eight articles in the Lancastrian manifesto, which chiefly aimed at Mortimer and the queen, who soon persuaded Edward that the real object of the advertisers was to deprive him of his crown. "I thought you were the parties pointed at," said the young king to his mother and her paramour; but the latter merely observing, "My dear fellow, they mean you, as sure as my name's Mortimer," soon taught Edward to believe that he was the object of the hostility of the rebellious nobles. Preparations were being made to chastise them, when Kent and Norfolk abandoned Lancaster, who justly complained of having been trifled with. The humiliated and humbugged Lancaster was glad to accept a pardon, and pay down a considerable sum towards the expenses which had been incurred in preparing for his own discomfiture. Mortimer did not forgive the parties who had contemplated his overthrow, but formed a determination to get hold of them when a good opportunity offered.

He received a number of anonymous letters, informing him that his brother, the late king, was alive in Corfe Castle. "Pooh, pooh," said Kent to himself, as he perused the first three or four epistles; "I'm not quite such a fool as to be taken in upon that point. I'm not going to believe my brother is alive, when I happen to have been present as chief mourner at his funeral." Every post, however, brought such a pile of correspondence upon the subject that he first began to believe that half of what he was told might possibly be true; and when credulity admits one half of a story, the other half soon forces an entrance. Kent's anonymous correspondents, not content with declaring the late king to be alive, gave the circumstantiality to their statement which is generally resorted to in the absence of truth, and indicated Corfe Castle as the place where the second Edward was "hanging out" at that very moment. The credulous Kent, being in doubt as to the fate of his brother, wrote at once to ask him whether he was really dead or alive, saying to himself, as he put the epistle into the post, "There! I've written to him now, and so we shall soon settle that question one way or the other."

The party being deceased, the letter came back to the dead-letter office, and fell into the clutches of Mortimer. Everything was done to humour the delusion of poor Kent, who, having been told that his brother was confined in Corfe Castle, sent a confidential messenger to make inquiries in the neighbourhood. It is even said that a sort of optical illusion, a jack-o'-lantern, or phantasmagoria, or dissolving-view, had been resorted to, for the purpose of showing a representation of Edward the Second sitting in Corfe Castle at his luncheon,[44] with a waiter or two in attendance, as a mark of respect to the unhappy sovereign.

The messenger returned with the news to Edmund, who determined to use his own eyes, by going to Corfe Castle and judging for himself. When he arrived and saw the governor, that wily official pretended to be much surprised at the secret having been divulged. He did not deny that Edward was at the castle, but merely remarked that the captive could not be seen. "At all events, you can give him this letter," said Edmund, putting into the governor's hands a *douceur* and a communication directed to the deceased monarch, offering to aid him in his escape from captivity.

The governor took the *billet* to the queen, and Edmund was arrested on a charge of endeavouring to raise a deceased individual to the throne. Poor Kent was put upon his trial, and his own letter having been produced, with witnesses to prove his handwriting, the case against him was complete. The whole proceeding was disposed of with the rapidity of an undefended cause; speedy execution was asked for and granted, but the headsman was nowhere to be found, though persons were sent to look for him all over Winchester. A delay of four hours was occasioned, and the generous British public began to expect that they should lose the spectacle they had assembled to witness, when a convicted felon came forward in the handsomest manner, at a moment's notice, to prevent disappointment, by undertaking the part of headsman. Thus, at the early age of twenty-eight, perished Prince Edmund, on the charge of having

---

44. Rapin, tom. iii., p. 152.

sought to put a sceptre in the hands of a spectre, and raise a phantom to the throne. He left two sons and two daughters, one of whom was a beauty whom we will not attempt to paint, for our inkstand is not a rouge-pot, and if it were we should be sorry to apply its contents to so fair a countenance. She married eventually the eldest son of Edward the Third, who became so celebrated as the Black Prince, and who was born at about the period (1330) to which our history has arrived. The king finding himself a father, determined to be no longer a child in the hands of a tyrannical mother, and he longed for some assistance from his subjects, to enable him to throw off the maternal yoke as soon as possible.

Edward at last opened his mind—a very small recess—to Lord Montacute. A Parliament was being held at Nottingham, where Mortimer and the queen had lodgings in the castle, while the bishops and barons took apartments in the town and suburbs. How to get hold of Mortimer was the great difficulty, for Queen Isabella had the keys of the castle brought up to her every evening, and placed at her bedside.[45] Her majesty had gone round as usual to see everything safe, and all the candles out; but of course, like other sagacious people, who examine minutely the fastenings of the doors, she never gave a thought to the cellars. Through one of these the governor (who, like all the great officers of that period—the founders of our illustrious families—was a sneaking knave, ready to do anything for money) admitted Montacute and his followers. They crawled along a dark passage, at the end of which they were met by Edward, who conducted them up a staircase into a room adjoining his mother's chamber. The queen had gone to bed, but Mortimer, the Bishop of Lincoln, and one or two others, were sitting—probably over their grog—in an apartment close at hand. Their language had all the earnestness that might be expected from the time of night, and the manner in which they were occupied. They were, in fact, all talking at once, when Montacute and party rushed in, knocking down two knights who sat near the door, and seized Mortimer, in spite of the entreaties of Isabella, who ran screaming out of bed on hearing the noise and confusion.

The favourite was dragged off to the nearest station-house, and Edward issued a proclamation the next morning, announcing his intention to try his own hand at government forthwith. A Parliament met at Westminster on the 26th of November, 1330, by which Mortimer was tried and condemned, though a short time before he enjoyed the command of a large majority. The favourite had, however, fallen into disgrace, and the old proverb, "Give a dog a bad name and hang him," was literally realised.

After the death of Mortimer, Queen Isabella was shut up in a place called the Castle of Risings, on a pension of three thousand a year, according to one historian, four thousand according to others, while Rapin unceremoniously cuts her down to the paltry pittance of five hundred per annum. It is probable that the last named sum is the nearest the mark, for all agree in saying that "she lived a miserable monument of blighted ambition," and it is obvious that a miserable monument would not require an outlay of three or four thousand a year to keep it in condition during an existence of rather better than a quarter of a century.

Though Edward had agreed to a truce with the Scotch, he did not scruple to take a favourable opportunity of breaking it. Though his sister was married to little Master David Bruce, the nominal king, Edward did not hesitate to turn that young gentleman off the throne, to make way for his creature, Edward Baliol. Young David was sent to France, while Baliol kept up a kind of semblance of royalty, but his rebellious subjects took every opportunity, when the backs of the English were turned, to fall upon and baste the bewildered Baliol. Edward was soon compelled to leave his vassal to get on as he could, for the entire throne of France appeared to be open to the ambition of the English sovereign. The French crown seemed to be "open to all parties and influenced by none," when Edward of England and Philip of Valois became candidates for the vacancy. The former claimed as grandson of Philip the Fourth, the latter as grandson of Philip the Third, and each party endeavoured to complicate the matter as much as he could by producing a number of perplexing and unintelligible pedigrees. Philip claimed through his grandfather, who was thought to be a sure card for the French king to depend upon; but Edward tried to play something stronger, in the shape of what he affectionately called that "fine old trump his mother." She, however, was objected to as a female, and the question was, to save further trouble, referred to the arbitration of the peers and judges of France, and was decided in favour

---

45. Homing, Knyght, Holinshed.

of Edward's opponent. The English king declared the French judges were no judges at all, and refused to be bound by the award; for it was the royal practice of those days to abide by an agreement only so long as might be convenient.

Edward having appointed the Earl of Brabant his agent, coolly demanded, through that individual, the French crown. The English seconded their sovereign in his preposterous request, and he took advantage of their acquiescence to squeeze out of them all he could in the shape of subsidies, tallages, and forced loans. He raised money by the most disgraceful means, and even pawned the crown with the Archbishop of Treves, who after trying the purity of the gold with the usual test, unpicking the velvet cap to examine the setting of the jewels, and submitting it to as many indignities as a hat in the hands of an old clothesman, consented to lend about one tenth of its value on the degraded diadem.

The conversation between the parties, though it has not been authentically handed down by the chroniclers, may be very easily imagined. It is probable that Edward, forgetting the dignity of the king in the meanness of the borrower, may have familiarly asked the Archbishop to "make it a trifle more" than the sum at first offered. It may be presumed that the greedy ecclesiastic would have objected that the crown had been very ill-used; that it got badly treated in the time of John, and that even Edward himself had had a good deal of hard wear out of it, which had rubbed off very much of its pristine brilliancy. But it was not to the comparatively honest expedient of pawning his own property that the king had recourse, for replenishing his exhausted treasury. When he had got all he could by pledging his own honours, and deposited the sceptre

Edward pawning the Crown with the Archbishop of Treves.

and single ball at the sign of the three, he began the old royal trick of plundering his people.

From the inhabitants of Cornwall Edward took nearly all their tin, and every part of England allowed itself to be fleeced for the purpose of affording one man the means of attempting to gratify his ambition at the expense of an entire people. The money thus obtained was devoted to the payment of foreign mercenaries, so that he robbed his own subjects for the double purpose of corruption and usurpation. To enable him to oppress the French, he bribed the Germans with money obtained by plundering the English.

He sailed on the 15th of July, 1338, with an army rather more select than numerous, and landed at Antwerp, where he had secured himself a friendly reception by sending emissaries before him to marshal the peasantry into enthusiastic groups, and "get up" the spectacle without regard to outlay. The burghers were called to numerous rehearsals before the appointed day, and on the arrival of the English king they were tolerably perfect in the parts assigned to them.

Edward engaged a few foreign potentates—principally small Germans—to aid him in his audacious enterprise. Louis of Bavaria, Emperor of Germany, came to terms; the Dukes of Brabant and Gueldres did not refuse his money; the Archbishop of Cologne consented to add a few pounds to his salary; while the Marquis of Juliers, and the Counts of Hainault and Namur, jumped at a moderate stipend for their services. Every adventurer who was to be had cheap, found instant employment, and James von Artaveldt, a brewer of Ghent, the Barclay or Perkins of his time, made an arrangement for farming out a few of his stoutest draymen. Philip availed himself of a couple of kings in reduced circumstances—those of Navarre and Bohemia—besides securing a few dukes who were in want of a little cash for current expenses. A rope of sand could scarcely have been more fragile than Edward's band of hired followers. Like a Christmas-pudding made of plums and other rich ingredients without any flour to bind it, his supporters, though comprising a compound of dukes, marquises and counts, with even an archbishop and an emperor, was not likely to hold together as long as it was deficient in the flower of an army, a zealous soldiery. The Flemings and Brabanters having spent his money sneaked off with a promise to meet him *next* year, and 1338 was consequently lost in doing nothing. By the middle of September, 1339, there was another muster of the mercenaries, with whom Edward started for Cambray, but happening to look back when he got to the frontiers of France, he saw the Counts of Namur and Hainault disgracefully backing out of the expedition. Having in vain hallooed to them, and finding that the more he kept on calling the more they persisted in not coming, he pushed on as far as St. Quentin, when the rest of his allies struck, and declared they would not go another step without an advance of wages. Edward, who had spent all his own money and a good deal of somebody else's—for he was fearfully in debt—could only say "Very well, gentlemen, I'm in your hands," and turn into the town of Ghent, where he took lodgings for a limited period. While here he amused himself by taking the title of King of France, and he had the French lily quartered on his arms; which, as Philip said when he heard of it, was "like the fellow's impudence."

Edward had previously endeavoured to draw his adversary into a battle, but the latter shirked the contest under various pretexts. Some say that he was ready for a terrific combat and was "just going to begin" when he received a letter predicting ill luck, from the king of Naples, who was looked upon as a sort of Wizard of the South, or royal conjuror. No fight took place, and Edward ran across to England in the middle of February, 1340, to make a call upon the pockets of his people. The Parliament foolishly throwing good money after bad, granted immense supplies, for which the king thanked them in the fulness of his heart, for the fulness of his pocket. Returning to Flanders, he met the enemy at the harbour of Sluys, on the 24th of June, 1340, when a battle ensued, in which Edward astonished his own followers by his most successful *début* in a naval character. He gave orders to the sailors as freely as if he had been playing in nautical dramas and dancing naval hornpipes from the days of his infancy. So complete was the victory of the English that nobody dared inform the French king of the extent of his calamity, until the court jester was fool enough to put the news in the shape of a conundrum to Philip. The latter was enjoying his glass of wine and his nut, when the buffoon in waiting declared that he had a nut to crack which would prove somewhat too hard for his royal master. "Were it a pistaccio or a Brazil," cried the king, "I would come at the kernel of it." When, however, the riddle was put and the sovereign had guessed it, the unhappy fool found it no joke, for he was sorely punished for his ill-judged pleasantry.[46]

Edward's success brought round him troops of friends, and finding himself strong, he wrote a letter addressed to Philip of Valois, offering to tackle him singly in a regular stand-up fight man to man, to pit a hundred soldiers against a hundred on the other side, or to pitch into each other's armies by a pitched buttle, embracing the entire strength of their respective companies. The French king, who was not disposed to give battle, which he thought might end in his taking a thrashing,

Edward's arrival at the Tower.

---

46. Rapin, vol. iii., p. 178. We have used every possible exertion to obtain a copy of this celebrated riddle, but without having succeeded. The nearest Approach we have made to it is an old conundrum in the fly leaf of the Statutes at Large, which is nearly as follows:—"What was the greatest fillip to the success of Edward!" There is no answer added, but there can be little doubt that some allusion to Philip's loss giving a fillip to Edward is intended.

evaded the matter, by saying that he had seen a letter addressed to Philip of Valois, but as it could not be meant for him, he should certainly decline sending an answer. This shabby subterfuge succeeded in baffling the English king, who consented to a truce and returned to his own country.

Edward arrived in London late one night in November, without a penny in his pocket. He went at once to the Tower, where everybody had gone to bed, for he was not expected, and where there were signs of culpable negligence. There was no fire in his room, and nothing to eat; which put him into such an ill-humour that he had three of the judges called up to be thrown into prison; he turned out the Chancellor, the Treasurer, and the Master of the Rolls, besides committing to gaol a number of subordinate officers. Those who had been employed in collecting the revenue were the especial objects of his rage, for he expected to have received a large sum, and was irritated beyond measure at the contemptible amount of available assets. Stratford, the Archbishop of Canterbury, on hearing of the king's arrival at the Tower—in what has perhaps been since called a "towering passion," from the historical fact—observed to his informant, "Oh! indeed. Well, I shall be off out of his way," and fled to his official residence. The king sent him a summons, which he refused to attend, and threatened with excommunication any rascally officer who might attempt to execute the process. Want of money soon softened Edward's heart, and Parliament refused a grant until there had been another confirmation of Magna Charta, which served the double purpose of a blister to draw the people's cash and a plaster to heal their wounded liberties.

In the year 1341, little David of Scotland came over with a little money and a few troops lent to him by the king of France, and with this assistance the Bruce made a tolerably decent appearance in his own country. Edward having projects of wholesale robbery abroad, gave up Scotland as a piece of retail plunder that was wholly beneath his attention, and concluded a truce with David, who compromised with Baliol, by appointing him to keep watch and ward against the Scottish borderers. A situation in the police seems to have been a sorry compensation for one who had aspired to a throne, but it is probable that the pride of Baliol was in some degree consulted by nominating him A 1 in his Dew capacity.

One would have thought that Edward had had enough of Continental warfare, and that "look at home" would have been his motto for the remainder of his reign, but he was soon induced to join in a squabble that had arisen about the crown of Brittany. John the Third, the late duke, had lately died, leaving one brother and a niece named Jane, who having the misfortune to be lame, had got brutally nicknamed *La Boiteuse*, in accordance with the coarse and unfeeling practice of that chivalrous period. The contest for the duchy was between this young lady, who had married Charles de Blois, the French king's nephew, and her uncle John de Montfort, who professed to have a superior claim, and who savagely pooh-poohed her pretensions by allusions to her infirmity. "Hers is indeed a lame case," he would fiendishly exclaim. "Why, by my troth, she hasn't got a leg to stand upon." This argument was the old rule of grammar that the masculine is worthier than the feminine; but this arrangement *La Boiteuse* determined to kick against. Charles de Blois, her husband, did homage to his uncle Phil for the duchy—Brittany being a fief of France—while John de Montfort propitiated Edward by doing homage to him as the lawful sovereign. Philip and Edward thus became bottleholders to the two competitors; but through the tardiness of the English king in supporting his man, De Montfort was taken prisoner. This gentleman had the advantage—or the disadvantage as the case may be—of being married to a high-spirited woman. It is fortunate for a man wedded to a vixen wife, when the affectionate virago, instead of making a victim of him, vents her fury upon his enemies.

Mrs. de Montfort had, according to Froissart, "the courage of a man and the heart of a lion." In addition to these fascinating qualities she had the tongue of a true woman. She went about with her child in her arms, holding forth in a double sense, for she held forth her infant, and was continually holding forth on the subject of her husband's wrongs to the populace. A pretty woman, who takes to public speaking, is always sure of an approving audience; but when she began to give recitations in character, by putting a steel casque on her head and a sword in her hand, the effect was truly marvellous. She took a provincial tour, with the never-failing motto of "Female in Distress" as her watchword; and a host of young men engaged themselves as assistants under her banner. She threw herself into a place called Hennebon, where she was besieged by the French, but she ran up and down the ramparts with all the agility of a young tigress. She stood firmly among a shower of arrows, and though danger darted across her every now and then—so much that her casque got a rapid succession of taps—she merely observed that she had never been afraid of a living beau and would certainly not shrink from a bow without vitality. Aid was expected from the English, but as it did not arrive the Bishop of Leon began to croak most horribly, and proposed to capitulate. The bishop had been to the larder, and finding provisions running exceedingly low, declared there was nothing left for them but to eat humble pie as speedily as possible. He had succeeded in raising an *émeute d'estomac* in the garrison, when the countess, who had begged the troops to hold out a little longer, saw the English fleet from the window of her dressing-room. "Here they are!" cried she as she ran downstairs; and the whole of the inhabitants were soon watching the arrival of the boats with intense interest. Sir Walter Manny commanded the squadron, and after a good night's rest and a capital dinner the next day, which concluded amid a slight shower from the French battering-ram, he declared that he would not run the risk of having any more batter pudding from the same quarter. "That ram," he exclaimed, "must not again disturb me over my mutton;" and he had no sooner dined than he went forth, followed by a few select soldiers, and broke the instrument to pieces.

The French, having raised the siege of Hennebon, left Lady de Montfort leisure to go over to England for the purpose of getting a present of troops that Edward had promised her. She was returning to France with her reinforcements when she fell in with a French fleet, and they fell out as a natural consequence. De Montfort's wife rushed on deck in a coat of mail over her petticoat of female, and fought with tremendous vigour.

One of the foe tauntingly told her the needle was a fitter instrument for her than the sword, when she rushed upon him, exclaiming, "I want no needle, fellow, to trim your jacket." She cut the thread of several existences, and there is no doubt that had the gun cotton been discovered in those days, she would have used it for the purpose of whipping, basting, hemming in, felling to the earth, and, in a word, sewing up her unfortunate antagonists. Darkness having set in upon this fearful set out, the battle was cut short, for night dropped her curtain in the middle of the act, and brought it to an abrupt conclusion.

Edward now came over to superintend the war in person, and he began by looking the danger in the face, which he accomplished by lying several weeks opposite the foe—an example that was followed by the other side; and thus the two armies continued to take sights at each other during the entire winter. At length a truce for three years and eight months was agreed upon; but its conditions were not attended to. John de Montfort was to have

Madame de Montfort astonishing the French Fleet.

been released from prison, according to the agreement; but Philip, by pitiful quibbles, found excuses for keeping him in closer custody. At length, the old gentleman escaped in the disguise of a pedlar; but he was cruelly hounded by his enemies, and with a pack at his back was for some time hunted about, until, by dint of the most dogged perseverance, he arrived safely in England. Coming to the door of his own house, he set up a faint cry of "Stay-lace, boot-lace, shoe-tie," in a disguised voice, which brought the mistress of the establishment to the window; but she merely shook her head, to indicate that nothing was wanted. Upon this the supposed pedlar threw off his hat and wig, and being instantly recognised, was dragged into the hall, to the surprise of the various servants, until the words, "It's your master come back," furnished a clue to the mystery. His wife's joy at meeting her "old man," as she affectionately called him, was extreme; but the excitement was too much for the veteran, who went bang off, like an exhausted squib, while Lady de Montfort fell in an explosion of grief by the side of her husband.

The fortune of war had been oscillating with the regularity of a pendulum between England and France, when the Earl of Derby threw himself into the scale with tremendous weight, and turned it completely in England's favour. In the emphatic language of the day, he was "down upon the French like a thunderbolt." Edward went off to Flanders to treat with the free cities for their allegiance, and, in fact, ascertain the price of those friends of Liberty. Louis the Count, though deprived of nearly all his revenue, kept up his independence, and refused to pay allegiance or anything else to Edward. The English king tried to effect a transfer of the loyalty of the Flemings from Louis, the Count of Flanders, to his own son, Edward the Black Prince; and with this view he obtained the support of his old friend James von Artaveldt, the brewer, whose stout gave him a great ascendency over the actions of the people. He addressed to them a good deal of frothy declamation, and endeavoured to brew the storm of revolution; but it ended in very small beer, amid which Artaveldt himself was eventually washed away through the impetuosity of the stream he had himself set in motion. A popular insurrection broke out, and the brewer behaved with great gallantry. He wore a casque on his head which pointed him out as a butt for the malice of his enemies. He was cruelly murdered, and Edward vowed vengeance when he heard that the lifeless bier was all that remained of his friend the brewer.

In 1346 the English king landed on the coast of Normandy, with an army containing not only the flower of his own troops, but a regular bouquet, in which the English rose was blended with the Welsh leek and a sprig of the Irish shillalah. He marched towards Paris, and his van had even entered the suburbs of that city; but, without attacking the capital, he contented himself with a little arson in the small towns in the neighbourhood. His antagonist was not inactive, and succeeded in getting the English into a corner, from which escape seemed almost impossible. It was necessary to cross the Somme; but Philip and the river were rather too deep for Edward and his soldiers. Having waited till the tide went down, they took a desperate plunge, and the foe having also resolved on making a splash, the two

Assassination of Artaveldt the Brewer.

armies met in the middle of the stream, where they fought with an ardour that was not damped by the surrounding element. Edward and his troops found as much difficulty in reaching the Bank as if they had made the attempt in an omnibus during one of the blockades of Fleet Street. At length they succeeded, and after travelling for some distance, they put up in the neighbourhood of the village of Cressy. On the 26th of August, 1346, the English sovereign took an early supper, and went to bed, having given instructions for his boots to be brought to his door by dawn the following morning. The whole army slept well, considering it was the first night in a strange place; and, having been called by that valuable valet, the lark, everyone was up and down by the hour of daybreak.

Breakfast was scarcely concluded when Edward ordered the army to arms, and sent for the herald in the hopes of getting the news; but from this quarter he learned nothing. At length he took up his post, and chose three leaders, a column being assigned to each of them. The first was under the command of his young Bon, Edward the Black Prince, a youth of fifteen, who held very high rank in the army, having been included in every brevet, notwithstanding the brevity of his service. Two experienced captains—the Earls of Warwick and Oxford—were employed under him to do the work, so that the boy prince had nothing to do but to reap the glory of his position. Heaping laurels under such circumstances was a common practice in those days; and the vulgar expression "with a hook" may have originated in allusion to the reaping of the harvest created by another's merit. It must, however, be stated in justice to the Black Prince that he proved himself quite equal to the position in which fortune had placed him. If we examine his character, we shall find in it many good points, and it may fairly be said that the Black Prince was by no means so black as history has painted him. The three divisions took up their position on the hill, and the archers stood in front, forming a semicircle or bow, from which they could more effectually discharge their arrows. The Battle of Cressy is perhaps one of the most interesting in English history; and though part of it was fought in a tremendous shower of rain, which has caused some frivolous writer of the period to give it the name of Water Cressy, we are not induced by this idle and impotent play upon words to lose our respect for one of the greatest exploits of our countrymen.

Philip slept at Abbeville on the 25th of August, and rising in a terrible ill-humour, set out early in the morning to give battle. He started off in such a fit of sulkiness that he did not even give the word to "march," and breaking suddenly into a run, his impatience carried him far in advance of his army. By the time he came in sight of the foe, he was ever so much ahead of his own troops, and was obliged to sit down quietly until they had come nearly up to him. By some mismanagement, the troops at the back started off quicker than those in front, who began to hesitate still more as they approached the enemy; and thus, one part of the army beginning to back off while those behind pressed forward, a state of confusion which can only be described as a dreadful squeege was the immediate consequence. "Now then, stupid," resounded from rank to rank, and comrade addressed comrade with the words "Where are you shoving to?" The king got hurried head foremost almost into the English camp, in spite of the vehement cries of "Keep back!" which, however, were no sooner acted upon than the rear ranks were seized with a panic, and the soldiery began tumbling over each other like those battalions in tin which in youthful days have fallen prostrate beneath the power of the peashooter.

Philip, who had never intended to take the honour of a foremost rank, was pushed willy-nilly into the front place, like a gentleman who happened to be walking down the Haymarket on an opera night, and found himself suddenly engulfed in a stream which washed him off his legs, and left him high and dry in a stall to which he had been driven by the impetuosity of the torrent. Finding himself in the heat of an engagement in which he had not intended to be so closely engaged, his French majesty called to the Genoese crossbow-men to advance, but they pleaded sudden indisposition and fatigue, when Philip's brother deeply offended them by exclaiming—"See what we get by employing such scoundrels, who fail us in our need!" The Genoese were rather nettled—that is to say, somewhat stung—by this remark, and made a rush which was worth no more than a rush, for they were really worn out with their morning's walk, and felt fitter to be in bed than in battle. Though their arms and legs were tired, they still had the full use of their lungs, and began to shout out with tremendous vehemence, in the hope of frightening the English. This horrible hooting had no effect, and a Scotch veteran, by happily exclaiming "Hoot awa!", turned the laugh in favour of the English. Upon this, the Genoese gave another fearful yell, when one of Edward's soldiers inquired whether the crossbow-men wanted to

Edward the Third on the morning of the Battle of Cressy.

frighten away the birds, and gave them the nickname of the heavy scarecrows. They advanced a step, when the English archers sent forth a volley of arrows, which fell like a snowstorm upon the Genoese, who, converting their shields into umbrellas, tried to take shelter under them. Philip was so disgusted with this pusillanimous conduct that he cried out in a fury, "Kill me these scoundrels, for they stop our way without doing any good!" And the poor Genoese caught it severely from both sides.

During the battle, Edward sat on the tip top of a windmill, situated on the summit of a lofty hill, where, completely out of harm's way, he could watch the progress of the action. While in this elevated position, he was asked by a messenger to send a reinforcement to the Prince of Wales, who was performing prodigies of valour. "I'm glad to hear it," said the affectionate father; "but," he added, "return to those who sent you, and tell them they shall have no help from me. Let the boy win his spurs," continued the old humbug, who was too selfish to put himself out of the way to assist his son, and would rather have let him perish than make any sacrifice to aid him in his arduous struggles.

When these unaided exertions came to a triumphant issue, the father endeavoured to gain a reflected glory from the brilliance of his son's achievements. It is, however, due to the reputation of the latter to assert that the glory was all his own; for his selfish father had taken care of himself, while the son fought the battle alone, and won it without any assistance that it was in the power of his parent to have afforded him.

Poor Philip fought desperately as long as he could, till John of Hainault, who had several times advised him to "go home and go to bed, for it was of no use," went up to the horse of the French king, seized the bridle, and quietly led him off in the direction of the nearest green-yard. Seeing it was a bad job, Philip requested to be taken to the castle of La Broye, but the gates were shut, and the chatelain, looking out of a window, inquired who was knocking him up at such an unreasonable hour. "Me," cried Philip, in the grammar of the period; but "Who's me?" was the only response of the governor. "Why, don't you know me? I'm Philip, the fortune of France."

"Pretty fortune, indeed!" muttered the chatelain, as he came downstairs, keys and candle in hand, to admit his unfortunate sovereign.[47] The king's suite had dwindled down to five barons, who turned in anywhere for the night, on sofas and chairs, while Philip took the spare bed usually kept for visitors.

Edward the Third at the Battle of Cressy.

Thus ended the memorable Battle of Cressy, from our account of which we must not omit the incident of the king of Bohemia, who, old and blind, was perverse enough to tie the bridle of his horse to those of two knights, and with them he plunged into the midst of the battle. Considering that he could not have seen his way, there is something very rash, though perhaps very valiant, in this behaviour. Nor should we in our admiration of the bravery of the king of Bohemia, forget to sympathise with the two knights, upon whom he must have been a precious drag, by tying his horse's bridle to theirs, and making them no doubt the victims of a most unfortunate attachment. The king of Bohemia of course fell, for the union he had formed was anything but strength, and the Prince of Wales picking up his crest—a plume of ostrich feathers—adopted it for his own, with the celebrated motto of *Ich Dien*.[48] The literal meaning of this motto is simply "I serve," but it has been very naturally suggested that "I am served out" would have been a more appropriate translation of the phrase, as long as it appertained to the unfortunate king of Bohemia. Rapin, the French historian, who is naturally anxious to make the best

---

47. Froissart.
48. Doubts have been lately cast on this old story. See the Cabinet Portrait Gallery of British Worthies, vol. i., p. 81.

case he can for his countrymen, attributes their defeat at Cressy to the use of gunpowder by the English, who introduced, for the first time in war, a small magazine of this startling novelty. Such a *magasin des nouveautés* of course would have taken the French by surprise, and would easily have accounted for any little deficiency of valour they might have exhibited. When the battle was over, Edward sneaked out of his windmill, where he professed to have been "overlooking the reserve," and joined his successful son, whom he warmly congratulated on his position.

The night after the battle was of course a gala night with the English, who lighted fires, torches, and candles, including probably "fifty thousand additional lamps," in celebration of the victory. So excellent, however, were the regulations on the occasion that we have not heard of a single instance of disturbance or accident. The day after the battle was disgraced by a series of attacks on some French unfortunates, who not knowing of the defeat of their king, were coming to his assistance. It happened that, as if to make the English quite at home, a regular English fog set in, and some French militia, not being able to see their way very clearly, mistook a reconnoitring party of the enemy for their own countrymen. The French hastened to join their supposed comrades, but soon found out their mistake from the cruel treatment they experienced. Other stragglers who had missed their way in the mist were also savagely attacked, and when Edward heard the facts, he sent out Lords Cobham and Stafford, with three heralds, to recognise the arms, and two secretaries to write down the names of those that had fallen. The party returned in the evening, with a list of eleven princes, eighty bannerets, twelve hundred knights, and thirty thousand commoners. We can only say that the herald of those days could not have been such a very slow affair as the *Herald* of these, and the secretaries must have written not merely a running but a galloping hand to have in so few hours deciphered the arms, and made a list of the names of such an enormous number of individuals.

Having remained over Sunday at Cressy, Edward set out on Monday morning for Calais, with the intention of besieging it. While he was occupied abroad, his enemy, little David Bruce, at the instigation of Philip, attempted to disturb England. After a brief campaign, in which the Scotch king was joined by the Earls of Monteith and Fife, David Bruce was placed in custody. Monteith lost his head for showing his teeth, and Fife would have had a stop put to him, but for his relationship to the Royal Family, his mother having been niece to the first Edward.

Calais was kept in a state of blockade, for the English king had resolved upon hemming in and starving out the inhabitants. John de Vienne, who was the governor, finding provisions getting low, turned what he called the "useless mouths" out of the place, and among these "useless mouths" were a number of women, who must have been rare specimens of their sex to have kept their mouths in a state of uselessness. The brutal policy of John de Vienne was to continue weeding the population as long as he could by turning out the old and helpless, the women and the children. Seventeen hundred victims were thrust from the town and driven towards the English lines by the Governor of Calais, who was reckless of the lives of the citizens so long as the sacrifice enabled him to hold out and gain a character for bravery.

It is easy for a military commander to win a reputation for extreme heroism if he is utterly regardless of the expense, and chooses to pay for it in the blood of those under his control; but it is the duty of the historian to audit the accounts and justly strike the balance. In looking into the case of John de Vienne we adjudge him guilty of fraudulent bankruptcy in his reputation, for he sought to establish himself in the good books of public opinion by trading on the lives of the citizens of Calais, which were his only capital. If he were now before us, we should assume the part of a commissioner, and should say to him, "Go, sir. We cannot grant you your protection from the heavy responsibilities you incurred when you wasted human life which you were bound to preserve as far as you were able. You have violated a sacred trust; and we must therefore adjourn your further examination *sine die*, for it is quite impossible to grant you your certificate."

As long as John de Vienne could find anything to eat, and could have his table tolerably well provided, he held out; but when starvation threatened himself as well as the citizens, he asked permission to capitulate. Edward, annoyed by the obstinacy of the resistance, refused to come to any terms short of an unconditional surrender, but he at length consented to spare the town on condition of six burgesses coming forth naked in their shirts, with halters round their necks, and without anything on their legs, as a proof of their humiliation being utterly inexpressible. When John de Vienne was apprised of this resolution, he called a meeting in the market-place, and stated the hard condition which Edward had imposed, but the governor had not the heroism to propose to make one of the party required for the sacrifice. He was exceedingly eloquent in urging others to come forward, and was loud in his protestations that such an "eligible opportunity," such an "opening for spirited young men" would never occur again; but the citizens turned a deaf ear to all his arguments. No one seemed inclined to set a noble example, but all the inhabitants gave way to a piteous fit of howling, until Eustace de St. Pierre, a rich burgess, drying his eyes and mopping up his emotion with the cuff of his coat, offered himself as the first victim. Five others followed his example, and the six heroes, taking off their trousers, prepared to throw themselves into the breach, and slipping off their slippers, went barefooted into the presence of the conqueror. He eyed the miserable objects with malicious pleasure, and according to Froissart, insulted the unhappy burgesses by a series of grimaces, like those with which the clown accompanies the ironical inquiry of "How are you?" which he always addresses to his intended victim in a pantomime. The wretched state of the burgesses shivering in their shirts—but not shaking in their shoes, for they were barefooted—had a softening influence on all but Edward, who with a clownish yell of "I've got you!" desired that the headsman might be sent for immediately.

The queen threw herself on her knees, and representing that she had never asked a favour of Edward in her life, entreated him to spare the trembling citizens. "Look at them!" exclaimed her majesty, as she dragged one forward and turned him round and round to show what a miserable object he was. "Look at them! and observe how piteously they implore mercy; for though their tongues do not speak, their teeth are constantly chattering." Edward looked at his wife, and then at the citizens. "I wish," said he to the former, "that you had been—— somewhere else; but take the miserable beggars and do what you can with them." Philippa instantly took the coil of rope from the necks that were so nearly on the point of "shuffling off the mortal coil," and told them to go and get rigged out in a suit of clothes each, which made the oldest of them observe that "the rigger of the queen was much less formidable than the rigour of the king, with which they had been so lately threatened."

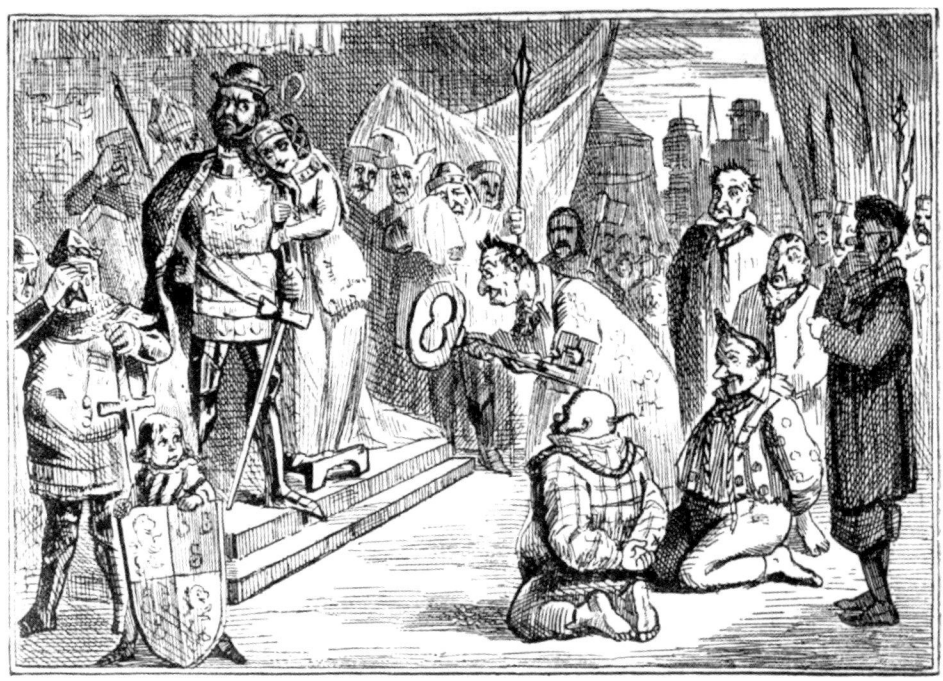

Queen Philippa interceding with Edward the Third for the six Burgesses of Calais.

The imbecility to which fear had brought their minds is fearfully shadowed forth in this miserable piece of attempted pleasantry, and it was perhaps fortunate that Edward did not overhear a pun, the atrocity of which he might have been justified in never pardoning. The six citizens having received their dressing, in a more agreeable shape then they had expected, and having sat down to an excellent dinner, provided at the queen's expense, were dismissed with a present of six nobles each that they might not be without money in their pockets. As they partook of the meal prepared for them, the wag of the party, whose vapid jokes had already endangered the lives of himself and his companions, ventured to observe that he should look upon the ordinary as one of the most extraordinary events in his life; but as none of the king's servants were at hand to overhear the miserable *jeu de mot*, it was not followed by the fatal consequences we might otherwise have been compelled to chronicle.

On the 3rd of August, 1347, Edward and his queen made their triumphant entry into Calais, which was transformed into an English colony; and as the residents of that early period were debtors to the generosity of the sovereign, the place has become a favourite resort for debtors even to the present moment.

Edward having returned to England began to try the squeezability of his Parliament, and got up various pretexts for demanding money. He pretended to ask advice about carrying on the war with France, but the Parliament suspecting his intention declined giving any answer to his message. He next had recourse to intimidation, by spreading a report that the French contemplated invasion; and though it was little better than a cry of "Old Bogey," it had the desired effect. There is no doubt that Edward was guilty of obtaining money under false pretences, for he and Philip had agreed between themselves for a truce, and yet each taxed his subjects under the pretence that war might be imminent.

About the year 1344, according to some, but in the year 1350, on the authority of Stowe, the celebrated Order of the Garter was founded. If we may put faith in an old fable, it originated in the Countess of Salisbury having danced her stockings down at a court ball; when the king seeing her garter dangling at her heels, took hold of it and gave it to her, exclaiming, *Honi soit qui mal y pense*, which was a cut at some females who pretended to be shocked at the incident. Their smothered exclamations of "Well, I'm sure!"

"Upon my word!" and "Well, really I never! Did you ever?" were thus playfully rebuked by Edward the Third, who afterwards made the words we have quoted the motto of the Order. We need scarcely tell our readers in this enlightened age that *Honi soit qui mal y pense* is equivalent to saying that those who see harm in an innocent act, derive from themselves all the evil that presents itself.

Origin of the Order of the Garter.

Edward's old enemy, Philip of France, was now dead, but his son and successor, John, continued the truce, or renewed the accommodation bill, which was entered into for the purpose of stopping proceedings on either side. In state affairs, as in pecuniary matters, these temporary arrangements are seldom beneficial, for they cause a frightful accumulation of interest, which must some time or other be paid off or wiped out at a fearful sacrifice.

The Continental successes of the English king were marred by the trouble that Scotland gave to him, and he was often heard to say that "though he could make the French poodle—by whom he meant the king of France—do as he pleased, he hated the constant barking at his heels of the Scotch terrier." He therefore determined on attempting to buy the country out and out. So, going over to Roxburgh, he asked Baliol point-blank what he would take for the whole concern, exactly as it stood, including the throne, the title-deeds of the kingdom, and the crown and sceptre. "Let me see. What has it cost me?" said Baliol, evidently contemplating a bargain; but Edward interrupting him with "A precious deal more than it is worth," somewhat modified the figure that was on the tip of the tongue of the Scotch sovereign. "Will fifty thousand marks be too much?" observed the vendor, with an anxious look. But Edward's rapid "Oh, good morning!" instantly told the wary Scot the shrewdness of his customer. "Stop, stop," said Baliol; "I like to do business when I can. What will you give? for I'm really tired of the thing, and would be glad to accept any reasonable offer." Edward resumed his seat, made a few calculations on a scrap of vellum with a pocket-stile, and then, jumping up, exclaimed, "I'll tell you what I'll do with you. I'll give you five thousand marks down, and an annuity of £2000 per annum."

The bargain was struck. With the title-deeds laden, Edward joyfully flew to his own country, and he had scarcely turned his back when "Adieu!" said Baliol; "you are not the first humbug who, coming to cheat, have got cheated yourself." The fact was that the Scotchman, with characteristic cunning, got the best of the bargain, for the crown had been fearfully ill-used, the sceptre had got all the glitter worn off by the hard rubs it had endured, and the throne would cost more to keep in substantial repair than twice its value.

Edward having bought up the country, began to exercise the right of ownership by setting fire to little bits of it. He marched through the Lothians, where he met with loathing on every side, and set Haddington as well as Edinburgh in flames, which caused Scotland to be prophetically called the Land of Burns by a sage of the period.

While the king was thus engaged at home, his son Edward, the Black Prince, so called from the colour of his armour, which he had blackleaded to save the trouble of keeping it always bright, was occupied in France, where he fought and won the famous battle of Poictiers. The truce had, with the customary faithlessness of royalty in those days, been broken. Young Edward, having a small force, made a most earnest appeal to his army, and said something very insinuating about "his sinewy English bowmen."

Before the commencement of the battle, a diplomatist of the name of Talleyrand, who seems to have been worthy of his celebrated modern successor, rode from camp to camp trying to arrange the affair, and making himself very influential with both parties. John was, however, so confident in the superiority of his numbers that he declined a compromise, except on the most humiliating terms, to the Black Prince, who looked blacker than ever when the degrading proposition was made to him.

On the 19th of September, 1356, the battle began with a duet played by two trumpets—one on each side—but this did not last long, for neither party desired to listen to overtures. The French commenced the attack, but they came to the point a little too soon, for they actually ran upon the arrows of the English bowmen. The Constable of France tried to inspire courage into the troops on his side by roaring out "Mountjoy! St. Denis!" but a stalwart Briton, telling him to hold his noise, felled him to the ground. A strong body of reserve, who carried their reserve to downright timidity, fled without striking a blow. They had scarcely drawn their swords, and received the word of command to "cut away," when they did literally cut away, and having cut refused to come again. John of France flourished his battle-axe with ferocious courage; but at last he received two tremendous blows in the face which brought him to the ground. His son Philip, a lad of sixteen, fought by his side, encouraging him with cries of "Give it 'em, father!" which aroused the almost exhausted John, and caused him to recover his legs. Every kind of verbal insults was offered to him by the enemy, and particularly by the Gascons, who indulged in a great deal of their usual gasconade. "Stand and surrender!" cried a voice; to which John replied, "If I could stand, I would not surrender, but I suppose I must fall into your hands." With this he tottered into a circle of English knights, by whom he was nearly torn to pieces in the scramble that arose for the royal captive. Some among the crowd of his victors endeavoured to induce his majesty to place himself under their charge, and one or two began to talk to him in bad French, when Sir Denis, a real Frenchman, who had been dismissed from the service of his own country and entered that of England, addressed the monarch politely in his native tongue. John was in the act of offering up his glove to this gentleman as a token of surrender, when the royal gauntlet was torn to pieces by the surrounding knights, who all wanted to have a finger in it. Everyone was eager to claim the French monarch, who seemed on the point of being torn to pieces like a hare by a pack of ill-bred hounds. "I took him," exclaimed fifty voices at once, when the Earl of Warwick, rushing into the front, thundered forth in a stentorian voice, "Can't you leave the man alone?" and drawing John's arm within his own, led off the conquered king to the camp of Edward. Warwick took little Philip by the hand, and presented father and son to the Black Prince, who received them with much courtesy.

He invited them both to supper, waited on the French king at table, and soothed his grief with probably such kind expressions as "Poor old chap!"

"Never mind, old fellow!" and other words of respectful sympathy. The Black Prince made them his companions to London, which they entered in the character of his prisoners, on the 24th of April, 1357. The pageant was very magnificent, the citizens hanging out their plate to do honour to the occasion; and the windows were filled with spoons, just as they are when a modern Lord Mayor's show is to be seen within the city. Edward had now a couple of kings in custody; but in November, 1357, one of them, David

Edward, the Black Prince, conducting his Prisoner.

Bruce, was released, upon drawing a bill for one hundred thousand marks on his Scotch subjects. There can be no doubt that the latter were regularly sold by their weak-minded monarch, who had become the mere creature of the English sovereign. John remained in captivity in London, while Edward carried the war into France; but having got nearly as far as Paris, he was caught in a shower, which completely wet him down, and diluted all the spirit he had, up to that point, exhibited.[49] The wind was terrific; but it was not one of those ill winds that blow nobody good, for the blow it inflicted on the courage of Edward made good for those he came to fight against. The French justly hailed the rain as a welcome visitor, for it completely softened Edward by regularly soaking him. On the 8th of May, 1360, peace was concluded, and John was set at large on condition of the payment of three million crowns of gold, which was rather a heavy sum forgetting one crown restored to him. Some hostages were given for the fulfilment of the bargain; but poor John found he had undertaken more than he could perform, and though he did not exactly stop payment, it was because he had never commenced that operation. He was exceedingly particular in money matters, and it annoyed him not to be able to fulfil his pecuniary arrangements. Some of his bail having bolted, he could bear the degradation no longer, and he voluntarily went over to London, where he put himself in prison, as a defaulter, though others say it was a love affair in England, rather than his honesty as a debtor, which brought him up to town. The royal insolvent did not long survive, for he died in the month of April, 1364, at the Palace of the Savoy; and it was tauntingly said of him by a contemporary buffoon that the debt of nature was the only debt he had ever paid.

The Black Prince, who had been created Duke of Aquitaine, governed for his father in the South of France, but was induced to espouse the cause of one Pedro, surnamed the Cruel, who, for his ferocious conduct, had been driven from the throne of Castile. Bertrand du Gueselin, a famous knight in his day, and Don Enrique, the illegitimate brother of the tyrant, had expelled him from his dominions, when the Black Prince, tempted by offers of an enormous salary, undertook to restore Pedro to his position.

---

49. Froissart, Knyght, Rynier, and Company.

Edward fought and conquered, but could not get paid for his services; and, as he had undertaken the job by contract, employing an army of mercenaries at his own risk, he was harassed to death by demands for which he had made himself liable. Captains were continually calling to know when he intended to settle that little matter, until he got tired of answering that it was not quite convenient just now; and he that had never turned his back upon an enemy, ran away as hard as he could from the importunity of his creditors. Pedro, abandoned by his chief supporter, agreed to a conference with his half brother Enrique; but cruelty seems to have been a family failing, for the couple had scarcely met when they fell upon each other with the fury of wild beasts, and Pedro the Cruel was stabbed by Enrique the Crueller, who threw himself at once upon the throne.[50]

Charles of France now thought that the harassed mind and declining health of the Black Prince afforded an eligible opportunity of attacking him. His Royal Highness resisted as well as he could; but he was so exceedingly indisposed that he was carried about on a litter from post to post, as if he had been compelled to rest at the corner of every street through sheer exhaustion. He marched, or rather was jostled, towards Limoges, the capital of the Limousin, which he stormed in two places at once; and at the sight of the pair of breaches he had made, the women fled in inexpressible terror and confusion. His conduct to these poor defenceless creatures was merciless in the extreme; and this one incident in the life of the Black Prince is sufficient to give to his name all the blackness that is attached to it. Some allowance may, however, be perhaps made for the state of his health, which now took him to England to recruit—not in a military but in a physical sense—but it was too late, for he died at Canterbury, on the 8th of January, 1376, to the great regret of his father, who only kept the respect of the people through his son's popularity.

Edward the Third had been for some time leading a very disreputable life, and had been captivated by one Alice Perrers, to whom he had given the jewels of the late queen, and who had the effrontery to wear them when abroad in the public thoroughfares. Among other freaks of his dotage was a tournament which he gave in Smithfield—the origin, no doubt, of the once famous Bartholomew Fair—where Alice Perrers figured in a triumphal chariot, as the Lady of the Sun, the king himself appearing in the character of the Sun, though it was the general remark that, as the couple sat side by side, the Sun looked old enough to be the father.

It was towards the close of this reign that Wycliffe, the celebrated precursor of Huss, Luther, and Calvin, as well as the curser of popery, began preaching against the abuses of the Catholic clergy. His cause was espoused by the Duke of Lancaster, who had been in power since the death of the Black Prince, and who is said to have taken Wycliffe's part so ardently, as to have threatened to drag the Bishop of London by the hair of his head out of St. Paul's Cathedral. Considering that the priest was all shaven and shorn, it would have been difficult for Lancaster to have carried out his threat by tugging out the bishop in the manner specified. It is a curious fact that this alleged attack on one of the heads of the church was soon followed by a general burden on the national poll, in the shape of a poll-tax, which was imposed to provide for the renewal of the war, as the truce in existence was on the point of expiring.

Edward had now become old and miserable; for having done nothing to gain the affection of others, he was abandoned at the close of his life, by even the members of his own family. One or two sycophants clung to him, in the hope of getting something; but his children had all separate interests of their own, for the cold and selfish conduct of their parent had driven them quite away from him. He endeavoured to give decency to the close of his existence, by a general amnesty for all minor offences; but it was now too late to gain him friends, and the wretched old man was left alone with Alice Perrers. He died in her arms at his villa at Sheen, near Richmond, on the 21st of June, 1377, and she took advantage of being by his side at his death, to rob him of a valuable ring, which she took from his finger in his last moments, when he was too weak to resist the robbery. Were the shade of Edward the Third to present itself before us for a testimonial, we should advise the spectre, for its respectability's sake, not to ask us for a character.

Much good was done in the reign we have been describing; but this is only another illustration of the well-known truth that the prosperity of a country does not always depend on the virtues of the

---

50. Froissart.—Mariana.

sovereign. Perhaps the most valuable measure passed by Edward was an act limiting to three principal heads the cases of high treason, of which a hundred heads, all filled with teeth, might until then have been considered symbolical. This wholesome statute had at least the effect of changing a Hydra into a Cerberus. The leash of crimes that this Cerberus was empowered to hunt down were, conspiring the death of the king, levying war against him, or adhering to his enemies. A curious question arose some time afterwards under the last of these three divisions, when a loyal subject was nearly being condemned for adhering to the king's enemies, though it appeared he had adhered only in the sense of sticking to them, with a view to punish them.

The conduct of Edward the Third to David Bruce, his brother-in-law, was unjust in the extreme; and though the Black Prince made his way by his own talents, he does not appear to have owed his advancement to any assistance that his father ever afforded him. Some useful alterations were made in the law, and the power of the Commons advanced; but the taxes were fearfully increased, as if the liberality of the people was expected as an equivalent for the liberality of the Government. The money collected was not altogether wasted in war, for some of it went in the building of Windsor Castle, of which William of Wickham was the architect. The first turnpike ever known in England was started also under Edward the Third, between St. Giles's and Temple Bar, where to this day the successor of the ancient pikeman rushes forth to levy a toll on carts that enter the city. On the same principle, that out of evil good often comes, Edward the Third may be regarded as a benefactor to his subjects.

CHAPTER THE FIFTH

RICHARD THE SECOND, SURNAMED OF BORDEAUX

f little and good were always identical, Richard the Second would have been a very good king, for he was a little boy of eleven years of age when the crane of circumstances hoisted him onto the throne of his grandfather. Young Richard was the only surviving son of Edward the Black Prince, and out of compliment to the juvenile monarch, his coronation in Westminster Abbey was made as gaudy as possible. No expense was spared in dresses and decorations; but the ceremony not being over till it was high time all children should be in bed and asleep, the boy king was completely exhausted before the spectacle was half over. Stimulants were administered to keep the child up; but when the heavy crown was placed on his brow, the diadem completely overbalanced a head already oscillating from side to side with excessive drowsiness. His attendants tumbled him into a litter, and hurried him into a private room, where, by dint of the most scarifying restoratives held to his nose, he so far recovered as to be enabled to create four earls and nine knights, partake of a tremendous supper, dance at a ball, and listen to a little minstrelsy.[51] It was at the coronation of Richard the Second that we first find mention in history of a champion rushing into Westminster Hall, throwing his gauntlet on the ground, and offering to fight any number—one down and another come on—who may dispute the title of the sovereign. The gallantry of the challenge is not very considerable, for it is a well-understood thing beforehand that the police will keep all suspicious characters out of the Hall, and the only difficulty required is in backing out of the Hall on horseback; as, if a claimant to the throne should actually appear, the champion would no doubt back cleverly out of his challenge. Even this trifling merit must, however, be assigned to the horse, who is generally a highly trained palfrey from the neighbouring amphitheatre, and is let out, trappings and all included, to the Champion of England for the performance in which his services are required.

Though Richard was not too young for the position of king, it was not to be supposed that a boy of his age could be of any use whatever, and twelve permanent councillors were therefore appointed, to do the work of government. It was expected that the Duke of Lancaster, *alias* John of Gaunt, would have been appointed regent, but not one of the king's uncles was named, and John, looking gaunter than ever,[52] withdrew in stately dudgeon to his Castle of Kenilworth.

The truce with France having expired, without renewal, some attacks were made on the English coast, and advantage was taken of the circumstance to ask the Parliament for a liberal supply. Every appeal to the patriotism of the people was in those days nothing more than an attack upon their pockets; and it is not improbable that, by an understanding among the various kings of Europe, one of them should be threatened with attack if he required a pretext for obtaining a subsidy from his subjects.

Notwithstanding the money taken from the public purse for the national defence, the work was so utterly neglected by the Government that John Philpot, a shipowner and merchant of London, equipped

---

51. We get these facts from Walsingham, who gives an elaborate account of the coronation. Walsingham says, they waltzed till all was blue, which means, until the coerulean dawn began to make its appearance.
52. John of Gaunt was not so called from his gaunt stature, as some suppose, but from Ghent, or Gand (then called Gaunt), where the gent was born.

a small fleet of his own, with which he captured several of the enemy's vessels. The authorities feeling the act to be a reflection on their own shameful dereliction of duty, censured Philpot for his interference; but the worthy alderman, by replying— "Why did you leave it to me to do, when you ought to have done it yourselves?" effectually silenced all remonstrance.

Young Richard, or those who acted for him, continued to make ducks and drakes of the money of the English, which was being constantly wasted in wanton warfare. The setting up of a duke here, or the taking down of a king there, though the English felt no interest whatever in either the duke or the king, became a pretext for levying a tax on the people. In order that none should

Fancy Portrait of the Champion of England.

escape, so much per head was imposed on every one from the highest to the lowest. The tax varied with the rank of the person; and while a duke or archbishop was assessed at six 'thirteen four (£6 13s. 4d.) a lawyer was mockingly mulcted of six and eightpence. Such was the unpopularity of the poll-tax that a regular pollish revolution speedily broke out, which was fomented by the exactions of some mercenary speculators to whom the tax had been farmed out by the Government. Commissioners were sent into the disturbed districts to enforce payment, and one Thomas de Bampton, who sat at Brentwood in Essex, with two serjeants-at-arms, was glad to take to his legs, to escape the violence of the populace, who sent him flying all the way to London, where he rushed with his two attendants into the Common Pleas, and asked for justice. Sir Robert Belknape, the chief, was sitting at Nisi Prius, when Bampton begged permission to move the court as far as Essex. The judge followed by clerks, jurors, and ushers, consenting to the motion, went off to Brentwood, where they had no sooner arrived, than poor Belknape was seized by the nape of the neck and forced to flee, while the clerks and jurors were much more cruelly dealt with.

Leaders were all that the people wanted, when a notorious priest who got the name of Jack Straw— from his being a man of that material—put himself at the head of the discontents. The throwing up a straw will often tell which way the wind blows, and the elevation of Jack certainly indicated an approaching hurricane. During the excitement, one of the tax-gatherers called upon one Walter the Tyler, of Dartford, in Kent, to demand fourpence, due as Miss Walter's poll-tax. Mrs. Walter, with the vanity of her sex, wishing to make herself out younger than she really was, declared that the girl was not of the age liable by law to the imposition. The collector made a very rude remark on that very tender point, the age of the elder lady, when she screamed out to her husband, who was tiling a house in the neighbourhood, to come and "punish the impertinent puppy." Walter, who had still his trowel in his hand, replied by crying out "Wait till I get at you;" and the tax-gatherer insolently calling out "What's that what you say, Wat?" so irritated Walter that he at once emptied a hod of mortar onto the head of the collector. The functionary was, of course, dreadfully mortar-fied at this incident, but the trowelling he got with the trowel completely finished him. Everybody applauded what Wat had done, and he was soon appointed captain of the rebels. They released from prison a Methodist parson named John Ball, or Bawl, whom they called their chaplain. A nucleus having been formed, the mob increased with the rapidity of a snowball, picking up the scum of the earth at every turn, until it arrived at an alarming magnitude. The Tyler first visited Canterbury, where he played some practical jokes upon the monks, and then came to Blackheath, where, finding the young king's mother—the widow of the Black Prince—he gave the old lady a kiss, and in this operation nearly every rebel followed his leader. Such were the liberties taken by the mob in their zeal on behalf of liberty, which they often affect to pursue by means of the vilest tyranny, cruelty, cowardice, and oppression. The insurgents made for London, when Walworth, the mayor, endeavoured to oppose their entrance; but his efforts were vain, and several parts of the city were burnt and plundered. The Temple was destroyed by fire, and the lawyers running about in their black gowns amid the flames suggested a very obvious comparison. Newgate and the Fleet prisons were broken into, when all the scamps from both places at once assumed the character of patriots, and joined the cause of the people.

It is astonishing how easily a scamp who is unfit for any honest occupation can at once become a friend of the masses. The prisons might at any time contribute a fresh supply, when the stock of lovers of liberty on hand may seem to be diminishing. Rapine and murder were pursued with impunity for some time, the Government leaving matters to take their chance; until a formal demand having been made by the mob for the heads of the Chancellor and Treasurer, it was thought high time to effect a compromise. A proclamation was issued announcing the king's intention to be at Mile End by a certain hour, and the people were politely requested to meet him there. On his reaching the spot where he intended to talk things over with his subjects, he found sixty thousand of them assembled; and as they all began talking at once, a little confusion arose until the appointment of a regular spokesman. At length the demands of sixty thousand tongues were reduced to four heads, and to these the king agreed very graciously. The dispute might have ended mildly at Mile End, but for the violent proceedings of those who kept away from the meeting. These got into the Tower directly Richard's back was turned, and the least of their offences was the rudeness they manifested towards the widow of the Black Prince, who had either dropt in to tea with the Archbishop and Chancellor or was permanently residing there. This lady had got the name of the Fair Maid of Kent, a title that had many local variations, according to the part of the county in which she was spoken of. Sometimes they called her the Dartford Daisy, sometimes the Canterbury Belle, sometimes the Greenwich Geranium, sometimes the Woolwich Wallflower, and occasionally, even the Herne Bay Hollyoak.

The rioters finding her in the Tower, treated the Fair Maid of Kent with excessive rudeness, comparing her lips to Kentish cherries, and making them the subject of the well-known game which is played by what is termed bobbing at the fruit specified. She was, in fact, nearly smothered in the Tower with the kisses of the malcontents. Her ladies were, of course, dreadfully shocked, and their screams of "Mi!" at the treatment of their mistress were truly terrible. When remonstrated with on the liberty they were taking, they declared liberty to be the sacred object they were bent on furthering. The Fair Maid of Kent was at length dragged away by her attendants, who concealed her in a house called the royal wardrobe, or perhaps put her into a clothes-cupboard, to keep her out of the way of the rioters.

The Mile End charter had been very nicely written out by order of the king, but Wat Tyler and his followers refused to have anything to do with it. Richard tried another charter with more concessions, but this had no effect; and at length he drew up a third, which went still further than the two first, for the king, or those who advised him, cared not how much was promised to answer a temporary purpose, as there was never any difficulty in breaking a pledge that might be found inconvenient. Whether or no Wat suspected the worthlessness of charters, which might be sworn to one day and treated as waste paper the next, he refused to be satisfied with either of the documents offered to his approval. Finding written communications utterly useless, Richard rode into town, with the intention of seeing what could be done by means of a personal interview.

On reaching Smithfield he met Wat Tyler, and drew up opposite the gate of St. Bartholomew's Hospital, which was in those days an abbey. The incident which then happened has been variously described by different pens, but unless we had at our command some of the Smithfield pens that happened to be present at the time, we could not vouch for the accuracy of any particular statement. Some say that Tyler came up in a bullying attitude, and flourished a dagger; others allege that he seized the king's bridle, as if he would take out of the royal hands the reins of power; a few hint that Wat was intoxicated, either with brief authority or something equally short; but all agree that he received his quietus at the hands of one of his majesty's attendants.

The merit or responsibility of the death of Wat Tyler has usually been assigned to Walworth, Lord Mayor of London, who is said to have killed the rebel with his mace; but it is doubtful whether the civic potentate would be carrying his mace about with him during a morning's ride.[53] The fall of the Tyler had a most depressing influence on his followers, and Richard, riding up to them, offered his services as their leader. "Tyler was a traitor," cried the king: "I will be your captain and your guide," when several of the mob consented to transfer themselves, like so many tools, from the hands of Wat to those of Richard. Some of the rioters sneaked quietly away, while those that remained were paralysed; for it was always the characteristic of an English mob to go on very valiantly as long as they had it all their own way, but to turn tail and flee on the very first symptom of earnest resistance.

Richard, finding himself once more powerful, instead of tempering justice with mercy, threw in a strong seasoning of the most highly spiced cruelty, and commenced a series of executions, in which there were nearly fifteen hundred victims to royal vindictiveness. As might have been expected from the state of royal honour at the time, he at once revoked all the charters to which he had agreed—an act which proved that Tyler took a very fair view of the worth of the concessions he had rejected. Jack Straw, one of the rioters, after being tauntingly told by the authorities that he, Straw, deserved to be thrashed, was among the sufferers by the law; and an act was passed by which "riots and rumours and other such things" were turned into high treason. Considering that rumour has an incalculable number of tongues, which are not unfrequently all going at once, there must have been plenty to do under the act by which all rumours were converted into high treason.

In the year 1382, Richard was married to Anne of Bohemia, a most accomplished Bohemian girl, and the daughter of Charles the Fourth, the highly respectable emperor. The king had in the commencement of his reign been surrounded by a low set, placed about him by his mother, the Princess of Wales, for the purpose of excluding his uncles, who could not be expected to mix with ministers and officers whose vulgarity was shocking, and whose meanness was quite detestable. One of these fellows, John Latimer, a Carmelite friar, and an Irishman, gave Richard a parchment containing the particulars of a conspiracy to place the crown on the head of his uncle, the Duke of Lancaster. The duke swore that the whole story was false; his accuser swore the contrary, and the dispute was at length settled by the strangulation of Latimer. Sir John Holland, the king's half-brother, was the alleged perpetrator of the savage act; and indeed this gentleman subsequently disgraced himself by a homicide in the royal camp, for he pounced upon and killed one of the favourites.

"You're no favourite of mine," roared Holland, as he perpetrated the ruffianly act; which proves the holland of that day to have been a very coarse material.

The Duke of Lancaster having gone abroad to urge a stale, and rather hopeless, claim to the throne of Castile, Richard was left in the power of his more turbulent uncle, the Duke of Gloucester. This unpleasant person at once proposed a permanent Council of Regency, to which the king objected, when, with dramatic effect, one of the commons produced from under his cloak the statute by which Edward the Second had been deposed, and holding it to Richard's head, implied that his consent or his life were his only alternatives. Upon this he gave his consent, but about two years afterwards, at a council held in May, 1389, he suddenly took what is commonly called a new start, and rising up, addressed Gloucester with the words, "I say, Uncle, do you know how old I am?"

"Of course I do," replied Gloucester, a little puzzled at the oddness of the question; "you are in your twenty-second year; and a fine boy you are of your age," continued the crafty duke; "but why so particular about dates at the present moment?"

"Because," replied the king, "I've been thinking if I'm not old enough to manage my own affairs now, I never shall be."

An expression of "hoity toity!" came into the countenance of the duke; but Richard continued, with much earnestness, that all the young men of his age were released from the control of their guardians, and he did not see why he should any longer be kept morally in pinafores. With this he thanked the council for their past services, which, however, he declared he should no longer require. Before there was time to prevent him, he had snatched the seals from the archbishop, and seized the bunch of keys

---

53. Others say that the mace in the hands of Walworth was not the official mace, but a mace belonging to a billiard marker in the mob. It is pretty certain that, wherever the mace may have come from, the insolence of Tyler furnished the cue.

from the Bishop of Hereford. Everybody was completely dumbfounded by this exhibition on the part of a lad who had never before been known to do more than stammer out a bashful "Bo!" to some goose he may have met with in his youthful wanderings. Gloucester was driven from the council, and the whole thing was done before anyone present had time—or if he had time he certainly omitted the opportunity—to say "Jack Robinson." An affecting reconciliation afterwards took place between Gloucester and the king; but we believe the reconciliation itself to have been more affected than the parties who were concerned in it.

Richard had soon afterwards the misfortune to lose his wife; and in 1394 he went over to Ireland with a considerable army, but, as it would seem, less for the purpose of making war than making holiday. The English king never struck a blow, and

I lchard thinks it high time he managed his own affairs.

the Irish did not resist, so that the whole affair was a good deal like that portion of the performance of Punch, in which one party is continually bobbing down his head, while the other is furiously implanting blows on vacancy. Richard entertained the Irish with great magnificence, and at one of the banquets said the evening was so pleasant he wished he could make several knights of it. Some of the guests taking up the idea, persuaded him to make several knights by knighting them, which he did with the utmost affability.

Richard did not remain very long a widower, for in October, 1396, he married Isabella, the daughter of Charles the Sixth, an infant prodigy, for she was scarcely more than seven, though a prodigy, according to Froissart, of wit and beauty. Our private opinion—which we do not hesitate to make public—is that there must have been some mistake about the infant's age, and that the parents and nurses of that period were not so particular in proving registers and records of birth as they might, could, or should have been. The wit of a child of seven must have been fearfully forced to have been so early developed: and in spite of the tendency there has always been to exaggerate the merits of royalty, we respectfully submit that the *facetiae* of a child of seven must have been of the very smallest description. The king, who had never been cordially reconciled to Gloucester, was annoyed by the opposition of the latter to the royal marriage, and resolved on striking a blow at his uncle as well as at one or two of his chief partisans. Richard's plan was to ask people to dinner, and in the middle of one of the courses, give a signal to a sheriff's officer, who was concealed under the tablecloth, from which he sprang out and arrested the visitor. He served the Earls of Warwick and Arundel one after the other in this way, having invited them each in turn to a chop, which it was designed that they should eventually get through the agency of a hatchet.[54]

His uncle Gloucester was not to be caught in this way, and declined several invitations to a *tête-à-tête*, when Richard, determined to accomplish his object, went to Bleshy Castle in Essex, where his uncle was residing. "As you won't come to see me, I've come to see you," were the king's artful words, when he was naturally invited to partake of that *fortune du pot* which is the ever-ready tribute of English hospitality. While Richard was doing the amiable with the Duchess, Gloucester, the Duke, was seized by one of the bailiffs in the *suite*—disguised, of course, as a gentleman of the household—and hurried

---

54. This must not be confounded with an old legend that he asked his friends occasionally to a chop at Hatchett's—the well-known hotel in Piccadilly.

to the Essex shore, where he was shoved off in a boat, and conveyed, almost before he could fetch his breath, to Calais.

It was the practice of Richard to do things by fits and starts; so that he accomplished an object very often by getting people to aid him without knowing exactly what they were about, in consequence of the suddenness with which he claimed their services. A few days after poor Gloucester had been "entered outwards" for Calais, the king went to Nottingham Castle, where, taking his uncles Lancaster and York by surprise, he pulled out a document, requesting them to favour him with their autographs. They could not very well refuse a request so strangely made, and it eventually turned out that they had put their names to a bill of indictment against Gloucester, Warwick and Arundel. A Parliament was called to try the traitors, who were condemned, as a matter of course; for Richard, walking into the house with six hundred men-at-arms and a body-guard of archers, was pretty sure of a large majority. Arundel was beheaded, and a writ was issued against Gloucester, commanding him to return from Calais, to undergo the same disagreeable process.

Fortunately, or unfortunately for the duke, he was dead before the writ could be served; but the Parliament, though they could not kill him twice over, indulged the satisfaction of declaring him a traitor after his decease, by which all his property became forfeited. This proceeding was a good deal like robbing the dead; but it was by no means contrary to the spirit of the period. Warwick pleaded guilty, and was sentenced to perpetual imprisonment in the Isle of Man—a sort of *lucus a non lucendo*, which was called the Isle of Man from there being scarcely a man to be seen in the place from one week's end to the other.

The peculiar richness of this reign consists in the historical doubts, of which it is so full that the chroniclers are thrown into a state of pleasing bewilderment. Nobody knows what became of Gloucester while in captivity at Calais; and therefore every writer is at liberty to dispose of the duke in any manner that may tempt an imagination inclining to riot and rampancy. The treatment of his Royal Highness becomes truly dreadful in the hands of the various antiquarians and others who have undertaken to deal with him. By one set of authorities he is strangled, in accordance with the alleged orders of the king: others kill him of apoplexy; a few poison him; ten or a dozen drown him; six or seven smother him; but all agree in the fact that he was, surreptitiously settled. We are the only faithful recorders of the real fact, when we state upon our honour that nobody knows the manner of the duke's death, which is involved in the dense fogs of dim obscurity. Into these we will not venture, lest we lose our own way and mislead the reader who may pay us the compliment of committing himself to our guidance.

Richard having got rid of Gloucester, was anxious for the removal of Norfolk and Hereford, whom he involved in a quarrel with each other, intending that they should realise the legend of the Cats of Kilkenny. When, however, they had entered the lists to decide their dispute by wager of battle, Richard thought it better to run no risk of either of them escaping, and he therefore sentenced both to banishment. Poor Norfolk, a pudding-headed fellow, who might have gone by the name of the Norfolk Dumpling, was soft enough to die of grief at Venice, on his road to Jerusalem, whither he contemplated a pilgrimage. Hereford remained in France, having been promised a pardon, but as it did not arrive he took French leave to return to England, in 1399, after scarcely more than a year's absence. His retinue was so small as to be utterly ridiculous, for it consisted of one exiled archbishop, fifteen knights, and a small lot of servants, who may be put down as sundries in the little catalogue. One fool, however, makes many, and one rebellious earl was soon joined by a number of other seditious nobles.

The plan of Hereford was that of the political quack who pretends to have a specific for every disease by which the constitution is affected. He published a puffing manifesto declaring that he had no other object but the redress of grievances, and that the crown was the very last thing to which his thoughts were directed. One of his confederates to whom Hereford was reading the rough draft of his proposed address, suggested that the disclaimer of the crown which it contained, might prove inconvenient, when the royal diadem was really obtainable. "Don't you see," replied the crafty Hereford with a smile, "I have not compromised myself in any way. I have only said it is the last thing to which my thoughts are directed, and so indeed it is, for I think of it the last thing at night as well as the first thing in the morning." Thus with the salve of speciousness, did the wily earl soothe for a time the irritations of his not very tender conscience.

The manifesto had its effect, for it is a remarkable fact that they who promise more than it is possible to perform, find the greatest favour with the populace; for an undertaking to do what cannot be done always affords something to look forward to. Expectation is generally disappointed by fulfilment, and the most successful impostors are consequently those who promise the most impracticable things without ever doing anything. The imposition cannot be detected until the impossibility of the thing promised is demonstrated; and this does not often happen, for the difficulty of proving a negative is on all hands admitted. It was therefore a happy idea of Hereford, as a political adventurer, to promise a redress of every grievance; and if he could have added to his pledge of interference *de omnibus rebus* an assurance of his ultimately applying his panacea to *quodam alia*, there is little doubt that he would have been even more successful than he was in augmenting the number of his followers.

Henry of Bolingbroke and the Duke of York transacting business.

By the time he reached London he had got sixty thousand men of all sorts and sizes about him, for the people in those days were fond of changing their leaders, and Hereford was popular as the latest novelty. The Duke of York—the king's uncle—moved to the West End, as Henry and his forces entered at the East; but Henry of Bolingbroke—alias Hereford, who was also the nephew of York—invited the latter to a conference. After talking the matter over, the worthy couple agreed to a coalition; the conduct of York being very like that of an individual left to guard a house, and joining with the thief who came to rob the premises.

Richard, who was in Ireland, knew nothing of what was passing at home, for in consequence of contrary winds, the non-arrival of "our usual express" was for three weeks a standing announcement with all the organs of intelligence. When he received the news from his "own reporter," he started for Milford Haven, where he was almost overwhelmed with disagreeable information from gentlemen who evinced the genius of true penny-a-liners in making the very most and the very worst of every calamitous incident. Richard's soldiers seeing that their king more than ever required their fidelity and aid, immediately, according to the usual practice, ran away from him. "They deserted," says the chronicler, "almost to a man," and it is to be regretted that we have not the name of the "man" who formed the nearly solitary exception to the general apostasy. Whoever he may have been, he must have exercised a great deal of self-command, for he was, of course, his own officer; he must have reviewed himself, as well as gone through the ceremony of putting himself on duty and taking himself off at the proper periods. We must not, however, take too literally the calculations of the old chroniclers, who reduce the number of Richard's adherents to an almost solitary soldier, for the truth appears to be that the king mustered almost six thousand men out of the twenty thousand he had brought with him from Ireland. Flight was therefore his only refuge, and selecting from his stock of fancy dresses the disguise of a priest, Richard, accompanied by his two half-brothers, Sir Stephen Scroop, the Chancellor, and the Bishop of Carlisle, with nine other followers, set off for the Castle of Conway. There he met the Earl of Salisbury and a hundred men, who had eaten every morsel of food to be found in the place, and Richard was occupied in running backwards and forwards from Conway to Beaumaris, then on to Carnarvon, then back to Conway again, in a wretched race for a dinner.

It is pitiable to find a king of England reduced to the condition described in the old nursery ditty. He went to Conway for provisions; but

"When he got there
The cupboard was bare;"

and the same result followed his visit to Beaumaris and Carnarvon. Notwithstanding the number of bones that his subjects had to pick with him, there was not one in the larders of the three castles he visited. "And so," in the emphatic words of the nursery rhyme, "the poor dog had none." So complete was the desertion of Richard that the Master of the Household, Percy, Earl of Worcester, called all the servants together, and broke his wand of office, accompanying the act by exclaiming, "Now I'm off to Chester, to join the Duke of Lancaster." This ceremony was equivalent to a discharge of all the domestics under him, and the king, had he returned to his abode, would have been compelled to "do for himself" in consequence of the disbanding of all his menials. The members of the establishment, fancying they had an opportunity of bettering themselves, did not hesitate to follow the example of their chief, and there is no doubt that a long list, headed *Want Places*, was at once forwarded to the Duke of Lancaster.

Having ransacked every corner of Conway Castle without finding any provisions, Richard had nothing left but an unprovisional surrender. He got as far as Flint Castle, which was only three miles from Chester, but he found the inhabitants had flinty hearts, and he met with no sympathy. Henry of Bolingbroke came to meet him, when Richard, touching his hat, bid welcome to his "fair cousin of Lancaster."

"My lord," replied Henry, somewhat sarcastically, "I'm a little before my time, but, really, your people complain so bitterly of your not having the knack to rule them, that I've come to help you." Richard gave a mental "Umph!" but added, "Well, well, be it as you will," for his hunger had taken away all his appetite for power. After a repast, unto which the king did much more ample justice than he had ever done to his subjects, a hackney was sent for, and Richard rode a prisoner to Chester.

No one pitied him as he passed, though the spectacle was a truly wretched one. The horse was a miserable hack, while Richard himself was hoarse with a hacking cough, caught in the various exposures to wind and weather he had undergone in his vicissitudes. The dismal *cortège* having put up at Litchfield for the king and his horse to have a feed, of which both were greatly in want, Richard made a desperate attempt, while the waiter was not in the room, to escape out of a window. He had run a little way from his guards, but a cry of "Stop thief!" caused him to be instantly pursued, and, when taken, he was well shaken for the trouble he had occasioned. He was treated with increased severity, and on arriving in London was conveyed, amid the hootings of the mob, to the Tower.

Richard the Second conducted a prisoner to Chester.

Parliament had been appointed to meet on the 29th of September, 1399, and on that day Richard received in his prison a deputation, to whom he handed over the crown and the other insignia of royalty. Not satisfied with the delivery of the sceptre as a proof of the king's abdication, a wish was expressed to have it in writing, and he signed, as well as resigned, without a murmur. His enemies had, in fact, determined on his downfall, and they seemed anxious to be prepared at all points for dragging the throne from under him. In order to make assurance doubly or trebly sure, an act of accusation against him was brought before Parliament on the following day, when Richard's conduct was complained of in thirty-three, or as some authorities have it, thirty-five separate articles.[55]

---

55. The Pictorial History of England, which is generally very accurate, mentions thirty-three articles. Rapin sets out substance of thirty-one of the articles, and adds that there were four others.

There is no doubt that Richard had behaved badly enough, but the articles, taking the definite and indefinite together, attributed to him a great deal more than he had really been guilty of. His punishment having taken place before his trial, it was of course necessary, for the sake of making matters square, that the offence should be made to meet the penalty. Had he been tried first and judged afterwards, a different course might have been taken, but as he had already been deposed, it was desirable—if only for the look of the thing—that he should be charged with something which would have warranted the Parliament in passing upon him a sentence of deposition. Upwards of thirty articles were therefore drawn up, for the great fact that in laying it on thick some is almost sure to stick, was evidently well known to our ancestors: he was charged with spending the revenues of the crown improperly, and choosing bad ministers, though he might have replied that bad had been the best, and that he and Hobson were, with reference to choice, in about the same predicament. He was accused, also, of making war upon the Duke of Gloucester, as well as on the Earls of Lancaster and Chester, to which he might have responded that they began it, and that it was only in his own defence he had treated them as enemies. It was alleged against him, also, that he had borrowed money and never paid it back again; but surely this has always been a somewhat common offence, and one which the aristocracy should be the last persons in the world to treat with severity. In one article he was charged with not having changed the sheriffs often enough, and, as if to allow him no chance of escape, another article imputed to him that he had changed the sheriffs too frequently. Some of the counts in the indictment were utterly frivolous, and the twenty-third stated that he had taken the crown jewels to Ireland, as if he could not legally have done what he pleased with his own trinket-box.

It must be presumed that Richard allowed judgment to go by default, for all the accusations were declared to be proved against him. If he had been assisted by a special pleader, he might have beaten his accusers hollow on demurrer, for many of the counts in the declaration were, in legal phraseology, utterly incapable of holding water.[56] Notwithstanding the weakness of the articles, they were not attacked by anyone in Parliament except the Bishop of Carlisle, who, in a miserable minority of one, formed the entire party of his sovereign. The venerable prelate, in a powerful speech, talked of Richard's tyranny, including his murder of Gloucester, as mere youthful indiscretion; and described his excessive use of the most arbitrary power, as the exuberance of gaiety. The bishop's freedom of speech was fatal to his freedom of person; for he was instantly ordered into custody by the Duke of Lancaster. No one followed on the same side as the prelate, whose removal to prison had the effect of checking any tendency to debate, and the articles were, of course, agreed to without a division. Sentence of deposition was accordingly passed on the king, who had been already deposed, and the people of England revoked all the oaths and homage they had sworn to their sovereign. Such, indeed, was the determination of his subjects to overturn their king, that his deposition was not unlike the practical joke of drawing the throne literally from under him. They knew he had not a leg to stand upon, and they seemed determined that he should not have a seat to sit down upon; for even established forms were overturned in order to precipitate his downfall.

What became of Richard after his having been deposed is a point upon which historians have differed; but the favourite belief is that he was cut off with an axe by one of his gaolers at Pomfret Castle, where he was kept in custody. Some are of the opinion that he was starved, and died rather from want of a chop than by one having been administered. Mr. Tytler believes that the unfortunate exmonarch escaped to Scotland, where he resided for twenty years; but the story is doubtful, for even in Scotland it is impossible to live upon nothing, which would have been the income of Richard after his exclusion from the royal dignity.

When we come to weigh this sovereign in the scale, we can scarcely allow him to pass without noticing his deficiency. He seems to have had originally a due amount of sterling metal, but the warmth of adulation melted away much of the precious ore, as a sovereign is frequently diminished in value by sweating. To this deteriorating influence may be added that of the clipping process, to which he was subjected by his enemies, who were bent on curtailing his power. He had by nature a noble and

---

56. Mackintosh, who keeps the facts always very dry, seems inclined to our opinion that the indictment would not have held water.

generous disposition, which might have made him an excellent monarch. But our business is with what he really was, and not with what he might have been. He was alternately cowardly and tyrannical, in conformity with the general rule—applicable even to boys at school—that it is the most contemptible sneak towards the stronger who is towards the weaker the fiercest bully. Wholesome resistance tames him down into the sneak again, and in pursuance of this ordinary routine, Richard, from an overbearing tyrant, became a crouching poltroon, when his enemies got the upper hand of him.

It was during this reign that the authority of the pope was vigorously disputed in England, chiefly at the instigation of John Wickliffe, who denied many of the doctrines of the Church of Rome, and protested against its supremacy. Its

A Practical Joke. Deposition of Richard the Second.

influence was, moreover, weakened by its being in some sort "a house divided." Avignon had been for some time the papal residence, but the Italian cardinals having persuaded the pontiff to return to Rome, the French cardinals set up a sort of opposition pope, who continued to live at Avignon. Urban did the honours with great urbanity in the Eternal City, while Clement carried on the papal business at the old establishment in France, and Europe became divided between the Clementines and Urbanists.

These two sects of Christians continued to denounce each other to eternal perdition for some years, and their trial of strength seemed to consist chiefly in a competition as to which could execrate the other with the greatest bitterness. This dissension was no doubt favourable to the views of Wickliffe, who, like other great reformers, renounced in his old age the liberal doctrines by which he had obtained his early popularity.

We have alluded in the course of this chapter to a combat which was about to take place between the Earls of Hereford and Norfolk, in pursuance of the practice of Wager of Battle, which was in those days prevalent. It may seem unjust and ridiculous to the present generation that the strongest arm or stoutest spear should have settled a legal difference, but even in our own times it is frequently the longest purse which determines the issue of a law-suit. The only difference is that litigants formerly knocked about each other's persons, instead of making their assaults upon each other's pockets, and the legal phrase, that "so-and-so is not worth powder and shot," preserves the allegory of a combat, to which an action-at-law may be compared with the utmost propriety. There has always been something chivalric in entering upon the perilous enterprise of litigation, and we are not surprised that the forensic champions of England should have been originally an order of Knights Templars. The only military title which is still left to the legal corps is that of Sergeant, and the black patch in the centre of their heads is perhaps worn in memory of some wound received by an early member of their order in the days of Wager of Battle. The sword of justice may also be regarded as emblematical of the hard fight that is frequently required on the part of those who seek to have justice done to them by the laws of their country.

Contemporaneously with the Wager of Battle, there was introduced during the reign of Henry the Second a sort of option, by which suitors who were averse to single combat might support their rights by the oaths of twelve men of the vicinage. Thus it was possible for those who were afraid of hard hitting to have recourse to hard swearing, if they could get twelve neighbours to take the oath that might have been required. These persons were called the Grand Assize, and formed the jurors—a word, as everybody knows, derived from the Latin *juro*, to swear—but the duty has since been transferred from the jury to the witnesses, who not unfrequently swear quite as hard as the most unscrupulous of our ancestors.

We have seen that there were very few improvements in the reign of Richard the Second; but we think we may justly say of the sovereign that though he did no good to his country, yet, in the well-known words of a contemporary writer, "He would if he could, but he couldn't."

CHAPTER THE SIXTH

ON THE MANNERS, CUSTOMS,
AND CONDITION OF THE PEOPLE

efore entering on the fourth book of our history, we may perhaps be allowed to pause, for the purpose of taking a retrospective glance at the condition, customs, candlesticks, sports, pastimes, pitchers, mugs, jugs and manners of the people. It is curious to trace the progress of art, from the coarse pipkin of the early Briton to the highly respectable tankard found in the ruins of Glastonbury Abbey,[57] which proves the teeth of the monks to have been decidedly liquorish. We must not, however, plunge prematurely into the pot of a more polished era: but we must go regularly back to the earthenware of our earliest ancestors.

The furniture of the Britons was substantial rather than elegant. A round block of wood formed their easiest chair, which, we need hardly say, was easier to make than to sit upon. The earth served the purpose of a bed, not only for the parsley but for the people; and in winter they made fires on the floor, till the Romans, who brought slavery in one hand, gave the brasier with the other. Thus did even subjugation tend to civilisation, and the very chains of the conqueror contained links for the enlightenment of the conquered.

The diet of the Britons was as poor as their apartments, and consisted chiefly of wild berries, wild boars, and bisons. We have no record of their cookery, and it is doubtful whether they cooked at all, though some antiquarians have endeavoured to find evidence of a stew, a roast or a curry, and have ended after all in making a mere hash of it. In clothes the Britons were by no means straight-laced, though their intercourse with the Gauls was of inexpressible advantage to them, for it introduced the use of Braccæ, or trousers made of fine wool woven in stripes or chequers.[58]

Of the domestic habits of the early tenants of our isle very little is known, and we regret to say there can be little doubt they might most of them have been indicted for polygamy had they lived under our present system of laws, for a plurality of wives was in those days nothing singular.

Their mode of bringing up children is wrapt in obscurity, but the treatment, if we are to believe a story told by Salinus, was rather less tender than vigorous; for the first morsel of food was put into the infant's mouth on the point of his father's sword, with the hope that the child would turn out as sharp a blade as his parent. The Saxons brought very material improvements to the mode of living in our island, though we cannot compliment them on the comfort of all their upholstery. Their chairs were a good deal like our camp-stools, without the material which forms the seat; for the Anglo-Saxons were satisfied to sit in the angle formed by the junction of the legs of the article alluded to.[59]

The drinking-cups in use at this period began to be very elaborate, and were made of gold or silver, while glass was a luxury unknown, though the Venerable Bede, who had a good deal of glass in his family, mentions lamps and vessels of that material. The Anglo-Saxons had beds and bolsters; but from illustrations we have seen in the Cotton MS., we think that if, as they made their beds, so they were

---

57. The tankard has no name distinctly bitten into it.
58. It is probable that we get out our own word braces from the Braccæ of our forefathers.
59. Pictorial History of England, vol i., book i., chap. vi., p. 129.

obliged to lie, our ancestors could not have slept very pleasantly. Some of the Saxon bedsteads were sexagonal boxes, into which it was impossible to get, without folding one's self up into the form of an S; and another specimen is in the shape of an inverted cocked hat, somewhat smaller than the person by whom it is occupied. Nothing but a sort of human half-moon could have found accommodation in this semilunar cradle, in which to have been "cribbed, cabined, and confined," could not have been very agreeable.

Costume could scarcely be considered to have commenced before the Anglo-Saxon period, for the Britons persevered in a style of un-dress which was barely respectable. It is therefore most refreshing to find our countrymen at last with stockings to their feet and shirts to their backs, in which improved case they are to be met with in the Anglo-Saxon period. The shoe also stands boldly forward at about the same time, and shows an indication of that polish which was eventually to take a permanent footing. Amid the many irons that civilisation had in the fire at this date, are the curling-irons for ladies' hair, which began to take a favourable turn during the Anglo-Saxon period. The armour worn by the military part of the population was very substantial, consisting chiefly of scales, which gave weight to the soldiery, and often turned the balance in their favour. This species of defence was, however, too expensive for the common men, who generally wore a linen thorax or "dickey," with which they offered a bold front to the enemy.

It would be exceedingly difficult to give an accurate account of Anglo-Saxon life, for there are no materials in existence out of which a statement could be framed; and though some historians do not object to have "their own materials made up," we should be ashamed to have recourse to this species of literary tailoring. We think it better to cut our coat according to our cloth; and we had rather figure in the sparest Spencer of fact, than assume the broadest and amplest cloak, if it were made of a yarn spun from the dark web of ambiguity. What we say, we know, and what we are ignorant of, we know much better than to talk about.

The Anglo-Saxon husbandman was little better than a serf who was paid for his labour by the landowner; but the former furnished the base, without which there would have been no *locus standi* for the latter's capital. It was customary in those days to encourage the peasantry by prizes, which did not consist of a coat for a faithful servitude of nearly a life, but a grant of a piece of the land to which the labourer had given increased value by his industry.

The proprietors of the soil had not yet learned the wisdom of trying how much a brute could be made to eat, and how little a human being could exist upon.

With reference to the domestic habits of the period, it has been clearly ascertained that people of substance took four meals a day, and as they took meat at every one, their substance can be no matter of astonishment. The Britons had not been in the habit of dressing their food, which is not surprising, for they scarcely dressed themselves; but the Anglo-Saxons were not so fond of the raw material. With them the pleasures of the table were carried to excess, and drinking went to such an extent that every monk was prohibited from taking any more when his eyes were disturbed, and his tongue began to stammer. The misfortune, however, was, that as all who were present at a banquet generally began to experience simultaneously a disturbance of the eye and a stammering of the tongue, no one noticed it in his neighbour, and the orgies were often continued until the stammering ended in silence, and the optical derangement finished by the closing of the organs of vision.

The chase was a popular amusement with the Anglo-Saxons, but it does not seem to have been pursued with much spirit, if we are to believe an illustration from the Cotton MS. of the practice of boar-hunting. Two men and one dog are seen hunting four boars, who are walking leisurely two and two, while the hound and the hunters are hanging back, as

Anglo Saxon Husbandman.

if afraid to follow their prey too closely. In another picture, from the Harleian MS., seven men are seen huddled together on horseback, as if they had all fainted at the sight of a hawk, who flaps his wings insolently in their faces. Nothing indeed can be more pusillanimous than the sports of the Anglo-Saxons as shown in the illustrations of the period. The only wonder is that the animals hunted did not turn suddenly round and make sport of the sportsmen.[60]

The condition of the great body of the people was that of agricultural labourers, who, it is said, were nearly as valuable to their employers or owners as the cattle, and were taken care of accordingly. In this respect they had an advantage over the cultivators of the soil in our own time, who remain half unfed, while pigs, sheep, and oxen are made too much of by constant cramming.

The Normans added little to the stock of English furniture, for we have looked through our statistical tables and find nothing that would furnish an extra leaf to our history. It is, however, about this time that we find the first instance of a cradle made to rock, an arrangement founded on the deepest philosophy; for by the rocking movement the infant is prepared for the ups and downs of life he will soon have to bear up against.

The reign of John introduces us to the first saltcellar on record, though, by the way, the first vinegar cruet is of even earlier date, for it is contemporary with the sour-tempered Eleanor, who is reported to have played a fearful game at bowls with the unfortunate Rosamond.

When Fashion first came to prevail in dress, Taste had not yet arrived, and the effect was truly ridiculous. It does not follow, however, that if Fashion and Taste had existed together, they would have managed to agree; for although there is often a happy union between the two, they very frequently remain at variance for considerable periods. Fashion being the stronger, usually obtains the ascendency in the first instance; but Taste ultimately prevails over her wayward rival. In nothing so much as in shoes, have the freaks of Fashion been exemplified. She has often taken the feet in hand, and in a double sense subjugated the understanding of her votaries. In the days of Henry the First shoes were worn in a long peak, or curling like a ram's horn, and stuffed with tow, as if the natural toe was not sufficient for all reasonable purposes. The rage for long hair was so excessive that councils were held on the subject, and the state of the crops was considered with much anxiety.[61] The clergy produced scissors at the end of the service to cut the hair of the congregation; and it is said of Serlo d'Abon, the Bishop of Seez, that he, on Easter Day, 1105, cut every one of the locks off Henry the First's knowledge-box.

We have hinted at the out-of-door amusements of the people, but those pursued within doors may deserve some passing notice. The juggler, the buffoon, and the tumbler were greatly in request, and we see in these persons the germ of the wizards, the Ramo Samees, the clowns, with their "Here we ares," and the various families of India-rubber incredibles, Mackintosh marvels, or Kensington untrustables that have since become in turns the idols of an enlightened British public. That there is nothing new under the sun, nor in the stars—at least those belonging to the drama—is obvious enough to anyone who will examine the records of the past, which contain all that are declared to be the novelties of the present. Learned monkeys, highly trained horses, and— to go a little further back—terrific combats, or sword dances, in which deadly foes go through

Fox-hunting Bishop of the Period.

---

60. Julius, A. 7.
61. At Limoges, in 1031, by Pope Gregory the Seventh in 1073, and at Rouen in 1095.

mortal conflicts in a *pas de deux*, are all as old as the hills, the dales, the vales, the mountains, and the fountains. Even the reading-easel—for those who wish to read easily—which was advertised but yesterday, and patented the other day, was a luxury in use as early as the fourteenth century. Even Polka jackets, imported from Cracow in Poland, were "very much worn," and, for what we know, the Polka itself may have been danced in all its pristine purity. In head-dresses we have seen nothing very elegant, for, during Richard the Second's reign, a yard or two of cloth, cut into no regular pattern, formed a bonnet or hood for a lady, while an arrangement in fur very like a muff, constituted the hat of a gentleman.

Out-of-door sports were much in favour during the fourteenth century, and the priesthood were so much addicted to the pleasures of the chase that a clergyman was prohibited from keeping a dog for hunting unless he had a benefice of at least ten pounds per annum.

The foxhunting parson is therefore a character as old as the days of Richard the Second, in whose reign the Bishop of Ely was remarkable for activity in the field, where the right reverend prelate could take a difficult fence with the youngest and best of them. He was particularly active in hunting the wolf, and he often said jestingly that the interests of his flock prompted him to pursue its most formidable enemy.

We have seen what our ancestors were in their habits, pleasures, and pursuits, none of which differed very materially from those that the people of the present generation are or have been in the habit of following. As the child is father of the man, the infancy of a country is the parent of its maturity. Reproduction is, after all, the nearest approach we can make to novelty, and though in the drama of life "each man in his time plays many parts," there is scarcely one of which he can be called the original representative.

Book IV

THE PERIOD FROM THE ACCESSION OF HENRY THE FOURTH TO THE END OF THE REIGN OF RICHARD THE THIRD, A.D. 1399—1485

CHAPTER THE FIRST

HENRY THE FOURTH, SURNAMED BOLINGBROKE

he wily Henry had now got the whip hand of his enemies, and had grasped the reins of government. He ascended the throne on the 30th of September, 1399, and began to avail himself at once of the patronage at his disposal by filling up, as fast as he could, all vacant offices. His pretext for this speed was to prevent justice from being delayed, to the grievance of his people; and by pretending there was no time to elect a new Parliament, he continued the old one, which was in a state of utter subservience to his own purposes. At the meeting of the Legislative Assembly, which took place on the 6th of October, Thomas Arundel, the Archbishop of Canterbury, made "the speech of the day," which was a powerful panegyric on the new sovereign. There is no doubt that the whole oration was a paid-for puff, of which the primacy was the price, for the prelate had been restored by Henry to the archiepiscopacy, out of which Richard had hurried him.

The new candidate for the crown gave three reasons for claiming it; but when a person gives three reasons for anything, it is probable they are all bad, for if one were good the other two would be, of course, superfluous. He declared his triple right to be founded, first on conquest, which was the right of the ruffian who, having knocked a man on the head, steals his purse and runs off with it; secondly, from being the heir, which he was not; and thirdly, from the crown having been resigned to him, which it certainly had been, when the resigning party was under duress, and when his acts were not legally binding. Upon these claims he asked the opinion of Parliament, which, having been cleverly packed by Arundel and his whippers-in, of course pronounced unanimously in Henry's favour. Upon this he vaulted nimbly onto the steps of the throne, and, pausing before he took his seat, he cried out in a loud voice, "Do you mean what you say?" when the *claqueurs* raised such a round of applause that, whispering to one of his supporters "It's all right," he flung himself onto the regal ottoman. Another round of applause from the privileged orders secured the success of the farce, and the usual puffing announcements appeared in due course, intimating the unanimous approbation of a house crowded to suffocation. This had been certainly the case, for the packing was so complete as to stifle every breath of free discussion.

A week's adjournment took place, to prepare for the coronation, which came off on the 13th of October in a style of splendour which Froissart has painted gorgeously with his six-pound brush, and which we will attempt to pick out with our own slender camel's-hair. On the Saturday before the coronation, forty-six squires, who were to be made knights, took each a bath, and had, in fact, a regular good Saturday night's wash, so that they might be nice and clean to receive the honour designed for them. On Sunday morning, after church, they were knighted by the king, who gave them all new coats, a proof that their wardrobes could not have been in a very flourishing condition. After dinner, his majesty returned to Westminster, bareheaded, with nothing on, according to Froissart, but a pair of gaiters and a German jacket. The streets of London were decorated with tapestry as he passed, and there were nine fountains in Cheapside running with white and red wine, though we think our informant has been drawing rather copiously upon his own imagination for the generous liquor. The cavalcade comprised, according to the same authority, six thousand horse; but again we are of the opinion that Froissart must have found some mare's nest from which to supply a stud of such wondrous magnitude. The king took a bath on the same night, in order, perhaps, to wash out the port wine stains that might have fallen upon him while passing the fountains. "Call me early, if you're waking," were the king's last words to his valet, and in the morning the coronation procession started for the Abbey of Westminster. Henry walked under a blue silk canopy supported on silver staves, with golden bells at each corner, and carried by four burgesses of Dover, who claimed it as their right, for the loyalty of the Dover people was in those days inspired only by the hope of a perquisite. The king might have got wet through to the skin before they would have held a canopy over him, had it not been for the value of the silver staves and golden bells, which became their property for the trouble of porterage. On each side were the sword of Mercy and the sword of Justice, though these articles must have been more for ornament than for use in those days of regal cruelty and oppression.

At nine o'clock the king entered the Abbey, in the middle of which a platform, covered with scarlet cloth, had been erected; so that the proceedings might be visible from all corners of the Abbey. He seated himself on the throne, and was looking remarkably well, being in full regal costume, with the exception of the crown, which the Archbishop of Canterbury proposed to invest him with. The people, on being asked whether the ceremony should be performed, of course shouted "Aye," for they had come to see a coronation and were not likely to deprive themselves of the spectacle by becoming, at the last moment, hypercritical of the new king's merits. We cannot say we positively know there was no "No," but the "Ayes" unquestionably had it; and Henry was at once taken off the throne to be stripped to his shirt, which, in the middle of the month of October, could not have been very agreeable treatment. After saturating him in oil, they put upon his head a bonnet, and then proceeded to dress him up as a priest, adding a pair of spurs and the sword of justice. While his majesty was in this motley costume, the Archbishop of Canterbury, clutching off the bonnet from the royal head, placed upon it the crown of Saint Edward.

Henry was not sorry when these harassing ceremonies were at an end, and having left the Abbey to dress, returned to the Hall to dinner. Wine continued to play, like ginger-beer, from the fountain; but the jets were of the same paltry description as that which throws up about a pint a day in the Temple. We confess that we are extremely sceptical in reference to all allegations of wine having been laid on in the public streets, particularly in those days, when there were neither turncocks to turn it on, nor pipes through which to carry it. Even with our present admirable system of waterworks, we should be astonished

Coronation of Henry the Fourth (from the best Authorities).

at an arrangement that would allow us to draw our wine from the wood in the pavement of Cheapside, or take it fresh from the pipe as it rolled with all its might through the main of the New River. Whether the liquid could be really laid on may be doubtful, but that it would not be worth drinking cannot admit of a question. Under the most favourable circumstances, our metropolitan fountains could only be made to run with that negative stuff to which the name of negus has been most appropriately given. Let us, however, resume our account of the ceremonial, from which, with our heads full of the wine sprinkled gratuitously over the people, we have been led to deviate.

Dinner was served for the coronation party in excellent style, but before it was half over it was varied by an *entrée* of the most extraordinary and novel character. It was after the second course that a courser came prancing in, with a knight of the name of Dymock mounted on the top of

Entrance of Dymock the Champion, at the Coronation Banquet.

the animal. The expression of Henry's astonished countenance gave an extra *plat*, in the shape of calf's head surprised, at the top of the royal table. The wonder of Henry was somewhat abated when the knight put into the royal hand a written offer to fight any knight or gentleman who would maintain that the new king was not a lawful sovereign. The challenge was read six times over, but nobody came forward to accept it; and indeed it was nearly impossible, for care had been taken to exclude all persons likely to prove troublesome, as it was very desirable on the occasion of a coronation to keep the thing respectable. The champion was then presented with "something to drink," in a golden goblet, and pocketed the *poculum* as a perquisite.

Thus passed off the coronation of Henry the Fourth, which is still further remarkable for a story told about the oil used in anointing the head of the new monarch. This precious precursor of all the multitudinous mixtures to which ingenuity and gullibility have since given their heads, was contained in a flask said to have been presented by a good hermit to Henry Duke of Lancaster, the grandson of Henry the Third, who gave it to somebody else, until it came, unspilt, into the possession of Henry of Bolingbroke. We confess we reject the oil, with which our critical acidity refuses to coalesce, and we would almost as soon believe the assertion that it was a flask of salad oil sent from the Holy Land by the famous Saladin.

The day after the ceremony, or as soon after as the disarrangement caused by the preparations for the coronation could be set to rights, the Parliament resumed its sittings. The terrible turncoatery of the last few years gave rise to fearful recriminations in the House of Lords, and the terms "liar" and "traitor" flew from every corner of the building. At one time, forty gauntlets were thrown on the floor at the same moment as pledges of battle, but there was as little of the *fortiter in re* as of the *suaviter in modo*, and the gloves not being picked up became, of course, the perquisites of the Parliamentary charwoman. Some wholesome acts were passed during the session, but the chief object of the new king was to plant himself firmly on the throne of England. A slip from the parent trunk was grafted onto the Dukedom of Cornwall, and the Principality of Wales, to both of which Henry's eldest son was nominated. No act of settlement of the crown was introduced, for his majesty wisely thought that it would only have proclaimed the weakness of his title had he made any attempt to bolster it. Had the question of legitimacy been tried, the young Earl of March would have turned out to be many steps nearer the throne than Henry, who, however, laughed at his claims, and the old saying of "as mad as a March hare," was quoted by a parasite, to prove the insanity of regarding March as a fit heir to the throne of England. Besides, the little fellow was a mere child, and was, of course, a minor consideration in a country which had a natural dread of a long regal minority. "A boy of eight or nine," said one of the philosophers of the day, "cannot sit upon the throne, without bringing the kingdom into a state of sixes and sevens." It was, however, to strengthen the presumed legitimacy of his family that Henry got his son created Prince of Wales, and though the circumstance is said to have weighed but as a feather in the scales, the Prince of Wales's feathers must always go for something in the balance.

Richard, who was still in custody, was kept continually moving about from castle to castle, like a spring van in town or country, until a few of the lords devised the plan of murdering Henry and restoring the late king, just by way of novelty. A tournament was got up, to which the king was politely asked, and the words, "Tilting at two. An answer will oblige," might be found in the corner of the invitation card. Henry "had much pleasure in accepting" the proposal to join the jousting party, but having received an intimation from the Earl of Rutland, his cousin and one of the conspirators, his majesty did not attend the *soirée*. The intention was to have hustled him and killed him on the spot, but he did not come, and the jousting was, of necessity, carried on for some time by the traitors at the expense of each other. At length, as the day wore on, they began to think it exceedingly odd that Henry had not arrived, when suspecting they had been betrayed, they determined to make for Windsor, where they knew the king had been passing his Christmas holidays. He had, however, received timely warning, and had left for London, so that the conspirators were utterly baffled.

On their arrival at Windsor, they hastened to surprise the Castle; but the greatest surprise was for themselves, when they heard of the escape of their intended victim. Henry had rushed up to town to issue writs against every one of the traitors, who ran away in all directions before he had time to return to Windsor. Some of them attempted to proclaim King Richard in every town they passed through; but they might as well have proclaimed Old King Cole, or any other merry old soul, for they only got laughed at and slaughtered by the inhabitants. Poor Richard was also a sufferer by his injudicious friends, for it was agreed that he would become an intolerable nuisance if he should serve as a point for the rebels to rally round. It was therefore thought advisable to have him abated, and according to the chroniclers of the day, who confess they know nothing about it, he was either starved or murdered. The condition of Richard's young wife, Isabella, a girl of eleven, the daughter of King Charles of France, was exceedingly deplorable. She had brought a large fortune to her husband, and upon his death, her father wished her to be restored to the bosom, and her money to the pockets, of her family. The young lady was promised by an early boat; but Charles insisted that she should be allowed to bring her dowry back with her. Henry, who had spent at least half of it, declined this proposal, and her papa, who had an eye to the cash, would not receive her without, so that she really seemed on the point of becoming a shuttlecock tossed between two immense battledores in the shape of Dover and Calais. Every kind of paltry excuse was set up to avoid payment of the demand, and the English pretended to find upon their books an old claim for the ransom of the French King, John, who had been taken by Edward the Third, and had never been duly settled for. This plea of set-off was overruled on demurrer by the French, who kept reiterating their applications for Richard's widow and her dowry, with a threat of ulterior proceedings if the demand was not speedily complied with. At length Henry agreed to restore her like a toad, "with all her precious jewels in her head." Her old father received her with the exclamation of "Oh, you duck of diamonds," in allusion, no doubt, to the valuable brilliants she carried about her; and there is every reason to believe that had her teeth been literally pearls, the king would have made copious extracts from the choice collection.

Henry now began to consider the best means for making himself popular, and after thinking it well over he came to the conclusion that a war would be a nice little excitement, of which he might reap the benefit. Upon looking about him for an eligible object of attack, Scotland seemed to be the most inviting; for Robert, the actual king, was old and helpless, while his eldest son David, Earl of Bothsay, was a drunken, dissipated, reckless, but rather clever personage. He had quarrelled with his uncle the Duke of Albey, who had acted as regent during the illness of the king, and who was himself a remorseless ruffian; so that the Scotch royal family consisted of a dotard, a drunkard, and a bully. Henry, though he wanted a war, wished to get it without paying for it, to prevent the odium he might incur by taxing the people. He therefore tried the old plan of feudal service, by calling upon all persons enjoying fees or pensions to join him in arms at York, under pain of forfeiture. The lay lords were ordered to come at their own charge with their retainers, but the result afforded a strong proof of the fact that a thing is never worth having if it is not worth paying for. Those who came in arms were fearfully out at elbows; and amid the owners of fees with their retainers, was perhaps some unhappy Templar, with his one fee and one retainer, urged by an ordinary motion of course, to appear in the great cause of the king *versus* Bruce, Rothsay and others.

Henry began boldly with a writ of summons directed to Robert, greeting, and ordering him to come to Edinburgh to make submission. The Earl of Rothsay entered an appearance for his father; a declaration of war ensued on Henry's part, when Rothsay, without putting in a plea, took issue at once, and threw himself upon the country. Henry, not expecting the action to come off so speedily, was but ill prepared, and after making a vain attempt at a fight—in the course of which he tried all his earls and failed on every count—he retired from the contest. He endeavoured, nevertheless, to make the best of it, and observed pleasantly to his followers, "Well, gentlemen, I told you we were sure to beat, and so we will yet. Come, let us beat a retreat; that is better than not beating anything." Thus ended, in a pitiable and most humiliating pun, a campaign commenced in pride, confidence, and insolence.

While Henry was fooling away his time and resources in the North, a little matter in the West was growing into a very formidable insurrection. Owen Glendower, esquire, a Welsh gentleman "learned in the law," who had held a place in the household of Richard the Second, perhaps as standing counsel, became involved in a dispute about some property with Lord Grey de Ruthyn. Mr. Glendower petitioned the Lords, who rejected his suit, which so irritated him that he instantly exchanged the pen for the sword, the forensic gown for the coat of mail, and dashing his wig violently on the floor, ordered a helmet to fit the head and the box hitherto devoted to peaceful horse-hair.

In the course of his legal studies he had learned something of the art of making out a title, and he immediately set to work to prove himself the lineal descendant of the native Welsh princes. By drawing upon fact for some portions, and his imagination for the remainder, he contrived to get up an excellent draft abstract, which he endorsed with the words "Principality op Wales. Grey Ruthyn *ats* self;" and adding the usual formula of "Mr. O. Glendower, to settle and advise, 2 *Guas.*; Clerk, 2s. 6d.;" he placed it among his papers. The Welsh peasants set him down as a magician at the least, and the barrister had no difficulty in placing himself in a little brief authority over them.

Assisted by his clerk the trusty Thomson, Mr. Owen Glendower armed himself for the contest upon which he had determined to enter; and the learned gentleman, who had never used any weapon more formidable than a file, upon which he had occasionally impaled a declaration, now girded on the sword, and prepared to listen to the war-trumpet as the only summons to which he would henceforth pay attention. Taking the somewhat professional motto of "deeds not words," he sallied forth, as he boldly declared, for the purpose of subjecting all his opponents to special damage.

He collected a small band, and made an attack on the property of Grey de Buthyn, for which the king had Mr. Glendower's name published in the next batch of outlaws. Irritated by this indignity, the learned gentleman declared himself sovereign of Wales, observing with much quaintness, "One may as well be hanged for a sheep as for a lamb, and why not for a Welsh rabbit?" Henry at once marched in pursuit, but the barrister was cautious enough to avoid an action, and led his antagonist all over the Welsh circuit, by which he continually put off the day of trial. Henry, who had a variety of other little matters to attend to, was compelled to allow the cause of himself *versus* Glendower to stand over to an indefinite period.

Among the businesses getting into arrears at home, was an absurd declaration of war by Walleran of Luxemburgh, the Count of Ligny and St. Pol, who had married a sister of the

Mr. Owen Glendower armed by his trusty Clerk.

deposed Richard, and was suddenly seized with a fit of fraterno-legal or brotherly-in-lawly affection, and began to talk of avenging his unfortunate relative. In spite of the recommendations of his best friends, who all urged him "not to make a fool of himself," he insisted on going to sea, where a fate a good deal like that of the three wise men of Gotham appeared to threaten him.

Conspiracies now sprung up on every side, and a rumour was spread that Richard was alive in Scotland, and was coming presently to England at the head of a large army, to play old Harry with Henry's adherents. Never was a cry of "Bogey" more utterly futile than this assertion, for Richard was really dead, though it suited a certain party of malcontents to resuscitate him for their own purposes. Henry was exceedingly angry at the rumour, and every now and then cut off some half-dozen heads, as a punishment for running about with a false tale, but there was no checking the evil.

At length an army came from Scotland, but Richard was not with it, and the Scotch no longer kept up the delusion, but, like the detected impostor who confessed "It is a swindle, and now do your worst," they acknowledged the hoax they had been previously practising. The Scotch proved mischievous, but impotent; and Henry was not far from the truth when in one of his remonstrances he remarked, "You are doing yourselves no good, nor me either." They were defeated at Nisbet Moor by the English, under the command of a disaffected Scot, the old Earl of March, who was piqued at his daughter Elizabeth having been jilted by the Earl of Bothsay, to whom she had been affianced. The Earl of Bothsay had made another, and let us hope, a better match, so that the action fought at Nisbet Moor was, as far as the Earl of March was concerned, in reality an action for a breach of promise of marriage. Young Bothsay had united himself to Miss Mariell Douglas, the daughter of old Douglas who had his child the husband—that was for his child the husband—that was to have been—of Earl March's daughter that was, but had also obtained for himself a grant of the estates of the father of Rothsay's ex-intended. Douglas, with ten thousand men at his heels, hurried to take possession, and they soon carried sword and fire—but we believe it was fire without coals—to Newcastle. Having completely sacked this important city—but mark I there were in those days no coals to sack—he returned laden with plunder, towards the Tweed, for which way he went, was—like Tweedle-dum and Tweedle-dee—a matter of pure indifference. The Duke of Northumberland, aided by his son, the persevering Percy, surnamed Hotspur, with the indignant March, had got an army in the rear, when Douglas, seeing a good position between the two forces, called Homildon Hill, was the first to take possession of it. Harry Percy was about to charge up the hill, when the Earl of March, seizing his bridle, backed him cleverly into the ranks, and advised him to begin the battle with his archers. The advice was taken; they shot up the hill, and success was the upshot. Every arrow told with terrific effect upon the Scotch, who presented a phalanx of targets, and the stalwart troopers became at length so perforated with darts that they looked like so many fillets of veal, skewered through and through by the enemy. Douglas was wounded in so many places that he resembled a porcupine rather than a Scottish chief, and he was taken into custody, regularly trussed like a chicken prepared for roasting. Among his fellow-prisoners were the Earls of Moray and Angus, who had tried daughter that was, but had also in vain to escape; but neither did Moray nor Angus reach their own quarters in time to escape the grasp of the enemy.

The battle of Homildon Hill, which we have thus faintly described, was fought on the 14th of September, 1402, while Henry himself was much less profitably occupied in hunting up his learned friend, or rather his knowing opponent, Owen Glendower. The lawyer-like cunning of this gentleman carried him triumphantly through all his engagements; and though good cause might have been shown against it, yet, by his cleverness and tact in Wales, he was nearly successful in getting his rule made absolute.

Henry's next annoyance was an impertinent letter from a former friend and "sworn brother," the Duke of Orleans, uncle of Isabella, the widow of the late king, and the acknowledged "female in distress," whom it was fashionable for the "recognised heroes" of that day to talk about avenging. The letter of the Duke of Orleans was a mixture of ferocity and facetiousness; it deplored the inactivity prevailing in the military market, and offered to do a little business with Henry, either in "lances, battle-axes, swords, or daggers." He sneeringly repudiated "bodkins, hooks, points, bearded darts, razors, and needles," as if Henry had been in the habit of arming himself with the fittings of a work-box or a dressing-case. An answer was returned in the same sarcastic strain, and an angry correspondence ensued, in which the parties gave each other the lie, offered to meet in single combat, and indeed entered into a short but sharp wordy war, which was followed by no more serious consequences.

Northumberland, who had struck for the defence of his country, now struck for his wages, which were unsatisfactory, and several other patriotic noblemen insisted on more liberal terms for their allegiance. Henry having resisted the extortion, gave, of course, great offence to his faithful adherents, who veered, at once, clean round to the scale of the king's enemies. In those days the principles of great men seemed to go upon a pivot, and Northumberland's swivel was evidently in fine working order on the occasion to which we have alluded. Scroop, the Archbishop of York, who might well have been called the Unscrupulous, advised that Henry should be treated as a wrongful heir, and that the young Earl of March should be rallied round, as the rightful heir, by the dissatisfied nobles. They sent a retaining fee to Owen Glendower, and marked upon his brief "With you the Earl of Northumberland and Henry Percy," and appointed a consultation at an early period. Earl Douglas was released from custody without payment of costs, on condition of his leaving the rebels, and O. Glendower, Esquire, married the daughter of his prisoner, Mortimer, the young Earl of March's uncle.

The conspirators having consulted, determined to proceed, and though Northumberland himself was kept at home by indisposition, Hotspur marched to meet Glendower. That learned gentleman, who had probably not received his "refresher," did not come, but young Percy, nevertheless, sent to Henry a written notice of trial. The king proposed referring it to arbitration, but the offer was treated with contempt; and he then rejoined that he had no time to waste in writing, but he would, "by dint of sword and fierce battle," prove their quarrel was false and feigned, "whereupon," as the lawyers have it, "issue was joined." Each army consisted of about fourteen thousand men, and on the morning of the 21st of July, 1403, both being full of confidence, began sounding their horns or blowing their own trumpets. Hotspur and Douglas led the first charge with irresistible vigour, and one or two gentlemen who had carried their loyalty so far as to wear the royal arms as a dodge, while the king fought in plain clothes, paid with their lives the penalty of their fidelity. Henry of Monmouth, the young Prince of Wales, got several slaps in the face, and once or twice exclaimed, in the Norman-French of the period, "Oh, *Mon mouth!*" but he nevertheless continued to the last, showing his teeth to the enemy. Douglas and Hotspur were not ably supported, and the latter was struck by an arrow shot at random, while Douglas, losing command over his head, took to his heels, and becoming positively flighty in his flight, fell over a precipice. This was his downfall, but not his death, for he was picked up and made prisoner. Old Percy, who had been absent from ill-health, but had now got much better from his illness, was marching to join the insurgents with a considerable force, and had paused on the road to take his medicine, when he was met by a messenger, who, glancing at the physic, exclaimed, "Ah! my lord, I've got a blacker dose than that for you!" With this, he administered two pills in the shape of two separate announcements of the deaths of Hotspur and Worcester, the son and brother of the earl, who, bidding "Good morning" to his retainers, all of whom he dismissed, shut himself up in the castle of Warkworth. The king soon routed him out, when Northumberland, like an old sycophant as he was, pretended that Hotspur had acted against his advice, for the venerable humbug, though eager enough to share in his son's success, was meanly anxious to repudiate him in his misfortunes.

By this paltry proceeding, Northumberland was allowed to get off cheap, and even to win commiseration as the victim of the imprudence of his heir, though the fact was that the latter had been completely sacrificed to his parent's selfishness. In the year 1404, the old cry of "Dick's alive" was renewed, and some people even went so far as to say that they had recently walked and talked with the deposed King Richard. The rumour ran that he was living in Scotland, and one Serle, an old servant, went over to recognise his majesty, but found in his place the court jester, who bore some resemblance to the unfortunate sovereign. Serle, however, determined on playing his cards to the best advantage, and thought it a good speculation to play the fool off in place of the king, a trick which was for a time successful. The buffoon humoured the joke, which was a sorry one for its author, who was executed as a traitor, and it might be as well if the same justice were dealt out to similar delinquents in the present day, for indifferent jokes are the madness of few for the gain of nobody.

Henry was now frightfully embarrassed by the quantity of bills pouring in upon him for carrying on the war in Wales, and every day brought him a fresh account which he had never expected. Even the musicians made a claim, and the king, running his eye down a long list of items, including a drum, a ditto, a ditto, a flute half a day, a pandean pipe, *et caetera, et caetera*, exclaimed mournfully to his treasurer, "Alas! I fear I cannot manage to pay the piper." In fact, the claims on account of the war left him no peace, and he proposed taking a quantity of the property of the church to settle with his creditors.

This proposition raised a perfect flame amongst the whole body of the clergy. The Archbishop of Canterbury instantly took fire, while the inferior members of the church were fearfully put out, and cold water being thrown on the attempt, it was soon extinguished. Fighting was still the business that Henry had on hand, for as fast as one of his foes was down, another was ready to come on with fresh vigour. Old Northumberland could not keep quiet, but Owen Glendower was perhaps the most troublesome of all the king's enemies. The rapidity of the learned gentleman's motions kept the other side constantly employed, for he never hesitated to change the venue, or resort to a set-off, when he wished to baffle his antagonists. At length, lack of funds, and its customary concomitant, the loss of friends, compelled him not only to stay proceedings, but to keep out of the way to avoid his heavy responsibilities. He is supposed to have been engaged for years in a protracted game of hide and seek, living at the homes of his daughters and friends, but disguised always in a shepherd's plaid, to prevent the servants from knowing him. What became of him was never known, and, unfortunately for the historian, there were in those days no registrars of either births, deaths, or marriages. Some say that Owen Glendower ended his days at Mornington, but they might as well say Mornington Crescent; and the place of his interment is no less doubtful, for where he was buried is now buried in obscurity.

There is a tradition that his tomb is in the Cathedral of Bangor, but this story is of little value to anyone except to the Bangor beadle, who makes an occasional sixpence by calling the attention of visitors to a spot which he, and Common Rumour, between them, have dignified with the title of the tomb of Owen Glendower. We all know the character which Common Rumour bears for an habitual violation of truth; and we are afraid that if she is no better than she should be, the Bangor beadle is not so good as he ought to be.

Henry was fortunate in overcoming his enemies, but his treatment of them was frequently cruel in the extreme. Poor old Robert, the nominal king of Scotland, was driven about from abbey to abbey, but had no sooner got comfortably settled in one, than a cry of "Here he is! we've got him!" drove him to take refuge in another. At last he hid himself in the Isle of Bute, where he is supposed to have remained to the close of his existence, and it is certain that he never addressed to the Isle of Bute the celebrated apostrophe, "Isle of Beauty, Fare thee well!" His eldest son Rothsay was imprisoned in the castle of Falkland (March, 1402), into which it is supposed he was pitched with a pitcher, containing about a pint of water, and furnished by a crusty gaoler, with a piece of crust. Even this miserable diet is said to have been very irregularly administered, and was of course insufficient for an able-bodied young man like Rothsay. He was treated like a pauper under the new Poor-law, and is believed to have died of inanition; for though the chronicles of that day attributed his death to starvation, the chronicle of our day prefers a genteeler term. The king of Scotland's second son, James, had been shipped by his father for France, to be out of the way, when the vessel was seized by the crews of some English cruisers.

Robert died of grief at the loss of young James, whom he called his precious jewel of a gem, and the little fellow, though a prisoner, was lodged and boarded in comfort, allowed masters, and instructed in all the usual branches of a sound education.

Constitutional liberty had in previous reigns taken very irregular hops, skips, and jumps; but, during the reign of Henry, it began taking rapid strides. During the latter part of his life the tranquillity of his own country gave him the power to lend out his soldiers to fight the battles of others; but it never paid him, for though there was a good deal owing to him, he was unable to get the money. His second son, the Duke of Clarence, had landed in Normandy with a large army, but finding that he could not get a penny to pay his troops, he began to insist on a settlement. He was insultingly told that he was not wanted and might take his army back again, but he soon brought the people to their senses by a little prompt pillage. The matter was arranged, and the Duke of Orleans brought all the ready money he could raise as the first instalment to the headquarters of the English. It is doubtful whether the payments were regularly kept up, but every possible precaution was taken that bail or bills could afford.

Henry's reign was now drawing to a close, and he became exceedingly sentimental in the latter years of his existence. He had discovered the hollowness of the human heart, together with its propensity for wearing a mask, and the keen perception of this perpetual fancy-dress ball of the finest feelings, rendered him gloomy, solitary, and suspicious. He was also in a wretched state of health, for nothing agreed with him, and he agreed with nobody. He became jealous of the popularity of his son, whom he declared to be everything that was bad, though the after life of the young man gave the perfect lie to the paternal libel. Many anecdotes are related of the low freaks of Henry and his companions, who seem to have been the terror of the police and the people. If we are to believe all that is said concerning them, we should look upon the Prince of Wales and his associates as the foes to that great engine of civilisation the street-door knocker, and the determined enemies to enlightenment by the agency of public lamps.

Anecdotes are told of their being brought before the Chief Justice Gascoigne, the Denman, Pollock, or Wilde of his day, who took cognizance of a case, which would induce either of these learned and upright individuals to exclaim to a complainant: "You must not come here, sir; we don't sit here to decide upon the merits of street rows." Gascoigne, who was a chief justice and a police magistrate all in one—like an article of furniture intended for both a bedstead and a chest of drawers, but offering the accommodation of neither—committed to prison some of the prince's associates. The learned judge, setting a precedent that might be followed with advantage in the present day, inflicted imprisonment, instead of a fine, on those to whom the latter would have been no punishment. The Prince of Wales, on hearing of the incarceration of his companions, rushed into court, demanding a *habeas corpus*, and drew his sword upon the judge when asked for a case in point. Judge Gascoigne ordered the usher to take the prince into custody, and the officer of the court having hesitated, young Henry, politely exclaiming, "I'm your prisoner, sir," surrendered without a murmur. When the king heard the anecdote, he became mawkishly sentimental, exclaiming, "Happy the monarch to have such a good judge for a justice, and happy the father to have a son so ready to yield to legal authority." If the latter is really a subject for congratulation, what happiness the police reports of each day ought to afford to those parents who have had sons confined in the station-house for intoxication, by whom the penalty of five shillings has been paid with alacrity. We can fancy the respectable sire of some youth who has formed the subject of a case at Bow Street, and who has submitted to the decision of the Bench; we can imagine the parent exclaiming, with enthusiasm, "Happy the Englishman to have such a magistrate to enforce the law, and such a son to yield obedience to its orders." Another anecdote is told of the amiable feeling existing between the sovereign and his heir, which we insert without vouching for its truth, though it is not by any means improbable. The king was ill in bed, and the Prince of Wales was sitting up with him in the temporary capacity of nurse. The son, however, seemed to be rather waiting for his father's death, than hoping for the prolongation of his life, and the king, having gone off into a fit, the prince, instead of calling for assistance, or giving any aid himself, heartlessly took the opportunity to see how he should look in the crown, which always hung on a peg in the royal bed-chamber. Young Henry was figuring away before a cheval glass, with the regal bauble on his head, and was exclaiming "Just the thing, upon my honour," when the elder Henry, happening to recover, sat up in his bed, and

Unseemly conduct of Henry, Prince of Wales.

saw the conduct of his offspring. "Hallo," cried the king, "who gave you leave to put that on? I think you might have left it alone till I've done with it!"

The prince muttered some excuse, which was not long needed, for on the 23rd of March, 1413, Henry the Fourth died, in the forty-seventh year of his age, and the fourteenth of his reign. The character of Henry the Fourth may be told in a few words, and the fewer the better for his reputation, inasmuch as it is impossible to furnish him with that passport to posterity with which it would give us pleasure to present the whole of our English sovereigns. Other historians have puffed him, but the only puffing we can promise him is a regular blowing up. He was cautious how he gave offence to his subjects, but this was less out of regard to their interests than care for his own. He knew that the hostility existing towards him among the nobles, on account of his usurpation, could only be counteracted by obtaining the support of the people. He therefore refrained from irritating the latter by taxing them heavily for his wars, but he never scrupled to help himself to the goods of the former whenever his exigencies required. The only difference between him and some of his predecessors in the practice of extortion and robbery, is in the fact that while others plundered principally the people, Henry the Fourth thought it better worth his while to plunder the nobles. Some of our predecessors have praised his prudence, which was unquestionably great; for never was a king more cunning in his attempts to preserve the crown he had unjustly acquired. He was not wantonly barbarous in the treatment of his enemies when he got them into his power, and, in this respect, his conduct presents an honourable contrast to that of the sanguinary monsters who committed the greatest crimes to surmount the smallest obstacles. He did not seek to stop the merest breath of disaffection by the most monstrous murders, nor to rid himself of the annoyance of suspicion by incurring the guilt of slaughtering the suspected. His treatment of his predecessor, Richard, and one or two others, who are yet unaccounted for, and returned "missing" in the balance-sheet of history, must always leave a blot, or, rather, a shower of blots, throwing a piebald aspect upon the character of Henry. Among the distinguished individuals who shed lustre on a reign which derived no brilliance from the sovereign himself, are the poets Chaucer and Gower, as well as William Wickham, and Richard Whittington, the Lord Mayor of London. We have been at some pains to trace the story of the latter, in the hope of being able to find accommodation for his cat in the pages of history. We regret to say that our task has ended in the melancholy conviction that the cat of Whittington must make one in that imaginary family which comprises the puss in boots of the Marquis of Carabas, the rats and lizards of Cinderella, and the chickens of Mother Carey.

Among the distinctions to which this reign is entitled, we must not omit to mention that it was the first in which the practice prevailed of burning what were called heretics. Had this circumstance occurred to us before we commenced the character of Henry, we think we might have spared ourselves the trouble of writing it. The burning of heretics ought, of itself, to brand his name with infamy.

CHAPTER THE SECOND

HENRY THE FIFTH, SURNAMED OF MONMOUTH

Henry the Fifth, on coming to the throne, pursued the policy of conciliation; but it so happened that his first act of magnanimity was bestowed in a quarter where it could do no good and excite no gratitude. The act in question, for which he has been greatly praised, was the removal of the body of Richard the Second from an obscure tomb in the Friars' Church, at Langley, to a place beside his first wife, the good Queen Anne, in the Abbey of Westminster. Had Richard the Second been aware of the honour reserved for him after his death, he might probably have requested the advance of a small instalment during his lifetime, when it would have been of some use to him. The greatest magnificence that can be lavished on a tomb will scarcely compensate for an hour's confinement within the dreariness of a prison. Had Richard been living, there would have been some magnanimity in restoring him to his proper position, but giving to his remains the honours due to sovereignty was only a confession on the part of Henry that he and his father had usurped the crown of one who, being dead, could no longer claim retribution for his injuries. It was a mockery to pretend to uphold the deposed king by the agency of an upholsterer, and the funeral was nothing more than another black job added to the many that had already arisen out of the treatment of poor Richard.

The release of the Earl of March from captivity, and the restoration of the son of Hotspur to the honours of the Percies, were acts of more decided liberality; but, if we are to believe the gossip of the period, these two young gentlemen were a pair of spoons, wholly incapable of making a stir of any kind. The Earl of March was, it is true, a spoon of the king's pattern, for he was a scion of a royal stock, but he nevertheless had enough of the fiddle-head about him to make it certain that he could be played upon, or let down a peg when occasion required.

From the wildness of Henry's life during his Welsh princedom, it was expected that his career as king would have been a series of practical jokes upon his officers of state and his subjects in general. He had, when a young man, "scrupled not," according to Hume, "to accompany his riotous associates in attacking the passengers in the streets and highways, and despoiling them of their goods; and he found an amusement in the incidents which the tears and regret of these defenceless people produced on such occasions." It was feared, therefore, that he would have continued to riot in runaway knocks, not only at the doors, but upon the heads of the public. Happily, he disappointed these expectations, for from the moment of his ascending the throne, he became exceedingly well conducted and highly respectable. He did not exactly cut his old friends, but told them plainly that they must reform if they desired to retain the acquaintance of their sovereign. He stated plainly that it would not do for the king of England to be figuring at fancy balls, and kicking his heels about at casinos, as in former times, for he was now no longer a man about town, but the sovereign of a powerful country. Poor Gascoigne, the Chief Justice, had approached the royal presence with fear and trembling, fully expecting to be paid off without any pension for having committed Henry, when Prince of Wales, but, to the surprise of everyone, the king commended the judge for his firmness, and advised him, in the words of the song—*"To do the same thing, were he in the same place,"* should he, the king, be placed to-morrow in another similar position.

In the first year of the new reign a commotion sprung up, which first developed itself in a violent fit of seditious bill-sticking. In the course of a night, some party succeeded in getting out an "effective poster," announcing the readiness of "a hundred thousand men to assert their right by force of arms, if needful." What those rights were the placards did not state, and probably this would have been the very last subject that the hundred thousand men would have proceeded to think about. They were supposed to have been instigated by the Lollards, one of whom, Sir John Oldcastle, their leader, was sent for by the king to have a little talk, in the course of which the wrongs of the Lollards might perchance be hit upon. Sir John Oldcastle, who was one of the old school, found plenty to say, but he never could find anyone to listen patiently to his rigmaroles. Henry the Fifth was obliged to cut the old gentleman short by hinting that the statute *de heretico comburendo* was in force, and Sir John, who had been about to fire up, cooled down very decidedly on hearing the allusion. Henry, finding nothing could be done with Oldcastle, who was as sturdy and obstinate as his name would seem to imply, turned him over to Archbishop Arundel. The prelate undertook to bring Sir John to his senses, but the junction could not be effected, for the objects were really too remote to be easily brought together. A writ was issued, but Oldcastle kept the proper officer at bay, and assailed him not only with obstructive missiles, but with derisive ridicule. At length, a military force was sent out to take the Oldcastle by storm, when Sir John unwillingly surrendered. Though taken, he refused to be shaken in his obstinate resolves, and he pleaded two whole days before his judges, in the hope of wearing them out and inducing them to stay the proceedings, rather than subject themselves to the fearful blow of his excessive long-windedness. He was, however, condemned, but the king granted a respite of fifty days, during which the old fellow either contrived or was allowed to escape from the Tower; and the probability is that the gaolers had instructions to wink, in the event of his being seen to pass the portals of his prison.

Oldcastle, or Lord Cobham, as he was also called, had no sooner got out of prison than he rushed into the flames of sedition, and illustrated by his conduct the process of a leap from the frying-pan into the fire. He appointed a meeting of his followers at Eltham for the purpose of surprising Henry, but the king observing the moves of the knight determined if possible to avoid being check-mated. His majesty repaired to Westminster, when Cobham, changing his tactics, fixed upon St. Giles's Fields as the place of rendezvous. The king thought to himself "Now we've got them there we'll keep them there," and shut the gates of the city. This was on the feast of the Epiphany, or Twelfth Day, 1414, and in the evening the Lord Mayor of London arrested several disreputable Twelfth-night characters. On the next day, a little after midnight, Henry went forth expecting to find twenty-five thousand men assembled in St. Giles's Fields, but he met only eighty Lollards lolling about, expecting Sir John Oldcastle. Several of them were hanged on the charge of having intended to destroy king, lords, commons, church, state, and all the other sundries of which the constitution is composed, and to turn England into a federal republic, with Sir John Oldcastle as president.

The idea of eighty enthusiasts meeting in a field near London to slice their country into republics, and make a bonfire of the crown, the sceptre, the throne, and the other appointments of royalty, is really too ridiculous to be entertained, though it is almost funny enough to be entertaining. Such, nevertheless, was the alarm the Lollards had inspired, that everyone suspected of Lollardism was condemned to forfeit his head first and his goods afterwards, though after taking a man in execution it was rather superfluous cruelty to take his property by the same process. Life, however, was held of so little account in those days that there was considered to be no such capital fun as capital punishment.

Henry had scarcely worn the English crown for a year, when, in the spirit of an old clothesman, who delights in a plurality of hats, he thought the crown of France might furnish a graceful supplement to his own head-dress. He therefore sent in his claim to the French diadem, making out a title in right of Edward the Third's wife, who had no right at all, or if she had, it is clear that Henry the Fifth had no right to the lady, whose heir was Edward Mortimer. France was in a wretched state when Henry put in his claim; for Paris was in one of its revolutionary

Lord Mayor of the Period arresting a suspicious Twelfth-night Character.

fits, and intrigue was rampant in the royal family. The dauphin, Louis, was continually fighting with his mother, and insulting his father, while the Duke of Orleans and his cousin the Duke of Burgundy were perpetually quarrelling. Each had his partisans, and those belonging to the latter were in the habit of declaring that an Orleans plum—alluding, of course, to the duke's vast fortune—was preferable to an entire dozen of Burgundy. In the meantime Paris was infested by a band of assassins, professing to be the friends of liberty, and wearing white hoods, which they forced onto everybody's head; and this act was no doubt the origin of the expression with reference to the hoodwinking of the people.

Before proceeding to arm, Henry proposed a compromise. He demanded two millions in cash, and King Charles's daughter, Catharine, in marriage. The latter offered the lady in full, but only a moiety of the money. This arrangement was scornfully rejected, and Henry held a council on the 17th of April, 1415, at which he announced his determination to go "over the water to Charley." Having resolved upon what to do, the next question was how to do it; and the first difficulty that occurred was the refusal of his soldiers to stir a step without an advance of three months' wages. He first tried the Parliament, and got a good supply, which was further increased by borrowing from or robbing his subjects. Even this would not do, and recourse was had to the common but disgraceful practice of unpicking the crown, for the purpose of sending the jewels to the pawnbroker's. A trusty officer was despatched to deposit with one of the king's relatives a brilliant, in the name of Bolingbroke. The news of the preparations being made in England spread terror in France, for the distant roaring of the British Lion came across the main, with portentous fury. The French King, Charles, was utterly useless in the emergency—for he was a wretched imbecile—and several artful attempts were made to get rid of his authority. Every now and then he was made the subject of a commission of lunacy, as a pretext for placing power in the dauphin's hands; and that undutiful son, having turned his mother out of doors, seized the contents of the treasury, which made him at once master of the capital. At one time, while the pusillanimous Charles was lying at Arras, an attempt was made to burn him out, by setting fire to his lodgings; but, having all the essential qualities of a perfect pump, he does not appear to have been of a combustible nature. He certainly was not of a very fiery disposition, and his enemies declared that he owed his escape from the flames to his being utterly incapable of enlightenment. Such was the king of France, and such the feeling entertained towards him by the majority of his subjects, when the English sovereign resolved on his aggressive enterprise.

Henry left London on the 18th of June, 1415, and proceeded to Winchester, where he was met by another offer of a compromise. This he refused, and rudely pushing the deputation aside, he pressed on to Southampton. Here his fleet awaited him, but receiving news of a conspiracy to take his life he, instead of putting off to sea, put off his departure. Sir Thomas Grey, the Lord Scroop, and the Earl of Cambridge were all in the plot; and the two latter having claimed the privilege of being tried by their peers, took very little by their motion, for they were condemned by a vote of wondrous unanimity. Having heard the heads of the treason, Henry cut off the heads of the traitors, and embarked, on the 10th of August, on board his ship the "Trinity." The scene on the Southampton pier was animated and brilliant when the sovereign placed his foot upon the plank leading to the vessel that was to conduct him to the shores of his enemies.

Gentle breezes were in attendance to waft him on his way, and Neptune, who is sometimes ruffled on these occasions, presented an even calmness that it was quite delightful to contemplate. An enthusiastic crowd on the shore burst forth into occasional cheers, which were succeeded now and then by the faint sob of some sentimental trooper, taking leave of the fond maid whose heart—and last quarter's wages—he was carrying away with him. The civic authorities were, of course, active in their demonstrations of loyalty on this occasion; and the Mayor of Southampton, in backing to make one of his sycophantic bows, sent one of the attendants fairly over the bows of the vessel. With this exception, no accident or mischance marked the embarkation of Henry, which seemed to proceed under the most favourable auspices.

His fleet consisted of more than a thousand vessels, and some swans having come to look at it, he declared this little mark of cygnal attention to be a capital omen. We must request the reader to bear in mind that though all the authorities justify us in announcing one thousand as the number of the ships constituting Henry's fleet, we should not advise anyone to believe the statement who has not had an

Embarkation of King Henry the Fifth at Southampton, A.D. 1415.

opportunity of counting the vessels. Either the ships in those days were very small, or Southampton harbour has been fearfully contracted by the contractors who have since undertaken to widen it. We have been accustomed to place implicit faith in the rule of arithmetic that "a thousand into one won't go!" nor do we feel disposed to alter our impression in favour of a thousand of Henry's ships being able to go into Southampton harbour.

We suspect that a hundred would have been nearer the mark, for posterity is greatly in the habit of putting on an O, and really believing there is nothing in it.

Whatever the numerical strength of Henry's fleet may have been, it is certain that he entered the mouth of the Seine, which made no attempt to show its teeth, and he landed on the 13th of August, three miles from Harfleur, without any resistance. He severely deprecated all excesses against the peaceful inhabitants, but he nevertheless besieged the fortress of Harfleur with tremendous energy; so that his conduct towards the natives was a good deal like that of the individual who knocked another downstairs with numerous apologies for being under the painful necessity of doing so.

The siege was under the conduct of "Master Giles," the Wellington of the period. Master Giles must have been somewhat of a bungler, for he was not successful until he had lost nearly all his men, and been six-and-thirty days routing out the garrison. Even then the foe surrendered through being too ill to fight, rather than from having got much the worst of it. Henry's army was also reduced to a pack of invalids, and his ships were turned into infirmaries for his soldiers. Though the troops were wretchedly indisposed, Henry himself was only sick of doing nothing, and he accordingly sent a challenge by a friend to the dauphin of France, inviting him to a single combat.

The feelings of Louis were not in correspondence with those of the English king, whose invitation to a hostile *tête-d-téte* was never answered. The friend sent by Henry was not by any means the sort of person to tempt the representative of Young France to a hostile meeting.

The bearer of the challenge was, in fact, a walking pattern of what the dauphin might expect to become in the event of his engaging in a duel. A countenance which looked more like a mug that had been cracked and riveted in twenty places, was the letter of recommendation presented by Henry's second. As the friend was evidently not a man to take a denial, Henry contented himself with scratching off a few hieroglyphics on a sheet of paper—to make believe that he was writing a note—and hastily seizing an envelope, he sealed and delivered the delusive missive. Henry's friend went away satisfied, with the full conviction that he was taking back an acceptance of his master's challenge, but when the communication came to be opened, the English king was indignant at the hoax that had been played upon him.

Finding himself foiled in an attempt to settle his dispute by single combat, Henry called over the muster-roll of his troops, which presented a frightful number of vacancies since the making up of his last army list. He had lost several hands from his first foot, and he was compelled to say to his adjutant, "Really, if we go on at this rate we shall be compelled to notify that *Nobody* is promoted *vice Everybody*, killed, or retired."

Henry the Fifth sends a Friend to the Dauphin.

His entire force having dwindled down to the mere shadow of its former self, he was advised to get home as speedily as possible. "No," he replied, "I have no notion of coming all this way for nothing, and I shall see a little more of this good land of France before I go back again." The army, which was nearly all under the doctor's hands, seemed, upon being drawn up in marching order, far fitter to go to bed than to go to battle. Every regiment required medical regimen, and when the soldiers should have been sitting with their feet in hot water and comforters round their throats, they were required, with a callous indifference to their state of health, to march towards Calais.

The journey began on the 6th of October, when the French king and the dauphin had a large force at Rouen, while the Constable of France was in front of the English, with an army consisting of the very pick of Picardy. In passing through Normandy Henry met with no opposition, but his movements were watched by a large force, which kept continually cutting off stragglers, or in military language, clipping the wings of his army. Those who lingered in the rear, or, as it were hung out behind like a piece of a pocket-handkerchief protruding from the skirts of the main body, were cut off with merciless alacrity. The English continued to be dreadfully ill, and were proper subjects for the *Hotel des Invalides*, but they nevertheless pursued their march with indomitable courage. In crossing the river Bresle, beyond Dieppe, they made a decided splash; but the garrison of Eu interrupted them in their cold bath, though with very little effect, for the French leader was killed and his followers were driven back to the ramparts. On reaching the Somme the English army found both banks so strongly fortified that had they resorted to the most desperate hazard, or played any other reckless game, breaking the banks would have been impossible.

Henry consulted with his friends as to the best means of getting across, but nothing was suggested, except to tunnel under the banks and dive along the bottom of the stream; but this was objected to for divers reasons. Henry kept marching up the left bank of the river, in the hope of finding a favourable opportunity to dash across; but every attempt terminated in making ducks and drakes of his brave soldiers. Wherever a chance appeared to present itself he tried it, but without success, for the river had been filled with stakes, though the extent of the stakes did not prevent him from carrying on the game as long as possible. At length, on reaching Nesle he hit the right nail on the head, for running across a temporary bridge near the spot, he found the accommodation passable.

The Constable of France, on hearing what had occurred, retired to St. Pol, like a poltroon, and sent heralds to Henry, advising him to avoid a battle, for the French fully intended to give it him. The constable then fell back upon Agincourt, in which direction the English army prepared to follow him. On the 24th of October, Henry and his soldiers came in sight of the enemy's outposts, and their columns served as advertising columns to indicate their position. During the night it is said that the

English played on their trumpets, so that the whole neighbourhood resounded with the noise; but as they were all very tired, and had gone to sleep, it is probable that the only music heard by the inhabitants emanated from the nasal organs of the slumbering soldiers. By the French the night was passed in noise and revelry; but the English were chiefly absorbed in repose, or occupied in making their last wills and testaments. These were far more suitable employments than the performance of those concerted pieces which would only have disconcerted the plans of their leaders.

The moon, which on that occasion was up all night, enabled the English officers to ascertain the quality of the ground that the French occupied. The constable stuck the royal banner into the middle of the Calais road, an achievement which the muddy nature of the soil, rendered softer by the drizzly rain, prevented from being at all difficult. The French took the usual means of counteracting the effect of external wet by internal soaking. "Every man," says the chronicler, "dydde drynke lyke a fyshe," though the simile does not hold, for we never yet found one of the finny tribe who was given to the sort of liquor that the French were imbibing before Agincourt. They passed round the cup so rapidly that, what with the clayey nature of the soil and the whirl of excitement into which their heads were thrown, they found it almost impossible to preserve their respective equilibria. They floundered about in the most disgraceful manner, and there was "many a slip 'twixt the cup and the lip" on that memorable occasion. In addition to the excesses of the table, they availed themselves of the resources of the multiplication table, by calculating the amount of ransoms they should receive for the English king and the great barons, whom they made sure of capturing. Thus, in the agreeable but delusive occupation of turning their imaginations into poultry-yards, and stocking them with ideal chickens that were never destined to be hatched, did the French pass the night before the battle. Still, there was a melancholy mixed with the mirth in the minds of many, who, in the midst of the general counting of the phantom pullets, found sad thoughts to brood over. It so happened that there were scarcely any musical instruments among the French, and their horses, it was remarked, never once neighed during the night, which was thought to be ominous of bad, for if a dismal foreboding intruded, there was not even an animal to say "neigh" to it. Some of the older and more experienced officers were seized with gloomy anticipations, but they were either coughed, laughed, or clamoured down; and when the veteran Duke of Berri ventured to allude to Poictiers, on which occasion the French had been equally sanguine, he was tauntingly nicknamed the Blackberry for his sombre sentiments. To add to the discomfort of the troops, there was a deficiency of hay and straw for the use of the cavalry. The piece of ground where the horses had been taken in to bait was a perfect pool, in which the poor creatures could be watered, it is true, but could not enjoy any other refreshment. The earth had proved itself indeed a toper, according to the song, and had moistened its clay to such a degree that everyone who came in contact with it found himself placed on a most uncomfortable footing. However resolved the French might have been to make a stand on the day of battle, it was impossible for them to make any stand at all on the night preceding it.

At early dawn Henry got up in excellent spirits, and declared himself ready to answer the communication of the French constable, which he had received some time before, advising him to treat or retreat, and which had hitherto remained unresponded to. A movement of astonishment was evinced by his followers at the announcement of the English king's intention to reply to the message he had received, but when he said, "I shall trouble him with three lines, which may extend to three columns," and proceeded to divide his army into that form, the gallant soldiers understood and cheered his meaning. The archers were placed in front, and every one of them had at least four strings to his bow, in the shape of a billhook, a hatchet, a hammer, and a long thick stake, in addition to his stock of arrows.

Having made these preparations, Henry mounted a little grey pony and reviewed his army. He wore his best Sunday helmet of polished steel, which had received, expressly for the occasion, an extra leathering, and on the top of that he wore a crown of gold richly set with jewels. In this headgear he presented such a dazzling spectacle to the enemy that it would have been almost as difficult to take an aim at the sun itself as at the blazing and brilliant English leader. As he rode from rank to rank, he had an encouraging word for every soldier; and his familiar "Ha, Briggs," to one; his cheerful "What, Jones, is that you, my boy?" to another; and his invigorating "Up, Smith, and at 'em!" to a third, contributed greatly to increase the confidence of his men and strengthen their attachment to their general. "As for me," he said, "you'll have to pay no ransom for me, as I've fully made up my mind to die or to conquer."

On passing one of the divisions, he heard Walter Hungerford—the original proprietor of Hungerford Stairs—regretting there were not more of them. "What do we want with more?" exclaimed Henry. "I would not have an *extra* man if you would give him me. If we are to fall, the fewer the better, and if we are to conquer, I would not have one pair of additional hands to pick a single leaf of our laurels." The French were at least six to one of the English, but the former were horridly out of condition on the night before the battle. They wore long coats of steel down to their knees, which gave them the look of animated meat screens, and the armour they carried on their legs served to complete the resemblance. "They wore a

Henry inspecting his Troops before the Battle of Azincourt.

quantity of harness on the upper part of their bodies," says M. Nicolas, but he does not tell us whether the harness consisted of horse collars, which by being grinned through would have enabled them to advance towards the foe with a smiling aspect. The ground was remarkably soft, and the French troops being exceedingly heavy, they kept sticking in the mud at every step, while the ensigns, who had the additional weight of their flags, got planted in the ground like a row of standards. The horses were up to their knees in no time, and when they attempted to pull up they found the operation quite impossible. Henry had declared he would roll the enemy in the dust, but the wet had laid all the dust, and he must have rolled them in the mud if he had rolled them in anything. The French are said by a recent historian[62] to have been suffering under a "moral vertigo," but as the vertigo had been brought on by drinking on the previous night, the morality of the "vertigo" will bear questioning. They had got themselves into a field between two woods, where they had no room to "deploy," and they were tumbling over each other like a pack of cards, or a regiment of tin soldiers. Though they had imbibed a large quantity of wine and spirits, the rain, which fell in torrents, only added water to what they had drunk, and threw them into what is technically termed a "groggy" condition. Henry compared them to so many tumblers of rum-and-water, so comical was their appearance as they fell about in a state of soaked stupidity. To increase their confusion, the Constable of France was unable to keep order, for several young sprigs of French nobility were all tendering their advice, and thus there were not only cooks enough to spoil the broth, but to make a regular hash of it.

At length, about the hour of noon, Henry gave the word to begin by exclaiming "Banners, advance!" and at the same moment Sir Thomas Erpingham, a grey old knight, who appears to have been a kind of military pantaloon, threw his truncheon into the air with true pantomimic activity. "Now, strike!" exclaimed the veteran, as he performed this piece of buffoonery, and followed it up with the words "Go it!" "At 'em again!" "Serve 'em right!" and "Give it 'em!" The French fought bravely, and Messire Clignet, of Brabant, charged with twelve hundred horse, exclaiming "Mountjoye, St. Denis!" when down he fell, on the soft and slippery ground, like a horse on the wooden pavement. Everywhere the French cavalry cut the most eccentric capers; and even when there was an opportunity of advancing, the advantage seemed to slip from under them, for the ground was as bad as ground glass to stand upon. The English archers rushed among the steel-clad knights, who were as stiff as so many pokers—though not one of them could stir—and they were thus caught in their own steel traps, or trappings. The Constable of France was killed, and the flower of the French chivalry was nipped in the bud, or, rather, experienced a blow of a fatal character.

"This is a very hard case, indeed," roared one of the victims, as he pointed to his suit of steel, which rendered him incapable of fighting or running away, though he was quite ready for either. But the hardest part of all was the softness of the ground, into which the French kept sinking so rapidly that

---

62. Macfarlane. Cabinet History, vol. v., p. 21.

they might as well have fought on the Goodwin Sands as on the field of Agincourt. The weight of their armour caused them to disappear every now and then, like the Light of All Nations, on the spot we have just named, and an old French warrior—one of the heavy fathers of that day—was seen to subside so completely in the mud that in a few minutes he had left only his hair apparent. The English, who were lightly clad, kept up wonderfully under the fatigues of the day, and some of them performed prodigies of valour. Henry himself seems to have acquitted himself in a Style quite worthy of Shaw, or Pshaw, the Life Guardsman. His majesty was charged by a band of eighteen knights, whom it is said he overcame, but it is much more likely that finding themselves ready to sink into the earth, they were compelled to knock under.

Their cause was desperate, it was neck or nothing with many; but as they became immersed in the soil by degrees, it was neck first, and nothing shortly afterwards. The Duke of Alençon made a momentary effort to be vigorous, in spite of his steel petticoats, and gave Henry a blow on the head that broke off a bit of the crown which he had been wearing over his helmet. This *embarras des chapeaux*, or inconvenient superfluity of hats, was a weakness Henry was subject to, and there was no harm in his being made to pay for it. The Duke of Alençon had no sooner broken the king's crown than he received a fracture in his own, which proved fatal. The battle was now over, and the English began to secure prisoners, taking from each captive his cap, or hat, but it is to be presumed giving a ticket to each, by which all would get back their own helmets. Henry having taken it into his head that the battle was going to be renewed, ordered the prisoners to be killed; but he afterwards apologised for his mistake, though posterity has never been satisfied with the excuse he offered. As far as we have been able to learn the particulars of this atrocious blunder, it arose in the following manner. The priests of the English army—with a sort of instinctive tendency to taking care of themselves—were sitting amongst the baggage. Henry, hearing a noise among the reverend gentlemen, looked round, and found them apparently threatened with an attack from what he thought was a hostile force, but which turned out to be a few peasants, who were scrambling with the priests for a share of the luggage. This attempted appropriation of church property was resisted by a vigorous ecclesiastical clamour, which led Henry to believe there had been a rally among the foe, and that the priests were giving the signal. Had he been aware that they were crying out before they were hurt, there is every reason to believe that he would not have issued the mandate which has so much compromised his otherwise fair average character. The French loss at the battle of Agincourt was quite incredible, but not a bit the less historical on that account, for if history were to reject all that cannot be believed its dimensions would be fearfully crippled.

The English, sinking under the weight of their booty, as well as the mud on their boots, marched towards Calais. Henry's army was reduced almost to a skeleton, but he used to say jocosely that with that skeleton key he would find an opening anywhere. Though rich in conquest, he was short of cash, and as England was always the place for getting money, he determined on hastening thither. The people received him with enthusiasm, and at Dover they rushed into the sea to carry him on shore, so that he literally came in on the shoulders of the people. Proud of this popular pickaback, he made a speech amid the general waving of hats, which was responded to by the gentle waving of the ocean. The tide, however, began to rise, when Henry cut short the proceedings of the meeting between himself and his subjects by exclaiming, "But on, my friends, to the shore, for this is not the place for dry discussion."

On his way up to town each city vied with the other in loyalty. Rochester contended with

English Soldier securing Prisoner at the Battle of Agincourt.

Canterbury, Chatham struggled with Gravesend, and Blackheath entered into a single combat with Green-wich; Deptford ran itself into debt, which it retains nominally to this day; and the Bricklayers presented their arms to Henry as he passed into the metropolis. In London he was met by the Lords and Commons, the mayor, aldermen, and citizens; but the sweetest music was that made by the wine as it poured down the streets, and caught a guttural sound as it turned into the gutters. Many a bottle of fine old crusted port was mulled by being thrown into the thoroughfare, and though it might have been good enough to have spoken for itself, it ran itself down through the highways with much energy. Nor was this enthusiasm confined to hollow words, for all the supplies which the king requested were freely voted him. It was only for Henry to ask and have, at this auspicious moment; and if, like some children, he had cried for the moon, it is not unlikely that his subjects, in the excess of their loyalty, would have promised to give it him.

In the spring of the year 1416, London was enlivened by a visit from the Emperor Sigismund. He imparted considerable gaiety to the season, and his entry into the city gave occasion for a general holiday. His object was to endeavour to effect a coalition between the two rival popes, and to get the kings of France and England to make it up if possible. He was followed by some French ambassadors who marred the harmony of the procession by looking daggers at the English nobles. Occasionally they proceeded from glances to gibes, which naturally led to pushes, that were only prevented from coming to blows by the sudden turning round of the emperor whenever he heard a disturbance going on amongst those who followed him.

During Sigismund's stay in town, the French besieged Harfleur, which was guarded by the Earl of Dorset and a most unhealthy garrison. Toothache, elephantiasis, and sciatica had so reduced the spirit of the English force that the Duke of Bedford, the king's brother, was sent to aid the Earl of Dorset, and the poor old pump was grateful for this timely succour. Bedford having put matters quite straight, returned to England, and Henry proposed a run over to Calais with his imperial visitor, Sigismund. Here a sort of Congress was held at which Henry made himself so popular that his rights to the French throne were partially recognised. France was at this juncture in a very unpromising condition, for the royal family did nothing but quarrel and murder one another's favourites. Isabella, the queen, lived in hostility with the king, who arrested several of his wife's servants, and had one of them, whose name was Bois-Bourdon, sewn up in a leather-bag and thrown into the Seine, from which the notion of giving a servant the sack, on the occasion of his getting his discharge, no doubt takes its origin.

The Dauphin John having died, he was succeeded by his brother Charles, a boy of sixteen, who was continually fighting with his own mother, and getting a good deal the worst of it. This state of things tempted Henry to bring an army into France in August, 1417, when, after the surrender of a few smaller places, he took Caen by assault, or rather by a good Caen pepper. In the ensuing year he undertook several sieges at once, and played with his artillery upon Cherbourg, Damfront, Lonviers, and Pont de l'Arohe as easily as the musician who plays simultaneously on six different instruments. His next important undertaking was the siege of Rouen, before which he sat down, and having looked at it through his glass, he made up his mind that starving it out was the only method of taking it. The inhabitants held out for some time on their provisions, but these being exhausted, they began to devour all sorts of trash that was never intended for culinary purposes. *Soupe au shoe* became a common dish, and though for a brief period they had mutton chop *en papillotes* they were at last reduced to the *papillotes* without the meat, but with their tremendous twists they of course could not be expected to make a satisfactory meal off curl-papers. They accordingly surrendered, and Henry, on the 16th of January, 1419, entered Rouen, where ambassadors from the various factions in France were sent to him. He was, however, quite open to all, but decidedly influenced by none, and had a polite word for each, but a wink for those in his confidence, as he administered the blarney to the various legates. At length it was agreed that he should have an interview with the king and queen of France and the Duke of Burgundy.

The French sovereign was not presentable when the day came, for excessive indulgence in wine had reduced him to a state from which all the soda-water in the world could not, at that moment, have recovered him. Henry, therefore, met the queen, who was attended by her lovely daughter, the Princess Catherine, and her cousin of Burgundy, while the English king was supported by his brothers, Clarence and Gloucester. The meeting was exceedingly ceremonious, and was conducted a good deal in the style of a medley dance, comprising the minuet, the figure *Pastorale* in the first set of quadrilles, and Sir Roger de Coverley. At a signal announced by the striking up of some music, Henry advanced first, performing as it were the *cavalier seul*, when the Princess Catherine and the queen, with the Duke of Burgundy between them, also advanced, until all met in the centre. Henry bowed to the queen, and took her hand, and then did the same with the Princess Catherine, a movement resembling the celebrated *chaine des dames*— and Burgundy fell in gracefully with what was going on by an occasional *balancez* to complete the action of the second couple.

This was the first occasion upon which Henry had seen his intended bride, and whether in earnest or in sham he appeared to be at once struck by her surpassing beauty. He enacted the lover at first sight with a vigour that would have secured him a livelihood as a walking gentleman, had he lived in our own time, and been dependent for support on his theatrical abilities.

The Duke of Burgundy introducing Queen Isabella and his Daughter to Henry the Fifth.

The whole day was spent in formalities, and Henry sat opposite to the princess till the close of the interview, looking unutterable things, for she was so far off that it would have been vain to have uttered anything. In two days afterwards Henry and the queen paid each other a second formal visit; but the English king looked in vain for the young lady, who like a true *coquette*, seems to have kept away for the purpose of increasing the impatience of her lover. Her mother, with the tact of an old matchmaker, tried to get the best possible terms from Henry; but with all his affection, he would not stir from his resolution, to insist on having the possession of Normandy and a few other perquisites as the young lady's dowry.

The French queen pretended to take time to consider his proposal, and seven formal interviews were held; but all of them were of so dull, stately, and slow a character that no progress was made at any one of them. The fact is that Henry was being humbugged, and if he had suspected as much during the seven first meetings, he was convinced of it at that, which should have been the eighth, for on going to keep his appointment he found neither the queen, the duke, the princess, nor any of the attendants of either of them. All ceremony was at an end, the diplomatic *quadrille* parties were broken up, and Henry, disgusted at having been made to dance attendance for nothing at all, became so angry that his brain began to reel on its own account, and he set off to his own quarters in a *galop*. He ascertained the truth to be that the queen and Burgundy had made it up with the dauphin, whom they had gone to join, and the precious trio having sworn eternal friendship to each other, added a clause to the affidavit for the purpose of swearing eternal hatred to all Englishmen.

Tired of kicking his heels about to no purpose, Henry determined on practising some entirely new steps; the first of which was to advance upon Pontoise and *chassez* the inhabitants. He then pushed on towards Paris, when Burgundy, fearful of a *rencontre*, retired from St. Denis, where he had taken up his position. Henry again offered to treat, but in sending in the particulars of his demand he added Pontoise to the list of places he should require to be transferred to his possession.

The alliance between the dauphin and the Duke of Burgundy was as hollow as the hollow beech tree rendered famous by a series of single knocks at the hands, or, rather, at the beak, of the woodpecker. After a little negotiation, and a great deal of treachery, Burgundy, in spite of the warnings of several of his servants, was induced to visit the dauphin at Montereau. The duke went unarmed, on the assurance that he should return unharmed, and instead of his helmet he wore a velvet cap, which one of his attendants declared was a wonderful proof of soft-headedness. Burgundy, on coming into the presence of the heir to the throne of France, bent his knee; when the President of Provence whispered something in the dauphin's ear, and both began winking fearfully at a man with a battle-axe. The man with the battle-axe gave a significant nod, and dropped his weapon, as if by mistake, upon Burgundy; when the Sire de Navailles, a friend of the duke, pointing to the fearful dent the axe had made, exclaimed, "This is not a mere accident." This was immediately obvious; for several others rushed upon poor Burgundy, who devoted his last breath to exclaiming to the dauphin, "You are an ass—ass—" for he died before he could get the word ass—ass—in.

Young Philip, the heir of Jean Sans-peur—-or Jack Dreadnought, as we should have translated this nickname of the Duke of Burgundy—succeeded to his father's estates, as well as becoming residuary legatee of the affections of most of his subjects. The dauphin's foul deed was execrated on all sides; for though the state of morals was low at the period of which we write, there was always a certain love of fair play inherent in the human character. The younger Burgundy was in a state of effervescence, and though he kept bottled up for a short time, his rage soon spirted out with fearful vehemence. He entered into a coalition with Henry, who stipulated for the hand of the Princess Catherine in possession, with the crown of France in reversion, and a few other trifling contingencies. In the year 1420, one day in the month of April—probably the first—the imbecile Charles, guided by Queen Isabella and the Duke of Burgundy, put his hand to the treaty. The unhappy monarch was in his usual state, when a pen having been thrust into his grasp, and while somebody held the document, somebody else directed the motion of the royal fingers. The treaty thus became disfigured by a series of scratches and blots which were declared to be the king's signature. An appendix to this document contained a fulsome panegyric on the English king, which wound up with a declaration of his fitness to succeed to the French crown, because "he had a noble person and a pleasing countenance." This shallow argument was intended to lead to the conclusion that he would treat his subjects handsomely; or that, at all events, should he ever reign over France, his rule would not be without some very agreeable features.

In May of the same year—1420—Henry started for Troyes, where the young Duke of Burgundy and the French royal family were sojourning. The English king was all impatience to see his bride, and he found her sitting with her papa and mamma in the church of St. Peter. They had intended a little surprise for their illustrious visitor, and everything being ready beforehand, he was affianced on the spot to the lovely Catherine. They were regularly married on the 2nd of June, and some of the gay young nobles hoped there would be a series of balls, dinner parties, and tournaments, in celebration of the wedding: Henry, however, declared he would have "no fuss," but that those who wanted to show their skill in jousting and tourneying might accompany him to Sens, which he purposed besieging on the second day after his marriage. He declined participating in the child's play of a tournament when there was so much real work to be done, "and as to feasting," he exclaimed, "let us give the people of Sens their whack, or, at all events, if we are to have a good blow-out, it must be by blowing the enemy out of the citadel." He proceeded at once with his beautiful bride from Troyes, and soon reaching Sens, he in two days frightened the inhabitants out of their Senses. They surrendered, and he then advanced to Montereau, which he took by assault—or rather, as one of the merry old chroniclers hath it, "which he took, not so much by assault as by a pepper." After besieging a few other places in France, Henry, in conjunction with Charles, the French king, made a triumphal entry into Paris. The inhabitants of that city gave him an enthusiastic reception, for, like the populace in every period, they were delighted at anything in the shape of change, and paid the utmost respect to those from whom they had experienced the greatest injury.

In January, 1421, Henry being very short of cash, determined on going home to England, which was even in those days the most liberal paymaster to popular favourites. Having with him a good-looking queen, his reception in his own country was most gratifying, for the old clap-trap about "lovely woman" was inherent from the earliest periods in the English character. This fascinating female was crowned at Westminster Abbey with tremendous pomp, and the happy couple went "starring it" about the country in a royal progress immediately afterwards. Their success in the provinces was immense; but their pleasant engagements in their own country were soon brought to an end by the announcement that France was still in a state of turbulence, requiring the immediate presence of Henry in Paris.

Having warmed his subjects' hearts, he struck while the iron was hot, and took an aim at their pockets. Parliament was in a capital humour, and came out splendidly with pecuniary votes for a new expedition. He left the queen at Windsor Castle, where she shortly after gave birth to a son; and having landed a large but very miscellaneous army at Calais, Henry marched to Paris, to reinforce the Duke of Exeter, who had been left there as governor. The English were successful at all points, and Queen Catherine having joined her husband, they held their court at the Louvre, where they sat in their coronation robes, with their crowns on their heads, as naturally as if they had formed a part of "the Royal Family at Home" in Madame Tussaud's far-famed collection of wax-work.

In the midst of his victorious career in France, Henry had started off to the relief of a town invested by the dauphin—an investment that was profitable to nobody. The English king had reached Corbeil, when he was taking suddenly ill, and throwing himself on a litter, he declared himself to be literally tired out with his exertions. Having been taken home to the neighbourhood of Vincennes, and put to bed, he summoned his brother, the Duke of Bedford, and some other nobles, to whom he recommended amity; but, above all, he advised them to continue the alliance with Burgundy, whose habit of sticking to his friends has given the name of Burgundy to the well-known pitch plaster. Having appointed his brothers Gloucester and Bedford regents, the one for England and the other for France, during the minority of his son, he seemed perfectly resigned; but his attendants literally roared like a parcel of children, so that he was compelled to tell them that crying would do no good to anybody. He died on the 31st of August, 1422, aged thirty-four, having reigned ten years with some credit to himself, and in full, as far as conquest may be desirable, with advantage to his country.

On the death of a king, it had been usual for the attendants to rush helter-skelter out of the room, and ransack the house of the deceased monarch, while his successor generally made the best of his way down to the treasury. Henry the Fifth was an exception to the rule, for he had earned so much respect in his lifetime that at his death there was no indecorum, but a desire was manifested to give him the benefit of a decent, and indeed a magnificent, funeral. When a king of England had died abroad on previous occasions, his remains were seldom thought worthy of the expense of carriage to his own country; but in this instance no outlay was considered too extravagant to bestow on the funeral procession of the sovereign. Hundreds of mutes followed, with that mute solemnity which is the origin of their name: and on this occasion there were hundreds of knights, all in the deepest mourning. Several esquires had their armour black-leaded, and their plumes dyed in ink, while the king of Scotland acted as chief mourner, and the widow of the deceased sovereign came in at the end of the gloomy retinue.

On its arrival in England, when it drew near London, fifteen bishops popped on their pontifical attire, and ran to meet it; while the abbots, taking down their mitres from the hat-pegs in the halls of their houses, sallied forth to join the sad procession. The remains of the king were carried to Westminster Abbey, and consigned to the tomb with every token of esteem, and the reverence it had been customary to show to the rising sun alone, was on this occasion extended to the luminary that had just set in unusual glory. The queen, desirous of evincing her affection for such a prince, caused a silver-gilt statue as large as life to be placed on the top of his monument. This piece of extravagance was, however, before the invention of British Plate, or that "perfect substitute for silver," which is a perfect substitute in everything but value, strength, purity, appearance, and durability.

In painting the character of Henry the Fifth, the English historians have used the most brilliant colours, while the French writers have thrown in some shades of the most Indian-inky blackness. The former have been lavish in the use of *couleur de rose*, while the latter have selected the very darkest hues, and, indeed, produced a picture resembling those dingy profiles which give a hard outline of the features, but render it impossible for us to judge of the aspect or complexion of the original. It is for us to look at both sides, like the apparently inconsistent pendulum, which, by constantly oscillating from right to left, becomes the instrument of furnishing a faithful record of the time.

Henry the Fifth was devoted to the happiness of his people; but he had sometimes an odd way of showing his attachment, by ill-using the few for the satisfaction of the many. Thus, he persecuted the Lollards in the most cruel manner, out of the purest condescension towards the clergy, who had got up a clamour against the sect alluded to. This obliging disposition may be carried too far, when it urges the commission of an injustice to one party, in order to favour another, and the persecution of the Lollards at the call of the clergy was a good deal like an acquiescence in a cry of "throw him over" got up in the gallery of a theatre, against some unfortunate who may have incurred the momentary displeasure of a "generous British audience."

The military exploits of Henry the Fifth have been praised by English historians, but the French writers have contrived to show that even the battle of Agincourt was nothing more than a mistake, like the one which happened at Waterloo about four centuries afterwards.

"He ought to have been conquered at Agincourt," say the annalists of France, but we are quite content that his conduct was not precisely what it ought to have been—according to them—on this great occasion.

Some praise has been given him for his tact in negotiating with the Duke of Burgundy and the dauphin at the same time, but we must confess that our notions of honour do not permit us to approve the act of temporising with two parties for the purpose of joining that which might prove to be the strongest. He was brave, beyond a doubt, but he was cruel in the treatment of some of the prisoners who fell into his hands, and we cannot give him the benefit of the presumption suggested by a French historian that if he hanged a quantity of unfortunate captives, he had probably very good reasons of his own for doing so.[63]

Among the other defects attributed to the character of Henry the Fifth is a degree of shabbiness towards the people in his employ, whom he is said to have paid very inadequately for their services. Considering, however, that the liberality of kings is often practised at the expense of the people, and that Henry was so crippled in his own means that the crown jewels were, on one occasion, pawned, we have no right to blame him for refusing to reward his soldiers with what could only have been the proceeds of plunder.

In person Henry the Fifth was tall and majestic, but his neck was a little too long, which may have given him that supercilious air for which some of his biographers have censured him. In his social habits he resembled the celebrated Mynheer Von Dunk, of antiintoxication notoriety, for Henry "never got drunk," even with success, which is of all things the most fatal to temperance.

---

63. Pour les autres qui furent exécutés dans le même temps j'en ignore les raisons, mais il est à présumer, &c., &c.— Rapin, tom, iii, p. 504.

CHAPTER THE THIRD

HENRY THE SIXTH, SURNAMED OF WINDSOR

enry the Sixth was not out of his long frocks when he came to the throne, for he had not yet completed the ninth month of his little existence. Though he succeeded peacefully to the crown, he was in arms from the first hour of his reign; and though he was not born literally with a silver spoon in his mouth, he had one there on his accession to the throne, for he was being fed at the very moment that the news of his father's death was announced in the royal nursery. It is easy to conceive the interesting proceedings that took place on its being proclaimed that the child, then in the act of having its food, had become the king of England. A clean bib was instantly brought, and he was apostrophised as a little "Kingsey Pingsey," a "Monarchy Ponarchy," and was addressed by many other of those titles of affectionate loyalty which are to be found nowhere but in the nursery dialect. A Parliament was summoned to meet in November, 1422, and, the regency being a good thing, there commenced a desperate struggle as to who should be allowed to have and to hold the baby. The Duke of Gloucester claimed the post of nurse, in the absence of his elder brother, the Duke of Bedford. The lords named the latter President of the Council, but while he was away the former was permitted to act as his deputy, and, what was more to Gloucester's purpose, he was allowed to receive the salary of £5333 per annum. Having got the money and the power, Gloucester was not particularly anxious to have the charge of the royal baby, who was accordingly handed over to the Earl of Warwick, jointly with Henry Beaufort, Bishop of Winchester, a half-brother of Henry the Fourth, who had also a high seat—convenient, by-the-way, for the infant king—in the council.

This Beaufort was the second son of John of Gaunt, and founder of the illustrious family of the Beauforts, who derive their original nobility from an ancestor who was *beau* and *fort*—strong as well as good-looking. If aristocracy in these days were derivable from the same source, the handsome and brawny drayman might take his seat in the House of Lords, while ticket-porters, coalheavers, railway navigators, and other representatives of the physical force party would constitute an extensive peerage, of what dramatic authors, when they write for the gallery, are in the habit of apostrophising as "Nature's noblemen." The Beauforts, besides the good looks and strength of their founder, had collateral claims to muscular eminence. The uncle of the first Beaufort was called John of Gaunt, from his gaunt or gigantic stature; and one of the family had been, in 1397, created Duke of Somerset, most likely on account of the somersets he was able to turn by sheer force of sinew.

We beg pardon for this slight digression, but as there are many who take a deep and reverential interest in everything appertaining to rank, it may be gratifying to them to know the precise origin of some of our most ancient and most aristocratic families.

Let us then resume the thread of our history. Bedford was still in France, and, in the month of October, King Charles the Sixth expired at Paris. The dauphin was at Auvergne, with a set of six or seven seedy followers, who could not muster the means of proclaiming him in a respectable manner. They hurried off altogether to a little roadside chapel, and having one banner among the whole lot, with the French arms upon it, they raised it amid feeble shouts of "Long live the king," aided by a few "hurrahs" from some urchins on the exterior of the building. This farce having been performed, and the title given to it of "The proclamation of Charles the Seventh," the party repaired to luncheon at the king's lodgings. Having come into a little money by the death of his father, he went with a few friends to Poictiers, where a coronation, upon a limited scale, was performed, at an expense exceedingly moderate.

While this contemptible affair was going on in a French province, the Duke of Bedford was busy, in Paris, getting up a demonstration in favour of the infant Henry. Fealty was sworn towards the British baby in various great towns of France; and Bedford, anxious to cement the alliance with Burgundy, married the duke's sister, Anne; though it seems strange that he should have calculated upon a marriage as a source of harmony. He must have had a strong faith in wedded life, to have anticipated a good understanding as the effect of that which so frequently opens the door to perpetual discord.

While Bedford was making strenuous exertions to promote the ascendency of the English in France, the nominal king of that country, Charles the Seventh, had given himself up to selfish indulgences. His energies were diluted in drink; but a few vigorous men, who were about him, forced him occasionally into the field, from which he always sneaked out on the first opportunity. He was compelled to engage in two or three actions, and was defeated in all, though he had the benefit of about seven thousand Scotch, under the command of the Earl of Buchan; and threatened to cure his enemies of their hostility by administering a few doses of Buchan's domestic medicine. After two or three reverses, Charles thought his army strong enough to attempt to relieve the town of Ivry, which, in the summer of 1424, was besieged by the Duke of Bedford.

Charles's force consisted of a strange mixture of Scotchmen, Italians, and Frenchmen, who were all continually giving way to their national prejudices, and quarrelling in broken French, broken Italian, or broken Scotch,—which is a dialect something between a sneeze, a snore, and a howl, spiced with a dash of gutturalism, and mixed together in a whine of surpassing mournfulness. The French declared the Scotch were mercenaries, who had an "itching palm;" but the Scotch savagely replied that "they came to the scratch with a true itch for glory."

While the three parties were engaged in a vigorous self-assertion, and were loud in praise of their own valour, they caught a glimpse of the English force—and, halting in dismay, retreated without drawing a sword. The garrison of Ivry, which had been waiting the approach of its friends, who were to do such wonders, and had been watching the scene with intense anxiety from the battlements, could only murmur out the words "pitiful humbugs," and surrender at discretion.

By some lucky chance—or, as other historians have it, by the revolt of the inhabitants—Charles and his mongrel army had got possession of the town of Vemeuil, which was a very strong position. They had scarcely got snugly in, when the Duke of Bedford presented himself before the walls, and a council was instantly held, to consider how they should get out again. Everybody talked at once, and a mixed jargon of Scotch and French, flavoured occasionally with a little Italian sauce, was the only result of the deliberation of the gallant army. At length, by common consent, they ran away, preferring to fight in an open field, if they must fight at all—for there would then be more margin for escape, or latitude for bolting, in the event of their getting the worst of it.

So rapid was their desertion of the town that they left behind them all their luggage, which was perhaps a wise precaution, for they were thus enabled to run the faster, in case of having to execute a retreat, which was one of the military manouvres in which they had had the most experience.

The two armies were now in presence of each other, and on both sides the feeling was like that of the young lady who "wondered when them figures was a-going to move," at an exhibition of wax-work. The Earl of Douglas, with Scotch caution, wanted to wait, but the Count of Narbonne, with French impetuosity, was for making a beginning, and rushed forward, shouting "Mountjoye St. Denis!"—which was synonymous, in those days, with "Go it!" in ours. The whole line followed, helter-skelter and pell-mell, so that when they got up to the stakes the English had run into the ground—to show, perhaps, they had a stake in the country—the French were out of breath, out of sorts, and out of order. They were miserably panting, but not panting for glory, and the punches in the ribs they got from the English made them roar out like so many paviours in full work—as they always are—down Fleet Street. Their temporary want of wind was soon changed into permanent breathlessness, and thus, in spite of all their boasting, there was a miserable end to their puffing.

The battle was very severe, for they had been "at it" for three hours. Douglas, it being before the time when "the blood of Douglas could protect itself," was slain. Buchan, who had been taunted by his allies with being nothing better than a buccaneer, also fell, and the French lost a countless number of counts, as well as a host of miscellaneous soldiers. The Italians, who had boastingly called themselves the Italian cream of the army, turned out to be the merest milksops, and kept as much out of harm's way as possible. The Duke of Bedford ordered the heads of several prisoners to be cut off, and the Bedford executions were so numerous that the heads-man's axe got the name of "the Bedford level."

The battle of Vemeuil had been fought on the 17th of August, 1424, and Charles the Seventh seemed on the eve of bankruptcy; both in cash and credit. His money was all gone, and his friends had—of course—gone after it. Fortune, however, favoured him, at the expense of his enemies, for they began to disagree with each other. To say that there was a quarrel is equivalent to saying that there was a woman in the case, and the woman was—upon this occasion—the celebrated Jacqueline of Hainault. This prize specimen of a virago was the daughter of the Count of Hainault, and the niece of John the Merciless, from whom she inherited all that coarse unwomanly bluster, which, in one of the fair sex, is called by courtesy "a proper spirit." She had been married to a little bit of a boy of fifteen, her cousin-german and her godson—an urchin commonly known as John Duke of Brabant. Jacqueline, who was beautiful and bold, was no match—or, rather, was more than a match—for a stripling not half way through his teens at the time of his marriage. The puny lad had got into bad company, and was surrounded by a set of low favourites. The masculine Jacqueline was not exactly the woman to submit tamely to any injury, and taking offence at one of her boy-husband's friends, she had him murdered.

This stamped her as that most objectionable of characters, an acknowledged heroine, and she became "a woman of strong mind" in all the chronicles of the period. Her liliputian husband was persuaded to retaliate by dismissing all his wife's ladies-in-waiting, upon which Jacqueline became a greater vixen than ever.

After a powerful scene of domestic pantomime, in which she alternately tore her hair and that of her husband, she declared her determination to leave him. "A thplendid riddanthe," lisped the aggravating boy; upon which Jacqueline, making another rush at his hair, and taking a large lock of it in her hands—not, however, to be preserved as a pledge of affection—she hurried off to Valenciennes, and thence to Calais. The runaway next made for England, where she remained on a visit with Henry's queen, Catherine, at Windsor Castle. Here she soon began flirting with the king's brother, the Duke of Gloucester, and though the poor man was not deeply in love with her, he was persuaded to agree to a marriage.

Jacqueline being already the wife of another, was compelled to seek a dispensation from Pope Martin V., but he looked at the matter with an unfavourable eye, when Jacqueline, making a coarse allusion to her own eye and a female branch of the Martin family, despatched a messenger to the opposition pope, the thirteenth Benedict. Being a Benedict he could not consistently oppose a marriage, and he granted the dispensation immediately.

Gloucester, who had determined on making his new wife profitable, if she could not be pleasant, claimed without delay her possessions in Hainault, Holland, and elsewhere, which she had inherited. It was a few weeks after the battle of Vemeuil, which we have recently described, that Gloucester and his considerably better-half—in quantity if not in quality—started off with a large army to take possession of Hainault. They soon frightened the inhabitants of the capital, of which they made themselves master and mistress, without any previous warning. Philip, Duke of Burgundy, the uncle of the boy-Duke of Brabant, was very angry at the lad's wife coming to cheat the boy, as it were, out of his property. After a good deal of hard struggling to keep his position at Hainault, Gloucester came to the determination that his wife was not worth the bother she occasioned him, and he accordingly went home, leaving her to defend herself as well as she could, when she was instantly besieged, given up to the Duke of Burgundy, by the inhabitants of Mons, and sent to Ghent in close imprisonment.

Neither bolts nor bars could restrain the impetuosity of this tremendous woman, who burst from her prison, and putting on male attire, which became her much better than her own, she escaped into Holland. It was not to be expected that a fighting woman would remain very long without followers, and the "Hainault Slasher"—as Jacqueline might justly be called—soon mustered a strong party in her favour. The novelty of going to battle with a woman for a leader told well at first, but as the attraction wore off her soldiers dwindled away by degrees, until her forces became utterly insignificant. Even her chosen Gloucester took advantage of her absence to treat his marriage as a nullity, and to unite himself with Miss Eleanor, the daughter of Lord Cobham. The desertion of the husband she preferred was in some degree compensated by the death of the husband she hated, for the boy-Duke of Brabant lived only until April, 1427, and thus, by the abandonment of one, and the decease of the other, she became doubly dowagered. Still she continued to struggle with the Duke of Burgundy, but she was now advancing in years, and her efforts became perfectly old-womanish.

The summer of 1428 was the means of bringing her to her senses, for she was severely drubbed by the duke, and finally quelled in a career as unbecoming to her age and sex as it was inimical to her interest. She agreed to recognise Burgundy as direct heir, at her death, to all she possessed, and he made her hand over everything at once, which was a capital plan for making sure of his inheritance.

We have, however, devoted to the Hainault vixen more time and space than she is perhaps worth, but we have thought it better to dispose of her off-hand, to prevent so disagreeable a person from again intruding herself on the pages of our history.

From the time the English took possession of Paris, Orleans, like a ripe and tempting Orleans plum, had been the object of their desires. The French knew the importance of the place, and had concentrated within it ammunition, eatables, and stores of every description. Barrels of beef, and barrels of gunpowder—hams and jams—wine for the garrison and grape for the foe—preserves for themselves and destructives for their enemies, were laid up in abundance in the city of Orleans. In addition to all these articles, enormous supplies of corn had been poured into the place, which contained something superior even to the corn, for it held all the flower of the French nobility. Regardless of these facts, the Earl of Salisbury began to attack the city, and the English commenced an attempt to scale the walls, but having some missiles thrown at them from above, those engaged in the scale soon lost their balance. Salisbury, nevertheless, persevered by attacking some other point; but the garrison determined to pay him off, and having recourse to their shells, they shelled out with such effect as to kill the English leader. Salisbury was succeeded by the Earl of Suffolk, who employed the winter of 1428 in cutting trenches round the city, and throwing up redoubts, which rendered him very redoubtable.

Orleans was thus cut off from the chance of further supplies, and the awful words, "When that's all gone you'll have no more," began to be whispered into the ears of the inhabitants. Charles himself was for surrendering, and several mealy-mouthed courtiers, who feared they should soon be without a meal for their mouths, seconded the king in his pusillanimous project. Others were for holding out instead of giving in, and Charles's fortune seemed to be at the lowest ebb, when a letter arrived from one of the posts to announce the prospect of an early delivery. This early delivery was not, however, to be looked for by the mail, but by that illustrious female, Joan of Arc, familiarly known as the Maid of Orleans.

Charles, who had little faith in the power of a female to get one out of a scrape, and who believed the tendency of the interference of the sex to be a good deal the other way, burst out into a fit of immoderate laughter at hearing the news that had been brought to him. "Never laughed so much in my life," occasionally ejaculated the French king, as the tears rolled down his cheeks, in double-distilled drops of the extract of merriment. He, nevertheless, granted her permission to give him a look-in when she was coming that way; but it was more from curiosity, or to have another hearty laugh at the Maid's expense, that he consented to an interview. Joan arrived, with her squires and four servants; but even this retinue, small as it was, must have been larger than her narrow circumstances could have fairly warranted. The two squires could have got in the service of two knights a certain sum per day, and the four servants, at a time when war was being waged, might have obtained better wages than a poor and friendless girl would possibly have paid to them. These, or similar reflections, occurred to some of the people about the court of Charles, who, considering that Joan must be an impostor, advised his majesty to have nothing to do with her. At all events, it was deemed as well that her previous history should be known; and as the reader may wish for the character of the Maid, before permitting her to engage even his attention, we will, at once, say what we know concerning her.

Joan was the child of a brace of peasants, in a wild and hilly district of Lorraine, on the borders of Champagne, a country of which she seems in a great degree to have imbibed the qualities. Living in the neighbourhood of the sparkling and effervescing Champagne, her head became turned, or, at least, began to be filled with those bold aspirations which the *genius loci* might have had some share in engendering. It is undeniable that when a mere child, she delighted to roam about for the purpose of drinking at the great fountain of inspiration, which Champagne so abundantly supplies, and she would often go on until she heard voices—or a sort of singing in her ears—which told her she was destined for great achievements. Her birth-place was a short distance from the town of Vaucouleurs, at a little hamlet called Domremy, into which faction and dissatisfaction had so far forced their way, that the children used to pelt the children of the next village with mud and stones, on account of their political differences. Joan's attachment to her native soil caused her to be among the foremost of those who took up earth by handfulls, and threw each other's birthplace in each other's faces. Being in the habit of holding horses at a watering-house on the Lorraine road, she frequently heard the conversation of the waggoners, and, amid their "Gee-wos!" the woes of France were sometimes spoken of. Invisible voices now began to tell her that she was destined to set everything to rights, and to be her country's deliverer.

Though her father called it "all stuff and nonsense," she had talked over an old uncle, a cartwright at Vaucouleurs, whom she persuaded of her fitness to repair the common weal, and the honest cartwright promised to assist her in putting a spoke into it. The brace of peasants were annoyed at the very high-flown notions of their offspring, and when she talked of going to King Charles, they asked her where the money was to come from for the purposes of her journey. Joan immediately had a convenient dream, appointing the governor of Vaucouleurs, one Sire de Baudricourt, her banker on this occasion.

Under the guidance of her uncle, she visited the Sire, and told him the high honour her visions had awarded him, in naming him treasurer to her contemplated expedition. The Sire, not at all eager to become a banker on such unprofitable terms, refused at first to hear her story, or indeed to allow her to open an account, so that the first check she received was somewhat discouraging. He suggested that she should be sent home to her father with a strong recommendation to him to take a rod and whip all the rhodomontade completely out of her. Joan, however, cared little for what might be in pickle for herself while she was bent on preserving her country. She went constantly to the house of the Sire de Baudricourt, but he never allowed her to be let in, for he verily believed it would only have been opening the door to imposition.

At length, more out of pity to his hall-porter than from any other motive, the Governor agreed to see that troublesome young woman who had given no peace to his bell since the first day of her arrival at Vaucouleurs. After the interview, Baudricourt came to the conclusion that Joan was crazed; but she declared she would walk herself literally off her legs, until they were worn down to the stump, if the Sire refused to stump up for the expenses of the journey. Some of the people beginning to believe the maid's story, she was enabled to get credit in Vaucouleurs for a few trappings as well as for a horse, and at the same time six donkeys, in the shape of two squires and four servants, consented to follow her.

On the 15th of February, 1429, the Maid began her journey, in the course of which her companions frequently came to the conclusion that she was a humbug, and on arriving at a precipice they often threatened to throw her over. At length, all difficulties being surmounted, she arrived at Chinon, near Orleans, where Charles was residing. "I won't see her," cried the king, upon hearing she had come; "I am not going to be bored to death by a female fanatic. A man who believes himself to be inspired is bad enough, but there is not a greater plague on earth than a woman-prophet." At length, after being pestered for three days, he consented to grant an interview to Joan, who stood unabashed by the sneers of the courtiers. Every word that flowed from her lips had the effect of curling fluid on the lips of those who listened. Some would have coughed her down, others began to crow over her, and the scene was a good deal like the House of Commons during the speech of an unpopular member, when Charles, who was a good deal struck by the assurance of the Maid, took her aside to have a little quiet talk with her.

"Well, my good woman," he observed, "what is all this? Let me know your views as briefly as possible." Joan explained that her views consisted of magnificent visions, but Charles declared them to be mere jack-o'-lanterns of the brain, which were not worth attending to. Nevertheless, the earnestness of her manner had its effect, and the king sent her to Poictiers, where there was a learned university, and, though Joan was rather averse to the fellows, she allowed them to question her. Some of them began to assail her with their ponderous learning, but she cut them short by acknowledging that she did not know a great A or a little a from a bouncing B. She declared herself, however, ready to fight, and the learned men, who were not anxious for a contest with the Maid in her own style, pronounced a favourable opinion on her pretensions. To raise the siege of Orleans, and take the dauphin to be crowned at Rheims, were the feats she undertook to perform. As one trial would prove the fact, Charles consented to grant it. The soldiers, however, refused to follow her until they had seen how she would manage a horse, and they consequently all stood round her while she went through a few scenes in the circle. One of them, who acted as a kind of clown in the ring, put a lance into her hand, which she wielded with great dexterity, while she was still in the performance of her rapid act of horsemanship.

Joan having passed her examination with success, was invested with the rank of a general officer. In spite of her masculine undertaking, there was still enough of the woman in her disposition to induce her to be very particular in ordering her own armour and accoutrements. She had herself measured for an entirely new suit of polished metal, her banner was white, picked out with gold, and her horse was as white as milk when properly chalked for metropolitan consumption. The Maid looked exceedingly well when made up, and people flocked round her with intense curiosity; for if even the man in brass at the Lord Mayor's Show will attract a mob, a woman regularly blocked in by block tin was a novelty that everyone would be sure to run after. Full of enthusiasm, she started off to the relief of Orleans, and the garrison, encouraged by her approach, sallied out upon the besiegers with unusual vigour, exclaiming "The Maid is come!" and the result realised the old saying that "where there's a will, there's a way," or in the Latin proverb, *possunt* (they can) *qui* (who) *videntur* (seem) *posse* (to be able).

With the aid of the *posse comitatus* the object was achieved, and it may, perhaps, have happened that the superstitious fears of the English had much to do with the result of the battle. They declared that she was a witch, and some of them pretended to have seen her looking at them with great saucer eyes, which was, in those days, a test of sorcery. The sentinels at night got so nervous that they used to be startled by their own shadows in the moon, and would run away, declaring that they were pursued by black figures stretched on the ground, from which there was no escaping. Others declared the stars were all out of order, and that they heard the band of Orion playing, out of tune, at midnight. Some declared they had seen a horse galloping along the Milky Way, and they inferred that Joan of Arc sent her steed along it at full speed to keep up his milky whiteness.

The English army had been completely panic-struck by the successes of Joan, which were owing nearly equally to the zeal she inspired in her friends and to the superstition of her enemies. She caused a letter to be written to the latter, in her name, strongly advising them to "give it up," and now she determined to give them a bit of a speech from the ramparts of Orleans. Taking her place on the top of a ladder resting against a high wall, she advised them to "be off;" "that it was no use;" they were "only wasting their time there;" and recommended that, if they had business elsewhere, they had better go and attend to it. Sir William Gladesdale, an English leader, rose to reply amid cries of "Down, down!" "Off, off!" "Hear him!" "Oh, oh!" and the usual ejaculations which a difference of opinion in a crowd has always elicited. As soon as Sir William could obtain a hearing, he was understood to advise the Maid to "go home and take care of her cows;" upon which Joan cleverly replied that if "a calf were an object of care as well as a cow, he (Sir William Gladesdale) ought to be placed at once in safe keeping." The knight, finding the laugh against him, sat down without another word, and Joan became more popular than ever after this little incident.

It was part of the plan of the Maid to work upon the imagination of the foe, and an amanuensis was employed to write another threatening letter, in her name, to the English soldiers. The communication was thrown into the midst of them, and Joan, being anxious to know what effect it produced, stood on the ramparts to overhear what they said to it. "Listeners never hear any good of themselves," and the Maid had the mortification of listening to some fearful abuse of herself, which, perhaps, served her right, for her behaviour was, to say the least of it, exceedingly unladylike. Vanity became one of her most powerful incentives, and she took upon herself to disagree with the Governor of Orleans, the great captains, and all the military authorities, on points of military tactics. Joan was, in fact, a very impracticable person, but it was necessary to let her have her way to a considerable extent, on account of her immense popularity with the soldiers. She insisted on making an attack which was considered very premature, and, while leading it in person, she got knocked over into a ditch by a dart, which set her off crying very bitterly. A valiant knight picked her up and placed her in the rear, consoling her by saying, "There, there you're not a great deal hurt. Come, come—dry your eyes. Don't cry, there's a good girl," and other words of encouragement. Joan, feeling that it would not do for a heroine to be found roaring and whimpering at the first scratch she received, soon recovered her self-possession, and was soon at the ditch again, but on this occasion it was less for the purpose of fighting herself than of urging on others to battle.

The English, though they did not know whether Joan was a witch or a what, were nevertheless ready to fight her on a fair field, if she would give them the opportunity. Her voices had not, however, given her the word of command, and she found it advisable to put a poultice on her neck, which rendered it necessary that she should keep for some days as quiet as possible. Her voices were often exceedingly considerate in refraining from advising her to go to battle when she might have got the worst of it. In this instance they were accommodating enough to give her the opportunity of nursing her neck for at least a limited period. The English waited a little time for the Maid, expecting that she would prove herself a "maid-of-all-work" by venturing to go single-handed into a very difficult place, but, as she did not make the attempt, they retired with flying colours. These colours, had they been warranted not to run, might never have left Orleans, but on the 8th of May, 1429, the siege was raised, and the reputation of the English army considerably lowered.

On the strength of this event, Joan went to meet King Charles, who received her very affably, and the courtiers proposed inviting her to a public dinner. This honour she politely declined, for—like the celebrated Drummond—she was "averse to humbug of any description" but that which she had made for her own use, and after-dinner speeches were matters she held in utter abhorrence. She objected strongly to that festive foolery which induces people who never met before to express hopes that they may often meet again, and which is the source of at least twenty proudest moments of about as many existences. Joan, therefore, urged her previous engagements as an excuse for going out nowhere, for she felt assured that if she encouraged a spirit of jolly-doeism among the troops, they would soon become neglectful of all their duties.

Charles, urged by the example of Joan, determined to do a little soldiering himself, and had his armour taken out of his box, the rust rubbed off, the shoulder-straps lengthened, the leggings let down, the breastplate let out, and other alterations made, to adapt it to the change in his figure since he had last worn his martial trappings. Though he took the field, it was in the capacity of an amateur, for his modesty—or some other feeling—kept him constantly in the background, and after the battle of Patay, which was fought and won by the French, the cries of "Where is Charles? What's become of the king?" were loud and general. The Maid found him reposing on his laurels, or, rather, under them, for he had concealed himself in a thick hedge of evergreens, from which he declined to emerge until his question of "Is it all right?" had received from Joan's lips a satisfactory answer. The object of her visit was to persuade him to accompany her to Rheims, to celebrate his coronation in the cathedral of that city. "It's not a bad idea," said Charles, "but premature, I'm afraid, and so at present we will not think of it." Joan would, however, take no refusal. On the 15th of July, 1429, the French king made his solemn entrance into that city. He was crowned two days after, and, though not one of the peers of France were present at the ceremony, it went off with quite as much spirit as anyone might venture to anticipate.

Philip, the Duke of Burgundy, declined an invitation from the Maid, who pointed out to him the folly of fighting against his own king, when, if he wanted war, the Turks were always ready to fight or be fought, to have their heads cut off, or oblige anyone else by making the thing reciprocal. The Duke of Burgundy still kept aloof, but Joan continued to be successful without his assistance, and took several towns, chiefly from the readiness with which they were given up to her. Many of the people looked upon her as something preternatural, and they even fancied her white banner was always surrounded by butterflies, though truth compels us to state that these fancied butterflies were probably harvest-bugs, which, at about the period of the year when the phenomenon was supposed to have been seen, were most likely to be fluttering blindly and blunderingly about the Maid's standard. Many of the French officers, jealous of her success, attempted to malign her character. No tiger could have stood up for his respectability more furiously than Joan defended her reputation; and, indeed, she made so much fuss, to vindicate her fair fame, that we might have suspected her of impropriety, had not all the historians agreed in coming to an opposite conclusion. It was evident that Joan, having made one or two lucky hits, was anxious to back out before she damaged her reputation by failure. When asked what she would do if allowed to retire, she declared she would return and tend her sheep; nor did the cruel sarcasm of "Oh, yes, with a hook!"—which some courtier would throw in—divert her at all from her humble purpose. Having the rank of a general, she might perhaps have claimed the right to sell out or retire on half-pay, but she was anxious to return to her lowing herds, which caused Charles to say that for her to go and herd with anything so low, would be indeed ridiculous. Her voices, however, began to confuse her, and perhaps to talk more than one at a time, as well as to say different things; for on one day she would speak of resuming her humble occupations, and on another day would make preparations for smashing the English.

Fortune seemed to have deserted the English in France, and Bedford, the regent—like others of his countrymen, when they found their numbers inferior to those of the foe—had the coolness to propose settling the dispute by single combat. This ingenious device is like that of the gamester who has but a single pound, which he proposes to stake against the pound of him who has a hundred more, with the understanding that if the party who makes the proposition shall win, he shall walk off with all that belongs to his antagonist. Charles was rude enough to make no reply to this offer, but about the middle of August, 1429, the English and French armies found themselves very unexpectedly in sight of each other, near Senlis. How they came to such close quarters no one seemed to know; but it is agreed on all hands that both sides would have been very glad to get back again. Neither would venture to begin, and Charles requested to know what Joan of Arc's voices had to say upon such an important occasion. The Maid had unfortunately lost whatever voice she might have had, and could find nothing at all to say for herself. The king was eager to know whether his army might commence the attack, but Joan's voices said not a word, and as their silence was not of the sort which Charles considered capable of giving consent, he did not permit any assault to be begun by his soldiers. After looking at each other during three entire days, each army marched off the field by its own road, and nothing had taken place beyond the interchange of an occasional "Now then, stupid—what are you staring at?" between the advanced guards of either army.

Though our business, as an historian, has taken us a good deal abroad, we must now return home, lest, in our absence, the thread of our narrative should have got into such a state of entanglement as to cause ourselves and our readers difficulty in the necessary process of unravelling it. The 6th of November, 1429, was set apart for the coronation of the baby king, at Westminster; and, in a spirit worthy of the rising generation of the present day, his infant majesty insisted on the abolition of the protectorship. The notion that he could take care of himself had got possession of the royal mind; but the sequel of his reign afforded bitter proof of the extent of the fallacy. In 1430, he embarked for France, but the privy purse was again in such a disgraceful state that the king had not the means of paying for his journey. The usual humiliating step was taken of sending the crown to the pawnbroker. We may here take occasion to remark that though we frequently hear of the crown being put in pledge, we have no record of its being ever taken regularly and honestly out again. There can be little doubt that the people were unscrupulously taxed to rescue the regal diadem, which was no sooner redeemed than royal extravagance, or necessity, placed it again in its humiliating position. Had the same crown been transmitted regularly from hand to hand—or, rather, from head to head—it would have been perforated through and through by the multiplicity of tickets that from time to time have been pinned onto it.

On this occasion, the jewels went to the pawnbroker's, as well as the crown, so that the regalia were huddled together as if they had been no better than a set of fire-irons. It is surprising, under all the circumstances, that the sceptre never figured in the catalogue of a sale of unredeemed pledges, and we cannot wonder that some of our sovereigns have chosen to rule with a rod of iron, as a cheap and durable but a most disagreeable substitute. In addition to the means already alluded to, for filling his purse, the young king hit upon another mode of making money. Everyone who was worth forty pounds a year was forced to take up the honour of knighthood, and made to pay exorbitant fees for the undesired privilege. In this manner, many persons were dubbed knights, for the express purpose of making them dub up; and there is every reason to believe that the word "dub" has taken its meaning in relation to pecuniary affairs, from the arbitrary practice we have mentioned. Those illustrious families who trace their genealogy up to some knight who flourished in the time of Henry the Sixth, will not, perhaps, after this disclosure, be so very proud of their origin. We have had in our own day one or two who have been dignified with knighthood by mistake, instead of somebody else, but those who had greatness thrust upon them only for the sake of the fees, were scarcely less contemptible.

CHAPTER THE FOURTH

HENRY THE SIXTH, SURNAMED OF WINDSOR (CONTINUED)

edford had for some time been struggling in France under the extreme disadvantage of shortness of cash, for the council being engaged in continual quarrelling at home, had become very irregular in sending remittances. He had gone week after week without his own salary, but he never grumbled at that until he found his army, from getting short of cash, beginning to fail in allegiance. Often, while reviewing the troops, if he complained of awkwardness in the evolutions, he would hear murmurs of "Why don't you pay us?" and on one occasion an insolent fellow, who had been bungling over the easy manoeuvre of standing at ease, cried out, "It's all very well to say 'Stand at ease,' but how is a man to stand at ease when he never receives his salary?" Upon another occasion, Bedford had given the word to "Charge!" when a suppressed titter ran through the ranks, and, on his demanding an explanation, he was told respectfully by one of his aides-de-camp that the troops thought it an irresistible joke to call upon them to "charge," when, if they charged ever so much, there was no prospect of their demand being satisfied. Bedford used to rush regularly every morning to the outpost, in the hope of finding a letter containing the means of liquidating some of the arrears of pay into which he had fallen with his soldiers. He was, however, always doomed to disappointment, for there was either no communication for him at all, or an intimation that "next week"—which never comes—would bring him the cash he was so eagerly waiting for. His repeated visits to the outpost usually ended in a shake of the head from the officer on duty, whose "No, sir; there's nothing for you," had in it a mixture of compassion and contempt, which are not always incompatible.

Bedford, the regent, having left Paris, Charles thought that, the cat being away, the mice might be at play, and that the city would be unprepared if an attack should be made upon it. Beauvais and St. Denis opened their gates, but the Parisians were not so complaisant, and Charles, unwilling to resort to force, tried the effect of flummery. He issued proclamations, full of the most brilliant promises to his "good and loyal city," but the inhabitants replied by hanging out an allegorical banner, representing an individual in the act of offering some chaff to an old bird, who was refusing to be caught by it. Stung by this sarcasm, Charles determined to make an attack, and on the 12th of September he commenced an assault on the Faubourg St. Honoré.

Joan threw herself against the wall, but could make no impression upon it, and she could only lament that among the French artillery there was no mortar to be brought to bear upon the bricks of the city. She then resorted to other steps—or, rather, to a ladder—and had reached every successive round amid successive rounds of applause from her followers, when she was stopped by a wound, which fairly knocked her over. A friendly ditch received the disabled Joan, who went into it with a splash, which caused all her companions to basely run away, lest they should participate in the consequences of her downfall. Drenched and disheartened, sobbing, and in a perfect sop, the Maid crawled out of the ditch and lay down for a little while; but suddenly rising, and giving herself a shake, she made another rush at the battlements. A few better spirits, ashamed of seeing the weakest thus a second time going to the wall, joined her in her advance, but, meeting with resistance, they rolled back like a wave of the sea, almost swamping the Maid, and carrying her violently away with them.

Joan's influence had now begun to decline, for, though a heroine is popular as long as she succeeds, a woman who fails in her performance of the part is always ridiculous. She had also lost the favour of the soldiers by attacking them behind their backs, for she had flogged them with the flat of her sword till she broke the blade over their shoulders. They openly called her an impostor, a humbug, and a do; so that, hurt in her feelings as well as in her neck, wounded alike in mind and body, she resolved to quit the army. She even went to the Abbey church, and, fixing up a clothes-line, hung her white armour before the shrine of St. Denis. Charles supposed the articles had been put there to dry after the soaking the Maid had experienced in the ditch, but when he heard that Joan, as well as her coat of mail, was on the high ropes, he determined to take her down a peg as gently as possible. She was persuaded to prolong her stay, or, rather, to renew her engagement; and though, even after her military *début* at the siege of Orleans, she had wished it to be her "positively last appearance on any ramparts," Charles had the satisfaction of announcing that she had in

Joan at the Walls of Paris.

the handsomest manner consented to remain in his company. A constant renewal of an engagement will dim the attraction of the brightest star, and Joan was evidently on the wane as a popular favourite.

In the beginning of 1430 there was a light cessation of hostilities, and Charles remained at Bourges, where he was suffering under a severe exhaustion of his means and a general sinking in all his pockets. At this juncture, Joan met with a rival in the shape of an opposition prophetess, for it is always the fate of merit and success to become the subject of base and paltry imitation. Catherine of La Rochelle was the name of the female counterfeit who adapted her inspiration to the exigencies of the time, and, knowing the king to be short of cash, she pretended to have fits of financial foresight. She was, in fact, a visionary Chancellor of the Exchequer, running about with an imaginary budget, and transforming Charles's real deficiency into an ideal surplus. She affected to hear voices and to see visions; but the former were rude shouts of I.O.U., and the latter represented to her certain hidden treasure, which was hidden so well that it has never been found from that time to the present. She had the art of extracting money for the king's use from those who had any money to give, and a single speech from her mouth was sufficient to fill with coin any soup-plate or saucer that might be handed round to the audience. She boasted that she could talk every penny out of the purses of her hearers, and whenever she appeared, there was a general cry of "Take care of your pockets!"

Joan called her an impostor, and was called "another" in return; but it was said by a quaint writer of the period that, whatever the Maid of Orleans might have done with the sword, the tongue of Catherine would give an antagonist a more complete licking than the most formidable weapon. Charles was attracted by the financial fanatic, but, still wishing to propitiate Joan, he ennobled her family, and declared that her native village of Domremy should forever be exempt from taxes. It thus became one of the greatest rights of this place to forget the whole of its duties.

At the opening of the spring, the French king advanced again towards Paris with two prophetesses in his suite, but, as two of a trade never agree—particularly if they happen to be of the gentler sex—the two young ladies were constantly quarrelling. It is probable that the presence of Catherine was the cause of putting Joan upon her mettle, for she marched to the relief of Compiegne with all her accustomed spirit. She had made up her mind to a repetition of the hit she had made at Orleans, but Victory did not answer her call or show any disposition to wait upon her. Joan fought with valour, but her soldiers had no sooner met the foe than they agreed that the chances were against them, and that the only way to bring themselves round was to turn immediately back, a manouvre which was performed by one simultaneous movement. Joan tried to rally them, but they were too far gone, and while she kept her face to the enemy, her old disaster befell her, for she backed into one of those ditches in which all her military exploits seemed doomed to ter-minate. There being no humane member of society, or member of the Humane Society, to give her the benefit of a drag from the water in which she was immersed, she was soon surrounded by her enemies. Her own companions had fled into the city and shut the gates upon her, against which she had not the strength to knock, when, mournfully murmuring out, "Alas! I am not worth a rap," she surrendered to her opponents. The sensation created by the capture of Joan of Arc was actually prodigious. The captains ran out of their positions, and the men left their ranks to have a peep at her. Duke Philip paid her a visit at her lodgings, in the presence of old Monstrelet, who was either so deaf, or so stupid, or so thunderstruck, that he could not relate what passed at the interview. The ungrateful French made no effort to release the Maid, and, indeed, there seemed to be a feeling of satisfaction at having got rid of her. Her captors showed a strong disposition to make much of her by turning the celebrated prophetess to a profit, and the person to whom she had surrendered—the Bastard of Vendôme—sold her out and out to John of Luxembourgh. Friar Martin pretended to have a lien upon her; but John, refusing to have the lot put up again, and resold—in accordance with the usual practice in cases of dispute—cleared her off to a strong castle of his own in Picardy. Another pretended mortgagee of the Maid then started up in the person of the Bishop of Beauvais, who claimed her on behalf of the University of Paris. John of Luxembourgh disposed of her to his holiness for ten thousand francs, rather than have any further trouble.

Poor Joan was committed to prison on the charge of witchcraft, and as a kind of preliminary to the proceedings in her own case, a woman who believed in the Maid was burned, *pour encourager les autres* who might put faith in her inspiration. The fate of Joan was for some time very uncertain; but the learned doctors of the University of Paris, and other high authorities, recommended her being burned at once, which would save the trouble and expense of a previous trial. The Bishop of Beauvais, who had become the proprietor, by purchase, of the illustrious captive, recommended the adoption of regular legal proceedings. Priests and lawyers and lettered men were summoned from far and near; many of the legal gentlemen being specially retained, and all being practised in the art of cross-examination, to which Joan was subjected by those who conducted the case for the prosecution. Her trial was, throughout, a disgraceful exhibition of forensic chicanery, for her opponents attempted to puzzle her with hard words, which, in spite of her being charged with magic spells, she had not the power of spelling. The pleadings were shamefully complicated; but she defended herself with spirit, and occasionally confounded the doctors, who were confounded knaves, for they tried to take every advantage of her unfortunate position. Sixteen days were consumed in taking the evidence, and Joan sometimes made a point in her own favour, when the Bishop of Beauvais, sinking the dignity of the judge in the temporary office of usher, began to call lustily for silence; and, according to the modern practice of the officer of the court, making more noise than everyone else by the loudness of his vociferations.

The bishop shouted and resorted to other ungentlemanly expedients, during the entire day, to damage the cause of Joan, who, nevertheless, proceeded as if in the midst of that silence which the usher in Westminster Hall is continually disturbing by loudly calling for. It was contended, on the part of the prosecution, that there was magic in her banner; but Joan, who had served the other side with notice to produce the banner, declared there was nothing particular in any part of it. The pole belonging to it was as plain as any other pike-staff, and the banner itself was formed of a cheap material, which Joan declared was all stuff; so that the banner was, of necessity, waived by her enemies. Her judges, nevertheless, declared there was sufficient evidence to support a charge of heresy, and began to deliberate on the manner of her punishment. While some recommended fire, others threw cold water upon it, and French, as well as English writers, have laboured to prove that their countrymen, at least, were averse to a proceeding from which the term "burning shame" no doubt took the signification it bears at present. Having already found her guilty, her persecutors tried their utmost to urge her to acknowledge her guilt, for in the absence of proof, it was thought advisable to get at least a confession.

At length, on the 24th of May, 1431, the Maid was brought up to hear her sentence, and the Bishop of Beauvais, taking out a pile of papers, endorsed *re* Joan of Arc, declared himself ready to deliver his judgment. An opportunity was, however, allowed her to stay execution, on giving a *cognovit*, or acknowledgment of every charge brought against her; and such a document being drawn up, she reluctantly permitted Joan of Arc, X, her mark—for she could not write—to be affixed to it. Her punishment was commuted to perpetual imprisonment, with "the bread of sorrow and the water of affliction," which consisted of a stale loaf and a pull at the pump once a day, as her only nourishment.

She found very few crumbs of comfort in her daily crust, and when the water was brought to her, she declared it to be very hard, which was certainly better than soft for drinking. It was a portion of her punishment to resume her female attire, which caused her considerable annoyance, and a soldier's dress having been left in her prison, she was one morning discovered wearing it. Her jailer, on entering, charged her with "trying it on," but added that it was anything but fitting, and told her that she would certainly be overhauled when he reported that he had seen her in a pair of military overalls.

Joan trying it on.

The circumstance was instantly turned against her, and the putting on of male attire, which she had worn before, was declared to be a revival of the old suit, to which she had been liable. Her re-appearance in the soldier's dress was looked upon as a proof of uniform opposition to the authorities; and her offence was described as "relapsed heresy," or double guilt, like the "one cold caught on the top of t'other" by the boy who had been suffering under several layers of those disagreeable visitors. Judgment was now finally entered up against the ill-used Maid, who, on the 30th of May, 1431, was brought in a cart to the market-place and burned at Rouen.

We would gladly draw a veil over the fate of poor Joan; but we are unwilling to spare those who were accessory to it, from the odium which increases whenever the facts are repeated. Cardinal Beaufort and some of the bishops who had been instrumental to the murder of the Maid, began to whimper when the ceremony commenced, and to find it more than their susceptible natures could bear to witness. They had ordered the atrocity that was about to take place; but conscience had made them such arrant cowards that they had not the courage to witness the carrying out of their own savage suggestions. If persons so hard-hearted as themselves could feel so much affected by the sacrifice they had ordered, we may imagine what opinion ought to be entertained of them for commanding an act of atrocity which they dared not remain to contemplate.

The conduct of Charles in not interfering on Joan's behalf is even more cruel and despicable than that of her avowed enemies. The French king finding the Maid of no further use, came practically to a free translation of *Non eget arcu* (there is no want of a Joan of Arc), and left her to the fate that awaited her. It would have been nothing but policy to have insured her life, which he might easily have done, even when she was threatened with burning, and her case became doubly hazardous.

The English were very anxious to get up a sensation in France by way of diverting the public mind from the fate of the Maid of Orleans. A coronation, which is always one of the best cards to play, being good for a king or queen at the least, was thought of and resolved upon. The affair was intended to eclipse the ceremony of which Charles had been the hero and Joan of Arc the heroine. Young Henry, who had been crowned already at Westminster, and had therefore rehearsed the part he would be called upon to play, was brought over to Paris with all the scenery, machinery, dresses and decorations, properties and appointments that had been used before, so that the coronation being in the *répertoire* of costly spectacles, the expense of its revival was moderate. The performance took place in November, 1431; but though the getting-up was very complete, the applause was scanty, and the attendance was by no means numerous. Cardinal Beaufort occupied a stall, and there was a fair sprinkling of people in the galleries; but the principal character being a spiritless and most unpromising boy of nine, the spectacle excited very little interest.

Things remaining in France in a very unsatisfactory state, Charles and Philip of Burgundy came to the resolution that it was folly to go on cutting one another's throats, and they consequently effected a compromise. Philip got the best of the bargain, which was solemnised by a great deal of swearing and unswearing; for as the parties had previously exchanged oaths of hostility toward each other, it was necessary to take the sponge and wipe out former affidavits, as well as to supply the blank with new oaths of an opposite character. There was a mutual interchange of perjury; and posterity, on looking at the respective culpabilities of the two parties, can only come to the conclusion that they were *beaucoup d'un beaucoup*, or much of a muchness.

The Duke of Bedford did not live long after this treaty, but died of indigestion, and considering that he had eaten an enormous quantity of his own words, the result is by no means marvellous. He finished up his existence at Rouen, on the 14th of September, 1435, having swallowed a parcel of his own oaths, some of which are supposed to have stuck in his throat, and caused his dissolution. The English in France soon felt the fatal consequences of being without a chief, for the columns of an army, like the columns of a journal, are incomplete without a leader. Deprived of Bedford, the English soldiers could no longer hold Paris—or, rather, Paris could no longer hold them—and they were consequently forced to surrender. The Duke of York succeeded to the command in France—if he can be said to have succeeded who failed in almost everything. A succession of reverses was the only thing approaching to success which he experienced; and a supersedeas was soon issued to overturn his commission.

Talbot, Earl of Shrewsbury, did something towards restoring the English ascendency in France; but Philip of Burgundy thought he would try his hand at a siege, and fixed upon Calais as being the most convenient. The Duke of Gloucester, hearing he had a tremendous army assembled in front of the town, sent over to Philip an offer to fight him. "Only stop there till I get at you," were Gloucester's words; to which Burgundy replied that he should be happy to wait the English duke's convenience. Four days, however, before the latter landed, the former was seized with a panic—and, taking suddenly to his heels, his thirty thousand men scampered wildly after him. Philip, who had set the example, and must have been flighty to have commenced such an insane flight, was completely run off his legs by the ruck of fugitives in his rear; and he was swept into the very heart of Flanders, before he could ascertain what his soldiers were driving at. Talbot, Earl of Shrewsbury, did something towards retrieving the failing fortunes of the English; but, as both parties were getting into a nervous state—running away through sheer panics, crying out before they were hurt, and flying before they were pursued—a truce was agreed upon. It was for two years, to expire on the 1st of April, 1446,—and there could not have been a more appropriate day than that devoted to All Fools, to renew hostilities which were injurious to all parties.

Henry, of Windsor, was now twenty-four; but, though a man in years, he was still an infant in intellect. He was physically full-grown, but mentally a dwarf; and what had been in childhood the gentleness of the lamb, became in manhood downright sheepishness. His conversational powers would not have allowed him to say "boo to a goose," had it been necessary for him to address to that foolish bird that unmeaning monosyllable. Even his mother had turned her back upon him, as a noodle she could make nothing of, and had married Owen Tudor, Esquire, an obscure gentleman of Wales, who boasted, nevertheless, a royal descent, or at least maintained that the Tudors were so called from being not above Two-doors off from such illustrious lineage. The Queen-mother had died, but had left a lot of little Tudors, under the care of O. T., her *bourgeois gentilhomme* of a husband.

Henry being a mere nonentity, it was resolved to try and make something of him by finding him a wife of spirit; as if small beer could be turned into stout by mixing a quantity of gin with it. Margaret of Anjou was selected for the formation of this deleterious compound. She was one of those intolerable nuisances—a fine woman, with a great deal of decision, which means that she was decidedly disagreeable. Her father was a nominal king of Sicily and Jerusalem; but he had no real dominions, and only rented, as it were, a brass plate, or had his name up over the door of the countries specified. He was as poor as a cup of tea after the fifth water, and ruled over about as much land as he could cram into a few flower-pots which adorned the window of his lodging. He kept a minister who answered the bell and the purpose at the same time, and was accustomed to wait at table. His majesty's apartment was furnished with a sort of dresser covered with green baize, which formed a board of green cloth; and he had several sticks-in-waiting in his umbrella stand. His *robe de matin* was his robe of state; he had a green silk privy purse, and an ormolu cabinet. He had a keeper of the great seal which hung to his watch; and his bureau comprised a secretary for the home department, in which he kept all his washing-bills. He dispensed with a master of the horse by keeping no horse of his own, and he always had plenty of gentlemen-in-waiting, in the shape of creditors. He saved the expense of a paymaster by paying nobody; and though he issued Exchequer Bills, they were not only at very long dates, but wholly unworthy of anyone's acceptance. He was his own Chancellor of his own Exchequer, for he used to declare, with much apparent integrity that his government should never be degraded by useless sinecures. "Whenever there is nothing to do," he would philosophically exclaim, "I consider it my duty to do it." He usually resided in Sicily when he was at home, but he kept in his court—at the back of his lodging—a few Jerusalem artichokes, to represent the interests of his other kingdom of Jerusalem. He used to make a financial statement every now and then, for the sake of clearing himself of his debts, which were the subject of an annual act of which he alone got the benefit. He used upon these occasions to profess a considerable anxiety to rub off as he went on, but his goings on and rubbings off were equally to his own advantage, and the cost of those who had trusted him. Never was political economy carried to such perfection as by the father of Margaret, the king of Sicily and Jerusalem.

It was hopeless to ask for a dower with the daughter of a man who had what is vulgarly termed "a sight of money," which means that he could have put the whole of his income into his eye without any detriment to his vision. Instead of asking anything from a sovereign more fitted to be upon the parish than upon the throne, a trifling settlement was made upon him that the king of England might not be said to have married the daughter of an absolute monarch and an absolute beggar. Anjou and Maine, which had been taken from him by main force, were restored to him, and a little money was advanced to him on account of his first quarter's revenue, to enable him to cut a respectable figure at his daughter's wedding.

Suffolk brought home the bride to England, where she was, of course, severely criticised. For many she was too tall, and her height was an objection that could not be overlooked very easily. The friends of the Duke of Gloucester—known as the good Duke Humphrey—declared he would have found a better queen; and Duke Humphrey paid her no attention, for he never even asked her to a family dinner, an omission which gave rise to a saying that is still current.[64]

The King of Sicily and his Household.

The good Duke Humphrey, though he gave no one a dinner, was anxious to let everyone have his desert, which made his royal highness very unpopular. His enemies began by charging his wife with necromancy, because she was in the habit of consulting the dregs of her teacup when turned out in her saucer—an act that was stigmatised as sorcery. She was also proved to have in her possession a large wax doll, resembling the king, which she was in the habit of placing before the fire for the purpose, it was said, of sweating her sovereign. This was interpreted into a desire to see him waste away, and she was

---

64. Dining with Duke Humphrey is a process that needs no explanation.

accordingly sentenced to perpetual imprisonment. Had she been able to melt the king himself as she melted his effigy, she might have been pardoned; but though the wax image was soft enough, he only waxed wroth when an appeal in her behalf was made to him. Her husband now became personally an object of persecution, and was arrested on a charge of treason, on the 11th of February, 1447, when he went to take his seat at the opening of Parliament. On the 28th of the same month, he was found dead in his bed, and of course the conclusion was that he had been murdered, though there were no signs of violence. There were various rumours as to the cause of Duke Humphrey's death, and despair, dyspepsia, apoplexy, and unhappy perplexity, or a broken heart, were equally spoken of as having occasioned his dissolution. It is strange that inanition was never thought of as a probable mode of accounting for the decease of Duke Humphrey, whose stinted diet has given to his dinners an unenviable notoriety.

The old rival and uncle of the good Duke Humphrey did not long survive his nephew, for the grasping prelate died on the 11th of April, 1447, at Winchester, where he had retired to his see, from which he was to the last straining his eyes towards the popedom.

Under the ministry of Suffolk the glory of England rapidly declined, and its possessions in France were daily diminishing. Parliament began to take the matter seriously up, and not a day passed without some awkward motion being made to embarrass the Government. At length, in January, 1450, Suffolk became so exasperated that he challenged his enemies to the proof of their accusations, which was equivalent to asking for a vote of confidence. The Commons replied by requesting the Lords to send him to the Tower, which they declared themselves most happy to do, if the Lower House would only send up a specific charge on which he might be committed. The Commons acceded with the utmost pleasure to the demand, and cooked up an accusation very promptly, for in those days such things were kept almost ready made, to be used at the shortest notice, for the purpose of knocking the head from off the shoulders of a minister. It was laid in the indictment against Suffolk that he had been furnishing a castle with military stores; or, in other words, ordering a quantity of gunpowder to be sent in for the purpose of assisting France against England. Though the accusation was wretchedly vague, it was sufficient foundation for a warrant, upon which Suffolk was seized by the scruff of the neck, and hurried to the Tower. Fearing that one bill of impeachment might be insufficient, his enemies published a series of supplements.

In his defence he noticed only the first set of charges, which accused him of a desire to put the crown on the head of his son; a freak that Suffolk never had the smallest idea of practising. On the 13th of March, 1460, he was brought to the bar of the House of Lords, and went down upon his knees like a horse—or rather like an ass—on the wooden pavement. He denied, ridiculed, and repudiated some of the articles in the impeachment, and accused the lords themselves of being his accomplices in some others. A proceeding which we can only characterise as a general row immediately took place, and the House of Lords became a perfect piece of ursine horticulture, or regular bear-garden.

Suffolk, though warmly defended by the court, was furiously attacked by the Commons, who declared they would not vote a penny of the supplies while the minister remained unpunished. The king, as long as it did not affect his pockets, was tolerably staunch towards his friend, but when no money came in, and the royal outgoings continued to be large, it was found expedient to throw the favourite over. Every fresh bill that was placed on the unpaid file at the palace shook the royal resolution; and when the eye of the king glanced over his huge accumulation of unsettled accounts, he began to think seriously whether it was not too great a sacrifice to lose his supplies for the sake of saving Suffolk.

The favourite was gradually getting out of favour, and was sent for by the king to a private interview, in the course of which it was intimated to the duke that he must be dropped, but that he should be "let down" as easily as possible. This private intimation kept Suffolk in a state of suspense considerably worse than certainty; for it is a well-established fact, given on the authority of those who have tried both, that a bold leap into the fire is preferable to a constant grill on the gridiron, or a perpetual ferment in the frying-pan.

On the 17th of March Suffolk was again brought up in presence of the king, at a sort of judicial "at home," given by his majesty. It took place, according to some authorities, in the sovereign's private apartments; but the chroniclers are mute as to which room—whether the two-pair back, the one-pair front, the *salle à manger*, or the *salon*—was the scene of the important interview. Suffolk threw himself once more at the feet of the king, who, it is to be hoped, had no corns; but Henry must have felt hurt at receiving a minister on such a footing. Suffolk, still at his master's feet, endeavoured to hit upon Henry's tender points, but the sovereign was on this occasion influenced by the impression made upon his understanding. He ordered Suffolk into banishment for five years, and gave him till the 1st of May to pack up for his departure.

The people were determined not to let the traitor off so easily, and no less than two thousand assembled to take his life, which he wisely abstained from placing at their disposal. He gave a farewell banquet at one of his country seats to his relatives and friends, and, upon his health being duly proposed as the toast of the evening, he swore, of course, that he was perfectly innocent. Finding it necessary to dodge the popular indignation, he started off to Ipswich, when he embarked for the Continent.

Banishment of Suffolk.

On the 2nd of May, as he was sailing between Dover and Calais, his convoy—consisting of a smack and punt for self and retinue—was hailed by a great hulking man-of-war from the hulks, which bore the name of *Nicholas* of the Tower. This was a sad blow to the little smack, which would have gladly gone off had it not been most vigorously brought-to by the larger vessel. The duke was ordered on board the *Nicholas*, and after the ship had stood off and on for three days, it turned out that the vessel was only waiting to take in an axe, a block, and an executioner. This dismal addition to the freight having at last arrived, it was immediately put in requisition, and, as Suffolk was very unpopular, nobody took the trouble to inquire what had become of him. The only account that could ever be given of him was that he had been taken away by the crew of the *Nicholas*, which was a very old ship, and the announcement that Suffolk had gone to Old Nick was all that was ever said concerning him.

We are soon about to enter upon those Wars of the Roses which planted so many thorns in the bosom of fair England. It is strange that out of *couleur de rose* should have emanated some of the most sombre and melancholy hues that ever darkened the pages of our history. "Coming events cast their shadows before," and the shade in this instance was one Cade, familiarly called Jack Cade by various authorities. This celebrated individual was a native of Ireland, who had served in France in the English army, so that he may be called a kind of Anglo-Irish-Frenchman, a combination that reminds us of the celebrated poly-politician, who, being desirous of being thought "open to all parties," with the vow of being ultimately influenced by one, gave himself out as a conservative-whig-radical. Jack Cade was a jack-of-all-trades, or, at all events, a jack of two, for he had been a doctor first and a soldier afterwards. Some have ironically contended that the change from a medical to a military life was only an extension of the same business, and that, in resigning the bolus for the bullet, the powders for the gunpowder, and the lancet for the sword, he was only enlarging the sphere of his practice. With that remarkable deference for the aristocracy they pretend to despise, which is only too common amongst demagogues, Cade tried to claim relationship even with royalty, and, giving himself out as a relation of the Duke of York, he assumed the name of Mortimer.

That Cade was a decayed scion of an illustrious stock may be doubted, and some, who have not been ashamed of an anachronism for the sake of a sneer, have gone so far as to say that the Cades were the earliest cads of which there are any records.

It has been well remarked somewhere, by somebody, that the men of Kent, though living near the water, were always very inflammable, and the Kentish fire is to this day proverbial for its intensity. Cade threw himself among these men, who made him their captain, and marched with him to Blackheath, from which he commenced a long correspondence with the Londoners. The Government, alarmed at an assembly of fifteen or twenty thousand men at a place where large assemblies were unusual, sent to enquire the reason of the good men of Kent having quitted their homes in such large numbers. Cade, who among his other restless habits, appears to have been troubled with a *cacoethes scribendi*, took upon himself to answer for the whole, and embodied their reasons in a document called the "Complaint of the Commons of Kent," which was of a somewhat discursive character. It commenced by alluding to a report that Kent was to be turned into a hunting forest, and remonstrated against the people being made game of in such a fearful manner; it then proceeded to abuse the Government in general terms, which have since been the stereotyped phraseology of nearly all the friends of the people; it complained of others fattening on the royal revenue, which forced the king to supply the deficiency by robbing his subjects, and to take their provisions wholesale as well as retail, without paying a penny for them. Allusion was then made to the lowness of the company admitted to court, though this seems to have been rather over-nice on the part of Jack and his followers. The document then came to the point, by intimating that the men of Kent had been subjected to extortion and treated with contempt, so that they had been, at the same time, overtaxed and under-rated.

When the court received this elaborate catalogue of ills, it was intimated to Cade and his companions that it would take some time to prepare the answer; but the authorities thinking that powder and shot would answer better than pen and ink, set to work to collect troops and ammunition in London. Cade could not resist his propensity to scribble, and sent in a second paper, headed "The Requests, by the captain of the great assembly in Kent." In his new manifesto Jack required an entire re-arrangement of the royal household even down to the minutest domestic arrangements; and it was even said that not a pie came to the king's table without Jack wishing to have a finger in it.

The court was now prepared with an answer in the shape of a large army, which advanced upon Blackheath, and caused Cade to be taken so regularly aback that he jibbed as far as Sevenoaks. Here he halted, and waited the attack of the royal army, a detachment of which came up and went down like a pack of cards, though as they had lost all heart there is something defective in the comparison. When the main army at Blackheath heard the fate of the detachment at Sevenoaks, the soldiers suddenly began to object to fighting against their own countrymen. The Court then found it time to make concession, and commenced by sending a few of its own party to the Tower, in order to propitiate the malcontents. Lord Say, an obnoxious minister, who was not merely a say, but a tremendous do, was at once locked up with some others who had rendered themselves unpopular.

Cade now made himself master of the right bank of the Thames from Greenwich to Lambeth, both inclusive, and made the celebrated incision into the latter, which retained the name of the New Cut to a very distant period. Cade took up his own quarters in Southwark, but went into London every morning, where he and his followers behaved very quietly for a few days, returning home regularly every evening to their lodgings in the Borough. Their first act of violence was to insist on the trial of Say, who was not allowed to have his say in his own defence, but was hurried off to Cheapside and beheaded. As too frequently happens with the promoters of the public good, Cade's followers could not keep their hands off private property, and a little pillage was perpetrated. Even Jack himself, who sometimes set a good example to his followers, was tempted to plunder the house at which he usually dined; and the citizens, feeling that as the spoons were beginning to go, their turn would probably be next, became indignant at the outrage. They consequently refused admission to Cade the next morning when he came to transact his city business as usual.

It was next determined by the court to delude the rebels by an offer of a pardon; and Cade caught at the bait with a simplicity less characteristic of a Jack than of a gudgeon. In two days, however, he altered his mind, and refused to lay down his arms or walk off his legs, until Government gave a guarantee for the fulfilment of its promises. With the customary hatred of each other, which too often prevails among the lovers of their country, the patriots commenced quarrelling. Cade began to fear that some disinterested friend of freedom would sell him for the thousand marks that were offered for his head; and Jack, from the idea of being apprehended, was thrown into a constant state of apprehension. Sneaking quietly downstairs in the night, he found his way to the stable, where he mounted a clever hack, and using what spurs he could to the animal's exertion, put him along at a slapping pace towards the coast of Sussex. He had not proceeded very far, when turning to look back on what he had gone through, he saw at his heels Alexander Iden, Esq. Jack had scarcely got out the words, "Is that you, Alick?" when a lick from Iden's sword revealed the purpose of his mission. "No, you don't!" cried Cade, parrying an attempt to plant a second blow, and putting in a slight poke with his battle-axe very efficiently. Were we to borrow the graphic style of the sporting chroniclers, in describing a fight, we should say that Iden came up smiling, and evidently meaning business, which he transacted by enumerating one, two, three, in rapid succession on Jack's chest, followed up by four, five, six, on the face, and seven, eight, nine, ten, eleven, twelve, in the stomach. Cade endeavoured to rally, but every effort failed; and Alexander Iden, Esq., claimed the thousand marks that had been advertised. The amount was large for a head with very little in it; but the tail, consisting of the riff-raff led on by Cade, formed the real value of the article.

A dispute now commenced between persons of higher degree; or, rather, it is to be suspected that Cade and his men had been used as the tools of some more exalted malcontent. It very frequently happens that political agitators in a humble rank of life are either cunningly or unconsciously playing the game of a political schemer of more exalted station; and while they are supposed to be working for the overthrow of one tyrant, they are preparing the way for the establishment of another.

The Duke of York was the individual who, endeavouring to profit by the recent revolt, left Ireland, of which he had been Lieutenant, and forced himself into the king's presence. "Now then, what is it?" cried Henry, annoyed at the sudden intrusion; when York replied he had come to extract something from the mouth of the sovereign. "A tooth, perchance?" ironically remarked the king; but his majesty was informed that a promise to summon a Parliament was the utmost that York required. This was acceded to, and, when Parliament met, one of the members proposed declaring the Duke of York heir apparent to the throne, but the proposer was indignantly coughed down, unceremoniously pulled out, and promptly committed to the Tower. The duke, discouraged at having a minority of one, which imprisonment had reduced to none, in his favour, repaired to his castle at Ludlow, where he collected a large army; but, by way of proving that he had no evil intentions towards the king, he took, every now and then, the oath of allegiance. This periodical perjury had very little effect, for York was better known than trusted, and an army was sent against him. As the forces went one way to meet him, he came up to London by another road, but the gates of the City were slammed in his face just as he came up to them. "Well, I'm sure!" was the indignant murmur of York, to which, according to an Irish chronicler who came from Ireland in the duke's suite, "You can't come in," was the only echo. Foiled in this attempt, he went to Kent, expecting Jack Cade's followers would rally round him, but beyond some half-dozen seedy scamps, belonging to the class excluded from kitchens under the general order of "No followers allowed," there were no adherents to York's banner. When Henry came up with him at Dartford, both of them, like two little boys who have met to fight and don't know how to begin, were anxious to negotiate. This was agreed to, and the duke having disbanded his army, by which, as the papers say when a theatre closes prematurely, "an immense number of persons were thrown out of employ," he went to Henry's tent for a personal interview.

The meeting was very unpleasant, for Somerset happening to be seated there, had the bad taste to assail York with a volley of vulgar abuse, which the latter repaid with interest. "You're a felon and a traitor, sir!" cried Somerset, as York came in, which elicited, by way of reply, "You're an old humbug," and other taunts, among which "Who embezzled the taxes?" was rather conspicuous. As the duke was about to depart, a tipstaff tripped up to him, and, begging his pardon, intimated that he was in custody. Somerset would have applied for speedy execution, but York compromised the affair by a little more perjury, for he swore a good batch—sufficient to last him a whole

Quarrel between Somerset and York.

year—of truth and allegiance. He then retired to his castle, where he may have amused himself with playing at "Beggar my Neighbour" with his porter, as far as we can tell, for his employment while in seclusion at Wigmore is not recorded in history.

Henry's utter incapacity to hold the reins, which were literally dropping out of his hands, began to give great uneasiness to the Parliament. York was wanted back, and Somerset was sent to the Tower, for the two rivals were like the two figures in the toy for indicating the weather. What brought one out sent the other in, and a storm was the signal for the entrance of York, while political sunshine was favourable to Somerset.

On the 14th of February, 1454, York opened Parliament as commissioner for the king, who was personally visited at Windsor by a deputation of peers, desirous of ascertaining his exact condition. They found Henry perfectly imbecile, and incapable of understanding a word or uttering a syllable. The deputation conceiving it possible that his majesty might be merely muddled, retired to give him time to come to, but on their return they found him in the same state as before, and *ditto* repeated on a third visit. The deputation, resolving unanimously that "this sort of thing would never do," reported the facts to Parliament, and Richard, Duke of York, was elected "Protector and Defender of the realm of England." In about nine months Henry was declared to have recovered his senses, such as they were, and the court claimed for him the return of the reins, which had been taken out of his hands by reason of his incapacity. York was instantly put down, and Somerset again taken up to occupy the box-seat as heretofore.

The ex-protector retired to Ludlow as before, but got together some troops, and poor Henry was put, or carried, or propped up, at the head of an opposing army. The duke having no fear of a force under such a tumble-down leader, met him near the capital, and sent a message, full of loyalty, to the king, but insisting on Somerset being sent back by return, to be dealt with in the most rigorous manner. An answer was returned in the king's name, declaring his determination to perish rather than betray his friend; but it was the friend himself who assigned to his majesty this very disinterested preference. The sovereign was indeed so imbecile that he knew not what he said, and understood nothing of what was said for him, so that when he asked if he would not rather die in battle than hand Somerset over to the foe, an unmeaning grin was the only reply of the royal idiot. A fight of course ensued, and York got the best of it. Somerset was among the slain, and the poor king, who was as innocent of the use of a sword as a child in arms, got a wound in the neck, which sent him howling and reeling away till he took refuge in a tan-yard. York found him hiding among the hides, and pulling him out with gentleness, conducted him to the Abbey of St. Alban's. Every care was taken of the wounded monarch, whose neck was duly poulticed, and whose feet were put in hot water, though indeed they were seldom out of it.

When Parliament met after this affair, theoretical allegiance was sworn to the king and prince, but practical contempt of their position was exercised. York was declared protector until Edward, the heir to the throne, attained his majority; but Henry was superannuated at once, for he was liable, like a hare in the month of March, to fits of insanity. He was sometimes sensible enough, but no one could elucidate the date of his lucid intervals; and as the sceptre is little better than a red-hot poker in a madman's hands, he was very properly deprived of that powerful instrument.

Things had been thus arranged, when, on the meeting of Parliament, in 1456, after the Christmas recess, Henry, to the surprise of everyone, rushed in, exclaiming—"I'll trouble you for that crown!" and "Oblige me with a catch of that ball!"—alluding to the orb which forms part of the regalia. No one disputed his restoration to sanity, and York resigned the protectorate, looking unutterable things, as if he had just been engaged in a speculation by which he had made a profit of eightpence and incurred the loss of a shilling.

The king now endeavoured to effect a reconciliation between the rival parties, who affected to make it up, but started at once to their respective castles, for the purpose of looking up materials and men for the renewal of hostilities. York sent his sword to the grinder's, his armour to the tin-plate-worker's, to be let out, pieced, and otherwise repaired—while the Lancastrian chiefs were, on their side, resorting to similar arrangements. At length they came to a battle, in September, 1459, and the Yorkists were in the better position, when Sir Andrew Trollop—either from blockheadism, or bribery, or both—deserted, with all his veterans, to the standard of Henry. York, taking a series of hops, skips and jumps over the

Welsh mountains, fled into Ireland. He ran so fast that the muscles of his leg were contracted; and it was said at the time that the York hams had as much as they could do to keep ahead of the Bath chaps, many of whom were engaged in the battle, from having lived not far from the neighbourhood. Warwick escaped to Calais, where he was exceedingly popular, and he soon collected forces enough to admit of his landing in Kent, where he stuck up his banner with the view of collecting a crowd, and then touting for followers. The project was successful, and by the time he reached Blackheath he had got thirty thousand men at his heels, according to the old chroniclers, who, it is only fair to say, have a peculiar multiplication table of their own, and who, whatever may be their aptitude at facts, certainly present to us some of the very oddest figures.

Warwick's reception was very enthusiastic. The archbishop ran out of Canterbury to meet him and shake him by the hand, Lord Cobham clapped him amicably on the shoulders, and five bishops, taking off their mitres, waved them as he passed in token of welcome. Warwick made at once for the midland counties, carrying with him the young heir of York, and meeting the Lancastrians at Northampton, a battle was fought which ended in the defeat of the latter. Henry was taken prisoner; but his wife Margaret of Anjou escaped with her son Edward, and encountered one of those adventures which season with a spice of romance the sometimes insipid dish of history. The story we are about to relate is offered with a caution to our readers, but it is too good to be omitted, and we are, moreover, afraid that were we to leave it out for the sake of correctness, we should be blamed for the omission. Use is second nature in literature as well as in anything else; and the public, being accustomed to falsehood, would regard the absence of even the most flagrant hoax as a curtailment of the fair proportions of history. It is, however, only under protest that we can lend ourselves to the gratification of this very morbid appetite, and we therefore advise the following story on the authority of *De Moleville*, to be taken not merely *cum grano salis*, but with an entire cellar of that very wholesome condiment.

The anecdote runs as follows: Margaret fled with her son into the recesses of a forest, like one of those which we see on the stage, where cut woods, canvas banks, and trees growing downwards from the sky-boarders furnish an umbrageous recess of the most sombre character. We fancy we see her advancing to slow music, laying her child on a canvas bank, and listening to the rattle of peas accompanied by the shaking of sheet iron, which form the rain and thunder of theatrical life, when suddenly a whistle is heard, and two figures enter whose long black worsted hair, wash-leather gauntlets, drawn broadswords, and yellow ochre countenances, bespeak that they are robbers of the worst complexion. The queen has, of course, all her jewels blazing about her, which the two men proceed to appropriate, and while they are quarrelling about the division of her booty, she contrives to escape.

This brings us to another part of the same forest, where the scenery is not quite so elaborate, but where Margaret, leading on her infant son, stumbles upon a sentimental robber with a drawn sword in his hand, a tear of sensibility in his eye, and in his mouth a claptrap. She appeals to his generosity in favour of a "female in distress;" he replies with some cutting allusions to the "man who—" compares himself to a melon, or a cocoa-nut, or anything else with a rough exterior, but with some sweetness or milk of human kindness within, and by way of climax, she exclaims, "Here, my friend, I commit to your care the safety of the king's son."

The honest fellow—by whom we mean, of course, the professional thief and casual cut-throat—goes down upon one knee in a fit of loyalty, and according to the scholastic versions of this little incident he is "recalled to virtue by the

Margaret of Anjou and her Child meeting the benevolent Robber.

flattering confidence reposed in him."[65] He went also a step further, and at once devoted himself to the service of the queen, magnanimously offering to share her fortunes, which considering the desperate nature of his own, was a proposition equally indicative of self-love and loyalty. Her majesty accepted the offer, and embarked for Flanders, of course paying all the expenses of her friend the sentimental robber, who became the companion of her flight, and a pensioner on her pocket.

Fighting between the adherents of York on one side, and of Lancaster on the other, continued with unabated fury, until York having gained a victory at Northampton, called a Parliament, and walked straight up to the throne. He took hold of the hammer-cloth, as if to mount, and looked round as much as to say, "Shall I?" but no "hears," "cheers," or "bravoes" encouraged him to proceed. Another battle was fought soon after at Wakefield Bridge, when Richard, Duke of York, was killed, and his son Edward succeeded to the title, which was very shortly afterwards exchanged for that of king, at a packed meeting of citizens. The question was put whether Henry was fit to reign, and the "Noes" had it as a matter of course, when a motion that Edward of York should ascend the throne was carried by a large majority.

Thus he who was not yet of age, and who had been recently nothing more than Earl March, was in early March, 1461, voted to the sovereignty by the acclamation of the people. Rushing into the House of Lords, he vaulted in a true spirit of vaulting ambition onto the throne, from which he delivered a discourse on hereditary right, making out every other right to be wrong, and maintaining his own right to be the only genuine article.

Poor Margaret made a futile attempt to rouse the loyalty of the citizens of London in a letter which she addressed to them,[66] but the style is so exceedingly vague that we do not wonder at the document having proved ineffectual. As far as it is possible to collect the meaning of the epistle to which we have referred, it trounces the Duke of York in a style of truly female earnestness. It calls him an "untrue, unsad, and unadvised person," who is "of pure malice, disposed to continue in his cruelness, to the utterest undoing, if he might," of the fair letter-writer and her offspring. Poor Margaret's state of mind may have accounted for the tremendous topsy-turviness—to use a familiar expression—of her sentences. The bursting heart cannot trammel itself by those fetters which grammarians and rhetoricians have forged to restrain language within its proper limits. That Margaret of Anjou was a woman of business is evident from a copy of one of her wardrobe books now, in a state of perfect preservation, in the office of the Duchy of Lancaster. This private ledger of the royal lady would be a model for the accounts of modern housekeepers.

It comprises a journal of payments even down to the accuracy of pence; and her gardener's wages, put down at a hundred shillings a year, may be considered a fair criterion of the average scale of her expenditure. She laid out little in clothes, though she kept twenty-seven valets as well as a number of ladies-in-waiting, and "ten little damsels," whose salaries and persons were no doubt equally diminutive. That her economy must have been wonderful is evident from the fact that she did it all for seven pounds a day, which she regularly paid to the treasurer of the king's household.

It has not often been our lot to begin with a new sovereign until we have finished with the old; but in the present instance we must drop Henry the Sixth before his death, according to the example set us by his ungrateful people. We have, perhaps, lingered too long over the downfall of Henry, and we are warned by a sort of mental shout of "Edward the Fourth stops the way" that we must drive on with our history.

---

65. See Pinnock's edition of Goldsmith's History of England, p. 143 of the thirty-second edition.
66. This letter, which is to be found in the Harleian MSS., No. 543, Fol. 147, is also given in Mary Anne Wood's interesting collection of Letters of Royal and Illustrious Ladies of Great Britain. The letter of Margaret of Anjou forms the thirty-eighth in the first volume of the work alluded to.

CHAPTER THE FIFTH

EDWARD THE FOURTH

dward, like the individual who having got such a thing as a crown about him, fully intended keeping it, lost no time in going into the provinces to enforce his claims. After killing twenty-eight thousand Lancastrians, and threatening a lesson on the Lancastrian system to anyone who might continue to oppress him, he returned to town, and was crowned on the 29th of June, 1461, in the usual style of magnificence.

Poor Henry, the deposed sovereign, was carried about at the head of his adherents, to give them something to rally round; but they might just as well have had a maypole, or any other inanimate object, for the ex-king was utterly imbecile. He could only be compared to a guy in the hands of the boys on the 5th of November; and sometimes, when his adherents were forced to run for it, they set him down to escape as he could, by which he was occasionally on the point of being taken prisoner.

Edward assembled a Parliament, which cut short all objections to the line of York by declaring that the three last kings of the line of Lancaster were intruders, and the grants they had made were of course reversed, in order to raise a fund for laying in a large supply of new loyalty.

Poor Henry, to whom peace and quietness were necessary, would have been very well satisfied to retire into private life, had not his impetuous wife, the tremendous Margaret, dragged him about with her at the head of a few proscribed and desperate nobles. Shortness of cash cramped the efforts of this impetuous female, who ran over to France, with the intention of begging and borrowing from all her relatives. The Duke of Brittany gave her a trifle, but Louis the Eleventh pleaded poverty, and even produced his books to show that he had not a penny beyond what he required for his own necessities. When, however, she talked of surrendering Calais, he produced twenty thousand crowns, which he had probably put by in an old stocking, and lent her the sum, with a couple of thousand men, under Peter de Brezé.

With this assistance Margaret burst into the northern counties, and, pushing poor Henry before her wherever she went, thrust him through the gates of a small series of castles which she had taken by surprise. These were soon taken back again, and Margaret, being obliged to fly, lost all her borrowed money in a storm at sea, which washed all her property in one direction and herself in another. After a few minor transactions, the 15th of May, 1464, was rendered famous by the battle of Hexham, at which the hiding or tanning of the Lancastrians was so complete that Hexham tan is to this day a leading article of commerce. Margaret escaped to her father's court, but poor Henry, after wandering about the moors of Lancashire, had found his way to Yorkshire, where he had gone out to dine at Waddington Hall, when a treacherous servant, or a traitor waiter, delivered him up to his enemies. The unhappy Henry was turned into the Tower, which, under all the circumstances, was the best place for him.

Edward, now adopting the sentiment of the vocalist, who, wishing to introduce a tender song in the character of a hero, modulates into a softer feeling by exclaiming, "Farewell, glory; welcome, love," resolved on paying those devotions to the fair which a necessity for encountering the brave had hitherto rendered impossible. He had intended to marry some foreign princess, and Warwick had engaged him to a young lady named Bona, daughter of the Duke of Savoy and sister to the Queen of France; but the king denied that he had ever given instructions to sue, and declined being bound by the act of his solicitor, who had solicited for him the hand of the fair princess. The truth was that his majesty had formed other views, or, rather, other views had been formed for him by an old match-making mother, who exhibited all those manoeuvring qualities which constitute, in the present day, the art of getting a daughter off to the best advantage.

The king, while hunting at Stony Stratford, pursuing a stag, came suddenly upon a pretty dear, who literally staggered him. The young lady was the widow of Sir Thomas Gray, and the daughter of Jacquetta of Luxemburg by her second husband, Sir Richard Woodville, afterwards Earl of Rivers. There is not the smallest doubt that Lady Gray and her mamma had arranged together this accidental interview. The young lady, who seems to have been a finished pupil in the school of flirtation, entreated the king to reverse the attainder passed on her late husband, to which Edward replied that "he must be as stonyhearted as Stony Stratford itself if he could refuse her anything." This rubbish ripened into a real offer of marriage, which was, of course, accepted, and Lady Gray was crowned Queen of England in the year following.

Edward the Fourth meeting Elizabeth Woodville.

Warwick was rather nettled at being, as he said, "made a fool of" by his royal master, and grew particularly jealous of the influence of the king's wife, who got off her five unmarried sisters upon the heirs of as many dukes or earls. He intrigued with the king's brother, the Duke of Clarence, and both of them, being denounced as traitors, were obliged to go abroad upon an order to travel. They visited France, where King Louis not only supplied them with board and lodging, but put Warwick in the way of a negotiation with Queen Margaret, which, it was thought, would be advantageous to all parties. It was arranged that another push should be made to push Henry onto the throne, but, as Warwick never did business for nothing, he stipulated for the marriage of his daughter with the queen's son, Edward.

Having reduced everything to writing, Warwick took his standard out of his portmanteau for the purpose of planting it, and on the 13th of September, 1479, he landed at Plymouth with a select but sturdy party of malcontents. The people, whose motto was "Anything for a change," were soon persuaded to join in a cry of "Long live King Henry," and he was taken out of the Tower for the purpose of being dragged about as a puppet to give a sort of legitimacy to Warwick's projects. This nobleman had got the name of the king-maker from a knack he had of manufacturing the royal article with a rapidity truly astonishing. He could coin a sovereign to order with a dispatch that the mint itself might fairly be jealous of. He could provide a new king at the shortest notice, like those victuallers who profess to have "dinners always ready;" and Edward having got into "very low cut," Henry was "just up" as the latest novelty from the *cuisine* of the ingenious Warwick.

When Edward saw what was going on he thought it high time for himself to be going off, and, with a few adherents who had not a change of linen in their trunks nor a penny in their purses, he got into a ship bound for Holland. The king himself had no money to pay his passage, and offered the captain, says Comines, "a gown lined with martens," as a remuneration for his services. Edward fled to Burgundy, where he persuaded the duke to advance a trifle in the way of ships, money, and men, with which the ousted monarch landed at Ravenspur. On his first arrival the people held back, saying, "Oh, here's the old business over again. We've had enough of this," and employing other expressions of discouragement. He, however, declared he had no intention of unsettling anything or anybody—except his bills, which remained unsettled as a matter of course—and was allowed to enter the capital, where he was once more proclaimed sovereign. It is an old commercial principle in this country that debt is a sign of prosperity, and Edward's success has been attributed to the fact of his owing vast sums to the London merchants. They were, of course, interested in the well-being of their debtor, and the hypothesis was thus proved to be true, that he who is worse off is in a better position than he who is well-to-do, and the man whose circumstances are tolerably straight is not so eligibly situated as the individual whose affairs are materially straightened. Edward, though not in clover, was obliged to be in the field, for Warwick fell upon his rear with alarming vehemence. They fought at Barnet on the 14th of April, 1471, in the midst of a mist, when poor Warwick was not only lost in the fog, but many of his friends were killed, and Edward obtained a decisive victory. The particulars of this battle have never been very accurately given, for the fog and the old chroniclers were almost equally dense; and between them the affair is involved in much obscurity.

It is easier to quell sixty thousand men than to subdue one troublesome woman, and Queen Margaret still gave "a deal of trouble" to the conqueror. She, however, ultimately fell into his hands, together with her son—one of the "rising generation" of that time—who, on being asked by Edward what he meant by entering the realm in arms, replied pertly, "I came to preserve my father's crown and my own inheritance."— "Did you, indeed, you young jackanapes?" cried Edward, "then take that," and he flicked the boy's nose with the thumb of a large gauntlet. The child set up a piercing yell, but this was not the worst of it, for some attendants, excited by the brutal example of their master, gave the lad a blow or two, which finished him.

Field of Battle (in a Fog) near Barnet.

Edward returned to town, and sent Henry, with his queen, to the Tower, from which the latter was ransomed by her relatives; but the former having no friends to buy him off or bail him out, remained in custody. He died a few weeks after his committal, and his death is attributed to the Duke of Gloucester, who from the peculiar conformation of his back, had shoulders broad enough to bear all the stray crimes for which no other owner may have been forthcoming. Accordingly, every piece of iniquity that can be traced to no one in particular is usually added to Gloucester's huge catalogue of delinquencies.

The Lancastrians were now regularly down, and every opportunity was taken for hitting them. Some were driven into exile, others were got rid of by more decided means, and a few, whose talents were worth saving, got purchased at a valuation, more or less fair, by the new Government. Sir John Fortescue, the Chief Justice to Henry the Sixth and the greatest lawyer of his time, was sold in this disreputable manner; for the judges of those days, unlike the pure occupants of the bench in our own, were as saleable as railway shares, and had their regular market price for anyone by whom such an investment was desired.

The prosperity of the House of York was now only marred by a quarrel between the Dukes of Gloucester and Clarence. The latter had married Warwick's eldest daughter, and claimed the whole property of his father-in-law, of which Gloucester naturally wanted a slice, and he struck up to Anne, a younger daughter, in order to derive some claim to a share of the family fortune. Clarence, anxious to baffle his brother, sent the young lady out to service as a cook, in London, when Gloucester—disguised probably as a policeman—found her out, and ran away with her.

He won her by alleging his heart to be incessantly on the beat, and by promising her the advantages of a superior station. He lodged her in the then rural lane of St. Martin's, and the king ultimately arranged the difference between his brothers by assigning a handsome portion to Lady Anne, and leaving Clarence to take the rest; while the widowed Countess of Warwick, who had brought all the money into the family, was obliged to leave it there, without touching it, for she got nothing.

In 1475 Edward began to form ambitious projects with regard to France, and sent off to Louis the Eleventh one of those claims for the crown which some of the preceding kings of England had been in the habit of forwarding. The letter was written in terms of marvellous politeness, and Louis having read it, desired the herald who brought it to step into the next room, where he was treated with great affability. Louis complimented the letter-carrier in the most fulsome manner, recommending him to advise his master to withdraw his claim as futile and ridiculous. "Bless you, he don't mind me," was the modest reply of the herald; but Louis remarked that the words of such a sensible fellow must have considerable weight, and slipped three hundred crowns into his pouch, with a wink of intense significance. The herald was regularly taken aback, and his bewilderment increased when his majesty, observing, "Dear me, what a shabby cloak you've got on," ordered three hundred yards of crimson velvet to be cut off from the best piece in the royal wardrobe. Garter—for such was the

Duke of Gloucester, disguised as a Policeman, discovering Lady Anne.

herald's rank—promised to do the very best he could; for the velvet had softened him down, or smoothed him over, to the side of Louis.

Edward nevertheless made extensive preparations to smash the French king, and strained every nerve to get the sinews of war, which he did by insinuating himself into the favour of his people. He emptied their pockets with considerable grace, and was the first to give the attractive name of Benevolences to those grants which were mercilessly extracted from the Parliament. Edward and Louis, though hating each other with the utmost cordiality, thought it prudent to negotiate—the former from mercenary motives, and the latter for the sake of peace and quiet. An interview was at last agreed upon, to take place at the bridge of Picquigny, near Amiens, across which a partition of railings had been thrown, to prevent treachery on either side. Louis came first, and looked through the bars, when Edward tripped gracefully up to the other side, bowing to within a foot of the ground, and paying a few commonplace compliments. Louis invited Edward to Paris, they shook hands through the bars, and the English king received a sordid bribe through the grating, "which," says the incorrigible Comines, "was exceedingly grating to the feelings of some of his nobles."

Several cruelties disgraced the latter part of Edward's reign; and one of the worst of his enormities was his treatment of Stacey and Burdett, two officers of the household of the Duke of Clarence. Stacey was accused of having dealings with the devil; but if he had, it was only the printer's devil; for Stacey was a priest of the order of Whitefriars, and learned in the typographic art, which had recently been discovered. No proof unfavourable to Stacey could be produced, but he was put to the torture by being made to set up night and day, which made him curse the author of his misery. Thomas Burdett, another gentleman of Clarence's household, was tried as an accomplice to Stacey, and these unfortunate men, having had their heads cut off, "died," according to the Chroniclers, "protesting their innocence." Clarence himself was the next victim, and on the 16th of January, 1478, he was brought to the bar of the House of Lords on a charge of having dealings with conjurors. It seems hard, in these days, when tricks of magic are exceedingly popular, that a person suspected of conjuring should be pursued with the vengeance of the law; and the hardship of the affair is particularly great in the case of Clarence, who was never known to make a plum-pudding in his hat, or perform any other of the ingenious tricks which have gained money and fame for the wizards of the present era. The unfortunate duke met all the charges against him with a flat denial, but he was found guilty, and sentence of death was passed upon him, on the 7th of February, 1478. His execution was never publicly carried out, and rumour has accordingly been left to run riot among the thousand ways in which Clarence might have undergone his capital punishment. The usual mode of accounting for his death is by the suggestion, that his brothers left the matter to his own choice, and that he preferred drowning in a butt of Malmsey wine to any other fatal penalty. The only objection to this arrangement appears to be that which occurred to an excellent English king of modern times, when he wondered how the apple got into the dumpling. However capacious the butt may have been in which Clarence desired to be drowned, it is obvious that he never could have entered the cask through its only aperture, the bunghole. When we witness the marvel of an individual getting into a quart-bottle, we shall begin to have faith in the story that Clarence met his death in the manner alluded to. If the wine was already in the cask before Clarence was immersed, there could have been no admission, even on business, except through the bunghole, and it is not likely that the vessel could have been empty before the duke took his place for the purpose of undergoing a vinous shower-bath.

Edward led for some time a life of luxury, which was now and then disturbed by wars with Scotland, though he never thought it worth his while to take the field in person, but always got his big brother, Richard Duke of Gloucester, to fight for him. Matters nevertheless took a fresh turn when the Duke of Albany, brother of James the Third, came over and declared he was entitled to the Scotch throne in preference to his elder relative. "I mean to swear he is illegitimate," said Albany, and he offered to give up Berwick to Edward, on condition of an army being lent to depose the reigning sovereign. A marriage with one of the English king's daughters was also proposed by Albany, who "thought it right to mention that he had two wives already;" but he did not seem to anticipate any objection on that account. Albany and Gloucester were successful in most of their joint undertakings, but they did not fight very frequently, for a treaty was soon concluded. Until this arrangement was carried out, Albany made every warlike demonstration, and produced a wholesome terror by the exhibition of a tremendous piece of artillery, familiarly known to us in these days as a cannon of the period. Its chief peculiarity was its aptitude—according to the engravings we have seen of it—for carrying cannon-balls considerably larger than the mouth of the piece itself, for we have often feasted our eyes upon very interesting pictures of a cannon-ball issuing from a cannon not half the circumference of the projected missile.

Whether it is that in those days expanding ammunition was provided, which increased in bulk twofold after leaving the cannon's mouth, we are unable to say at this period; but the illuminations of the time undoubtedly present this striking phenomenon. The dust of ages lies unfortunately on many of our facts, and though we might, it is true, take up a duster and wipe the dust of ages off, there is a pleasure in the imaginative which the actual could never realise.

Edward having been duped by his allies in France, on some matters almost of a private character, took the deception so much to heart that he put himself into

Cannon and Cannon-ball of the Period.

a violent passion, and died of it with wondrous rapidity. Instead of a raging fever, he caught the fever of rage, and died on the 6th of April, 1483, in the forty-first year of his age, and twenty-first of his reign.

The assassination of sovereigns was then so common that Edward the Fourth lay in state for some days, to show that he had not come to his death by any but fair means, for he was a king that merited severe treatment, at least as much as some of his predecessors; and it was, therefore, presumed that he might have come in for his share of that fatal violence which it was usual to bestow on kings in the early and middle periods of our history. In concluding our account of this reign, we may, perhaps, be expected to give a character of Edward the Fourth; but, *ex nihilo nihil fit*, and upon this principle we are unable to furnish a character for one who had lost in the lapse, or rather in the lap of time, whatever he may once have possessed of that important article.

CHAPTER THE SIXTH

EDWARD THE FIFTH

 ad the crown been always adapted to the head on which it devolves, the diadem would have been in very reduced circumstances when it descended on the baby brow of the fifth Edward. Almost bonneted by a bauble considerably too large for his head, and falling over his eyes, it was impossible that the boy-king could enjoy otherwise than a very poor look-out on his accession to the sovereignty. He had been on a visit to his maternal uncle, the Earl of Rivers, at Ludlow Castle, but he was now placed under the protection of his paternal uncle, Richard, Duke of Gloucester, as a sort of apprentice to learn the business of government. Richard, who was at the head of an army in Scotland at his brother's death, marched with six hundred men to a *maison de deuil*, where he insisted on having ready-made mourning for his followers. The astonished tradesman, exclaiming, in the language of one of our modern poets,

> "Five minutes' time is all we ask
> To execute the mournful task,"

prepared at once the melancholy outfit. Richard led his adherents to York, where a funeral service was performed, and the troops, looking like so many mutes, completely dumbfounded the populace. Their conduct and their clothes combined—for their designs seemed to be as dark and mysterious as their habits—obtained for these soldiers the unenviable name of the black-guards of the Duke of Gloucester.

Richard's next care was to swear loyalty and fealty to his young nephew—which went far towards proving the absence of both; for those who wish a little of anything to go a great way, generally make the utmost possible display of it. Notwithstanding the continued show of attachment evinced by the uncle for the nephew, it soon began to be noticed that Richard was a good deal like a snowball, for he picked up adherents wherever he moved; and as he went rolling about the country, he soon swelled into a formidable size with the band that encircled him. He, however, calmed suspicion by declaring that he was only collecting supernumeraries for his nephew's coronation. The fact is that Richard was all the time plotting with that discontented fellow Buckingham, the well-known malcontent, of whom it has been justly said that he liked nothing nor nobody.

Gloucester arrived at Northampton on the 22nd of April, 1483, about the same time that Rivers and Gray had "tooled" the baby-king by easy stages as far as Stony Stratford. The two lords came to Northampton to salute Richard, who asked them to supper at his hotel, when Buckingham dropped in and joined the party. The four noblemen passed the evening together very pleasantly, for the song, the sentiment, the joke and the jug, the pitcher and the pun, were passed about until long after midnight. Stretchers for two were in readiness, to take home Gray, who looked dreadfully blue, and Rivers, who was half-seas over, while the two dukes, who had kept tolerably sober, remained in secret debate, for they did

> "Not go home till morning,
> Till daylight did appear."

On the morrow, the whole party started off, apparently very good friends, towards Stony Stratford, to meet the young king, who was immediately grasped by his uncle Gloucester.

The royal infant naturally gave a sort of squeak at the too affectionate clutch of his uncle, who, pretending to think that Gray and Rivers had alienated the boy's affection from himself, ordered them both into arrest, when Gloucester and Buckingham fell obsequiously on their knees before the child, whom they saluted as their sovereign. Their first care was to ascertain who were his favourites, for the purpose of getting rid of them. Two of the royal servants, Sir Thomas Vaughan and Sir Richard Hawse, were dismissed not only without a month's warning, but, as they were sent off to prison at once, "suiting themselves with other situations" was utterly impossible. Young Edward was kept as a kind of prisoner, and Elizabeth, his mother, when she heard the news, set off to Westminster, with her second son and the five young ladies—her daughters—after her. The queen-mother had no party in London, and her arrival with her quintette of girls created no sensation.

In a few days young Edward entered the city, but more as a captive than as a king, and lodgings were immediately taken for him in the Tower, where he was to be boarded, and, alas! done for by his loving uncle. Gloucester was named protector to the youthful sovereign, and moved to No. 1, Crosby Place, Bishopsgate (the number on the door), where, instead of behaving himself like a gentleman "living private," he held councils, while Hastings, who began to doubt the duke's loyalty, gave a series of opposition parties in the Tower. At one of these, Richard, who had never received a card of invitation, walked in, and voted himself into the chair with the most consummate impudence. In vain did Hastings intimate that it was a private room, or that Gloucester must have mistaken the house for there he sat, exclaiming, "Oh no, not at all," begging the company to make themselves at home, as he fully meant to do. He was particularly facetious to the Bishop of Ely, asking after his garden in Holborn, and proposing to the prelate to send for a plate of strawberries.

These were soon brought, and Richard indulged in "potations pottle deep" of strawberries and cream, declaring all the while that the fruit was capital, and that of all wind instruments there was none he liked to have a blow out upon so much as the hautboy. The Protector having gone away for a short time, returned in a very ill humour, with his countenance looking exceedingly sour, as if the strawberries he had eaten had disagreed with him and the cream had curdled. He gave his lips several severe bites, and altogether appeared exceedingly snappish. Presently he asked what those persons deserved who had compassed or imagined his destruction. Hastings observed, "Why, that is so completely out of my compass

The Bishop of Ely presenting a Pottle of Strawberries to the Duke of Glo'ster.

that I can scarcely guess, but I don't mind saying off-hand that death is the least punishment they merit." The Protector declared his brother's wife—meaning the queen—and Mrs. Shore had between them twisted his body, which would, indeed, have been doing him a very bad turn; and, pulling up his sleeve, he exhibited his left arm, declaring there was something not at all right about it. The council agreed that the limb was a good deal damaged, and Hastings added that "*if* Mrs. Shore and the queen had really had a hand in Richard's arm, they certainly deserved grievous punishment."

"What!" roared the Protector, "do you answer me with 'ifs'? I tell you they have, and no mistake." Whereupon he banged his fist down upon the table with tremendous violence, giving himself as well as Hastings a frightful rap on the knuckles. Thereupon a door opened, and "men in harness came rushing in," according to More, and, being in harness, they proceeded to fix the saddle on the right horse immediately. The Protector exclaimed "I arrest thee, traitor," and pointed to Hastings, who cried out "Eh! What! Oh! Pooh! Stuff! You're joking! Arrest me? What have I done? Fiddlestick!" To pursue the elegant description given by More, we must add that "another let fly at Stanley," who bobbed down his head and crawled under the table.

The officers, after some trouble, pulled him out by the leg—having first drawn off his boot in a futile attempt to secure him—and carried him away in custody. Richard then had another turn at Hastings, who was in a sort of hysterical humour, at one moment treating the matter as a joke, and at another not knowing exactly what to make of it. "You may laugh," at length roared Richard, "but I'll tell you what it is, my Lord Hastings, I've ordered my dinner to be ready by the time I get home, but by St. Paul I'll not touch a mouthful—and I own I'm deuced hungry—until I've seen your head."

Arrest of Lord Hastings and Lord Stanley.

Hastings replied that such a condition was easily fulfilled, and thrusting his head into Richard's face exclaimed "There, my lord, you've seen my head, so now go home as soon as you like, and get your dinner." The Protector pushing him aside, expressed contempt for the paltry quibble, and amended the affidavit by inserting the word "off" after the word "head," and exclaiming "I'll see Hastings' head off before I touch a bit of dinner." Hastings was seized, and the purveyors for the Protector soon brought him the *avant goût* which he had required as a provocative to his appetite. Richard's violence had thus come suddenly to a head, and Earl Rivers, with Sir Thomas Vaughan and Sir Richard Hawse, were executed on the same day at Pontefract.

A few days after these executions, Richard went to the sanctuary at Westminster, arm-in-arm with the Archbishop of Canterbury, and called for the little Duke of York, who, they said, would be wanted for the coronation. Consent was somewhat unwillingly given, and Richard having got the child away, made him a prisoner in the Tower. An affecting anecdote is told of the ruse that was resorted to by Gloucester and his friend, the archbishop, to entrap their juvenile victim into going quietly with them towards the gloomy scene of his destined captivity. They lured him on from place to place by pretending that they were going to treat him to some wonderful show, and they took all sorts of roundabout ways to prevent him from suspecting the point they were really driving at. When the poor child was becoming tired of his walk, and surrounding objects had lost the attraction of novelty, he began crying after his mamma, with that filial force which is peculiar to the earliest period of infancy. Gloucester began to fear they should get a mob after them, if, as he savagely expressed himself, "the brat continued to howl," and the little fellow was promised, for the purpose of "stopping his mouth," that he should see his mother immediately. After walking him nearly off his little legs through back streets and alleys, they brought him out upon Tower Hill, and Richard, no longer disguising the fact that he was acting the part of the cruel uncle, snatched up in his arms the trembling child, who presently found himself in one of the gloomy apartments of the Tower.

Richard's next artifice was to practise the "moral dodge," which seldom fails to tell upon an indiscriminating multitude. Jane Shore, who had been seduced by the late king, was fixed upon as a mark for plunder and persecution by Richard, who first robbed the poor woman of all she had and then sent her to prison. He professed to be so shocked at some of the incidents of her past life that, as a moral agent or acting member of society for the suppression of vice, he could not allow her to escape without some heavy punishment. She was proceeded against in the Ecclesiastical Courts, and ordered to walk about London with a lighted rushlight in her hand and wearing nothing but a pair of sheets or a counterpane. The Hammersmith Ghost and Spring-heeled Jack are the only legitimate successors of Jane Shore in this remarkable proceeding, and might have cited her case as a precedent for their own unlawful practices.

Richard also entered into an arrangement with Doctor Shaw, a popular preacher, who was to preach down, or, as it was then called, depreachiate the two young princes. The Reverend Doctor then threw a doubt on their legitimacy, and declared their late father Edward was not a bit like his reputed father, the Duke of York, and pulling out two enormous caricatures from under his gown he asked the crowd whether any likeness could be traced between them. "Instead of the eyes," he exclaimed, "being as like as two peas, these eyes are not even as like as two gooseberries!" He then asked his hearers to compare notes by comparing the noses of the two portraits he held in his hand; and, pointing to the picture of Richard, Duke of York, he reminded them that the bridge of the nose was exactly like that of Richard, Duke of Gloucester. "There, my friends," he roared, "there is a bridge that I think there is no possibility of getting over!" The allusion created a laugh, but no conviction; and the failure was rendered more annoying by the Protector not arriving in time, as had been previously arranged, to enable Dr. Shaw to point out the striking likeness. By some mistake Richard missed the cue for his entrance, and did not come in until the comparison had passed, when upon Shaw endeavouring to recur to it, the trick was so obvious that the people only stared at each other, or passed their right thumbs significantly over their left shoulders. The Protector vented his disappointment and anger on the preacher, whom he denounced as an old meddler who did not know what he was talking about, and Doctor Shaw sneaked off, amid derision, shouts of "Pshaw! Pshaw!" and the jeers of the populace.

On the following Tuesday Richard got his friend Buckingham to go down to Guildhall to give him a regular good puff, at a meeting of the citizens. Buckingham's speech was listened to with a deal of apathy, and there were numerous cries of "Cut it short," responded to with a faint shout of "Hear him out," and an occasional ejaculation of "Now then, stupid!" Buckingham persevered, and at the close of his address somebody threw up a bonnet, exclaiming "Long live King Richard!" The bonnet belonged evidently to a person of straw, and excited little more than ridicule.

The speech of Buckingham to the citizens assembled in Guildhall was a rare specimen of the eloquence of humbug; and it evidently formed a model for the discourses sent forth by auctioneers from the rostrum at a later period, The whole system, indeed, pursued by the Duke of Buckingham on the memorable occasion of his putting up the claim of Richard to the suffrages of the bystanders, was evidently in accordance with that by which bad lots are frequently got off at the highest prices.

When there was a faint snout of "Long live King Richard," from a solitary individual, Buckingham adroitly multiplied the exclamation by declaring that he heard it "in two places," though he knew perfectly well that a solitary puffer, in his own employ, had been the only one who raised a shout for Gloucester. "What shall I say for Richard?" he lustily vociferated. "Look at him, gentlemen, before you bid. There's nothing spurious about *him*. Come, gentlemen, give me a bidding." At this juncture, one of the duke's touters cried out, from the bottom of the hall, "I'll bid a crown," and a slight titter arising, Buckingham took advantage of the circumstance to assert that "a crown was bid for Richard in several places at once;" whereupon the tyrant was said to have been accepted at that price, and the business of the day concluded.

On the next day a deputation was got up to wait on Richard at his lodgings, when he at first declined seeing them. His servant returned to say the gentleman particularly wished an interview, and Gloucester desired they might be shown up, when Buckingham and a few of the deputation were admitted to his presence. They handed him

The Citizens offering the Crown to Richard.

a paper, inviting and pressing him to accept the crown; but he observed, with assumed modesty, "that if he had it, he really should not know what to do with it."

"Clap it on your head, of course," said Buckingham; and, suiting the action to the word, he thrust the bauble on the brow of his friend, observing, "Upon my honour, he looks well in it, don't he, Shaw?" and he turned to the Lord Mayor for approval. Richard, however, shook his head, and remarked that "he could not think of it;" when Buckingham, by a happy turn, suggested that "they had thought of it for him, and therefore, he might as well do it first and think of it afterwards."

"But the little princes," remarked Richard, "whom I love so much." This caused Buckingham to say, in the name of all present, that "they had determined not to have the little princes at any price." Upon this, Gloucester replied, "that he must meet the wishes of the people, and if they must have him, they must, but he, really, had a good deal rather not;" when, amid a quantity of significant winking on all sides, an end was put to the conference.

This scene was enacted on the 24th of June, 1483, which was the last day of the nominal reign of the fifth Edward. It is impossible to give any character of this unfortunate king, whose sovereignty was almost limited to the walls of his own nursery. He might sometimes have played at sitting on a throne and holding a sceptre in his hand, but he never exercised the smallest power. He may, upon one or two occasions, have been allowed to dissolve Parliament; but it was only in the form of the cake so called, which he might, perhaps, be permitted to dissolve by the force of suction.

CHAPTER THE SEVENTH

RICHARD THE THIRD

ichard, on coming to the throne, rushed into Westminster Hall, and took his seat on a sort of marble slab or mantel-piece, between the great Lord Howard and the Duke of Suffolk. The precious trio looked like a set of chimney ornaments, of which Richard formed the centre. He declared that he commenced his reign in that place, because it had been once a judgment-seat, and he was anxious to administer justice to his people. Ten days after, on the 6th of July, he was crowned in Westminster Abbey, and to prevent any murmurs at his usurpation, he was lavish of gifts, promotion and bribery. The Duke of Norfolk, the celebrated jockey mentioned by Shakspeare, who had put Richard in training for the throne, became Earl Marshal, and his son was created Earl of Surrey, in honour, perhaps, of the surreptitious manner in which the crown had been obtained for his master Richard. The Archbishop of York and the Bishop of Ely were set at liberty, "which caused them to dance with joy," according to one of the chroniclers, though we cannot imagine a pair of prelates indulging in Terpsichorean diversions on their release from prison.

In the course of the summer, Richard made a royal progress, and was enthusiastically received, though it is believed that much of the enthusiasm was got up by frequent rehearsals with a set of supernumeraries, who were sent on before from town to town, to give a reception to the new sovereign. If Richard was expected to arrive anywhere at two, the populace would be called at one, to run through—in rehearsal—the cheers and gestures of satisfaction that were required to give brilliance to the usurper's entry. When he arrived at York, a wish was expressed by the inhabitants to see a coronation; and though the ceremony had already been performed in London, it was announced that the spectacle would be repeated, "by particular desire of several families of distinction."

While Richard's starring expedition was most successful in the provinces, things in London were by no means looking up, for conspiracies were being formed to release the two young princes from the Tower. The usurper, not relishing these proceedings, sent a certain John Green—whose unsuspecting innocence has made viridity synonymous with stupidity ever since—as the bearer of a message, the purport of which he was wholly unconscious of. It was addressed to Sir Thomas Brackenbury, the governor of the Tower, requesting him to put to death the two royal children, by smothering them—in onions, or anything else that might be found convenient. Brackenbury refused the commission, not so much out of regard to the little princes as from fear on his own account, and he sent back the monosyllable "No" as an answer to the sovereign. Green, who knew not the purport of the message, returned with the curt reply, and upon his reiterating "No" as all he was desired to say, Richard angrily desired him "not to show his nose again at court for a considerable period." The tyrant was not, however, to be daunted, and he called his Master of the Horse, Sir James Tyrrel, whom he desired to go and lock every door in the Tower, and put the keys in his pocket. One night in August, Tyrrel took with him a fellow named Miles Forrest, a professional assassin, and John Dighton, an amateur, a big, broad, square, and strong knave, who, notwithstanding his squareness, was living on the cross for a long period. The precious trio went together to the Tower, and Tyrrel waiting at the door, Miles Forrest entered with John Dighton, who jointly smothered the children in the bedclothes.

Dighton and Forrest entered with savage earnestness into this horrible transaction, and conducted themselves after the cruel fashion of a clown and pantaloon in a pantomime when an infant falls into their formidable clutches. Dighton danced on the bed, while Forrest flung himself across it with fearful vehemence. Tyrrel, who was standing outside, acted the part of an undertaker in this truly black job, and buried the princes at the foot of the staircase.

Various accounts have been given of this atrocious deed, and antiquarians have quarrelled about the form of the bed the princes used to sleep upon. Some declare it was a turn-up, in which the children were suddenly inclosed; whilst others affirm that the princes had the thread of their existence cut on that useful form of bedstead familiarly known as the scissors. Thus, to use the language of the philosopher, a feather-bed and pillows were made to bolster up the title of Richard, who from his artifice was exceedingly likely to have recourse to such a downy expedient. We may be excused for adding from the same high authority we have taken the liberty to quote that this assassination on a palliasse was an act that nothing could palliate.

Richard, by whom the outward decencies of life were very scrupulously observed, in order to make up for the inward deficiencies of his mind, determined to go into mourning for the young princes and repaired to the same *maison de deuil* which he had honoured with his patronage on a former occasion, when requiring the "trapping of woe" for himself and his retainers on the death of his dear brother.

Another competitor now appeared for the crown, in the person of Henry Tudor, Esquire, commonly called the Earl of Richmond, who came with a drawn sword in his hand and a pedigree already drawn up in his pocket. He was considered to represent the line of Lancaster by right of his mother, who was a great-granddaughter of John of Gaunt, whose extreme tallness proved him to be a worthy scion of the house to which the title of Lanky-shire—as it then might have been spelled—was obviously appropriate. In order to strengthen Richmond's party and give him a spice of Yorkism, a marriage was proposed with

The Duke of Gloucester goes into mourning for his little Nephews.

Elizabeth, of York, on the same principle that beef is sometimes cut with a hammy knife to give it a flavour. Richmond was joined by several nobles hitherto favourable to Richard, and even Buckingham, who had been indebted to him for wealth and office, suddenly turned against him. When Richard heard the news he put a price on the heads of all the leaders of the insurrection; and Buckingham's head, though a very empty one, was ticketed at a considerable figure.

Henry, Earl of Richmond, appeared with a fleet off Devonshire, but finding no one on the coast to meet him, he sailed back to St. Malo. Buckingham, who ought to have been on the look-out, was blundering about the right bank of the Severn, which he was unable to cross in consequence of the rains, when his army, finding themselves short of rations, declined continuing such a very irrational enterprise. Buckingham was left without a man, except his own servant—a fellow of the name of Banister—upon whose fidelity he threw himself. He soon found that he had been leaning upon a fragile prop, for this Banister broke down and betrayed his miserable master. Buckingham was accordingly captured, and sneakingly solicited an interview with Richard the Third, who, on hearing of his being taken, coolly drew on his glove and roared with a stentorian voice, "Off with his head!—so much for Buckingham!"

Richard now came to town, and summoned a Parliament, which was exceedingly complaisant; declaring him the lawful sovereign, by birth, by election, by coronation, by consecration, and by inheritance. Thus the usual attempt was made to make up by quantity for the deficiency as to quality in the title of the usurper, and the Princedom of Wales was settled on his boy Edward. Attainders were dealt out pretty freely among Richard's opponents, who were pronounced traitors in the usual form, which was kept to be filled up with the name of the unsuccessful party; while oaths of loyalty were always to be had—in blank—for the use of that numerous class which followed the crown with the fidelity of the needle to the pole—the pole being the head that happened to be wearing—*pro tem.*—the precious bauble.

Richard, being afraid that Richmond would gain strength by the project of marriage with Elizabeth of York, determined on marrying the young lady himself; an idea which both herself and her intriguing old mother most indelicately jumped at. The king being already married, difficulties arose, but it was proposed to poison Lady Anne, which, as quack medicines had not been yet invented, was a somewhat difficult process. There was no specific then in existence for curing every disease, or the matter might have been arranged at once; nor had the fatal art of punning become known, or Richard might have placed the author of the triple *jeu de mot* in attendance upon the Lady Anne, to be, in time, the death of her. The quarrelsome and cat-like disposition of this unhappy female may account for the tenacity of life which she exhibited; and the young Elizabeth kept continually writing up to inquire why the queen took so much time in dying. It was now the middle of February, 1484, and Lady Anne was still alive; but her obstinacy was soon cured by her husband, and in the course of March she was got rid of. Richard immediately opened to his friends and admirers his scheme for marrying Elizabeth; but they strongly opposed it, and he then pretended that he had never meant anything of the sort, but that the minx—for as such he stigmatised the young lady—had for some time persisted in setting her cap at him.

Henry was now preparing to make a descent upon England, when Richard did all he could to damage him by proclamations, in which Richmond was alluded to as "one Tudor," and his adherents were stigmatised as cut-throats and extortioners. Had this been the fact, it was certainly a case of pot pitching into kettle; and the usurping saucepan poured out its sauce with wondrous prodigality. Numerous were the expedients resorted to for the purpose of damaging the cause of Henry Tudor. Descriptions of his person were issued, and the people were warned against admitting to their confidence the individual of whom a caricature representation, or rather mis-representation, was sent abroad, to give an unfavourable idea of Richmond's exterior. Among other schemes to obtain popularity, Richard affected the character of a practical man, and personally attended to the administration of justice in a few cases, where, having no interest of his own to serve, he gave somewhat fair decisions.

His efforts were now directed to putting the country in a state of defence, and he sent his friends to the coast to bear the brunt of the first attack, while he smuggled himself up pretty comfortably in the middle of a large army in the centre of the kingdom. Several of his friends

Henry Tudor, Esq.

betrayed him, while others sent excuses on the score of ill health, and Stanley apologised in a coarse note, declaring he was confined to his bed by "a sweating sickness." Richard merely muttered, "Oh! indeed, and I suppose he sends me a wet blanket to prove the fact;" but he, nevertheless, ordered Stanley to be closely looked after. Henry landed at Milford Haven on the 7th of August, 1484, with about five thousand men, and on the 21st of the month the two armies met in a field near Bosworth. There a battle was fought, of which Shakespeare has furnished a series of pictures, which, on the stage, attempts are frequently made to realise. The contest, according to this authority, appears to have been carried on amid a mysterious flourish of drums and trumpets, to which soldiers, on both sides, kept running to and fro, without doing any serious mischief. Richmond's people, to the extent of about ten, then encountered about an equal number of Richard's adherents, and striking together, harmlessly, the tips of some long pikes, the two parties became huddled together, and retired in the same direction, apparently to talk the matter over and effect a compromise.

The field then seems to have become perfectly clear, when Richard ran across it, fearfully out of breath, fencing with a foil at nothing, and calling loudly for a horse in exchange for his kingdom, though there was not such a thing as a quadruped to be had for love or money. He then seems to have shouted lustily for Richmond, and to have asserted that he had already killed him five different times, from which it is to be inferred that the crafty Henry had no less than half a dozen suits of armour all made alike to mislead his antagonist. Richard then rushed away, with a hop, skip and jump, after some imaginary foe; and Richmond occupied the field; when Richard, happening to come back, they stood looking at each other for several seconds. We may account for Gloucester's temporary absence by referring to the historical authorities, for he had probably chosen the interval in question to make Sir John Cheney bite the dust, a most unpleasant process for Sir John, who must have ground his teeth horribly with a mouthful of gravel.

The two competitors for the throne then stood upon their guard, and a beautiful fencing-match ensued, to which there were no witnesses. A few complimentary speeches were exchanged between some of the home thrusts, and the combatants occasionally paused to take an artistical view of each other's gallant bearing. Business is, however, business in the long run, which, in this instance, ended in Richard being run through by the victorious Richmond. The soldiers of the latter, who appear to have been waiting behind a hedge to watch in whose favour fortune might turn, ran forward at the triumph of their master being complete, and formed a picture round him, while Stanley, taking the battered crown which Richard had worn in battle, placed it—in its smashed state looking like a gilt-edged opera hat—on the head of Richmond. The manner in which Stanley became possessed of the ill-used bauble is quite in accordance with the dramatic colouring that tinges and tinfoils this beautiful period of our history. It is said that an old soldier kicked against something in an adjacent field, and began actually playing at football with the regal diadem. Placing his foot inside the rim, he sent it flying into the air, when a ray of sunshine, lighting on one of the jewels, revealed to him that it was no ordinary plaything he had got hold of. Running with it as fast as he could to Stanley, the honest fellow placed it in his lordship's hands, with a cry of "See what I have found!" after the manner of the pantaloon under similar circumstances in a pantomime. Stanley was about to put it in his pocket, when another noble roared out, "Oh, I'll tell!" and a cry of "Somebody coming!" being raised, the diadem was ingeniously dropped onto the head of Richmond. The crown was fearfully scrunched by the numerous heavy blows its wearer had received, and Henry the Seventh, taking it off for a moment to push it a little into shape, exclaimed—half mournfully, half jocularly—"Well, well, to the punishment of the usurper this indenture witnesseth." The Duke of Norfolk—our old friend the jockey—shared his master's fate, or rather had a similar fate all to himself, though as he received the fatal crack, he expressed a wish that he might be allowed to split the difference.

The fierce and interesting battle we are now speaking of was one of those short but sharp transactions, which leave their marks no less upon posterity than upon the heads and helmets of the warriors engaged in the fearful contest. The great importance of the event deserves something more than the prosaic narrative in which we have recorded it; and having sent our boy to the Pierian spring with a pitcher, for the purpose of getting it filled with the source of inspiration, we proceed to attempt a poetical account of the Battle of Bos-worth. The celebrated Mr. Thomas Babington Macaulay has, we acknowledge, kindled our poetic fire, by his "Lays of Ancient Rome;" and our imagination having been once set in a blaze it must needs continue to burn, unless, by blowing out our brains, we put a suicidal extinguisher on the flame. Philosophy, however, teaches us that *"L'ame est un feu qu'il faut nourrir"* (Voltaire) and *alere flammam* is a suggestion so familiar to our youth that we do not scruple to throw an entire scuttle of the coals of encouragement upon the incipient flame of our poetic genius. We know that poetry is often an idle pursuit, and that he is generally lazy who addicts himself to the composition of lays, but the Battle of Bosworth Field is an event which fully deserves to have poetical justice done to it. Following the example of the illustrious model, whose style we consider it no humility, but rather an audacity, to imitate, we will suppose the recital to be made some time after the event has occurred, and we will imagine some veteran stage manager giving directions for, or superintending the rehearsal of, a grand dramatic representation of one of the grandest and—if we may be allowed the privilege of a literary smasher in coining a word—the dramaticest battles in English history.

> "Ho! trumpets, sound a note or two!
> Ho! prompter, clear the stage!
> A chord, there, in the orchestra:
> The battle we must wage.
>
> Your gallant supers marshal out—
> Yes, I must see them all;
> The rather lean, the very stout,
> The under-sized, the tall:
> The Yorkites in the centre,
> Lancastrians in the rear,
> Not yet the staff must enter—
> The stage, I charge ye, clear
> Those warriors in the green-room
> Must have an extra drill;
> Where's Richard's gilt-tipp'd baton?
> They charged it in the bill.
>
> Those ensigns with the banners
> Must stand the other way,
> Or else how is it possible
> The white rose to display?"
>
> Thus spoke the old stage manager,
> The day before the night Richard and
> Richmond on the field Of Bosworth had to fight.
> And thus the light-heel'd call-boy
> Upon that day began
> To read of properties a list—
> 'Twas thus the items ran
>
> "Four dozen shields of cardboard,
> With paper newly gilt,
> Six dozen goodly swords, and one
> With practicable hilt;
> The practicable hilt, of course,
> Must be adroitly plann'd,
> That when 'tis struck with mod'rate force,
> 'Twill break in Richard's hand.
> Eight banners—four with roses white,
> And four with roses red—
> Six halberds, and a canopy
> To hang o'er Richard's head;
> A sofa for the tyrant's tent,
> An ironing-board at back,
> Whereon the ghosts may safely stand,
> Who come his dreams to rack;
> A lamp suspended in the air
> By an invis'ble wire,
> And—for the ghosts to vanish in—
> Two ounces of blue fire."

Thus spoke the gallant call-boy,
The boy of many fights;
Who'd seen a battle often fought
Fifty successive nights.

The moment now approaches,
The interval is short,
Before the fearful battle
Of Bosworth must be fought;
Now Richmond's gallant soldiers
Are waiting at the wing,
Expecting soon that destiny
Its prompter's bell will ring;
Now at the entrance opposite
The troops of Richard stand,
Two dozen stalwart veterans—
A small but gallant band.

Hark I at the sound of trumpets,
They raise a hearty cheer,
Their voices have obtained their force
From recent draughts of beer.
Their leader, the false Richard,
Is lying in his tent,
But ghosts to fret and worry him
Are to his bedside sent.

Convulsively he kicks and starts,
He cannot have repose,
A guilty conscience breaks his rest,
By tugging at his toes.

A gentleman in mourning,
With visage very black,
When the tent curtain draws aside,
Is standing at the back;
And then a woman—stately,
But pale as are the dead—
Stood, in the darkness of the night,
To scold him in his bed.

There came they, and there preached they,
In most lugubrious way
Delivering curtain lectures
Until the east was grey;
Or rather, till the prompter,
Who has the proper cue,
Had quite consumed his quantity
Of fire, so bright and blue.

The conscience-stricken Richard
Now kicks with greater force,
Bears up, and plunges from his couch,
Insisting on a horse;
When, hearing from the village cock

A blithe and early scream,
He straightway recollects himself,
And finds it all a dream.

Now, on each side, the leaders
Long for the battle's heat,
But, by some luckless accident,
The armies never meet;
We hear them both alternately
Talking extremely large,
But never find them, hand to hand,
Mixed in the deadly charge.

"March on, my friends!" cries Richmond,
"True tigers let us be;
Advance your standards, draw your swords—
On, friends, and follow me!"

'Tis true, they follow him indeed,
But then, the way they go
Is just the way they're not at all
Likely to meet the foe.
So Richard, with his "soul in arms,"
Is "eager for the fray,"
But, with a hop, a skip, and jump,
Runs off—the other way.

He's to the stable gone, perchance,
Forgetting, in his flurry,

He has kept waiting all this time
His clever cob, White Surrey.
The brute is "saddled for the field,"
But never gains the spot,
For on his way Death knocks him down
In one—the common—lot.
Richard, a momentary pang
At the bereavement feels;
But, being thrown upon his hands,
Starts briskly to his heels.

And now the angry tyrant
Perambulates the field,
Calling on each ideal foe
To fight him or to yield.

"What, ho!" he cries, "Young Richmond!
But, 'mid the noise of drums,
Young Richmond doesn't hear him—
At least he never comes.

Now louder, and still louder,
Rise from the darken'd field
The braying of the trumpets.
The clang of sword and shields
But shame upon both armies!

For, if the truth be known,
'Tis not each other's shields they smite—
The clang is all their own;
For six of Richmond's people
Are standing in a row
(Behind the scenes), and with their swords
They give their shields a blow.

Wild shouts of "Follow, follow!"
Are raised in murmuring strain,
To represent the slayer's rage,
The anguish of the slain.

But now, in stem reality,
The battle seems to rage;
For Catesby comes to tell the world
How fiercely they engage.

He gives a grand description,
And says the feud runs high:
We won't suppose that such a man
Would stoop to tell a lie.

He says the valiant king "enacts
More wonders than a man; "
In fact, is doing what he can't,
Instead of what he can.

That all on foot the tyrant fights,
Seeks Bichmond, and will follow him
Into the very "throat of Death"—
No wonder Death should swallow him!

Now meeting on a sudden,
Each going the opposite way,
Richard and Richmond both advance,
Their valour to display.

Says Richard, "Now for one of us,
Or both, the time is come."
Says Bichmond, "Till I've settled this,
By Jove, I won't go home."

One, two, strikes Richard with his foil,
When Richmond, getting fierce,
Repeats three, four, and on they go,
With parry, quatre, and tierce.

Till suddenly the tyrant
Is brought unto a stand;
His weapon snaps itself in twain,
The hilt is in his hand.

The gen'rous Richmond turns aside,
Till someone at the wing
Another weapon to the foe
Good-naturedly doth fling.

Richard advances with a rush;
Richmond in turn retires;
Their weapons, every time they meet,
Flash with electric fires.

Posterity, that occupies
Box, gallery, and pit,
Applauds the pair alternately,
As each one makes a hit.

Now "Bravo, Richmond!" is the cry,
Till Richard plants a blow
With good effect, when to his side
Round the spectators go.

As fickle still as when at first,
The nation, undecided,
Was 'twixt the Roses White and Red
Alternately divided,

So does the modern audience
Incline, with favour strongest,
To him who in the contest seems
Likely to last the longest.

Then harsher sounds the trumpet,
And deeper rolls the drum,
Till both have had enough of it,
When Richard must succumb.

Flatly he falls upon the ground,
Declaring, when he's down,
He envies Richmond nothing else,
Except the vast renown
Which he has certainly acquired
By being made to yield
Himself, that had been hitherto
The master of the field.

And then the soldiers, who have stood
Some distance from the fray,
Rush in to take their portion of
The glory of the day.

And men with banners in their hands,
At eighteen-pence a night,
Some with red roses on the flags,
And some with roses white,
By shaking them together,
The colours gently blend,
And the Battle of the Roses
Is for ever at an end.

The Battle of Bosworth Field terminated the War of the Roses, or rather brought the roses into full blow, and cut off some of the flower of the English nobility. Richmond was proclaimed king on the field, as Henry the Seventh; and as the soldiers formed themselves into a *tableau* the curtain descended on the tragedy of the War between the Houses of York and Lancaster.

Richard had reigned a couple of years and a couple of months when he received his *quietus* on the field of Bosworth. If ever there was a king of England whose name was bad enough to hang him, this unfortunate dog has a reputation which would suspend him on every lamp-post in Christendom. The odium attaching to his policy has been visited on his person, and it has been asserted that the latter was not straight because the former was crooked. His right shoulder is said by Rouse, who hated him, to have been higher than his left; but this apparent deformity may have arisen from the party having taken a one-sided view of him. His stature was small; but in the case of one who never stood very high in the opinion of the public, it was physically impossible for the fact to be otherwise. Walpole, in his very ingenious "Historic Doubts," has tried to get rid of Richard's high hump, but the operation has not been successful, in the opinion of any impartial umpire. Imagination, that tyrant which has such a strange method of treating its subjects, has had perhaps more to do than Nature in placing an enormous burden on Richard's shoulders. His features were decidedly good-looking; but on the converse of the principle that "handsome is as handsome does," the tyrant Gloucester has been regarded as one of those who "ugly was that handsome didn't."

It is a remarkable fact that Richard the Third during his short reign received no subsidy from Parliament, though we must not suppose that he ruled the kingdom gratuitously; for, on the contrary, his income was ample and munificent. He got it in the shape of tonnage and poundage upon all sorts of goods, and when money was not to be had he took property to the full value of the claim he had upon it. The result was that his treasury became a good deal like an old curiosity shop, a coal shed, or a dealer's in marine stores, for anything that came in Richard's way was perfectly acceptable. The principle of poundage was applied to everything, even in quantities less than a pound, and he would, even on a few ounces of sugar, sack his share of the saccharine. If he required it for his own use he never scrupled to intercept the housewife on her way from the butcher's and cut off the chump from the end of the chop; nor did he hesitate, when he felt disposed, to lop the very lollipop in the hands of the schoolboy. This principle of allowing poundage to the king was in the highest degree inconvenient. It rendered the meat-safe a misnomer, inasmuch as it was never safe from royal rapacity.

It has been said of Richard that he would have been well qualified to reign, had he been legally entitled to the throne; or, in other words, that he would have been a good ruler if he had not been a bad sovereign. To us this seems to savour of the old anomaly—a distinction without a difference. He certainly carried humbug to the highest possible point, for he exhibited it upon the throne, which serves as a platform to make either vice or virtue—as the case may be—conspicuous.

The trick by which he obtained possession of his nephew, the young King Edward, whose liberty was likely to prove a stumbling-block in Richard's own path to the throne, is remarkable for its cunning, and for the intimate knowledge it displayed of the juvenile character. Proceeding to the residence of the baby monarch's mamma, he began asking after "little Ned" with apparently the most affectionate interest. He had previously provided himself with a lot of sweetstuff as he came along, for it was his deep design to intoxicate with brandy-balls the head of the infant sovereign. "Where is the little fellow?" inquired Richard, who would take no excuse for his nephew not being produced, but declared that being in no hurry, he could wait the convenience of the nursery authorities. Finding further opposition useless, Elizabeth reluctantly ordered the boy to be brought down, when Richard asked him "Whether he would like to go with Uncle Dick?" and got favourable answers by surreptitiously cramming the child's mouth with lollipops.

"Would York like to go with his Uncle Dick?"

Whenever the little fellow was about to say "He would rather stay with his mamma," the Protector called his attention (aside) to a squib or brandy-ball, and York consented at last to go with his uncle. "Oh! I thought you would," cried the wily duke, as he clutched his little nephew up and jogged with him to the Tower. Such was the artful scheme by which the tyrant originally got possession of the subsequent victim of avuncular cruelty. It has been urged in extenuation of his cruel murder of the little princes that their deaths were a necessary sequel to those of Hastings and others; but it would have been a poor consolation to the victims had they known that they were only killed by way of supplement. We cannot think that any portion of the catalogue of Richard's crimes should be printed in colours less black because it formed a continuation or an appendix to his atrocities; nor can we excuse Part II. of a horribly bad work because Part I. has rendered it unavoidable.

It is urged by those writers who have defended him that the crimes he committed were only those necessary to secure the crown; but this is no better plea than that of the highwayman who knocks a traveller on the head because the blow is necessary to the convenient picking of the victim's pockets. Richard's crimes might have been palliated in some trifling degree had they been essential to the recovery of his own rights, but the case is different when his sanguinary career was only pursued that he might get hold of that which did not belong to him. It is true he was ambitious; but if a thief is ambitious of possessing our set of six silver tea-spoons, we are not to excuse him because he knocks us down and stuns us, as a necessary preliminary to the transfer of the property from our own to our assailant's possession. The palliators of Richard's atrocities declare that he could do justice in matters where his own interest was not concerned; but this fact, by proving that he knew better, is in fact an aggravation of the faults he was habitually guilty of. It has been insinuated that when he had got all he wanted, he might have improved, but that by killing him after he had come to the throne, his contemporaries gave him no chance of becoming respectable. It must

"Ya-ah! Macker—el!" William of Trumpington, the Abbot of St. Alban's.

be clear to every reasonable mind that the result, even had it been satisfactory, would never have been worth the cost of obtaining it, and that in tolerating Richard's pranks, on the chance of his becoming eventually a good king, his subjects might well have exclaimed *le jeu n'en vaut pas la chandelle*. In the *vexata questio* of the cause of the death of the princes, the guilt has usually been attributed to Richard, because he reaped the largest benefit from their decease; but this horrible doctrine would imply that a tenant for life is usually murdered by the remainder-man, and that the enjoyer of the interest of Bank Stock is frequently cut off by the reversioner who is entitled to the principal. We admit there is a strong case against Richard upon other more reasonable evidence: and thus from the magisterial bench of History do we commit him to take his trial, and be impartially judged by the whole of his countrymen.

CHAPTER THE EIGHTH

NATIONAL INDUSTRY

Let us now turn from the turmoil of war, and apply our eye-glass to the pursuits of peace; for, having been surfeited for the present with royal rapacity, it will be refreshing to take a glance at national industry.

London was at a very early period famous for the abundance of its wool, and it has been ingeniously suggested that the great quantity of wool may account for a sort of natural shyness or sheepishness among our fellow-countrymen.

The Bill of Exchange was a luxury introduced in the beginning of the thirteenth century, for the accommodation of our forefathers, who had learned the value of a good name, and perhaps occasionally experienced the inconveniences of a bad one.

There is nothing very interesting in the history of Commerce until the time of Whittington, whose cat, we have already said, was a fabulous animal, though it has taken its place by the side of the British Lion in our English annals. We are inclined to believe that there is some analogy between these two brutes, and that both are meant to be the types respectively of our political and commercial prosperity. We have sometimes thought that the British Lion, from its plurality of lives, ought rather to be called the British Cat, especially from its readiness to come to the scratch when the altar or the throne may seem to be in jeopardy. Whatever may be the exact nature of the beast, it is certainly a very highly trained and somewhat harmless animal, for any statesman may place his head in the British Lion's mouth, and remove it again without suffering the slightest injury. The creature will roar loudly enough and show an ample expanse of jaw, but it is frequently *vox et praterea nihil* with the noisy brute, whose grumbling is often indicative of his extreme emptiness.

Whittington was certainly three times Lord Mayor of London, and we find him "doing a bill" for Henry the Fourth to the tune of a thousand pounds, and taking the subsidy on wool—out of which the sovereign generally fleeced the people—as collateral security.

In the reign of Henry the Fifth considerable advance was made in the art of ship-building, though from the pictures of the period it would seem that the craft exhibited very little of the workman's cunning. One of the ships of war of the fifteenth century, described in the Harleian MS., has all the appearance of a raft constructed of a few planks, with a sort of sentry-box at one end for the accommodation of the steersman. In the larger vessels the entire crew will be found always crowding the deck in a dense mass; for the rules against taking more than the number were not enforced, and an ancient ship, like a modern carpet bag, was never so full but something additional could be always crammed into it.

In this age commerce was so highly respectable that even kings carried it on; and the highest ecclesiastics were in business for themselves as tradesmen of the humblest character. Matthew Paris tells us of an abbot of St. Alban's who did a good deal in the fish line, under the name of William of Trumpington.

His chief transactions were in Yarmouth herrings, and the worthy abbot undertook to put upon every breakfast table as good a bloater as money could procure, at a very moderate figure. The benevolent dignitary had come to the conclusion that the cure of herrings would pay him better than the cure of souls, and he accordingly added the former lucrative branch to the latter employment, with a pompous declaration that the two might be considered analogous. This habit among the churchmen, of making all fish that came to their net, was by no means popular and it was said in a lampoon of the day that the (chap. viii.) next thing to be done would be the conversion of a prebendal stall into an oyster stall.

Among the other disreputable sources of revenue to which the ecclesiastics devoted themselves we must not omit to mention smuggling, which they carried on to an alarming extent in wool; for after going wool-gathering in all directions, they padded themselves with it and stuffed it under their gowns for the purpose of eluding the Customs' regulations, to which the article was subjected.

Edward the Fourth was a true tradesman at heart, and, had he been a general dealer instead of a king, he would have been quite in his proper station. Nature had fitted him for the counter, though Fortune had placed him on the throne; but even in his commercial transactions he was guilty of acts that were quite unworthy of the high character of the British tradesman. The butt of Malmsey in which he caused his brother to be drowned was, it is believed, actually sold as a full fruity wine with "plenty of body in it," after poor Clarence had been in soak till death relieved him from his drenching. Edward the Fourth had also the disagreeable habit of enriching himself by money which he borrowed from the merchants, and never thought proper to return to them himself; but if he paid them at all, he, by laying on taxes, took it out of the people. It was also a fraudulent propensity of some of our early kings to depreciate the coin of the realm, and Edward the Third managed to squeeze two hundred and seventy pennies, instead of two hundred and forty, out of a pound, which enabled him to put the odd half-crown into his own pocket. Henry the Fourth carried the sweating process still further, by diluting a pound into thirty shillings, a trick he excused by alleging the scarcity of money; though the expedient was as bad as that of the housewife who, when the strength of the tea was gone, filled up the pot with water for the purpose of making more of it. Edward the Fourth, considering that his predecessors had not subjected the pound to all the compound division of which it was capable, smashed it into four hundred pennies, which was certainly proving that he could make a pound go as far as anyone.

In speaking of the industry of the people, we may fairly allude to what was regarded at the time as a great drag upon it in the shape of a fearful increase of attorneys, who in 1455 had grown to such an extent in Norfolk and Suffolk that those places were literally swarming with the black fraternity. In the city of Norwich the attorneys were so plentiful that the evil began to correct itself, for they commenced preying on each other, like the water-lion "Ya-ah! Macker!" water-tiger in the drop of stagnant fluid viewed through the solar microscope. They were in the habit of attending markets and fairs where they worked people up into bringing and defending actions against each other, without the smallest legal ground for proceedings on either side. A salutary statute cut down the exuberance of the attorneys by limiting their numbers, and six were appointed as a necessary evil for Suffolk; six as a standing nuisance in Norfolk; while two were apportioned under the head of things that, as they "can't be cured must be endured," to the city of Norwich. Such was the state of national industry up to the period at which we have arrived in our history.

CHAPTER THE NINTH

OF THE MANNERS, CUSTOMS,
AND CONDITION OF THE PEOPLE

Notwithstanding that in a previous book we brought down the fashions and furniture of our forefathers to the fourteenth century, in the present chapter we shall have the pleasure of laying before our readers some considerably later intelligence. We left our ancestors lying upon very uncomfortable beds, but the year 1415 introduces us to some luxuries in the way of curtains and counterpanes. The Duke of York set forth his bedding in his will, which bears the date we have named, and he seems to have died worth some thousands of pounds—of superior goose feathers. At a somewhat later period the sheet burst upon the page of history, and a blank is supplied by the sudden appearance of the blanket.

It was about the same period that clocks with strings and weights began to have a striking influence on the time, and Edward the Fourth used to carry one about with him wherever he went, but we do not believe that he wore it in a watchpocket, from which, instead of key and seals, there hung a couple of weights and a pendulum.

Costume seems to have been curtailed of very little of its exuberant absurdity in the reigns of Henry the Fourth and Fifth, though reform was carried to extremes, for it cut off the surplus hair from the head, and took away at least half a yard from the foot by relieving the shoes of their long points, a fashion which had always been remarkable for extreme pointlessness.

In the reign of Edward the Fourth there appears to have been a practice prevalent of making a shift to go without a shirt, when those who had such a thing to their backs were seized with a spirit of self-assertion, and began to slash open their sleeves for the purpose of showing their possession of that very useful article. The desire to prove the plenteousness and perhaps also the *propreté* of the under linen, led to a further ripping up of other parts of the dress, and the fops of the day began to outslash each other by opening the seams of their clothes in the most unseemly fashion.

Richard the Third and his "cousin of Buckingham" were notorious for their love of finery, and the term "buck," which is used in the present day, is evidently an abbreviation of Buckingham. Richard, probably, invented the Dicky or false front, which gave him the appearance of having always a clean breast, though the fact is that he was reduced to the expedient of wearing a false front, because the stains of guilt upon his bosom were utterly indelible.

The appetite of the fifteenth century seems to have been uncommonly good, for we find our ancestors eating four meals a day, beginning with breakfast at seven, dinner at ten, supper at four, and a collation taken in bed—oh, the cormorants!—between eight and nine in the evening. The meal taken in bed may have consisted of a *blanquette de veau*, or perhaps now and then a bolster pudding, while the ladies may have indulged themselves with a *côtelette en papillotes*. Earl Percy and his countess used to absorb between them a gallon of beer and a quart of wine, and before being tucked up for the night would tuck in a loaf of household bread, with other trifles to follow. A dinner in the days to which we are reverting generally lasted three hours, but tumblers and dancers were employed to amuse the feasters, so that a kind of caper sauce was served out with every dish that came to table.

Nothing in the whole annals of ancient and modern gluttony can exceed the dinner said to have been given by George Neville, the brother of the King-maker, on his induction to the Archbishopric of York, in the fifteenth century. It opened with a hundred and four oxen (*au naturel*), six wild bulls (*a la ménagère*), three hundred and four calves (*en surprise*), with innumerable *entrées* of pigs, bucks, stags, and roes, to an extent that is not only almost but quite incredible.

The pictures of the period represent a very inconvenient mode of laying the table, for we find a fish served up in a slop-basin, or rather laid across the top of that article of china-ware, which was much too small to admit the body of the animal. As far as we can discern the intention of the artist, we fancy we recognise in one of his pictures of a feast a duck lying on its back in a sort of sugar-basin or salt-cellar. This and a kind of mustard-pot, with an empty plate and half of a dinner-roll, may be said to constitute the entire provision made for a party of seven, who are standing up huddled together on one side of the table, in an existing representation of a dinner of the period.

The sports of the people were very numerous in the fifteenth century; but if we may judge by the pictures we have seen of the games, there was more labour than fun in the frolics of our forefathers. The contortions into which they seem to have thrown themselves while playing at bowls are quite painful to contemplate; and the well-known game of quarter-staff consisted of a mutual battering of shins and skulls, with a pole about six feet in length and some inches in circumference. Tennis was introduced at this early date, and it is therefore erroneous to assign its invention to Archbishop Tennison—a report which has been spread by some unprincipled person, whose career of crime commencing in a pun has ended in a falsehood.

The professional fool was a highly respectable character in the middle ages; and the court jester was a most influential personage, who was allowed to criticise all the measures of the ministry. He was a sort of supplementary premier; but, in later administrations—the present always excepted—the office of fool has merged among the members of the Government. It is a curious fact that, judging from the portraits which have been preserved, the fools seem to have been the most sensible-looking persons of their own time; and the proverb that "it takes a wise man to make a fool" was, no doubt, continually realised. The practical jokes of the jester were sometimes exceedingly disagreeable, for they consisted chiefly of blows and buffets, administered by a short wand, called a bauble, which he was in the habit of carrying. It was all very well when the fool's sallies happened to be taken in good part, but a witticism coming *mal-a-propos* would often prove no joke to the joker, who would get soundly thrashed for his impertinence. An ancient writer[67] describes the functions of a fool to have consisted chiefly of "making mouths, dancing about the house, leaping over the tables, outskipping men's heads, tripping up his companions' heels," and indulging in other similar *facetio*, which, though falling under the head of fun for the fool himself, might have been death to the victims of his exuberant gaiety. His life must have been one unbroken pantomime; though its last scene was seldom so brilliant as those bowers of bliss and realms of delight in the island of felicity, which owe their existence to the combined ingenuity of the painter and the machinist.

The spirit of chivalry had already begun to decline, or rather chivalry had lost its spirit altogether, for when it once became diluted it took very little time to evaporate. The few real combats that were fought referred chiefly to judicial proceedings, in which points of law were decided by the points of lances. The combatants probably thought they might as well bleed each other as allow themselves to be bled by the hands of the lawyers. The tournaments had dwindled down into the most contemptible exhibitions, for the spears used were entirely headless, and an encounter generally ended in the clashing together of a couple of blunted swords or the flourishing in the air of a brace of huge choppers, so that as the antagonists kept turning about, they might be said to revolve round each others' axes.

Before concluding our chapter on the manners and customs of the people at the date to which our history has arrived we may notice some regulations for apparel, by which it was ordered, not only that every man should cut his coat according to his cloth, but should select his cloth according to the means he had of buying it. Apparel was not the only thing with which the law interfered, but some Acts were passed, fixing the rate of meals to be allowed to servants, and thus ameliorating their condition. Articles of dress were subjected to the most stringent legislation, and tailors were of necessity guided by Parliamentary measures; carters and ploughmen were limited by law to a blanket, so that the lightness of the restrictions permitted a looseness of attire, which was highly convenient. Persons not of noble rank were prohibited from wearing garments of undue brevity; and it was only those of the highest standing to whom the shortest dresses were permitted.

---

67. Lodge, author of the Wit's Miserie, 4to, 1599.

It was in the period to which the present chapter refers that English pauperism first became the subject of legislation; and it was an acknowledged principle that the land must provide the poor with food and shelter, for civilization had not yet required the suppression of destitution by starvation and imprisonment.

We have now brought down our account of the condition of the people, from the highest to the lowest, from the king on his throne to the pauper on his parish, from the royal robber in the palace to the sturdy beggar in the public thoroughfare. We have seen how England was torn to pieces by the thorns belonging to the Roses, and how, after fighting about the difference between white and red, the union of both taught those who had been particular to a shade the folly of observing so much nicety. Future chapters must develop the influence which this union produced, and will show the effect of that junction between the damask and the cabbage roses, which had only been brought about by dyeing them in the blood of so many Englishmen.

End of Volume One